NO MAN IS AN ISLAND

No man is an Island, entire of itself; every man is a piece of the Continent, a part of the main.

JOHN DONNE *DEVOTIONS XVII*

No Man is an Island

A study of Singapore's Lee Kuan Yew

JAMES MINCHIN

ALLEN & UNWIN
Sydney London Boston

© James Minchin 1986
This book is copyright under the Berne Convention. No reproduction without permission. All rights reserved.

First published in 1986
Third impression 1987
Allen & Unwin Australia Pty Ltd
An Unwin Hyman company
8 Napier Street, North Sydney NSW 2060 Australia

Allen & Unwin New Zealand Limited
60 Cambridge Terrace, Wellington, New Zealand

Unwin Hyman Limited
37-39 Queen Elizabeth Street, London, SE1 2OB England

Allen & Unwin Inc.
8 Winchester Place, Winchester, Mass 01890, USA

National Library of Australia
Cataloguing-in-Publication entry

Minchin, James.
  No man is an island.

  Bibliography.
  Includes index.
  ISBN 0 86861 906 X.

  1. Lee, Kuan Yew, 1923– . 2. Prime ministers—Singapore—Biography. 3. Singapore—Politics and government. I. title.

959.5'705'0924

Set in 10.5/11.5pt Garamond, Linotron 202 by Graphicraft Typesetters, Hong Kong

Endpapers: Courtesy of the Ministry of Communications and Information, Singapore
Front endpaper: Singapore, Seafront, central business district, 1959
Back endpaper: Singapore: Seafront, central business district, 1985

Contents

    ACKNOWLEDGEMENTS *vii*
    INTRODUCTION *ix*
    Singapore *xvi*
1 The Man and the Island *1*
2 War and Self-Preparation *31*
    Biographies *51*
3 Preparing a Movement *59*
4 Preparing for Self-Government *81*
5 Preparing for Merger *101*
6 Into Malaysia *125*
7 Out of Malaysia *141*
8 A Place in the Sun *163*
    Biographies *197*
9 More Than Survival *199*
10 Less Than Paradise *239*
11 Words and the Man *275*
12 Lee the Man *291*
13 No Man is an Island *321*
    POSTSCRIPT *343*
    ABBREVIATIONS *347*
    ENDNOTES *349*
    BIBLIOGRAPHY *363*
    INDEX *369*

Acknowledgements

From this author's point of view, any list of acknowledgements naturally begins with all those who, from early 1968, made the next three and a half years so rich and formative: members of St Andrew's Cathedral, Our Saviour's Church and the Diocese of Singapore; those I met while visiting hospitals, institutions and homes of every type throughout the island; university staff and students; and many in West Malaysia.

Special thanks go to friends who have been generous with their time and hospitality over the intervening years. They often encouraged and questioned me, but never interfered with my work. Likewise, although the Prime Minister's Press Office arranged an interview and supplied copies of speeches, no advance notice was claimed of what I might write.

I owe much to Dr Graham Little, of the University of Melbourne Politics Department, for supervising the thesis on which this book is based. Distance kept our meetings few and far between, yet each time we talked I was greatly stimulated both by his suggestions about how I might interpret data and by the articles and books he commended to my attention. I hasten to add that I am fully responsible for the end result.

Friends and colleagues from the Asian Bureau Australia and from kindred organisations have been a constant inspiration.

The Anglican parishioners of St Arnaud and Geelong West have been intrigued at their pastor's interest in the leader of an island that they associate not only with Lee Kuan Yew but with Changi prison, Raffles Hotel, tropical heat and fabulous shopping. I thank them for their generous and kindhearted support when pressures of writing were upon me.

Finally, I want to place on record my gratitude to my wife, Maureen, and our three children, Without them the practice of mental bi-location would have been quite unsustainable.

The author gratefully acknowledges the following poets' permission to use copyright material: Lee Tzu Pheng 'Left hand, right hand', 'My country and my people', 'Bukit Timah Singapore' and 'Lines' from *Prospect of a Drowning* (Singapore, Heinemann, 1980); Edwin Thumboo '9th of August I and II' from *Gods Can Die* (Singapore, Heinemann, 1977); 'May 1954' and 'Ulysses by the Merlion' from *Ulysses by the Merlion* (Singapore, Heinemann, 1979); Robert Yeo (excerpt) 'Leaving Home, Mother' from *and napalm does not help* (Singapore, Heinemann, 1977); Fernandez, G. ed. *Poets of Singapore* (Singapore, Society of Writers, 1983); Mohamad Haji Salleh 'Do not say' from Thumboo, E., ed. *Seven Poets: Singapore and Malaysia* (Singapore University Press, 1973), and D. J. Enright 'Yussoff the Bold' *Foreign Devils* (London, Covent Garden Press, 1972).

Introduction

In a mid-1984 issue of Singapore's *Sunday Times*, Dr Yeo Ning Hong* recalled his first meeting with the Prime Minister and senior Cabinet members: it filled him with an 'immense sense of awe'.[1] Even a foreigner like myself can testify that Lee Kuan Yew, whom I interviewed briefly in 1976, comes across as no ordinary human being. To be on the receiving end of his anger must be quite terrifying. Even when he is talking calmly, there are hints that the volcano remains active underground.

By Southeast Asian standards, Lee is unique. He is a ruler to the fingertips, yet he was not born to rule. By race he is Chinese, although born locally and Westernised through upbringing and education; but Zhou Enlai's gibe that Lee is like a banana—yellow of skin, white underneath—is unfair to one who always keeps his own counsel and is the patriot of no fatherland so much as his own will. He has long been a formidable speaker and debater in English, of world class among politicians on a stage where English has only recently become the first language. He has mastered from scratch the other tongues needed for communication with his people. He is *the* patron of Singapore politics: spotting, hiring and firing top talent; commanding the apparatus of power and various alternative sources of information; able to choose freely when to let well enough alone or when to intervene.

---

* Now a full Cabinet Minister in the Government elected December 1984.

Some commentators exaggerate his capacity to be a one-man band, a saviour figure. According to Richard Nixon, 'the fact that a leader of Lee's breadth of vision was not able to act on a broader stage represents an incalculable loss to the world'.[2] Yet it is inconceivable that Lee could be Prime Minister or President of any country but Singapore, however much his admirers crave his style of leadership for their own countries. His star and that of the island republic have merged almost beyond distinction.

Together with a band of colleagues, particularly the former First Deputy Prime Minister Dr Goh Keng Swee, and supported by a remarkable workforce at all levels, Lee Kuan Yew has presided over the transformation of Singapore into far more than the ideal port and commercial centre that Stamford Raffles intended it to be when purchasing the island in 1819.

What are the reasons for Lee's extraordinary dominance at such a time of change? Is it because his is the exotic plant of civilised leadership that Raffles envisaged might one day emerge from the inhospitable tropical soil, producing its own special bloom?

What makes Lee more than an opportunist, a clown or a stooge, three types of character who, in his view, have crowded the political stage of Singapore? Surely he is not less willing or less able than others to seize opportunities for attaining his goals. It is not that his personality has been matched to the demands of his rise to power or his present undisputed position without moments of play-acting and absurdity. Neither has it been true that he has always been recognised as his own master.

Has his special endowment been, as an Indian MP put it in 1966, a revitalising love for his people?[3] If so, his love has been of an unusual kind—berating, despising, exhorting various groups and, although sometimes exulting in and congratulating the people, finding few individuals to like or appreciate more than briefly.

How important is his intellectual stature? He has observed that Singapore's intellectuals have not come to the fore in the service of their country and their people, and he does not class himself among them.

Is he a creature of chance? Lee may be the only person who can pinpoint the role of fortune at any stage in his career.

What puzzled me after living in Singapore for some years (1968–71) was that no one seemed to be asking these questions. Lee and his colleagues were somehow 'there', indestructible parts of the landscape, eminences all the more influential for being grey and understated. Rumours ebbed and flowed about them, but did not come to much. The minority I met who hated the People's

Action Party (PAP) leaders resorted to name-calling or worked up a case for the prosecution based on examples of high-handed political behaviour, an exercise that could be transposed to almost any other technocratic setting. A greater number rejected particular policies but expressed no need to investigate the men who framed them.

This is not to say that I was at ease with Singapore's politics. I was already inclined to be sceptical about manmade social systems. I became more sharply so, being a pastor in the midst of Singapore's teeming life and a Christian wary of selective morality and secular pragmatism. I found it hard to esteem those who looked down on citizens with a lordly air of approval or blame.

Why were Singaporeans so reluctant to examine for themselves the character, the values and the history of their masters, especially Lee Kuan Yew? Were they mesmerised by the speed of the transformation going on day by day before our very eyes? Could they not guess that the extensive engineering of their society would have far-reaching consequences?

Two years after returning to Australia and being unable to put Singapore out of my mind or to shelve the many questions that had arisen, I decided to undertake a piece of postgraduate research that could form the basis of a book. The project would give me a chance to examine and share with others what I had experienced and observed. Its gestation has been very slow because of other more immediate responsibilities, but regular visits to Singapore quickened my resolve to bring the project to birth.

> Mr Lee is a much misunderstood man in spite of Mr Alex Josey's efforts, possibly because of them.
> Goh Keng Swee, *The Economics of Modernization*, 1970, page 177.

Alex Josey's huge *Lee Kuan Yew*, published in 1968, was my first resource. It contained thick slabs of Lee's speeches over the years of power, sandwiched between thin slices of dry narrative and flavoured with the spice of personal detail. Josey had been a confidant of Lee's from the 1950s to the mid-1970s, one of his most regular golfing partners and an admirer of Lee's blend of gradual socialism and definitive leadership.

Unfortunately, his book was hard to digest. A second edition, which appeared in 1971, brought the record up to date but left out many of Lee's more fiery speeches from the self-government and merger periods (1959–65).

Then in 1973 T.J.S. George's book, *Lee Kuan Yew's Singapore*, appeared. On hearing that it was a perceptive if critical study, I wondered if my own undertaking might now be unnecessary. A couple of readings, however, convinced me to press on. Whilst it was lively, thoughtful and written with flair and wit, the book was a hatchet job. Its information could be taken as broadly accurate in the absence of libel action from the Prime Minister, but the selection and linkage of facts were forced far too quickly into a negative picture. I believed, and still do, that George got the portrait mostly right; yet it was debased by the uniformly dark colour of the brushstrokes.

Josey's rejoinder to George's book—same format, same price, but half as thick again—was first published in 1974. *Lee Kuan Yew: The Struggle for Singapore* showed signs of hasty scissors-and-paste arrangement of material, there being many jumps and about-turns in the text. However, it was a welcome abridgement and regrouping of the previous work, and quoted a wider range than before of critics' views of Lee—though not George—some of which it rebutted. An extra chapter was added to a later edition to take in Lee's assessment of the region and the world following the communists' mastery of Indo-China. Then 1980 saw the second volume of Josey's original (revised) *Lee Kuan Yew*. Again heavy going, its main value was to record the Prime Minister's words to the end of 1978 and to provide more raw material for analysis.

Many other writers and journalists have described Lee Kuan Yew, but only in passing.[*] Did their curiosity wane, or was it stifled by lack of fresh leads? Where their focus was not on the man, perhaps all they needed was sufficient clarity about Lee to support their gut reaction for or against him.

Again and again I found myself hankering after insights into a person seemingly rendered more opaque by each new item of exposure and publicity. As far back as 1968, Willard Hanna's field report, *The Privacy of the Prime Minister*, (1968), had offered a mixture of gossip and fact. The drought in studies of Lee and Singapore's other leaders following Hanna's, Josey's and George's efforts eventually broke in 1984, but the drought-breakers added little to the public's understanding at a biographical level. John Drysdale's work, *Singapore: Struggle for Success*, despite being the best sourced book available on the period 1945–65 and

---

[*] e.g. Ronald McKie, Dennis Bloodworth, C. Northcote Parkinson, Denis Warner, Robert Gamer, Iain Buchanan, Noel Barber, Richard Hughes, D. J. Enright, Thomas Bellows, Rene Peritz, Nancy Fletcher (see bibliography).

Introduction xiii

drawing extensively on the Prime Minister's recollections, does not attempt to go behind Lee the politician. Joan Hon's *Relatively Speaking*, a memoir of her father Hon Sui Sen (former Finance Minister and a family friend of the Lees for forty years) avowedly kept personal references to a minimum. To his new book, *Governing Singapore*, Raj Vasil appended a revealing series of conversations he had recorded with the Prime Minister in 1969, but his emphasis was on political institutions and methods rather than on psychological exploration. Chan Heng Chee's study of David Marshall, Singapore's first Chief Minister, was published under the title *A Sensation of Independence*. Unlike the series of very competent if dispassionate treatises she and others had previously written on government, the book offered a close look at its subject—and left Lee intact!

There were times when the sheer mass of undigested material opening up to me gave me pause. How could I ever extract insights comparable to those of people native to the region or long versed in its affairs? Moreover, like Josey and George before me, I did not speak or read Chinese, to the detriment of a more stereoscopic vision.*

Still and all, a certain momentum had built up; and for that reason, or because they were convinced such a project was worthwhile and no one else was doing it, my Singapore friends and acquaintances reinforced my own urge to persevere, and have done so even more vehemently over the last few years.

I was also encouraged to go ahead by the quality of some of the interviews I was given from 1975 onwards. Cabinet Ministers, senior officials, professionals and academics, political adversaries in Malaysia and Singapore talked freely on and off the record. Only three times did I wangle an interview to have it terminated abruptly—once in visible fear of Lee and twice in violent hostility to the man and my espousal of a moderate approach to his biography. Several of Lee's past or present associates refused to grant an interview at all, although a few eventually relented.

The other great windfall was the public dossier of Lee's speeches. Supplemented by the materials already collected, by academic texts and by personal reminiscences, it formed a comprehensive picture of Lee Kuan Yew's performance under the spotlight from 1955

---

* There does not appear to be any substantive portrait of Lee composed in Chinese, Malay or Tamil. Is he even more enigmatic to other linguistic groups than to the English-speaking?

onwards. The resources tapered off as one pushed back to earlier days, but not completely.

How have I sifted all the data that I have accumulated? Without the luxury of direct personal knowledge of Lee Kuan Yew, I have had to proceed experimentally, using various lines of inquiry and cross-checking them. But the book seeks to make a virtue out of necessity: its interpretation has not been allowed to control its story too tightly.

It begins with a composite picture of the Prime Minister in recent times and sketches the context of Singapore society in which he came to prominence.

In Chapter 2 the focus shifts to the Japanese Occupation, the impact of which is supposed to have goaded Lee into politics. From there his career is traced chronologically up to 1966, a period that is well covered both by official and independent sources.

Chapters 8 to 10 adopt a thematic approach to the significant changes Lee has orchestrated in Singapore's geopolitical stance and domestic policy.

The concluding chapters assess the evidence of word and deed and what they tell us about the man, and some attempt is made to project a future for Singapore with and without Lee Kuan Yew.

I have tried not to let the scant personal details bear greater weight than the prolific public record. Impressions and hunches are set down as such. If nothing else, I hope *No Man is an Island* may do, perhaps in a more disciplined and systematic way, what any citizen should have the right and the appropriate knowledge to do in a democracy—move on from a spontaneous opinion of his or her leaders towards a more careful appraisal, whether it strengthens loyalty or not.

The initiative for this book, its contents and views, is entirely my own. Of course I have been influenced greatly by others through countless conversations and in what I have read. But I would not expect anyone to endorse every word I have written, least of all close friends in Singapore.

My aim is to provoke further investigation, not stifle it. There is a great risk of failure for those who would see contemporary leaders and events whole, or discern trends and the forces shaping them. Yet any writer or academic whose heart has gone out to people in a particular society will surely not want to hide behind the risk and avoid tackling research and communication. In this case the man and the island are far too compelling, far too fascinating, for withdrawal to be a temptation.

I do not believe in telling university researchers where they go wrong. They write all kinds of spurious silly articles or books. They get MAs and PhDs for them . . . I laugh away. But I never tell them why they are wrong. Because I am an Asian. I am not a Westerner. This is an Asian situation and do not be clever . . . Be modest. Just keep quiet. If they want to be wrong headed, wish them luck.

LEE KUAN YEW,
PARLIAMENT, 23 February 1977

1
The Man and the Island

> Any time, every time, you can damn the Prime Minister and so long as it is not a lie and a criminal lie, nothing happens to you. You can say a lot of things. You can write books about him, damning him. So long as it is not a libel, go ahead.
>
> LEE KUAN YEW,
> PARLIAMENT, 23 February 1977

This book attempts to portray the man who has been Singapore's Prime Minister for well over a quarter of a century: Harry Lee Kuan Yew. As far as possible, it is free of lies. Whether it damns him, even with faint praise, or whether its portrait is a caricature, the reader must judge. But, apart from the natural justice owed to anyone, we would be foolish to underestimate a man of such staying power in such volatile circumstances.

Neither should we underestimate the people of Tanjong Pagar constituency who have, without fail, elected Lee to represent them since 1955, and the people of Singapore who have chosen Lee's party to govern them at each election from 1959 onwards.

Lee is not—yet—President of Singapore. He has not been appointed for life with the backing of a military junta or elected for a fixed term in his own right. He stands or falls with his party. He is certainly not a dictator in the technical sense of the word: he can be voted out of office by his Central Executive Committee (CEC), by the People's Action Party (PAP) cadres, by his constituents or by the citizenry as a whole.

Under his tutelage, it is true that party and government machinery have been interlocked to a remarkable degree and that cabinet ministers, members of parliament, cadres and civil servants have not challenged their leader head-on. Moreover, Lee is now the only foundation member left on the Central Executive Committee and he keeps the cadre list to himself. It is true that the composition and performance of the judiciary have been somewhat noisily monitored by the Prime Minister within a tightened framework of legislative prescription. It is true that all modes of communication between the people and their leaders have been manipulated to reinforce dependence in the one and control by the other. Even the pronounced increase in emphasis on the armed forces and police has only altered the power equation further to the Prime Minister's advantage. Internationally he has become Mr Singapore, the astute geopolitician, the socialist come to his senses; the domestic impact of such a reputation has been invaluable.

Nevertheless, Singapore remains in form a democratic state, with 79 electorates for its 2.5 million people. Lee's party currently holds 77 of the 79 seats in the unicameral Parliament, the other 2 having been won in the December 1984 general elections by leaders of two of the opposition parties which, despite harassment and internal weakness, remain in existence.

Lee Kuan Yew in government

Lee and his People's Action Party swept into office at the end of May 1959. There have been six general elections since then, all won by the PAP and all built on a clear majority of votes, except in 1963.

During the thirty-odd-year history of the Party, Lee has made most of the running. Even after the executive committee elections of 1957 when he refused to stand as Secretary, he could have had the position back had he wanted it. Until recently, he has chosen to make much of his solidarity with Cabinet, or at least his chief colleagues within it. That people still cast him in the role of a one-man band, an autocrat, is testimony that his drive for power strikes true, not his capacity for restraint or co-operation.

From the outset, the PAP leadership has had a conscious but qualified commitment to the electoral process. In Lee's words, 'we have taken office because we believe that the PAP is the party most capable of discharging the duties and responsibilities of the government'.[1] Suitability for office does not come from popular support. On the other hand, power by itself is useless; it is the power to improve a society that counts, and this can be effective only if it carries the people. An electoral mandate is the sign of that. Yet Lee has said, 'If I were in authority in Singapore indefinitely, without having to ask those who are being governed whether they like what is being done, then I have not the slightest doubt that I could govern much more effectively in their own interest'.[2] Lee has not hesitated to steer the electorate with all means at his disposal, especially if he feels that others are doing the same.

The policy of the PAP Government, relatively unfettered since 1965, has been to develop and administer a modern, technically advanced, secular and independent republic, multiracial and politically plural so long as communalism or communism is not contemplated. Corruption has been kept to a minimum, and the Government has promoted the ethic of hard work, excellence and skill deserving rewards set by international demand and supply.

The state's supremacy is asserted by extensive economic and social engineering on the part of the Government and underpinned by a substantial defence effort. The Singapore version of socialism encourages private capital and ownership, whether domestic or transnational, as an efficient way of acquiring skills and markets and generating economic growth in the desired sectors. But every effort is made to keep private interests subordinate to those of the state. Overall policy is to be accomplished as much as possible in tandem with the democratic one-man-one-vote system.

The translation of policy to fact is achieved by a judicious mixture of the carrot and the stick. 'First what we know must be done, we explain, and then enforce', Lee has said.[3] The virtues that figure in his definition of Singapore's development are all somewhat Spartan: orderliness, cleanliness, discipline, intensity, virility. They correspond to Lee's own practice of life since childhood, though his is a more fastidious version than could be managed by a Spartan warrior or Singapore worker in the sweat and heat of the day.

The leaders' images of Singapore itself tend to be those of the machine or computer. The current Senior Minister, Rajaratnam, for instance, used the illustration of a jet fighter, as automated as possible with back-up and fail-safe devices, but requiring a trained pilot to show its full range.[4] Through education, through appeal to self-interest, through sanctions, people must be brought to accept their part in the whole as digits or ciphers. The rights of individuals beyond the ballot box are acknowledged; but they must not contradict the national goals defined by the leadership. To add to the complexity and energy of effort needed for technocratic government—running a tightly organised machine whose moving parts are voters and people—Singapore had to be geared up to merge with Malaya, a state of affairs Lee believed natural, only to face the profound readjustment of suddenly becoming a separate nation on 9 August 1965.

Lee is no less the pilot now than he was back in 1959. His success has not been primarily due to charisma, some supernatural endowment of personality that bewitches his followers. He does command fear from his subordinates, fear of his disfavour and its consequences. He commands respect that has bordered on veneration for his durability, the high quality of his performance and his self-renewing ability to calculate several moves ahead. But there is no evidence of Lee wanting a cult of himself via personal mementos and populist public relations. Nor is he interested in making hard news.

There have been moments of play-acting in Lee's political career. For instance, in September 1957 he denied his faction's access to intelligence about pro-communists in their midst; he sent up a cloud-seeding plane in 1963's long drought; he threatened several times during the 1960s to close the Singapore British bases; and he has frequently boasted of leaving 'no hostages to fortune' (are there none to leave, or have they all been pushed out of sight or neutralised?).

Even these pretences may be principled in Lee's eyes: the product of desperation when he has been in a tight corner, or of an opportunism more careful and patriotic than his enemy's. He can hardly sneer as he once did: 'Please remember we do not pretend to be virtuous. Hypocrisy is not a feature of Singapore's leadership'.[5]

But in general he is the practitioner of substantial politics. He ensures delivery of what he promises. He does not create false expectations, nor does he appeal to them.

The pleasure of electoral popularity, the subjective gratification that one's power and influence are recognised by others, do not sustain Lee at any conscious level. Whether out in front or behind the scenes, he has sought the real power that defines the shape and detail of a political community. His sphere of operation now is much smaller than the Malaya and Malaysia of earlier times. But to him the important thing is to do his best to set little Singapore up properly and hand her over to competent successors. Then he may withdraw from the strains of being helmsman: 'I do not find it difficult to envisage relinquishing that kind of power.'[6] Even so, he will practise real power until the day he dies, with whatever status or title destiny affords.

The political scientist Chan Heng Chee once described in conversation Lee's unique asset as his freedom to punish and reward. This asset is still present in almost absolute form. From a historical perspective, the absence of contenders is surprising—Lee has made some monumental errors of judgment in choosing political juniors and successors, civil servants or party functionaries, and in handling his opponents of the Malaysia period. But so far he has outlasted or outwitted them all: he has been well served by his dedication to political power and all its techniques, his control of the instruments of state, his foreign connections and his ruthlessness both in ferreting out skeletons in opponents' cupboards and leaving none himself. Most of those who have challenged him or his programmes have capitulated, been absorbed, are in exile, detention, limbo, or disgrace—or dead of natural causes. The only Singaporeans known to have challenged or bypassed him with some success are Goh Keng Swee, who used to delay putting his case until the heat from a particular argument had subsided, or Toh Chin Chye, who waxed petulant but then withdrew, and Lee's wife. Goh is now almost off the scene and Toh has been pushed from centre stage and become disaffected. Then again, Lee has not always been inflexible—he has backed off many times before disputes could go public. Nor has his patronage always been assertive; colleagues such as Haji Ya'akob, Rajaratnam or Lim Kim San were given a free hand, within limits, to carry out their subordinate roles. Self-discipline has been possible wherever Lee's own position has not been under threat. For example, he recognised in Goh Keng Swee the administrative overseer *par excellence* who unearthed talent and ideas with uncanny skill and saw them through to making or breaking point.

Lee has always been able to trade patronage. At the beginning of his political career, he could already offer a basic prescription, formidable forensic skills and good British connections. Even groups like the Progressives, who were probably glad to have his services withdrawn in 1951, knew that they were losing something. He was rarely forced to beg favours or negotiate from weakness in the manoeuvres of the 1950s and is even less vulnerable in the unbalanced relationships of today.

There is no question that Lee Kuan Yew has become fine-tuned to exercise leadership and to shape human affairs in Singapore. His own personality and his way of acting upon others and his society at large, radiate a confidence that makes resistance seem tedious or even pointless.

The man on stage

Despite long periods of uninterrupted progress in Singapore's economy, the charting of our principal actor's careers is not so straightforward. The story of Lee Kuan Yew, like that of any flesh-and-blood person, is shot through with contradictions and paradoxes at every turn. Farce and tragedy, elements noble and sordid, puncture the efficient calm of the passing years. How often and to what degree they appear will emerge, at least partly, as the random effects of one man's unpredictable moods, wishes and nightmares. Never let it be said that Singapore politics result simply from rational calculations, initiatives and responses, working themselves out mechanically and inevitably. Some cameos from recent years illustrate the point.

On 28 March 1985 Dr Yeoh Ghim Seng, the Speaker in Singapore's Parliament, announced that President Devan Nair had resigned on medical grounds. Most members of the House were present and were stunned by the news. There was more to come. Prime Minister Lee rose to his feet and with brutal frankness reported the attending doctors' diagnosis that 'the President was suffering from an acute confusional state due to alcohol superimposed on a long-standing condition caused by alcohol dependency'.[7] Lee went on to give his version of recent personal conversations between himself and the President, the doctors and Devan Nair's wife. Clearly affected by what he saw as an old friend's betrayal of his trust, Lee delivered judgment and sentence in the spirit of a father who tells his son, 'This beating hurts me as much as it hurts you.'

When Devan Nair was invited in 1981 to be President, both husband and wife told friends they would accept the post only for their partner's sake. Lee was seeking to upgrade the presidency, gradually to give it a more political character with more teeth. But the risks must surely have been all too apparent to the Nairs: promotion could well be the kiss of death for their relationship with the Lees or for their public standing. Any distinctive actions and attitudes, not to mention peccadilloes or bad habits, would be under extra scrutiny. Closeness had thus far existed on the presumption of their visible subordination to the Lees.

So it was that within eighteen months the President's residence, the Istana, became for Devan Nair a prison no less confining than the cells he had occupied at Changi or on St John's Island, only escaped through rest cures overseas after minor medical procedures. According to reliable sources, his designated heir in the trade union movement was removed from office the same way Lee had installed him, by getting Devan to make the arrangements; and in a related move the Prime Minister stopped the President's informal lunches with friends and former union colleagues. Hostility grew between the two men, and when Devan's alcoholism came out in a bizarre incident during a visit to Sarawak, the stage was set for a showdown.

At about 4 am on the morning of Sunday 23 December 1984, Yoshida Makoto of the *Asahi Shimbun* newspaper injected a friendly note into what had become an earnest media conference following the announcement of election results: 47 seats won by the PAP out of 49 contested, the other 30 already unopposed PAP victories—but a significant 12.6 per cent swing by voters against the Government. 'Prime Minister, I feel you are too much of a perfectionist. Relax. Relax.'[8] Makoto made complimentary remarks about the Prime Minister's son Hsien Loong and asked the Prime Minister to stay in office beyond the age of sixty-five (1988). Lee and his younger colleagues laughed once or twice, a change of mood after an hour and a half of biting statements and frequent interruptions by Lee at a table he shared with Goh Chok Tong, One Teng Cheong, Tony Tan and Dhanabalan. He had refused to congratulate the Opposition, talking instead of legal action for alleged defamation and of their turning politics into a snake pit that would scare off decent candidates. He had confirmed withdrawal of meet-the-people sessions from the two lost constituencies.

As in 1980, the election campaign had been the responsibility of the younger team under Goh Chok Tong. In 1980 Lee had intervened at the last minute, appearing at Fullerton Square to climax a major PAP rally. The rain dripped from his face as he continued well beyond his expected time at the microphone; the crowd remained for this one-man wrenching back of initiative in what had been a feeble lacklustre campaign. During the 1984 election he intervened three times, again at the last minute—once at Fullerton Square, once at a follow-up press conference and then in a written message released on the morning of the vote itself. It is unlikely that he helped at all—if anything, he contributed to the swing against the PAP. He insulted the electors by threatening retribution in constituencies that returned an Opposition candidate. (The threat was ambiguous: would Party or Government services be withdrawn? In the event both were downgraded to teach voters a lesson.) He insulted them again by mocking the O-level results of one of the Opposition leaders, Chiam See Tong. And he was hardly implying confidence in the quality of his own appointees when, to justify the choice of his son as a candidate, he quoted Rajaratnam's opinion: 'You must be mad if you don't. You know we are short.'[9] The 1984 election showed a Prime Minister for the first time out of sync with his people and his government colleagues.

Several thousand citizens, elite or party faithful, packed the National Theatre on a mid-August night every year from 1967 to

1983 for a rally addressed by the Prime Minister. His last performance in the theatre, due for demolition because its partly open structure was unsafe, was televised live over the government-controlled system. It was vintage Lee. Beginning with a compact outline in Malay of the points he wanted to make, the Prime Minister then spoke at greater length in Mandarin, involving more of his audience. Finally he moved into English and delivered a major statement off the cuff, despite having prepared a script in the hope that careful wording might better assist the redress of adverse trends in the marriage and maternity patterns of tertiary-educated women. 'I want all reproduced, but in proportion!' he declared, wanting to ensure that standards do not go down and the next generation makes it in the age of computers and robotics.[10]

There is no doubt that Lee Kuan Yew's prowess as a speaker has been a significant factor in mobilising Singapore behind the PAP and behind his leadership. For thirty years the people have listened to this remarkable man acquire from scratch a thorough facility in Mandarin, then Hokkien, polish his Malay and enlarge the range of his English. It was even rumoured—wrongly—that he had learned Tamil.

At this rally, Hokkien was not to be heard. Dialects are no longer accorded status in the Government's drive to make Mandarin the only acceptable form of Chinese language. The Prime Minister's Malay sounded more anglicised and perfunctory than during and before the Malaysia period when he strove to speak it better than many of his Malay counterparts.

Lee's English was measured, but compelling, and quite distinctive. Nowadays the fires flare up less often in his public speaking, but when he is emotionally involved with his subject, he has an almost hypnotic effect. That night was an example. The Prime Minister needs both an audience and a controversial cause to get his adrenalin pumping. But even his duller speeches reveal the right he has won to teach his people, and it will be some time before that right can be squandered or lost.

On 13 February 1984, Lee held a joint press conference with Australia's Prime Minister, Robert Hawke. Lee gave the appearance of being quite positive towards his counterpart and new-found friend from Down Under, but the heartfelt effusiveness was Hawke's. Lee's urbanity and control of language, his droll realism about Australia's defence contribution, contrasted with the Australian's tortured syntax and laboured answers, and he managed to put down Hawke's predecessor, Liberal Malcolm Fraser, for failing to keep a boast. Nicknamed by sections of the press 'the Harry and Bob show', the meeting left no doubt who was its effortless front runner.

When the Prime Minister's mother, Madam Chua Jim Neo (Mrs Lee Chin Koon) died in 1980, the funeral was the Christian ceremony she had requested. But it was her free-thinking son who gave the eulogy. Overcome with emotion, he stumbled through a short speech extolling her virtues. Whilst being Chinese in tenor, the speech presented one of those rare, although recently more frequent, opportunities to observe the man, apparently off guard, expressing his instinctive outlook. He remarked on his mother's closeness to her grandchildren, in several cases a closer relationship than they enjoyed with their own mothers. Equally pointed was his omission of any reference to his father's presence and grief.[11]

I met Lee Kuan Yew in 1976. At first his press officer, James Fu, saw little chance of an interview. I understood, having heard stories of other post-graduate students getting short shrift from Lee in their pursuit of him. An American PhD candidate had gained access in Lee's earlier, more ingenuous days; it had all been carefully arranged from the United States. The interview began, a victorious moment for the American, and then fell apart when the Prime Minister decided from a few questions that the student had no idea what he was talking about. Persistence was met with almost forcible ejection.

My glimmer of hope came when I mentioned casually to Fu that I had been approached by a publisher to submit a manuscript. Eventually, and with a few hours' notice, Lee granted a small space in his diary. This was after several days of the interview being on, then off, and on and off again, when I was convinced I would have to make do with the material I already had, indirect as it was. Now I was to have ten minutes with the Prime Minister for background. My questions had to be submitted in writing beforehand; they were not permitted to be personal.

Dressed as instructed in jacket and tie, I turned up at the press office underneath City Hall late on the afternoon of 5 April. We drove the two kilometres or so to the Istana through the traffic in Fu's modest car, making conversation *en route*. Fu said how much he respected the Prime Minister and I asked if Lee took a keen personal interest in his staff. Fu told me of Lee's recent expression of concern at his press officer's tiredness after a heavy eight-day schedule they had shared. The note of surprise in his voice gave me its own answer.

We went briskly past the guards at the busy Istana entrance and up a long, winding drive through the tranquil grounds and golf course to the annexe where Lee has had his office since 1971.* The building was guarded by Gurkhas, stocky Nepalese mercenaries. After some delay, I entered a lift with Fu and we went up a couple of floors to the foyer of the office. It was very cool. The visitor's book had an incredible collection of signatures, mostly those of foreign luminaries. Again there was a delay, and then I was ushered into Lee's office. The door opened onto a small alcove that made an L shape of the huge room. Being sparsely furnished, its size was highlighted. Lee's desk top in the far corner was all but empty of papers.

Lee Kuan Yew was at his desk; he stood and walked over to me slowly. I was struck by the disproportionate visual impact of his head—its high forehead and grizzled hair and familiar features. It made him seem taller than his 179 centimetres. He took my hand limply without a word of greeting, personal inquiry or glance at me, and the three of us sat around a low table. Lee said in English and Mandarin that he did not want a tape taken and it was not to be a formal interview. His manner was weary. My heart sank. I realised how keyed up I was in anticipation.

I launched into the prepared questions, which ranged over the local political scene. Quickly the Prime Minister slipped into a monologue, putting together prefabricated phrases and lecturing me about Western academics' innocence before the many faces of communism. Having heard this line before, and annoyed that it was tangential, my impulses got the better of me. Abandoning my script, I broke into the flow of words when I decently could and sought to bring the focus back to Singapore. Fortunately the Prime Minister accepted. By then he was talking in a much livelier vein. We exceeded our time limit—the press officer was looking at his watch—but still he continued, instructing me not to quote him when, to my surprise, he described certain vivid fears he had. It was fascinating. Fu made to leave—I could have killed him!—and this time the interview was over. We parted smoothly, impersonally, as ships that had passed in the night.

I have subsequently read or heard of other occasions when similar fears have been expressed, so I cannot claim privileged

---

* Previously at City Hall, the office was moved because of downtown traffic jams—and in line with security advice.

treatment. What was unexpected was the sudden transition to frankness that rescued the interview from its unpromising start.

There are times when watching Lee Kuan Yew in action leaves an uncanny sensation that here is a being not quite of this planet. His mannerisms are somehow private: sipping plain water; puffing out his cheeks in some intimate routine of checking the breath and expelling contaminants; smiling at unusual points and without necessarily consenting to an atmosphere of wit or jollity. It is as if his speaking, jogging and other movements proceed before an accidental audience. His reactions tend to be atypical, and his outlook more abstract and calculated than most others'. So the signs of obvious and powerful emotion in him either provoke the quite unfair charge of pretending or increase bewilderment.

He is not considered a warm person, for instance. There are countless stories of his anger, derision, indifference towards his fellows. Yet he speaks tenderly of his wife and children; and a whole range of younger politicians, both local and more recently even foreign, can attest to periods when he welcomed them into his counsel, his family circle, his precious time: Fong Swee Suan, Dominic Puthucheary, Ong Cheng Sam, Wee Toon Boon, Lim Chee Onn, Tony Tan, Andrew Peacock are names that come to mind without effort. He often used to declare his affectionate regard for Devan Nair after the latter hitched his wagon to Lee's star in the late 1950s. Political defectors or delinquents have caused him distress. As colleagues and associates have slipped away through illness or death, he pays open and touching tribute to those he has liked—the eulogies of President Sheares or Hon Sui Sen, late Minister for Finance, for example, or the letters of thanks or condolence sent privately and then released to the press.

One very striking feature of Lee is his almost complete lack of a sensing apparatus for non-verbal cues from others. His face is set with an extraordinary degree of self-containment. Messages from the outside world must have to go through an elaborate screening and connection process before Lee's instinctive and pre-emptive responses are adjusted or moderated at all. This is certainly not to say he is incapable of sympathy; just that he is accustomed far more than most to getting his own way, living on the terms he sets. Is he also protecting himself from constant demands for his wisdom, his judgment, his favour? In his world, very few people want nothing from him and there are few who, he believes, have anything to offer him beyond performance of a specific task.

T.J.S. George draws attention to his isolation and inner drive: 'Lee Kuan Yew is a man marked by the fact that he does not quite belong anywhere and has had to produce himself—his style and attitudes—out of his own deep mind. Thus he has the unpredictability of a man with a mission but no power brakes. When he talks of creating a new Singapore, he means, of course, creating a new society which will justify his own attitudes to life. His concept of "Singaporeanism" and of "the rugged society" is only partly a political device to ensure Singapore's separate identity; partly it is a way of compensating for his alienation by making a society in his own image—the projection on to the national scene of an individual's complex psychological problems.'[12]

But the reader puts George's book down little wiser as to what Lee's problems are, how they are projected, and whether Singaporeans can do anything about them except pray for his speedier departure from the scene. Far more evidence will need to be marshalled if George's throwaway hunch, intuitively right as it appears, is to lead to understanding.

Outside the inner circle

Lee Kuan Yew aims at leaving Singapore better than he found it. For him the business of government is to maximise the potential of the people. All is to be done for their sake, today's and tomorrow's generations and beyond, and for the sake of the nation that gives them cohesion, like components in a jet fighter.

How well has he related to 'the people'? The short answer is: successfully, but with indications that the rapport is diminishing. Through television and radio, through the press, through personal appearances and speeches at ceremonies, rallies or dinners, he is directly present to them. His general utterances are long on demand, short on praise. Almost always there are groups to warn or castigate. He is increasingly at odds with the younger generation that he set out to create.

The mode of contact is one-way. For many years the people have had little personal access to their Prime Minister. There are exceptions; sometimes he calls up community leaders or members of an interest group or association. More rarely, petitions to see him are granted. Those with experience of such gatherings say that the Prime Minister talks at people rather than to or with them. Most harrowing of all, Lee has cross-examined individuals opposed to legislative or policy changes he is promoting. After one such, when the then Dean of Law, Mrs Thio Su Mien, was harangued by

Lee over her objections to the permanent appointment of current cabinet ministers to the minority rights 'watchdog' Presidential Council, the Minister for Law, E.W. Barker, was overheard apologising to her for his leader's behaviour. Occasionally, Lee has gone walking and spot-visiting high-rise flats unannounced and with security entourage, but he has been dismayed at not finding more evidence of culture—books and so on—and has not repeated the venture too often.

In one of a series of radio 'Portraits of our Time', broadcast on 17 May 1971, BBC reporter John Tusa recalled: 'I have also seen him electioneering, which is rather a different situation. He was electioneering in Singapore, using three languages, very fluently. And what really impressed me was that he was in a poor part of Singapore and he really seemed to be getting close to the people he was talking to. He didn't seem embarrassed by it at all. He really had no difficulty at all in asking them about their problems, appreciating what their problems were and giving often very sensible and plain advice and encouragement to them.' Again, the problem with direct two-way contact is that most of those who come to Lee are supplicants. He mentioned in late 1965, when the strain of Singapore's separation from Malaysia was still bearing heavily on him, that he was 'shedding the load' of some of his duties, 'otherwise my life will become a misery and I will do nothing but meet people'.[13]

There is an extensive maypole system to bring the people of Singapore within Lee's grasp. He keeps abreast of Parliament by electronic means, he sits on select panels such as the Defence Committee, and his office receives countless spoken and written reports from parliamentarians, citizens' consultative committees and residents' committees, the People's Association, Party cadres, statutory bodies and government departments. Of great importance is the Special Branch briefing, which monitors not only individuals but coffee shop gossip. So a jigsaw picture of the 'ground' is assembled for the Prime Minister. What are the grumbles, the rumours, the fears and hopes? Chan Heng Chee has provided ample documentation of the type of politics implied by this information system in her book *The Dynamics of One-Party Dominance*.

Singapore being where it is, Lee also finds it easy to keep up with those visiting or passing through. Either by his invitation or their request, people distinguished in many fields—politics, commerce, the professions, military, academic—meet him at the Istana. Over and above these, protocol provides extra opportunities and obligations for encounters with the diplomatic and expatriate community which he can resist or choose to accept.

Lee himself has become a diligent world citizen and traveller, since his first proper overseas trip as a student in 1946. Once he found his feet not in grey, war-weary London but in Cambridge, he made many friends in the self-consciously egalitarian and anti-colonial atmosphere of the time. British Labour Party stalwarts, contemporaries at university, even his teachers, became his original points of reference and then valued contacts in an expanding network.

Now he ranges over the globe, paying special attention to the big powers and superpowers; he can be sure of a welcome almost anywhere in the anti-communist world. His recent devotees are more often from the Right than formerly, and he is in some demand as a speaker, seminar participant and consultant. He has drawn to himself what he describes as 'dog goodwill' which may not convert into 'cat goodwill', applicable to Singapore's leaders generally. In the hope that it may, he usually brings an entourage of younger ministers and officials with him.

Whether travelling on business or holiday, the Prime Minister prepares his itinerary according to complex calculations. Some plans are made or changed at the last minute in deference to one constant: security. The timing of Lee's absence from Singapore is important, particularly during the more turbulent period of his leadership (up to the late 1960s). With the desire to seek refuge and regain composure, there appear to be elements of diversion, lobbying and even catharsis.

In earlier days, Lee and his family would escape for an annual 'breather' in the Cameron Highlands. The climate, the smallness of the island and the unremitting pressure of demands make him claustrophobic. Nowadays travel takes him away from Singapore regularly, often for extended periods. He has enjoyed mini-sabbaticals in North America. Britain is as important as ever — catching up with old friends or his children when studying there, receiving the freedom of London and other honours, or perhaps overseeing the home he has bought near Cambridge. The nearest 'overseas' centre, Kuala Lumpur, was officially out of bounds from 1965 to 1972, and it took some little time for his interest in the other ASEAN capitals to be revived, aroused or expressed. Although he did not go to China until 1976, he has kept close contact with various East Asian centres by trips there and other means.

It requires real imagination for ordinary citizens to grasp the full value of overseas connections to someone like Lee. He has lived at rarefied heights for so long that the required breathing adjustments are second nature to him. One can construct a mock Baedeker that lists the printable factors by which each destination might be rated.

1. Access to special knowledge or classified intelligence and to the VIPs who possess it. Reinforcement of Lee's views on genetics, medicine, etc. is a bonus, although experts can sometimes be annoyingly reluctant to confirm his interpretation of their data and theories.
2. Facilities to map out the several chessboards on which Singapore plays, to analyse a nation's or bloc's prospects and to project scenarios.
3. A potential beach-head for Singapore—military training; acquiring needed resources of technology software and hardware, personnel including guest workers and professionals, raw materials, knowhow, markets, trading partners or investment targets; lining up alliances or UN votes; provoking a response in a third party by visiting a second.
4. Demand for consultancy (Bangladesh, China, Sri Lanka, Brunei, parts of Latin America and the Pacific are among countries that already benefit from this).
5. A platform to purvey hard truths, more in sorrow than anger, either directly to the people/nation concerned or via another audience.

With regard to meetings between Lee and foreign executive leaders, further observations will be made in the course of the book, notably in Chapter 8. For some visits, Lee goes to a lot of trouble in advance. Using a range of intermediaries he inquires about biodata and background details—from preferred diet and leisure pursuits through to profiles of trusted counsellors and confidants. When Jimmy Carter was President of the United States, for example, Lee was sufficiently bemused to write personal notes to men he thought would be in the know, seeking clarification about the new State Department and presidential advisers.

Lee has perfected the official speech of welcome or reply to an international dignitary. Since he respects few people unreservedly, he has evolved a repertoire of alternatives, tactful or ironic, to fill the bill. He may compliment his addressees on what he would acknowledge as their good points. He may lavish the sort of praise on them that their own or a generous observer's perspective would allow, even if his would not. He may link their nation's importance to Singapore and their own ideological acceptability to him with sufficient emphasis to dispel the qualms he has about their intelligence. His speeches to Reagan and Thatcher are good examples of this treatment.

In dealing with the world outside his immediate circle, Lee has a blunt instrument that he attempts to use selectively and sharply; the journalist. There are many stories of him attacking the very men on whom he relies to get his message of the moment across. 'I don't need to be interviewed by you,' is one of his favourite opening gambits. On the other hand, because of his frankness with them over the years, some senior journalists have become almost confessor figures, receiving his latest collection of shrewd and peculiar insights, of brilliant logic and perilous lateral thinking, of data evaluation and personality gossip, in the certainty that such comments can never be printed.

Lee and his workaday world

What are the routines and interactions that constitute Lee's normal day when he is in Singapore?

He is a late riser. After aerobic exercises (weights, skipping, rowing or bicycle machine) and a light breakfast, he reads the newspapers and considers his schedule for the day. Agenda matters from the previous twenty-four hours have already been taken off for processing. These are likely to include numbers of 'rockets' demanding correction of specific faults Lee has just noticed. Later in the morning there may be meetings or briefings. Lunch is sometimes a working meal, and it is followed by a lull in activity. Then more exercises (swimming or jogging, formerly golf) gear Lee up for the rest of the day. He may have more meetings, courtesy calls, special dinners or public engagements; he may manage some time with his family at Oxley Road, catching the BBC world news and some edifying conversation. Staff are summoned whenever needed and at whatever hour. The Prime Minister stays up late at night to deal with despatch boxes and papers. His working environment is maintained smoke-free at 22°C, or 19°C for sleep. He has a favourite cook prepare food (avoiding spicy ingredients), and consumes little hard liquor, Chivas Regal scotch being the main exception.

It would be wrong to assume that the routine is intense throughout: there are plenty of opportunities for what Lee calls 'dawdling' (which used to include time with Alex Josey on the golf course). The enthusiasm of the moment can be followed up by reading or by consulting someone who is passing through town, even if other appointments have to be altered.

Many have echoed Goh Keng Swee's view that Lee long ago ceased to talk with Singaporeans outside the upper reaches of the Party and the administration. When he has been among university dons or students, he has come away disappointed. Very few ancillary relationships draw Lee out in a personal way, except when he recognises people who do their jobs with substained competence; or, by contrast, when he feels compelled to criticise those who are not up to the mark 100 per cent of the time. Lee's personal staff are terrified of him; he is likely to bear down on them, demanding instant and total compliance with his orders. Only his wife can check him, and news of her accompanying local or overseas expeditions is greeted with relief. His senior aides have a strong loyalty and regard for his abilities, although departures and changes are not uncommon. For his part, Lee expresses far less interest in them than in their optimum performance.

The concern for performance overrides the civilities traditionally expected of younger men to older men in Chinese and other Asian cultures. Lee has no hesitation about dressing down a civil servant or member of staff, however senior in rank or age. 'You duffer', has been a common insult. Such behaviour—the refusal to allow his elders to save face—combines with Lee's lack of traditional pieties, filial and otherwise, and his latter-day acquisition of Chinese language and history, to bring down the proverbial accusation that he is a man who has forgotten his ancestors.[14]

Two other problems arise from Lee's concern for performance. He is forever interfering and cutting across lines of authority with a pet project or whim, demanding just as much obedience in carrying it out as in completing arrangements made carefully and with due consultation. He tends to single out the obsequious for promotion beyond their abilities, only to react against the sycophancy that cannot conceal their incompetence when they are nearer to him.

Several top civil servants or private sector technocrats have been co-opted into Cabinet, often joining the PAP just before their election to Parliament. They are very capable men, well known to Lee or Goh beforehand, or spotted by the various committees set up for the purpose. They pose no threat to Lee's authority, but their appointment illustrates the ambiguities and strains of an administrative state being a democracy: the mindset of a civil servant or corporate executive is not by training attuned to the people on the 'ground'. Howe Yoon Chong is a good example of a civil servant whose insensitivity to his parliamentary constituents caused problems for the PAP at election time.

The Party has undergone several changes. For eleven years (1954-65) it was all-important to Lee as his base of operation and ascendancy, and the period 1961-65 saw him consolidate clear gains for his faction. Then followed a long phase when the struggles shifted from the political domain to the social and economic. Gradually the PAP turned into what Lee had always mocked—a vote-cranking machine, dormant between elections. It was not easy to keep morale high. The stalwarts of the branches and headquarters have had to look on while outsiders, often youngsters, joined or were brought into the Party, gaining virtually overnight preselection for Parliament and perhaps the promise of a portfolio in the next shuffle. Although Lee has insisted that newcomers learn the ropes of representing their constituencies and working with the relevant secondary associations, the process has undoubtedly rankled with the old guard.

When Toh Chin Chye finally stepped down from the PAP chairmanship—and for some time Lee had been seeking to shunt him to a diplomatic posting or statutory board—the latest phase of party evolution set in, sealed by the subsequent resignation of all Lee's original colleagues and of the complement of second-string Central Executive Committee members who had come in to preserve continuity and Lee's hegemony. Now the Party offers some scope for leaders of the younger generation to test their mettle, to recruit, to try proposals on each other before going to Cabinet and running their leader's gauntlet. But the ultimate power remains, uncontested, with the Secretary-General, who could engineer the necessary party changes whenever he tires of Goh Chok Tong and company or believes they are wrecking the apparatus of state he has so carefully built up.

The atmosphere of government in Singapore has come to bear a remarkable resemblance to that of an imperial court. Its only member who still has independent status is Rajaratnam. His choice, however, has not been to fight Lee but to act as resident philosopher, dressing up decisions and policies, prophesying after the event and putting the appropriate gloss on history or current affairs. The craft of spinning words and designs has occupied Raja's energy and, although he is shrill in criticism of the latest villain, he has had a weak stomach for heated argument or face-to-face attack. He combines an amiable disposition with a capacity for sharp character assessment.

Apart from Lee himself, by far the most important palace figure is his wife. She has risen by degrees, with little evidence of scheming. Her role began to grow from the moment she first curbed her husband's outbursts. From being chief custodian of the children's upbringing, advising on the aptness of certain speeches and helping to keep the peace or vet budding politicians' wives, Kwa Geok Choo has reached the point where she alone is the indispensable confidante to her husband and to that rising star, their son, Lee Hsien Loong. Over the years she has strenuously denied any political interest, wish to interfere, or ambition on her part. 'I walk two steps behind my husband like a good Asian wife,' she said once.[15] But the logic of her position as wife and mother does not allow her the luxury of such detachment. Capable of being charming and viperish, homely and sophisticated, courteous and resolute, she has a brilliant intellect that those placed to know have compared more than favourably with Lee Kuan Yew's. Even if she never assumes a more explicit role in government—conceivable only to tide over an emergency transition period—her nod of approval is seen to be crucial among the younger generation of leaders who crowd the antechamber to the throne room and will do so until the genuine succession is decided, probably by 1988. (A lot will depend on the shakedown of the presidency after Wee Kim Wee's interim tenure.)

The First Deputy Prime Minister, Goh Chok Tong, is, to change the metaphor, having a turn at the helm. His high profile is only puzzling to those who set much store by it. It needs to be remembered that his base is the PAP as it currently operates: he has done sterling work in rebuilding the Party's sense of purpose and has won colleagues' loyalty, but he is still at the beck and call of the Prime Minister. Nor is he perceived by the people to be much of a leader—he is too awkward—and has insufficient clout in his own right to enable tough policies to be framed and seen through. To have won skirmishes and disagreements in Cabinet, to have been given a few months or even years to tinker with policy and present a more accommodating image says nothing of final victory or the old man's reserve powers. All of Goh Chok Tong's other principal colleagues have very good points: Ong Teng Cheong is from the Chinese-educated side, a distinction fast being blurred although still advantageous; he works smoothly with others, is colourless, perhaps, but very competent. Tony Tan is brilliant at assessing feasibility and drawing up blueprints for the future; he has something of the late Hon Sui Sen about him: the essential technocrat, obedient to the limits of his conscience but not beyond and arousing the suspicion that he shows human warmth when off duty and among his family. Dhanabalan, well aware that as an Indian he cannot expect to be Prime Minister, is shrewd, very bright, and in full command of whatever brief he receives, though sometimes impatient of the pretences and protocols required for domestic and foreign show.

These men are accepted as having great integrity and being conscientious to a fault. But the mantle of top leadership does not appear to sit naturally on any of them, with the possible exception of Tony Tan. They are the creatures of the Prime Minister and Dr Goh Keng Swee, which makes it hard for them to have the drive, flair or freedom to emerge in their own right.

Certainly, there are ambitious PAP men coming on stage or waiting impatiently in the wings. Good examples of each kind are Yeo Ning Hong and Ng Pock Too. Yeo is clever, quite dashing, and has made a strong bid to be identified with the armed forces and their strong defence approach. It remains to be seen whether the 1985 bungling of the taxi-fare issue (within his Communications portfolio) has set him back. Ng is tough and unattractive; however erroneous the parallel, it is hard to avoid seeing something of Phey Yew Kok's over-confidence in him.*

A revealing comment about the present period of transition in Singapore's leadership was made by the Prime Minister during his Indonesian tour of April 1985. Whatever imagery of Lee as goalkeeper and himself as centre forward Goh Chok Tong had been promoting, Lee indicated that he retained control of 'the direction in which policies will go, because we are able to induct a group of younger men and convince them that what we've been doing makes sense, and they should not lightly throw overboard policies which have been successful'. He considered that the reward 'for going earlier than we need to' was that 'we have more say in policies after we are no longer in charge. I think that is a fair trade-off'.[16]

The crown prince of Singapore is Lee Hsien Loong. Always referred to as Brigadier-General (Reservists) or B-G Lee for short—a rank to which he was promoted in 1984 some three months before handing in his regular commission to enter politics—he is an exceptional young man. It is impossible to forget he is the Prime Minister's son, and it is doubtful that he would have risen to prominence quite so rapidly without the (unsolicited) special attention and goodwill of his military superiors and peers. It is also unlikely that he would have had his upbringing and education from any other father. But no one can gainsay Hsien

---

* Phey Yew Kok was the erstwhile trade union boss and MP who disappeared overseas in 1980 while facing charges of misappropriation of funds.

Loong's formidable brain and his achievements; no one can overlook his own unusual degree of self-possession, astuteness and managerial ability, coupled with a feline grace, modest demeanour and orientation to civic service. He represents the best of both parents and his worst is not yet known. He does not seem to hunger for unmerited recognition and only the lionising of the media and the people singles him out whenever he appears in public.

Lee Kuan Yew is known to be relieved beyond words that his son has abandoned earlier slow preparation plans and come on stage without further ado. While everyone else is bound to be a little more edgy having to contend with two Lees rather than one (or three rather than two), the boost to long-term international confidence and the reduction of his need to manhandle the succession alone have clearly cheered the Prime Minister's spirits.

Cabinet was for some years virtually synonymous with the CEC. This strange phenomenon was partly a ploy to subordinate the Party to government, especially when its Chairman was the argumentative and fiercely independent Toh Chin Chye. The Prime Minister retained the whip hand in his capacity as head of Cabinet.

Several categories of courtier have backed and filled in Cabinet and senior posts since 1963: Goh Keng Swee's or Lee's friends such as Lim Kim San and Hon Sui Sen, family members such as Yong Nyuk Lin, recruits from Lee and Lee (the Prime Minister's law firm) such as Eddie Barker and Chua Sian Chin, party offsiders and subordinates such as Jek Yeun Thong or Lee Khoon Choy. Many have stepped down: Wong Ling Ken, Lee Chiaw Meng, Tan Eng Liang, Lim Chee Onn, for example. Malays have come and gone—Othman Wok, Rahim Ishak—without entering the innermost circle, and their current Cabinet representative, Ahmad Mattar, was only made a full Minister after years in an acting capacity.

Lee was given the nickname of 'Thunderclap' by other Cabinet members, and for the sake of the nation and their own skin they have put up with a great deal. The problem is that most of them have had a narrow base—no emergence out of party or political organising experience, inadequate linguistic skills, lack of specific expertise in relevant areas—and have risen to ministerial rank by direct patronage.

But in the absence of friendship or personal bonds, several potent factors prevent membership of the Cabinet, or CEC for that matter, from being a bleak exercise. Commitment to some or most of the leadership's principles may provide motivation. There is the stimulus of planning and implementing, of testing ideas against penetrating scrutiny. Another stimulus is being at the top of the pyramid, even if a little precariously. And the constant pressure on Singapore can give a heady, global sense of importance to deliberations.

Despite these benefits and the lesser perquisites of office, the strain of being one of the elite demands a strong constitution. Nepotism and corruption must have played a smaller part in Singapore's development than almost anywhere else in the world. Meritocracy prevails. But if one's virtue is no longer deemed virtue, the only hope of remaining in court (and not all persist in that hope) is to have some claim on the patronage of the extended government family.

The most interesting relationship in Singapore's political history has been that of Lee Kuan Yew and Goh Keng Swee. It has had a dynamic equilibrium missing in Lee's regular dealings with others. Goh is much more of a professional mandarin than the Prime Minister. His mind teems with ideas and his intellectual curiosity remains at the ready. He laments the lack of time to explore archives or to branch out elsewhere, beyond the call of duty. He has given free rein to those whose skills he has admired, yet he has been quite ruthless in cutting losses or casting off those who have failed to justify his confidence. He is less inclined than Lee to idealise or condemn others arbitrarily. His standing in his predominantly Cantonese constituency, Kreta Ayer, remains excellent. He has been relaxed about himself and, whilst admitting that he would perhaps have liked to be Prime Minister (having often acted or deputised for Lee), he has never pushed himself forward. And he 'wouldn't have done things differently'.[17] His distaste for rhetoric and populist appeal has undoubtedly been a factor in his staying behind the throne, as well as recurring bouts of ill-health.

He believes that Lee Kuan Yew is the best thing going for Singapore. Lee for his part must miss Goh both in the Cabinet 'where the big issues are thrashed out and major decisions taken' and in the 'benign tension' of day-to-day discussion and planning. In a letter of tribute to Dr Goh, published after the latter's retirement in December 1984, the Prime Minister wrote glowingly of his deputy's 'stupendous exertions', laying the foundations of modern Singapore's economy and, as well, catering for the aesthetic dimension of life (in the form of commercially risky ventures such as the Jurong Bird Park and the establishment of the Singapore Symphony Orchestra). 'Your robust attitude encouraged me to press on against seemingly unwinnable odds . . . Your biggest contribution to me personally was that you stood up to me whenever you held the contrary view. You challenged my decisions and forced me to re-examine the premises on which they were made.'[18]

Despite the deep bond between them, the two men have not been close friends. Although both are unconventional, even impious, in outlook and both are committed to rationalising society around a vanguard of enterprising and far-seeing leaders, their personalities manifest themselves quite differently. Lim Kim San characterised Goh as 'introvert', Lee as 'extrovert'; the terminology is a bit loose but it does point to their contrasting complementary qualities.[19]

For a friend's view of Lee in his normal milieu, we can do no better than to look through the eyes of Devan Nair, Singapore's recently resigned President. Of all the interviews conducted for this book, his was the only one unreservedly enthusiastic; and although Devan's circumstances have changed, sadly for the worse, we cannot discard the views of a person who has been so close to our subject. The interview took place on 3 April 1976 in Devan Nair's NTUC office.

Given Devan Nair's own religious convictions, my approach was to ask if the political arena was a proper milieu in which to pursue spiritual aspirations and what Lee's spirituality was. This is a summary of Devan's reply:

> Maybe only exceptional individuals like Gandhi can bring spiritual concerns directly to bear on politics. But the quality of any leader is directly related to his spiritual aspirations and inner life. Lee Kuan Yew has an intense inner life, one not defined by any particular religion. It is evident from the very high standards he sets himself in both private and public domains.
> There is a world of difference between those who like to be seen on top—their motives are egoistic—and those who have the inner capacity to be on top. Lee stands out from the run-of-the-mill politician because he can look beyond tomorrow, make projections, develop a vision and ignore or bypass the trivia of the present. But in so doing he may give the impression of lacking sensitivity, being aloof.
> Mind you, he is very effective at a popular level. He doesn't resort to oratory. He doesn't aim for the solar plexus. He converses, shares his analysis and appeals to the mind, so that even the least intellectual Singaporean begins to understand.
> His shortcomings are those of a man who is quicker on the uptake.

I have the highest esteem for Kuan Yew as a politician, a man and a friend.

Many who have intense desires to achieve give way to self-pity when they meet obstacles. Lee doesn't take blocks in his path, things going wrong, personally.

Again, once he accepts the bona fides of an individual, such as Goh Keng Swee, Rajaratnam or myself, he gives implicit trust. If he has reservations about a person, he is prickly, like a porcupine.

Whatever the uncertainties or absurdities about him, there is commitment.

His spirituality is expressed in his concern for people. Why else would he insist on such high standards for himself, his family, friends, the Government and the people of Singapore? These standards are necessary to the desired quality of life.

Kuan Yew can perceive quality in others—he is aware, for instance, of the strength of inner life in Roman Catholics.

The new elite emerging in Singapore troubles him. He is striving to create a new Jerusalem and it turns out to be a new Babylon! What is intended is very different from the result!

In the matter of Lee's own beliefs, I asked if the rumours of his interest in astrology were true. Devan Nair said that some close to Lee took it seriously.

On one occasion P. Govindaswamy, [late] MP for Anson and Kuan Yew's deputy at meet-the-people sessions in Tanjong Pagar, claimed, despite Lee's affectionate teasing, that the stars showed there was something clogging the Singapore River: unless it was removed, economic progress would be impeded.

Devan Nair gathered also that one or two of the women in Lee's family had sought to have his fortune told by astrologers.

Talking of his family, his wife is a marvellous breakwater for him. He doesn't appreciate what an overwhelming influence he has.

When he consciously wants to exercise influence he is terrific. With downright dishonesty he is quite ruthless. But it costs him heartache and sadness. Take the case of Wee Toon Boon:* I saw tears in Lee's eyes when he resolved that he could not avoid decisive action any longer.

---

* Wee Toon Boon was imprisoned in 1976 on four counts of corruption. He was a Minister of State and a 'friend' and 'comrade' of Lee's, going back to 1957 and the City Council elections.

The really great stand alone. Like the English military gentleman who is afraid to be seen reading Keats and Shelley, so goes to the toilet to do so, Lee doesn't wear his heart or his culture on his sleeve!

My last question dealt with the influences that have shaped Lee. Devan Nair responded:

> His relationship to his parents is not close. It could be described as conventional.
> Some of his teachers have been very influential. His world-view owes a great deal to his British education. Since then, he has been mainly affected by Gandhi and Nehru and some of the Chinese classics.

Devan Nair ended our interview with a joke; he told me it was one of a number about Lee Kuan Yew's adventures in Heaven and Hell. I was so surprised I stopped taking notes! Instead here is an excerpt from another, recounted on the occasion of Lee's fiftieth birthday.[20]

> St Peter found Lee knocking at the gate of Heaven after a long and richly satisfying life on earth. On hearing Lee's entry qualifications, St Peter thought for a while, then said, 'The divine decree has gone forth that creation's purpose will not be fulfilled until Hell is transformed. Since you have put a God-forsaken place like Singapore right, you might try your hand with Hell.' True to character, Lee did not wait to argue with St Peter. He set off. Twenty-four hours later, there was a frantic knocking at the Pearly Gates. St Peter opened them to find that it was Lucifer, flabby with self-indulgence, perspiring profusely, heaving and panting, and begging for refuge in Heaven. 'What's all this?' asked Peter. 'My God!' exclaimed Lucifer. 'Twenty-four hours ago you sent down a man by the name of Lee Kuan Yew. He has taken over. And you know what? He expects even *me* to work!'

C. Northcote Parkinson, who met Lee in the 1950s during the latter's periodic visits to Singapore's university, observed him cutting students down to size and doubted that he was a man even capable of friendship. Devan's testimony is eloquent rebuttal of the aspersion. On the other hand, friendship is a thin strand in Lee's life among his peers. He has always talked freely of friends, and rarely in sarcastic vein: but few graced with the title return it in kind.

Lee and his context

Understanding of Lee Kuan Yew would be incomplete if we ignored the context in which he has operated with what appears such a free hand.

There have, in fact, always been limits to the power he has been allowed to exercise. One of the harshest lessons he received in the Malaysia years was that whatever long-term ambitions he might entertain for himself or his policies, he was being deliberately frustrated in the short term with a determination that became no less furious than his own.

Many years ago, he was approached as a possible candidate to be United Nations Secretary-General. Although he toyed with the thought, he refused; not surprisingly in view of his preference for real, versus titular, power. His ventures into geopolitical analysis and manoeuvring are rooted in the desire for his Singapore to get the best deal. The UN post would not have given him the resources and sanctions necessary to achieve this.

It would be ridiculous to describe the transformation of Singapore from 1959 to today simply as the result of Lee's—and Goh's—efforts, in close collaboration with invaluable colleagues. To say that Lee is isolated and beholden to very few is only to describe the mode of his power. Without active co-operation, the Party would never have got off the ground, the civil service and business communities would never have rallied, and the people of Singapore would have become so frustrated that no one could have prevented their protest. In 1972, Iain Buchanan predicted that unrest and violence would shortly erupt onto the streets of Singapore because Lee had suppressed all normal channels of opposition.[21] His prediction was wrong. While that may suggest increased tyranny, it may also be because few Singaporeans yet believe they have anything to gain by rebellion.

Lee came upon the political scene when the colonial powers that had brought Singapore into being had forfeited credibility. They were beginning to withdraw, however reluctantly, to minimise damage to their fundamental economic interests. Other local alternatives were politically inept, corrupt, or less acceptable to the British. At stake was an island that, whilst closely linked to its hinterland, had a distinctive identity because of its strategic importance as a military base, its character as middleman *entrepôt* port and its predominantly Chinese composition. When Singapore and Malaya were split and administered separately in 1946, many preferred it so.

The Chinese who migrated and came to Singapore had left China to make good, or even to survive, rather than to stagnate or perish amid the turmoil and privations of their home provinces. They hoped to return to their homeland sooner or later. Away from the peasant economy of southern China, some had again taken up farming or fishing, but many became artisans, labourers, traders and adventurers. They retained their customs, their dialects, their clan associations, their religious practices, their artefacts and their secret society connections. But these did not form the cutting edge of their life overseas, only some of its driving force. This is confirmed by two related facts. Many of the cultural and ritual constructs they brought with them to alien lands were 'frozen' and tended to become tests and rewards of their loyalty to the past. And when the quest for prosperity became the cutting edge, some of the migrants (and increasing numbers with later generations) were willing to let their children embrace the languages and social mores of the new land's masters in order to succeed. Even the price of estrangement from family and culture was not considered too high.

The *towkays*,* the Straits-born and the King's Chinese formed three overlapping circles closest to the centre of British patronage in the settlements of Singapore, Penang and Malacca. Their relative cultural disorientation fitted well enough with the restless energy of the Caucasian entrepreneurs whose capitalistic urges and hopes of adventure had brought them east to open up the colonies. However little love might have been lost between the various elites, Asian and European, they were all able to flourish under the colonial governments' protection: that is, until the Japanese Occupation of 1942–45.

There have probably been few tribes on earth better poised to take advantage of commercial opportunity and rapid urbanisation than the overseas Chinese in Southeast Asia. They had no scruples or taboos about handling money and practising usury, and from the centres where they first gathered and established themselves, their kinship networks gave the more venturesome courage to fan out and develop a complex trading structure right down to village level, connected by land transport and shipping to all the regional ports. The contrast between them and the Muslim and animist peasants of Malaya and Indonesia was stark from the outset.

The traditional Chinese trust in the upward force of education also held sway among those who had migrated, with an inbuilt bias

---

* *towkay* = leading Chinese merchant.

towards equipping their children for a brighter future. Although much prodding by the government of Lee Kuan Yew was required to shift the ethnic Chinese emphasis from solely entrepreneurial and servicing occupations to include industry and manufacturing, modernisation meant no quantum leap for them as it did for the Malays in the *kampongs** or Tamil labourers on the plantations and railway gangs.

The East Asian civilisations of Japan, China and Korea set great store by each unit of society pursuing the means at its disposal to achieve a beneficial harmony with its milieu. Lee has spent much of his life pondering the reasons for this—genetic endowment, nurture, climate, force of history? Whatever the reasons, the result is that these cultures have an inherent pragmatism—seek what works and what works best, and use it. Despite strains and modifications, Japan has been more easily able to retain her traditional values and social structures because of her linguistic homogeneity and her isolation and because the national identity around the Emperor still has some cohesive force. Modernisation has proceeded with cultural contamination being reduced or Nipponised. Lee's Singapore is not nearly as isolated, and it comprises many fragments, but among the Chinese there is some basis for co-ordinated progress because they have been free to recognise that commercial and technical skills currently provide the best avenues to prosperity.

There are sections of Singapore society, the Malays for instance, who have seen the creation of a new national identity as brutal, and they have clung to deep roots of their own to resist the complete undermining of their self-confidence. There are, as well, many individuals who never make the grade, or who drop out along the way. The longer term significance of those outside the prevailing ethic will be considered later.

Basically, however, Lee has not had the completely impossible task of going against the grain of all his people all the time. Far from it. In 1959 he was able to take over the umbrella that had shielded the people of Singapore for 140 years. The authoritarian measures the British had adopted to keep the peace suited him well, and by and large he maintained them, even refined and extended them. The initial justification he gave—the prospect of merger with Malaya—removed the colonial stigma. After Separation, Lee was in a strong enough position to preserve repressive measures on his own authority. The chief objections to British rule had been to foreign cultural imperialism, or to law and order imposed from

---

* *kampong* = rural village, settlement.

outside—not to law and order themselves. By contrast, the Marxists suffered from being seen as the group willing to destabilise an economic system that was not completely uncongenial to the rest of the population.

Lee has two further advantages in his political management of today's Singapore. Once a society takes out a stake in the methods and benefits of being a technocracy, the inevitable outcome is an increase of central control at a national or corporate level. The international economy that Singapore serves has become too complex and too mesmerising for village, dynastic or municipal politics to influence to any great extent. Thus far, the purpose of large-scale technology has not been to increase political freedom on the ground.

Moreover, a small island state cannot expect to preserve its accustomed manner of existence and livelihood in a problematic world and alien region if there is no discipline or restraint. Whatever the gaffes and indiscretions of his behaviour towards the outside world, Lee is still perceived to be the person best equipped for handling the thorns of the foreign relations garden so that Singaporeans may pluck or at least sniff the roses.

Today's Singapore and the government of Prime Minister Lee Kuan Yew have reached a state of transition. Such are the demands of the present and the immediate future that it is tempting to forget the past. The temptation may become irresistible to any citizens further wearied by the 'correct' versions of history lately rolling off the presses. Yet there has never been a greater need than now for a careful tracing of Lee's journey to power and of its context at each stage. The social shapes and directions spun from his ambition as much as from the circumstances he found teach precise lessons that must be learned if whoever forms a successor government is to be any the wiser for Lee's long tenure of office.

By Lee's own repeated assertion and by general consensus, the starting point for our investigations is the Japanese Occupation of 1942–45.

LEFT HAND, RIGHT HAND

and we would plant our hearts
in the dark of our neighbour's ground
tending our secret fear-wish
that he may discover we cared

and we would plant our hate
in the dark of our enemy's ground
and blow him sky-high in the morning
that he will discover we dared

LEE TZU PHENG

2
War and Self-Preparation

> My colleagues and I are of that generation of young men who went through the Second World War and the Japanese Occupation and emerged determined that no one—neither the Japanese nor the British—had the right to push and kick us around. We determined that we could govern ourselves and bring up our children in a country where we can be proud to be a self-respecting people.
>
> LEE KUAN YEW,
> *The Battle for Merger*, 1961, pp. 10–11

The colonial realities of Malaya were exposed and upended by the Japanese Occupation. The Europeans in Lee Kuan Yew's words, 'were stripped literally naked as prisoners of war, and became ordinary people. It was the Japanese ten-cent storeman who, backed by Japanese military might, suddenly became the big boss who occupied a big house and had a better life'.[1]

The War and the Japanese Occupation

Of Malaya's major races, the Chinese were the most dramatically affected. The various responses to Japanese incursion seen in China—ranging from violent resistance to obsequious collaboration—were repeated in Malaya. But the political texture and the setting were quite different and much more complex.

Partly by design, partly by accident, the British had presided over a society consisting of radically different races and cultures. The policy of the colonial government was to protect the major races' separate development, moving gradually towards a degree of integration, with the benefits of rubber and tin extraction meanwhile flowing back to the metropolis. This balancing act was not only disrupted but fatally undermined by the Japanese capture of Malaya that culminated in the fall of Singapore on 15 February 1942.

The Malays made up half the mainland population. They subsisted in rural areas and were ruled by sultans and traditional leaders. Islam and local custom shaped their societies. Under the British, the Malays had been given greater political latitude than the other Asian races. Apart from the predominantly Chinese Straits Settlements (Singapore, Penang, Malacca), Malaya had become a federation of states. Each retained its own character under its sultan. The Japanese preserved this *status quo*. However, administrative needs pushed them to rely more on Malay civil servants and the mainly Malay police force was used in suppressing the Chinese, a disaster for race relations. The generally preferential treatment accorded the Malays had an added impact in Singapore, where they were very much in the minority.

As for Malaya's Indians, the Japanese sought to harness them, together with fellow expatriates, in the subjugated territories as far west as Burma. Substantial numbers were mobilised for the strategic task of defeating the British in India. From July 1943 and again from May 1945, Subhas Chandra Bose, the militant anti-British Bengali, made Singapore his base. 'Netaji', as he was reverently known, commanded the Indian National Army.[*] Collaboration, willing or expedient, was the prudent course; those who dissented were forced underground and could offer little co-ordinated resistance.

The Eurasians, concentrated in urban centres such as Singapore, were awkwardly placed during the Occupation. By definition their relations with the new regime were difficult. Little trust or acceptance came to them from any quarter.

Through the period in question, the Chinese comprised about 70 per cent of the population of *Syonan* (the Japanese name for Singapore). They formed the backbone of the economy and the Japanese rode them roughshod, extracting their wealth directly or making use of their inventiveness and enterprise whilst taking ownership control. A purge immediately after Occupation destroyed any chance of willing co-operation between most of the Chinese and their new masters. Those who collaborated were loathed. The Straits-born Chinese, known as Babas, who had already relinquished much of their racial identity and acquired a distinctive cultural heritage with Malay and English their principal languages, were in a particularly self-conscious and defensive position. They resented reprisals that should have been vented, if at all, on recent immigrants still connected to the struggles in China. They feared contempt and persecution on two opposite fronts: from the Japanese for being lackeys of the British, and from the

---

[*] He ended his life in an air crash out of Formosa *en route* to Japan, August 1945.

'proper' Chinese for holding on to former privileges in business and administration under their new colonial masters.

Lee and his family during the War

As with many of the Straits-born families, the King's Chinese in particular, the outbreak of the European war was a blow to the Lee Chin Koon family. The eldest son, Harry (Kuan Yew), had topped Malaya in the Senior Cambridge examinations of 1939, and his parents had saved money to help him go to England in pursuit of a legal career. Now he had to wait.

Apart from courses in medicine and dentistry offered by King Edward VII College, the only local opportunities for higher education lay at Raffles College. It had been founded in 1928, with Baba pressure and finance, to train young men and a few women for teaching, for middle-echelon posts in the civil service and to bridge the gap between secondary education in Malaya and the British universities. Harry enrolled to study there.

At Raffles College, the sixteen-year-old Harry encountered a new world of people and opportunities. Years later he identified two permanent benefits: he met his future wife and gained a grounding in economics. There were other formative experiences. As a resident of the College he was confirmed in his dislike of separation from the creature comforts of home. He also had to cope with being ostracised for his dogged avoidance of the customary fresher 'ragging'—acts of humiliation at the hands of seniors.

His academic subjects were economics, mathematics and English literature. He stood out in the select company of Raffles College, not only for his formal success as a student but as a budding orator who took over the debating society to sharpen and display his prowess. The elite social setting introduced him to a number of the people—teachers and students—who would be significant in the course of his own and Malaya's political development.

Many found Harry hard to take; he was a young man who swung between being friendly and loud-mouthed and competitive and solitary. Abdul Razak, for example, later to be Malayan and Malaysian Prime Minister, looked at him askance, no doubt with the eyes of a traditional Muslim and a person of markedly different temperament.

This buoyant and assertive phase of Harry Lee's life ended abruptly when the Japanese bombed Singapore. He was enlisted as a mobile medical orderly in the civilian organisation. Only weeks later he witnessed with bewilderment British surrender of an island believed unassailable. Empire troops marched dejectedly past his house into captivity. The whole framework of his elaborate planning—his facility in English, his thoughts of a legal career, his acceptance of his family's hopes for him (although on his own terms)—was dashed to the ground. In an interview broadcast over New Zealand television in April 1975, he said:

> I think the single most important event in my life was the Japanese entry into Singapore when the Imperial Guards set up sentry points at every bridge, chased me into a corner of my room whilst the officers and men took over the house and billeted themselves and I was generally knocked about. I wondered why it should be so. I think that was the single most traumatic experience.

Two other early incidents brought home to Lee how precarious his life could be at the mercy of crass foreign soldiers. In February 1942, he was ordered onto a lorry at the Weld Road—Jalan Besar Concentration Centre exit point, 'presumably to do some work for the Japanese. But somehow I felt that particular lorry was not going to carry people to work'.[2] He asked permission to collect some belongings first, and to his surprise it was given. He went on his way, and did not return. The people on the lorry were carted off and never seen again. Lee had escaped a fate that befell many young Chinese males.

Again, a Japanese sentry at the Red Bridge in Norfolk Road near his home made the youngster ride a bicycle round and round in circles, encouraging the bystanders, mostly children, to clap and jeer. He might also have been beaten by the soldier on that occasion, an incident he recalled years later.

On the whole, however, Lee and some of his colleagues who founded the People's Action Party survived the war with less physical distress than a good many of their compatriots. Raffles College became the Japanese military headquarters two days after British surrender. But the students had left and most of them had resources and connections to fall back on. Take the case of Goh Keng Swee: as a member of the Singapore Volunteer Corps, he should have been liquidated. But fate was kind. He stayed on to complete a game of bridge when he should have reported to the Japanese with his fellow volunteers for screening. The others were all executed. He was shielded by a friend, given work in the War Tax Department, and went on to marry a local Japanese woman.

Although Harry's future brother-in-law was shot and killed, he himself and his family managed quite well. They continued to live in their Norfolk Road home, taking in boarders including the late Hon Sui Sen, who was a junior civil servant at the time. Later in the war, when Allied bombing intensified, they moved to the top floor of the China Building, the premises of the Garden Club, where Harry's father was appointed caretaker.

One of the main reasons why the Occupation was relatively bearable for the Lees was because of the help of Tan Chong Chew, a wealthy Harbour Board contractor who had been Harry's mother's special friend for some years. Tan prospered at his business during the war years. Another reason was Harry's work as a stenographer and then translator with the Japanese news agency Domei. He had quickly applied himself to learn written and spoken Japanese.

The agency work gave him up-to-date world news. Once the tide turned and the Allies were winning the Pacific war, he began to circulate information contradicting Japanese propaganda. His masters eventually became suspicious of him and he slipped away from Domei early in 1945. Warned against seeking refuge in the Cameron Highlands whilst on his way there, he hid in Singapore to await the return of the British.

Free of Domei, Harry could devote more time to business, selling gum, a venture shared with his future wife, whose wealthy family had been reduced to living frugally but resourcefully in Tiong Bahru. In common with many better off Malayans, Harry profited from black market dealings—the sale of looted furniture and other goods. His mother supervised these operations.

T.J.S. George records the speculation of a 'leading British journalist' that during his employment with Domei Harry was also in contact with the British.[3] The journalist wondered if Lee might not have been receiving payment for services rendered when he had such surprising success soon after the war in arranging passage to the United Kingdom aboard a troopship, the *Britannic*. It is not impossible. But a more prosaic explanation could lie in the family link with Tan Chong Chew: because he was deemed to be a collaborator, he did not dare show his face in the Harbour Board once the Japanese had left. Harry took on his work and made quite a lot of money. And he would have found the appropriate transport officer who could secure a cheap berth on one of many ships taking troops home to Britian.

Whatever explanation is correct, there are, as George says, many gaps in information about Lee's career which fuel rumours of covert activities.[4] The themes of secrecy and loaded silence recur.

After the Occupation

> When the war came to an end in 1945, there was never a chance of the old type of British colonial system ever being recreated. The scales had fallen from our eyes and we saw for ourselves that the local people could run the country.
>
> Lee Kuan Yew, *The Battle for Merger*, 1961, p. 11

As a result of the Occupation, racial divisions in Malaya were sharpened and the forces of Marxist–Leninist revolution gained momentum. It is intriguing to contemplate how different the course of history would have been had the Pacific war ended a little later.

The Japanese had supported the idea of a Greater Indonesia to embrace Malaya. A faction of radical Malays wanted to make a last-minute bid, through Hatta in Taiping negotiating with the Malayan Communist Party (MCP) and Soekarno in Saigon with the Japanese High Command, to have Malaya included in the Indonesian declaration of independence. The plan was thwarted both by surrender and by the MCP's insistence that the Malays be disarmed.

With British assistance, the MCP had built up a tough fighting force, mostly Chinese. Why did the communists fail to take advantage of the Japanese surrender to seize control of Malaya? Did savage Malay resistance to their 'liberation' endeavours in Johore give them pause? Was there too little time? Did the treacherous Lai Teck's counsel prevail—to await the British and work for power constitutionally?*

Even though Malaya emerged from Occupation under neither Indonesian nor MCP dominance, the reactions and attitudes of the British were no longer the ultimate determining factors in Malayan politics. Many other groups and classes came to the fore with demands for political rights.

British plans for postwar Malaya had been made in the Colonial Office and War Cabinet, without serious attention to local viewpoints. Consultation had been envisaged but was forgotten in the rush to resume control after the Japanese had capitulated.

Both prongs of postwar policy—Singapore to be reserved outside Malaya, and the loosely federated states of Malaya to be made into a union with common citizenship for the locally born of

---

* Lai Teck was MCP leader at the time; he later defected and was discovered to have been a double agent for the British and the Japanese.

whatever race—provoked hostile reaction. But the Malayan Union proposal drew most fire. Racial politics came to the fore, with the United Malays' National Organisation (UMNO) being formed to safeguard Malay rights.

In this rapid polarisation, the Malay masses were further lost to the MCP, which was clearly seen to be Chinese. The small Malay Nationalist Party, successor to previous Malay pro-communist groups and with cadres drawn mainly from intellectuals and journalists, could not make much headway against an UMNO backed by the traditional rulers.

Almost overnight the political centre of gravity moved across the Causeway from Singapore. The island began to look more like a Chinese Gibraltar than the headquarters of the peninsula, with organic control of its economic, administrative and military affairs. From that time, attempts to bring Singapore back into Malaya or to intensify the contradictions of Malayan society and consolidate the struggle of urban or rural poor could be frustrated by the threat of racial tension. The government in power could also have a ready-made excuse to delay reform and to justify suppression.

The parting gift of the Japanese to the British was a Pandora's box not just of anti-colonialism but of heightened communalism. Lee said, 'Such was their blindness and brutality, they never knew what they did to a whole generation like me. But they did make me, and a whole generation like me, determined to work for freedom —freedom from servitude and foreign domination. I did not enter politics: they brought politics upon me. I decided that our lives should be ours to decide ... that we should not be the pawns and playthings of foreign powers.'[5]

The beginnings of a political career?

> Because of his wartime experiences, Lee became the first overseas Chinese, that is to say a person of Chinese origin, in Southeast Asia, to devote his life to politics.
>
> Alex Josey, *Lee Kuan Yew: The Struggle for Singapore*, 1974, p. 21

Lee Kuan Yew and all those who have written about him explain his involvement in politics as a result of the war, but unfortunately this explanation raises as many questions as it answers.

No one would deny that the postwar period saw an explosion of political consciousness in Malaya. Not only were memories of the Occupation fresh, the return of the British and the period of their military administration saw mismanagement and corruption flourish on a grand scale. (The joke going the rounds was that BMA stood for Black Market Administration.) T.H. Silcock, the late economist and academic, who lived through it all, was one of many who believed that the British put paid to their colonial cause in Malaya far more effectively after the war than the Japanese had done over the previous three and a half years.[6]

The Malays were rallied by their leaders to protect a position the British seemed to be downgrading. Many looked anew to Indonesia to underwrite their security and a few still hoped she would provide the base for a homegrown, potentially Marxist independence.

Some urban Indians were anxious to participate in India's struggles but their circumstances as poor aliens and their minority status in Malaya dictated more modest ambitions. They formed unions and political ginger groups and came under British socialist influence.

The Chinese had been cruelly treated, particularly recent immigrants. Their ties to the homeland, their deep resentment at foreign oppression, made them responsive either to the rising star of Mao Tse Tung* or, less and less, to Chiang Kai Shek.

Among all the races there was also a contrary spirit, one of withdrawal: in relief at war's end and in hope of pursuing private fortunes again or regaining normalcy.

The least likely sources of political activists with mass appeal were the Straits-born Chinese and the English-educated. Their cultural isolation made them specially and often willingly dependent on European patronage.

Yet it was from among them that Lee came. They were not beyond the reach of Western or regional ideologies of revolt: consider the handful of anti-colonial radicals such as P.V. Sharma, Lim Kean Chye, Joseph Tan, John Eber, Samad Ismail and Devan Nair. But on the whole the English-educated Malayans' political ambitions, where they existed, were not especially serious; they presupposed independent means and continuing British rule. Lee was to prove one of the rare exceptions, neither an out-and-out radical nor a political dabbler.

There is no reason to doubt that by 1945 Lee was already convinced he must help Malayans run their own country. Yet he did not plunge into any organised local political activity until 1950, and then within the gradualist Progressive Party. He and his

---

* Hereafter Mao Zedong (the Pinyin literation).

colleagues were to rise to power from being, in his words, 'a bunch of armchair critics of British colonialism'.[7]

Lee faced this paradox publicly on 24 November 1966 when one of his regular tirades against the English-educated provoked a university student in the audience to ask what had made him so different. He began his reply by noting the trauma of the Occupation, then went on, 'Either you form a new set of values or you are a broken personality ... I formed a new set of values and I questioned what went before and have never ceased to question it.'

T.J.S. George provides a clue why Lee changed his outlook: the Occupation had a profound effect on him because he 'was a naturally sensitive boy'.[8] He reacted strongly against the physical violence of the Japanese and dramatised what happened to others as adding vicarious injury to the insults he himself suffered. He decided that henceforth he would espouse reason, argument and persuasion, the politics of a civilised man. He was not the first overseas Chinese to devote his life to politics—men such as Chin Peng (Ong Boon Hua) born at Sitiawan, Perak, in 1921, had been seasoned MCP operatives before the Japanese invasion. But he was the first to take the Westminster system of parliamentary democracy as his point of departure for a full-blown career.

By twenty-two years of age, Harry emerged from the Occupation determined to be some sort of political leader. It was a project for a lifetime, and thorough preparation was needed.

At this point, fundamental questions must be asked. What in Lee disposed him to respond as he did to the war years? What 'visceral urges' drove him to scale the rarefied heights of governing other people's lives and reshaping a whole society? Such ambitions were certainly not the norm in postwar Malaya.

What may be published or known of Harry Lee's childhood does not give sufficient basis for answering these questions. So we are obliged to move forward in time, to examine the leading features of his public career as it unfolds. Only then will the meagre clues of the childhood years take their rightful place in our quest for understanding.

Lee overseas

From September 1945 Lee organised a study programme at his home, inviting his old tutor, Lim Tay Boh, to give a series of informal lectures. Lim was an economist who had taught at Raffles Institution* and had then been seconded to Raffles College on the

---

* Singapore's foremost government-run secondary school.

outbreak of war. He would later be appointed Vice-Chancellor of the University and then be discarded by Lee for not being tough enough. His outlook was that of a Fabian socialist, promoting the gradual evolution of a more just and equal society.

As well as his studies, Harry had work to do in the port. He also came in contact with the fledgling Malayan Democratic Union (MDU). His parents were friends of Philip Hoalim Senior, a London-educated lawyer from Guiana who had ended up in Singapore through Penang family connections. Hoalim was asked to be founding Chairman of the new party. According to John Drysdale, Harry took a part in drafting the MDU constitution;[9] if so, it was in a minor capacity and by courtesy of Hoalim.

During the year between Japanese surrender and his departure for Britain, Harry's position was that of a keen observer. Although quite well off himself, he nevertheless took to heart fellow Malayans' privations caused by British bungling and petty corruption. He knew some of the chief Singapore-based political actors and could therefore mentally assimilate their endeavours to his own zeal for independence.

His long-postponed overseas plans, however, now forged ahead. On his birthday, 16 September 1946, he left behind the turbulence of Singapore for four years. He embarked on the *Britannic* for the journey to London. T.J.S. George reports what one of Lee's shipmates from Hong Kong remembered of the voyage and of Lee. Each day Harry would use up more than six people's strict rations of fresh water. This won him no friends, but he seemed not to mind; he took for granted the satisfaction of his wants and struck the others as spoiled and selfish. He also played cards for small stakes, and had accumulated £20 in winnings from one soldier; he was persuaded to forget the debt, which he did.[10]

He arrived at Liverpool. No one met him, no one knew he was coming. Almost everything became an ordeal in the spartan environment of postwar Britain—finding accommodation with some privacy, looking after himself, cooking, keeping clothes and body clean, coping with the vast labyrinth of London, 'a grimy, sooty, bomb-scarred city'.[11]

Although he had gained admission to the Middle Temple and had used his letter of acceptance as *bona fides* in seeking a place on the *Britannic*, his academic studies began at the London School of Economics, where left-wing luminaries such as Harold Laski held sway. Whatever part law still played in his ambitions, the impact of the war made him pick up the threads of economics from Raffles

College. What better place for a young idealist than the London School of Economics?

But the passage from a fortunate position in the familiar tropical surroundings of Singapore, where Harry could choose his company, to the foreign, crowded, frugal world he now entered on the brink of winter made the vision of a Utopian future seem absurd and fanciful. 'I thought I was going absolutely crackers. This wasn't my idea of university life. I think it got me down a bit—buses, fumes, tubes—and I tried for Cambridge.'[12]

Perseverance was needed for him to secure a place at Cambridge, given that Harry had not completed a diploma from Raffles College. To lack of entrance qualifications could be added lack of referees, and he was reduced to invoking credibility through other Malayan students already at Cambridge. Eventually he was accepted at Fitzwilliam Hall. Messrs Thatcher, Censor at the Hall, and Turner, Director of Studies, gave the young man his chance, without charging him fees. It is probable that this change of fortune followed the bitter experience of being rejected a number of times.

Thatcher and Turner specialised in Roman law, and it was law that Harry read at Cambridge. He has not discussed the reasons for abandoning economics. Was it sheer necessity—the one tenuous link to acceptance in Fitzwilliam's and Cambridge's eyes? Was it disillusion with the London School of Economics in particular, with economics as a discipline, or simply with the whole London experience?

Cambridge was crucial to Harry Lee's development. Thatcher in particular came to assume a special significance, which Josey records,

> I think [Lee] would admit that William S. Thatcher influenced his thinking, his subsequent pattern of thought, and some of his values and beliefs, probably more than any other man, except possibly his paternal grandfather. Thatcher, as Lee found him, ... cared about students, especially those willing to work. He explained, he argued things through; and he encouraged. Lee Kuan Yew was impressed with Thatcher's mind, his ability to teach, and his knowledge, and also with his dignified and philosophical attitude towards life, which had not treated him particularly well. Thatcher had been badly wounded in the First World War, and his speech was affected, his face disfigured, and he suffered from asthma. At times he had to leave the room to seek relief. He would return as though nothing had happened. He bore his handicaps and his sufferings privately. He behaved as a normal person and

expected others to treat him as such, ignoring his illnesses and his disfigurement.[13]

There were other lessons that Lee absorbed from Thatcher and that he acknowledged after the latter's death in 1966. The two had maintained contact over the twenty or so intervening years. 'He taught me about people. He taught me to avoid self-pity. What is past is past. What has happened has happened. That is that. It's the future that counts, that makes life worth living.'[14] It should be noted that Thatcher's impact was largely through unconscious example, which Lee translated into a deliberate and tough personal style unencumbered by physical handicaps. The disciple was very different from the master.

Harry had been blessed with good mentors before, but at Cambridge the seal was set on his admiration of the Mr Chips mode which had aroused his best and noblest qualities.

The reputation of brilliant Malayan radicals, lawyers and personal acquaintances, men like John Eber or Lim Kean Chye, who preceded Lee to Cambridge, might have revived his flagging political ambitions. In a wistful speech opening a Singapore careers exhibition on 1 September 1965, just after the trauma of Separation from Malaysia, Lee said that twenty years earlier he had wanted to be a comfortable lawyer with no idea of responsibility directly for two million people and indirectly for nine million more. There probably was a crisis period late in 1946 and early in 1947 when Lee had little sense of commanding his own future, let alone anyone else's.

Be that as it may, his university days brought him into contact with all kinds of political activists, local and foreign. Josey reports: 'During his studies in Britain he was approached, as are most students from the Colonies, by the Communists.'[15] There is no evidence that he was ever seriously attracted to their ideology, intellectually or personally; he remained his own man and chose what influences to heed. In his own caustic words: 'Having been brainwashed in bourgeois British institutions about civilisation . . . I am hoping the [Marxist–Leninist triumph] is not predetermined.'[16] He became involved with the British Labour Party, meeting many of its up-and-coming leaders, and he campaigned in Somerset. The socialism he observed was democratic and gentlemanly.

Meanwhile, his nationalist zeal was growing. Even at recreation with overseas Chinese in the London clubs appointed for the purpose, he realised that he had more in common with Malayans of other races than with Chinese from, say, Mauritius or the West Indies.

War and Self-Preparation

He was away from home at a critical time. He described it vividly in a 1961 broadcast.

> Three years after the end of the Second World War a violent revolution started in Malaya. The Communists, who were almost a non-existent force in the years before the war, were allowed to arm themselves as a force just before the British surrendered. They went underground with those arms.
> Over three and a half years, partly with the arms they took underground and partly with more arms parachuted in by the Allies, they built up a tough little army in the jungles.
> With the surrender of the Japanese, they came out into the towns. For the first time, the MCP emerged as a legally recognised political force in our country. But it was not for long. In 1948 they retreated to the jungles and the armed insurrection which the British called the 'Emergency' started.
> That was a fierce and grim revolt. The angry young men from the Chinese middle schools, who hated colonialism and the British, joined the Communists to rid the country of British imperialism.
> In those tough years, 1949 and 1950, we got our first taste of the practical realities of politics. We had learned the theories of socialism, communism and capitalism in books, and read the histories of revolutions. But we now began to understand the meaning of revolution in terms of life and blood, liberty and incarceration, hate and fear, love and comradeship.[17]

The 'we' above must be primarily a reference to later colleagues such as Rajaratnam and Devan Nair, then in Singapore. Although Lee was keeping an eye on Malayan developments, it was not until he returned home that he began to feel their full significance. His perspective was conditioned by his own upbringing and, especially at a distance, he had little grasp of movements among the Chinese masses back home. By contrast, one wonders what he made of the Malayan Democratic Union's self-extinction in 1948, since he had personal links with several of its members.

Cambridge saw the flowering of his relationship with Kwa Geok Choo, begun somewhat inauspiciously at Raffles College and pursued through the war years. She came to Girton College in the autumn of 1947, having completed an Arts Diploma at Raffles College and won a Queen's scholarship. The competitive edge between them was maintained with the 'proper' bias when they both graduated in 1949 with first-class honours and Harry received a star for special distinction, the first ever awarded to a Malayan.

It was rich time personally. As well as courting Kwa Geok Choo, Harry learned to study hard with very little sleep. There are tales of his sizing up who would be his most likely Malayan competitors, men of the calibre of Fred Arulanandom (later a Malaysian judge) and distracting them with idle activity until eleven o'clock or so at night. Then he would go off and work at his desk for hours in order to gain a lead. As things turned out, it was hardly a necessary ploy. He formed a society for Malayan Chinese students and became its first president. He was elected Vice-President of the University Law Society. He took up golf, a game that was far to exceed the benefits and purpose he attached to it in those days. He travelled throughout Britain by motor bike or train and went sightseeing to the Continent.

Lee still shows the marks of his Cambridge days: his way of speech, his organisation of time and work output, his constant measuring of himself against peers, his self-assurance after overcoming obstacles and succeeding so well against world-class competition. Above all, he came to realise his own intellectual strength. The scope of his mastery would henceforth be subject only to his choices and those forces of circumstances that even the superhuman cannot match.

In 1970 he told an interviewer in Hong Kong that he had enjoyed Cambridge by and large with its hard work and play, its intense and often unpleasant 'glandular activity'. He was not sure which Cambridge influences still shaped him, since life was a constant process of action and adaptation. Some of the habits of thought remained, and perhaps superficial mannerisms. He found the interviewer's questions hard to answer: 'I am not very good at this sort of self-analysis'.[18]

The Malayan Forum and the 'Returned Students' speech

Harry and Geok Choo left Cambridge covered in glory. One of his tutors bade him 'keep the flag flying' as he set out on his career; he replied that his chief aim was to take it down. Full of confidence, the two young graduates moved to London for their professional law training in mid-1949. That year six students in London formed a club called the Malayan Forum to discuss and promote national independence for their home country. Though later to be captured by Marxists such as John Eber and Lim Hong Bee, it began as a politically mixed group, with Goh Keng Swee and Abdul Razak two of its leading lights. Harry made or re-established contact with some of its members and often went on pub crawls. He was invited to share his views at a Forum meeting. The speech he gave in January 1950 revealed the extent to which his outlook had matured: it was not only a thoughtful analysis of the prospects for Malayan independence, it was also a telling account of the place and perspective of politically conscious students returning from the imperial centre to their home, as he was about to do.

Here is a resumé of the speech including some direct quotes.[19] 'Returned students in any British colony fall broadly into two classes: the rich man's son, and the impecunious government scholar.' Both groups can do well, the former as capitalist entrepreneurs, the latter as subordinate administrators. Their time in England gives them the advantage over their fellow Asiatics. On returning to Malaya, they both find themselves a part of the vested interest of the country. They approximate more nearly to the model of perfection constituted by the ruling English caste. The same was true in the few years of Japanese rule. 'Had they stayed long enough, I have no doubt that those of us who could speak Japanese, who behaved like Japanese, and who had been educated in Japan, would have been the most favoured class of Malayan ... Many of us will remember the unhappy spectacle of English-speaking, Western-educated colleagues suddenly changing in their manner of speech, dress and behaviour, making blatant attempts at being good imitation Japs.'

The British effort, since resuming control of Malaya, has been to re-establish the 'pleasant orderly society of 1939', with the returned students again forming 'the uppermost crust'. Yet Malaya is the last colonial territory in Southeast Asia apart from French Indo-China. The newly independent countries of the region have been led out of colonialism by their returned students. In Malaya's case the difficult racial problem has delayed national mobilisation against the British, but cannot do so indefinitely. Subjugation 'is only possible where the subject race is inherently, both mentally and physically, inferior. Colonial imperialism in Southeast Asia is dead except in Malaya, and our generation will see it out'.

Let the returned students not lapse into visions of future greatness. The straightforward pattern of independence elsewhere will not repeat itself in Malaya. British rule must be accepted for some while yet. During this period 'we can attain a sufficient degree of social cohesion, and arouse a sufficient degree of civic and political consciousness among the various races ... This time is vital if we are to avoid a political vacuum that may otherwise follow British withdrawal from Malaya'.

'The two things we the returned students can help to decide are: firstly, how soon and orderly the change will be, and secondly, whether we shall find a place at all in the new Malaya.' Only the Communist Party is organised sufficiently to force the British to leave, and to run the country. It would be a mistake to dismiss MCP adherents as so many bandits. 'Theirs is a tightly knit organisation making their bid for power.'

In the other ex-British colonies of the region, the returned students had time to organise before communism became a threat, so they came to power with nationalist governments. But now the internationally co-ordinated communist challenge is the greatest threat facing them. 'How far these governments can counter the appeal and force of communism will depend on how far they are bold enough to carry out social reforms in the teeth of their own vested interest.' Amongst Malaya's neighbours, the native capitalists have supported the national aspirations. It is a moot point, though, whether long-overdue reforms will be carried through and the masses provided for without the communist religion.

With the disappearance of the British raj the Malayan vested interests realise very clearly that the great inequality in wealth of the peoples of Malaya must also disappear. 'For any independent Malayan government to exist, it must win popular support, and to gain any popular support it must promise, and do, social justice.'

'We, the returned students, would be the type of leaders that the British would find relatively the more acceptable. For if the choice lies, as in fact it does, between a communist republic of Malaya and a Malaya within the British Commonwealth led by the people who, despite their opposition to imperialism, still share certain ideals in common with the Commonwealth, there is little doubt which alternative the British will find the lesser evil . . . But if we do not give leadership, it will come from the other ranks of society, and if these leaders attain power, as they will with the support of the masses, we shall find that we, as a class, have merely changed masters. The difference between the British, the Japanese and the new masters who will arise if we remain unorganised will be a difference only of degree and not of kind.'

The two basic challenges facing returned students are racial harmony between Chinese and Malays and the development of a strong enough united political front to demand a transfer of power without resorting to armed force. 'If we who are thought of as the intelligentsia of Malaya cannot make a sincere start now towards a solution of these problems, the future is grim.'

More so the Malays than the Chinese, the two main racial groups have already organised their own nationalist movements. The others will surely do so. Whether the end result is another Palestine or another Switzerland remains in the balance. There is no question in anyone's mind of the non-Malays being deported. 'Since, therefore, the non-Malay communities must be accepted as part of the present and future Malaya, it follows that unity must be attained.'

There is still time for the returned students to organise themselves into a force in Malaya. 'But the final question is what each individual returned student will do when he goes back to Malaya, for, in the last eventuality, any party, any society, any body politic, consists of individuals.'

The British, whatever their political complexion, can never of their free will give independence to Malaya. 'For them Malaya means dollars.'

'But our trump card is that responsible British leaders realise that independence must and will come to Malaya and that therefore it will be better to hand Malaya to leaders sympathetic to the British mode of life, willing for Malaya to be a member of the British Commonwealth, and what is most important, willing to remain in the sterling area. For the alternative is military suppression, a policy which another imperialist power has found impossible in Indonesia.' Besides, 'no one can concede more graciously an already untenable position than the English'. The student's duty will be to help bring about social cohesion and make it clear to even the most diehard imperialist that his is an untenable position.

'What actual steps we take when we get back will depend on the political temper at that time. Whether we can openly advocate and propagate our views, or whether we should be more discreet and less vociferous, is something that can be answered only when the time comes. ... We must break the soporific [sic] Malayan atmosphere and bring home the urgency of the problems facing us ... If every returned student makes known his convictions to his own immediate circle, the cumulative effect will be tremendous ...'

'If we fail to fulfil our duty, the change that still will come must be a violent one, for, whatever the rights and wrongs of communism, no one can deny its tremendous appeal to the masses. Whatever our political complexion, from deep blue Tory to bright red Communist, we must all remember that we are not indispensable in this struggle for freedom ... What the individual returning home chooses to do is a question of personal inclination, economic circumstances and political convictions. But if the majority of us choose to believe that Malaya can be insulated from the nationalist revolts that have swept the European powers from Asia, then we may find that there is no place for us in the Malaya that is to be after the British have departed.'

Some observations must be made about this remarkable speech.

Lee used the parlance of his time, no longer strictly accurate, that treated Singapore as part of Malaya. He viewed communism from outside, and did not identify with those who might have been attracted to it because they were disturbed or downtrodden by injustice: its force was as a growing threat to the British and to any who might aspire to succeed them in orderly fashion.

Behind his words, there was only a faint awareness of the cultural strength of the Chinese masses in Singapore and Malaya. Their admiration for those with a British education was not at all unqualified, as Lee discovered in due course. Perhaps he discounted them as being out of bounds or largely under the communists' influence: whatever the case, he did not portray them as part of an orderly movement towards national independence. This was a major mistake he recognised and set about rectifying.

Lee's neat and neutral racial logic in the Malayan Forum speech contrasts with his belief, more widely known years later, that some of Malaya's races are superior to others. His contempt was directed more at groups or individuals—for example, his gibe at 'imitation Japs'—without trace of self-mockery for his own behaviour in Occupation days.

However, the core of his argument was rock-solid: returned students owed it to themselves to take leadership in the Malayan independence struggle. Otherwise 'we shall find that we, as a class, have merely changed masters'.

Lee categorised the returned students as broadly of two kinds. Interestingly he fitted neither exactly—the rich man's son or the impecunious government scholar. The consciousness of being among but not of the elite has continued to appear as a constant feature of Lee Kuan Yew's life. The solitariness, the uniqueness of his perspective enabled him to gain purchase on a situation far more than those who became bogged down in their sectional interests.

The speech was really a programme for political action, with Lee himself at or near its centre. He realised that the returned students had great advantages on the road to post-colonial leadership: relative acceptability to the British, good standing locally as the best equipped wealth makers, access to national movements among the students' various races, the vital capacity to function and organise multiracially. The students' Achilles' heel would be their reluctance 'to dislodge the system under which they enjoy' the privileges afforded or enhanced by their overseas education, wealth and status. Lee pressed his longer range view with frequent reminders that complacency and short-term self-interest would spell the ruin and the subjugation of the returned students by the communists. He might well have been admonishing himself no less than others, for he enjoyed the bourgeois life and could be lulled into forgetting that it could be lost without vigilance.

There is only the merest hint of socialism in this speech, the emphasis is more on pragmatic realities. Whatever the domestic complexion of British governments, he argued, they would wish to retain Malaya within their sphere of influence. Post-colonial British involvement went without saying, short of revolution. Again, 'for any independent Malayan government to exist, it must win popular support, and to gain any popular support it must promise, and do, social justice'. The important goal was an independent Malayan government. As a means to that end it would have to attempt, like other regional states, 'to do all that a communist state can for the masses', but 'without the communist religion'. Lee noted 'the active support of native capitalists' among Malaya's neighbours 'in the national aspirations of their fellow countrymen'. Such support and such a path to independence would have to be pursued: they would not be automatic. The alternative was stark: the disappearance of the British and total upheaval. There was still, according to his speech, just enough time to avoid such an outcome.

The 'actual steps' that he hoped would be taken in this interim period would also have little to do with socialism. They would consist of infusing a spirit of co-operation and political independence, breaking 'the soporific Malayan atmosphere'—the Emergency notwithstanding!—and eroding 'the belief that we are inferior and will always remain inferior to the European'.

The immediate task on return from study would be assessment of the 'political temper'. A united front with the communists was not envisaged, just linkage with other returned students and the mobilising of national ethnic movements.

History, as usual, turned out differently. Most of the returned students refused the challenge thrown down to them by Harry Lee, both in that speech and later, even though it was a challenge to preserve the supremacy of their own class. Lee was forced to risk being yoked unequally with the communists. Apart from those far more radical than himself, and apart from a small group of like-minded men, Lee's fellow scholars in Singapore and England joined the ranks of the dilettantes.

As the years went by, Lee reserved his greatest contempt for the English-educated and the returned students, men without 'ballast', willing to surrender their freedom for the sake of wealth or security. They were, in his oft-repeated words, 'emasculated', 'devitalised'.

Poised to return home, Lee showed at the Malayan Forum that he had invested a great deal of himself in preparing for a political independence consonant with his own autonomy. He wished no masters on himself and he set out to be a disinterested but caring mentor for the Malayan people. Generously, he was sharing his treasury of wisdom with all who had ears to hear.

Biographies

GOH KENG SWEE

Goh Keng Swee was born in Malacca on 6 October 1918. Though his cousin was Tan Siew Sin (Malaysia's finance minister from 1959–74), son of the wealthy and influential Tan Cheng Lock, Goh Keng Swee's own parents were of relatively modest means. Goh was educated at the Anglo-Chinese School and Raffles College, Singapore; on gaining his diploma, he joined the colonial civil service. During the Occupation he managed to keep up social welfare research. After the war and some work in emergency relief, he went to the London School of Economics and graduated with first-class honours. While there he helped establish the Malayan Forum, a political discussion group for expatriate Malayan students, and was its first chairman. Once back in Singapore, he engaged in doing innovative official research (especially of urban incomes and housing), localising the administration and planning for the PAP. He returned to England in 1954 on a postgraduate scholarship and again studied at the University of London, obtaining a PhD in economics.

In May 1959 he was elected to the urban constituency of Kreta Ayer (he held this Chinatown-based seat for the whole of his parliamentary career) and was immediately appointed Minister for Finance. At various stages after independence he held the Finance, Defence and Education portfolios; he was named Deputy Prime Minister in 1973 and First Deputy Prime Minister in 1980. He stepped down from Parliament before the December 1984 poll. He was a member of the PAP Central Executive Committee from 1959 until 1982 and it's Vice-Chairman for most of that period.

Dr Goh has received numerous international awards for his contribution to Singapore's economic planning. He has also held several consultancies, and is at present being retained by the People's Republic of China. He is Deputy Chairman of both the Monetary Authority of Singapore and the Government Investment Corporation. Married during the Occupation, he has one son.

SINNATHAMBY RAJARATNAM

S. Rajaratnam is a Tamil. He was born in Jaffna (Sri Lanka) on 23 February 1915. The family moved to Malaya and settled in Negri Sembilan, where his father became a prosperous rubber planter. He was educated at three of the best local schools: St Paul's Institution, Seremban, Victoria Institution, Kuala Lumpur, and Raffles Institution, Singapore. He proceeded to King's College, London, and embarked on law studies. He did not complete a degree; instead, he spent his time as an active propagandist and pamphleteer in left-wing politics. After World War II he returned to Malaya and was for a brief period secretary of the Malayan Indian Congress. He took up a journalistic career and moved to Singapore. He was sacked after being associate editor of the *Singapore Standard* for almost five years (during which time he met Lee Kuan Yew) and in 1954 he joined the editorial staff of the *Straits Times*. He served a term as President of the Singapore Union of Journalists. He sat on the Malayanisation Commission in 1955 and on the Minimum Standards of Livelihood Committee in 1956.

Rajaratnam was one of the principal convenors and founding members of the PAP, and only in 1982 did he step down from its Central Executive Committee (CEC). In 1959 he resigned from the *Straits Times* and was duly elected to the Legislative Assembly for the Kampong Glam constituency (where he is still the well-respected and popular sitting member). He was appointed Minister for Culture. After Separation he transferred to foreign affairs, taking on the Labour portfolio as well for three years (1968–71). He was designated Second Deputy Prime Minister (Foreign Affairs) in June 1980. Following the 1984 general elections, he became Senior Minister in the Prime Minister's Office.

He married a Hungarian woman he had met in England during the war years, they have no children. Rajaratnam is appreciated as a generous and hospitable friend, one who has willingly made his home available to others and who is unfussed about money or possessions. His wide reading is revealed by his use of illustration and his cultivated turn of phrase. He was a heavy smoker, but in 1984 underwent a coronary bypass operation; partly as a result, he may not see out the full parliamentary term that is due to finish in 1989.

TOH CHIN CHYE

Toh Chin Chye was born on 10 December 1921 to well-to-do Perak (Northern Malaya) parents of Amoy origin. Prior to the Occupation he read science at Raffles College, where he met Lee Kuan Yew. After the war he studied at the University of London's Institute of National Medical Research and completed a PhD with distinction. He participated in the Malayan Forum and was one of its chairmen for a time. He was appointed a lecturer (and later reader) in physiology at the University of Malaya in Singapore on the strength of his substantial and creative research into the chemistry of the nervous system and its transmission of impulses. He joined enthusiastically in the discussions that led to the formation of the PAP and was the Party's founding Chairman, a post he held until 1981. (He stood down from the CEC in November 1982). He looked after party organisation, policy formulation and discipline. In 1959 he was elected to the Legislative Assembly for Rochore and still represents the constituency, nowadays as a backbencher. At its peak, the range of his responsibilities was formidable: Deputy Prime Minister from 1959 to 1968, Chairman of the Polytechnic 1959–75, Vice-Chancellor of the University of Singapore 1968–75, Minister for Science and Technology 1968–75 and Minister for Health 1975–81. Toh Chin Chye married in 1962; he and his wife have a daughter.

K.M. BYRNE

A Eurasian Catholic, K.M. Byrne was born in Malaya in 1912. In 1947 he went to England, read law and arts at Christ Church, Oxford and, on graduating, was admitted to the Middle Temple at the same time as Lee Kuan Yew and Kwa Geok Choo. Following his return to Singapore in 1950 he was appointed to the senior administrative post of Clerk in the Legislative Council and Executive Council. Very active in politicising the Singapore civil service (through the Senior Officers' Association and the Council of Joint Action), Byrne worked behind the scenes to plan and found the PAP; he served on its CEC from 1959 until 1966. After holding various positions in the colonial administration, he resigned to contest the 1959 elections for the seat of Crawford. When the PAP won government, Lee appointed him Minister for Labour. He lost his seat in the Assembly at the 1963 elections. Later he served substantial terms as Singapore's High Commissioner to New Zealand and India. He is now retired.

ALEX JOSEY

An Englishman of Jewish background, Josey was born in April 1910. He spent most of World War II and the years immediately afterwards in the Middle East, where he was engaged in secret service and psychological warfare work. J.B. Smith's 1976 book *Portrait of a Cold Warrior* (New York: Putnam) relates an intriguing assessment of Josey offered by an American intelligence operative, Al Ulmer, who had been with him in a composite OSS-SOE unit in Cairo during the war. Its context was the author's informal briefing of Ulmer; the latter was passing through Singapore in 1956 and was expressing curiosity about the up-and-coming Lee Kuan Yew, having already heard that the local CIA station and the American Consul-General were both worried over Lee's close collaboration with 'known' communists. When mention was made of Lee's constant companion of recent months, 'a rather erratic freelance British writer named Alex Josey' who drank prodigious quantities of beer and showed up at regional Socialist International meetings, Ulmer immediately put his fellow Americans fears to rest: 'I don't think you have to worry too much about Mr Lee anymore. MI6 has a damned good case officer working on him. Josey's always been great at the vagabond leftist act' (page 207).

Having been his commanding officer in Palestine, Sir Henry Gurney, who was Britain's High Commissioner to Malaya from October 1948 until he was ambushed and killed on 6 October 1951, summoned Josey and his 'psywar' skills to help deal with the Emergency. Josey's cover was to be the post of chief editor for Radio Malaya. In June 1950 he was appointed Staff Officer (Emergency Information) assisting Sir Harold Briggs, Director of Operations. He soon fell foul of the British community in Malaya when he asserted on air that the country's economic conditions were fuelling the guerrilla war then in progress; in his view, the gap between workers' and managers' rewards from rubber prices (booming because of the Korean War's impact) was great enough to make a plausible case for nationalising the rubber industry. Questions were asked back home in the Commons and it was not long before he was replaced. His friends were surprised when he suddenly switched to journalism, joining the 'Tiger Balm' Aw family's *Singapore Standard* and corresponding or stringing for many foreign newspapers and journals over the next decade or more. Together with Rajaratnam he was a founding member and onetime President of the Singapore Union of Journalists. The two of them met and became firm friends in the late 1940s, and Josey lived at Rajaratnam's house from the mid-1950s until his expulsion from Malaysia in 1965 (see Chapter 7).

For fifteen years Josey acted as Lee Kuan Yew's semi-official press officer and publicist. Besides producing books that focus on Lee and his speeches, Josey has written about many other aspects and sidelights of postwar Singapore. He was also for some years a consultant with the British-dominated Singapore International Chamber of Commerce. Unmarried, he had a sturdy reputation for enjoying female company. Health problems have apparently rendered his future in Singapore uncertain.

C.V. DEVAN NAIR

Devan Nair is a Malayalee, his parents having come from Kerala in south India. He was born in Malacca on 5 August 1923, one of nine children. His father, a plantation clerk, was unemployed for three years as a result of the Depression-induced collapse of the rubber market, and the family lived in a garage at Muar. In 1933 they moved to Singapore and Devan began his schooling at Rangoon Road Primary School. He completed his Senior Cambridge at Victoria School in 1940. During the Occupation he provided food and information to members of the Malayan People's Anti-Japanese Army and was lucky enough to escape betrayal or harm. With the war over, he began training as a teacher; subsequently he taught English mostly at St Andrew's School among upper secondary level students. He joined the Singapore Teachers' Union and came under the influence of P.V. Sharma, one of its leading lights and already a convert to Marxism. Devan followed Sharma into the Anti-British League and underwent initiation into a secret cell group with its rigorous cadre formation. Soon he was espousing a Stalinist line. He was detained by the British in January 1951, and spent seventeen of the next twenty-six months 'quarantined' with other political prisioners on St John's Island. (Lee Kuan Yew offered a dramatic and probably fanciful reconstruction of his first sighting of Devan there when, in Parliament on 23 October 1981, he proposed Devan's election as President.) After his release Devan resumed teaching and union activity. He also married his childhood sweetheart, Avadai Dhanalakshmi (despite the misgivings of her wealthy high-caste Tamil family); she bore him four children.

Devan Nair was one of the convenors of the PAP. In 1955 he stood unsuccessfully for the Assembly. Deeply embroiled in organising and advising unions such as the Factory and Shop Workers' Union over the turbulent eighteen months that followed the elections, he was again detained. Braced by his wife, he backtracked from his initial decision, born of frustration, to capitulate and travel overseas for study; instead, he saw out another two and a half years in Changi prison. It was at this time that he decided to accept what he had formerly regarded as Harry Lee's *petit bourgeois* brand of democratic socialism and submit his allegiance to the right wing of the Party. Released after the PAP's victory at the polls of mid-1959, Devan was briefly a political secretary to the new Government but then returned to teaching. He launched the Adult Education Board, chaired a Prisons Enquiry Commission, visited China (meeting some of the revolutionary leaders through the good offices of his old comrade P.V. Sharma, exiled there) and strove to build up a viable non-communist union movement loyal to Singapore and Lee. In the wake of the PAP split (which he helped engineer), he became secretary-general of the National Trade Unions Congress (NTUC).

He was disqualified by Malaysian regulations from standing for the September 1963 Singapore elections; his wife contested and won the seat (Moulmein) for him. However, instead of the PAP adhering to its announced intention that he should replace her in December of that year, as soon as he was eligible, Devan was put up as a candidate for the Malayan parliamentary elections of 1964 (his wife stayed on as a Singapore MP until 1968). In reversal of the 1955 Assembly results, he was the only successful PAP candidate. He represented the Kuala Lumpur constituency of Bungsar in the federal Parliament for five years. Demands on his time were numerous—attending parliamentary sittings, leading opposition to the Alliance Government, establishing the Democratic Action Party (DAP) as Malaysian replacement for the PAP, keeping in touch with Singapore trade union colleagues and issues—and his constituency work (and family life) must have suffered.

In 1969, Lee persuaded him to return to Singapore and resume the secretaryship of the NTUC, so that he could spearhead the modernisation of the union movement and its integration into the Government's plans. After ten years more of devoted service, he relinquished his NTUC post to allow Lim Chee Onn, Lee Kuan Yew's chosen technocrat, to succeed him. A few months earlier he had been drafted into Parliament through a by-election for the seat of Anson. However, he was not able to escape the NTUC for long, being pressed to assume its presidency when Phey Yew Kok, previous holder of the office, fled the country.

There was more to come. Less than two years passed and he was sworn in on 24 October 1981 as Singapore's third President, eleven days after quitting the Parliament and the PAP. Things did not work out well and in March 1985 he resigned, apparently as a result of alcoholism. Following an ironically successful course of rehabilitative treatment in the United States, he went back there and was in the USA at the time of writing. He plans to earn a living through writing and lecturing—he refused the conditional pension offered by the Government.

Devan Nair is a prodigious reader with a bent towards philosophising. For many years he has been an ardent admirer of the syncretistic universal religion enshrined in Sri Aurobind's teachings and practised by the guru's followers at the Auroville *ashram* in India.

SAMAD ISMAIL

Abdul Samad Ismail, a Malay of Javanese descent, was born in Singapore in February 1924. Educated in Malay and English, he joined the Malay newspaper (Jawi script), *Utusan Melayu*. He was greatly influenced by Ishak bin Haji Muhammad (Pak Sako), who showed him how political beliefs—in this case anti-colonialism and socialism—could be expressed through the verbal arts of a particular culture. He made comradely cause with other committed Malays, some of whom were arrested by the British just before the Japanese invasion began. During the Occupation he worked on the staff of the Japanese-sponsored *Berita Malai* and became a member of several militant Malay groups linked to Indonesia (in anticipation that Malaya would be absorbed into an independent *Indonesia Raya* or Great Indonesia). When the Japanese surrender and the British return put paid to these hopes, Samad, having reverted to *Utusan Melayu*, helped found the Malay Nationalist Party (MNP). This was one of a number of groups that coalesced to promote the radical Malay cause and co-operate with non-Malays in organising political agitation. He was given the code name Zainal within the MNP, but was not, as Lee and the British Special Branch alleged, a full cadre member of the MCP—relations between the MNP and MCP were never very easy. (Zainal spelt backwards is Laniaz, which is how Lee referred to Samad in his 1961 'Battle for Merger' radio talks.) He was detained for three months by the British in 1948 after the declaration of the Emergency and again for two years in 1951 (with Devan Nair, to whom he became friend and adviser, P.V. Sharma, John Eber and others), this time for his alleged involvement with the Anti-British League.

He met Lee Kuan Yew in 1951 when Lee was appointed his legal adviser, but Lee did not begin cultivating him until the following year. Released in 1953, he was of vital help to Lee and his colleagues in the planning of the PAP—he was one of the Party's convenors—and in the co-opting of significant left-wing figures, not so much Malays as Chinese and others. He drifted away from the PAP, probably realising that the British and Lee between them would never allow the left wing of the Party to triumph, and he spent some time in Indonesia and Britain. In 1958, after returning to Singapore and Malaya, he was appointed editor of *Berita Harian*, a Malay newspaper within the *Straits Times* group. He also joined the more conservative Malay party, UMNO.

Lee came to consider him a dangerous influence, and lobbied at every opportunity to have him arrested. While it is true that Samad was a powerful figure because of his political commitment, his pioneering literary and journalistic skills and his extraordinary range of contacts with radical left-wing Indonesians and Malayans of all races (including the leader of the Brunei revolt of 1962, A.M. Azahari), it is also true that the UMNO leaders were not as dependent on him as Lee suspected: being aware of his past radicalism, they only sought or took Samad's advice if it suited their own purposes.

Samad rose to be managing editor of the UMNO-controlled *New Straits Times* group. It came as a great shock to the public when, in 1976, he was detained under the Internal Security Act (on the grounds that he was engaged in communist subversion of the Malays). He was restored to favour by Musa Hitam and Mahathir when they came to power. In 1982 he performed the *haj* (pilgrimage to Mecca and the Muslim holy places) and now acts as adviser to a government-linked commercial media conglomerate in Kuala Lumpur. Samad is reputed to be a gregarious but independent man who has woven his own way through the intricacies of regional politics. It is hard to believe his 'confession' of 1976, that he was the mainstay of a scheme to radicalise colleagues and juniors and, through them, the Malays as a whole.

3

Preparing a Movement

> Let me take my story back to 1950 when I began to learn the realities of political life in Malaya. At that time, every genuine nationalist who hated the British colonial system wanted freedom and independence. That was a time when only weak men and stooges came out and performed on the local political stage. Fierce men were silent or had gone underground to join the Communists.
>
> LEE KUAN YEW,
> *The Battle for Merger*, 1961, p. 14

Lee Kuan Yew returned home with Kwa Geok Choo in first-class comfort on the Dutch luxury liner *Willem Ruys*. Goh Keng Swee and K.M. Byrne were among their companions on the voyage. They reached Singapore on 1 August 1950. Fifteen years later, Lee recalled the scrutiny he received from a Mr Fox when immigration checks were being carried out; no doubt intelligence reports had preceded Lee and other returning nationalists. Moreover, his brother Dennis Lee Kim Yew had recently gone to Bulgaria and out of suspicion, confusion or both, Harry's belongings were searched.

Home and new stirrings of life

Lee joined the law firm of Chan, Laycock and Ong whose partners were involved in the 'weak men and stooges' politics of the Progressive Party (PP) and Straits Chinese British Association (SCBA).

He and Geok Choo were formally engaged on 11 August and married on 30 September 1950. They held a lavish reception with four-tiered wedding cake and their master of ceremonies, Yap Pheng Geck, a leading businessman and pillar of the Singapore Chinese Chamber of Commerce, toasted them with the prediction that one of them would be Prime Minister one day.

The Lees settled into Harry's family bungalow at 38 Oxley Road, and Harry became a breeder of Alsatians and proud owner of a Studebaker. His law work began, mainly with bread-and-butter cases. He and his wife were presented to the Singapore Bar by John Eber's father R.L. Eber on 7 August 1951, but Geok Choo practised law only intermittently until after the birth of their third child in 1957.

From this comfortable domestic base, Lee set out to assess the political temper. The signs in late 1950 were not encouraging. While the Emergency dominated Malaya, Singapore was strangely quiet. Because (it transpired) the entire Singapore City Committee of the Malayan Communist Party had been picked up in one fell swoop, little or no unrest and disruption occurred, and the Chinese masses seemed dormant. The political division of the island from the peninsula reinforced a sense of unreality about events across the Causeway.

Violence erupted momentarily in the Maria Hertogh riots of December 1950, which brought Malays and Europeans into confrontation but offered no tenable handle for opening up political awareness or co-ordinating anti-colonial sentiments among other races. The riots were triggered by a photograph in *Utusan Melayu*, the Jawi script Malay newspaper, showing a Dutch girl in a convent where she had been sent by a European judge, despite being fostered by Malays during the war years and brought up as a Muslim. Lee was disturbed by the trials that ensued in 1951, because he and others succeeded and were obliged to succeed in using the process of law to mete out false justice so that hysteria might be damped down. He was paid to act for some Muslims charged with murdering Europeans, and managed to have them acquitted.

Lee's first political steps were tentative and hardly leftward. At the suggestion of his employers and possibly his new family*, Harry took up with the SCBA and the PP, becoming Secretary of the former and campaigning for the latter in the Legislative Council elections of early 1951. He also joined the People's Education Association, an expatriate-dominated group which did some discreet nation-building under the cover of literacy work; he was its Secretary in 1951. With Geok Choo on a trip to the Federation of Malaya he met Dato Onn bin Jaafar and other committee members of the new Independence of Malaya Party; he sought to convince them of the mistake of separating Singapore from Malaya. Onn was impressed by his fluency and earnest approach.

---

* His brother-in-law Yong Nyuk Lin was a Progressive with modest Malayan Democratic Union credentials.

Preparing a Movement 61

What drew Lee to flirt with political forces he soon came to despise or reject? And why did he not link up with the Singapore Labour Party (SLP) since it was modelled on the British original that he had joined and actively supported during his overseas student days? The latter question is easy to answer: the SLP was small, faction-ridden, undisciplined and dominated by argumentative Indians with an inadequate union base. It was also willing to accept merger with Malaya under Kuala Lumpur rule.

Perhaps he was just being 'malleable', to use his implausible description of himself as he looked back on his association with the Progressive cause. Its attraction lay in its view that Singapore was the central and most sophisticated unit of British Southeast Asia; the Party proposed, a little naively, a Greater Malaya based on Singapore and including the three North Borneo territories.

However attractive the major plank of its platform was, the PP discredited itself in Lee's eyes by its leaders' game-playing and resorting to petty bribery in order to create an audience. Moreover, its electoral base was small—the enfranchised and therefore the privileged.

> There were the Progressive Party and their feeble leaders. There were the clowns of the Labour Party of Singapore. When I met acquaintances like Lim Kean Chye and John Eber and asked them what they were doing, why they were allowing these things to go on, they smiled and said, 'Ah well! What can be done in such a situation?'
> One morning in January 1951, I woke up and read in the newspapers that John Eber had been arrested, that Lim Kean Chye had disappeared and escaped arrest. Shortly afterwards a reward was offered for his arrest. Politics in Malaya was a deadly serious business. These are not clowns or jokers. They had decided to go with the Communists.[1]

Lee's first public steps took him, not (as Josey says) 'relentlessly towards his objective',[2] but along blind alleys with men whom he saw lacked political acumen and stamina. He himself did not exactly fit the radical mould—prosperous, well-connected, keen about golf and fast cars. He was a curious mixture, by turns true and alien to communal type; sometimes good-natured and companionable, sometimes bristling with contempt. He could be relentless in his commitments and then lapse into dilettantism. But, as always, he kept his own counsel.

By contrast Goh Keng Swee and K.M. Byrne quickly found their level. They entered the civil service and looked for ways of mobilising discontent. Goh took on research in the Department of Social Welfare and Byrne was Clerk of Council. Despite understandable reluctance and opposition from some of the most senior officers, the public sector was to prove a ready recruiting ground. Toh Chin Chye became a lecturer at the recently established University of Malaya in Singapore, but had limited opportunity to cultivate dissent on campus. He and Byrne set up the University of Malaya Society as a graduate forum.

By no means was the early running for a new political force made by Lee. In the period 1950–53 his active colleagues did not hesitate to dismiss some of his ideas as rubbish, knowing that, however good his analysis and rhetoric, he still had no following and no practical experience or prospect of turning theory into political fact. The rumours that Special Branch was interested in him also created problems. There were even times when the wives of former London and Malayan Forum student friends would chase him away if he arrived at their quarters to meet old drinking partners and continue discussion and planning.

In hindsight the best contacts of his first eighteen months home came with and via newspapermen and (despite the irony of the rumours) the Special Branch. Yusof Ishak, later to be Head of State and Singapore's first President, was founder and owner of *Utusan Melayu*, a paper strongly identified with Malay nationalism. An old boy of Raffles Institution, although of an earlier generation than Lee, Yusof was well-connected within and beyond the Malay community. He retained the young lawyer to advise *Utusan* in the wake of the Hertogh riots.

Yusof introduced Lee to the spectrum of Malay politics and politicians. He had ready access to Tunku Abdul Rahman and the Malayan United Malays National Organisation*, but his own philosophy of multiracialism and secular modernisation put him at odds with entrenched privilege and protected tradition as the means of improving the Malays' lot rather than their own efforts and better educational attainment. (Yusof's youngest brother, Rahim Ishak, a teacher, later joined the People's Action Party and was one of its leading Malays, eventually becoming a Minister of State.)

More important was the editor of Yusof's newspaper, Samad Ismail. He had a craftsman's facility with words both in English and Malay. Fiercely nationalist and Marxist, he was detained for the third time by the British in their round-up of Anti-British

---

* Not established in Singapore until 1952.

League members, January 1951. Over the years he had come to know a whole range of left-wingers of all races and in Indonesia as well. Yusof instructed Harry Lee to act for Samad.

Contact began in 1951 or 1952, and through Richard Corridon in Special Branch Lee received background briefings to complement his own relationship with Samad. Friendship and respect developed on Lee's part to an unusual degree towards this man whom Corridon described as 'the most brilliant Communist I know'.[3] Samad introduced Lee to Devan Nair, also in detention at that time. The two would shortly reappear on centre stage when Lee's career entered its decisive phase.

Corridon himself proved an invaluable confidant and link man. After years as a policeman in south India, where he learnt Tamil, he came to Singapore and was assigned to the Special Branch so that he could monitor Indians in trade unions and political movements. Surprisingly for someone in intelligence work, he was a member of the Fabian Society, had a keen sense of social justice and appreciated the desire for independence from colonial rule. His Director, Alan Blades, meticulous, mild-mannered, more conventional in outlook, was a fine linguist (Japanese and Mandarin); interned during the Occupation, he was also amenable to prudence in dealing with dissent. So he accepted Corridon's recommendation not to arrest Lee Kuan Yew and Goh Keng Swee on their return to Singapore but to wait and see how they shaped up. Corridon had received a letter from a London Fabian, the wife of a former Hong Kong Governor, inquiring after these two brilliant young men.[4]

Corridon and Blades would both develop close working relationships with Lee and Goh over the years ahead, but it was Corridon who handled contact at the outset. He enjoyed articulate left-wing ideologues and another such was a journalist, Sinnathamby Rajaratnam. This Jaffna Tamil, who was with the *Singapore Standard* when he met Lee in 1951, was a staunch anticolonialist. During his abortive student days in wartime Britain, and following his return to Malaya, he looked for a political movement he could serve as a propagandist. His quarters in Singapore were a meeting place, if not temporary home, for many students, journalists, unionists and the like.

On Rajaratnam's suggestion, Lee Kuan Yew was approached in February 1952 by the leaders of the Uniformed Postal Staff Workers' Union who were preparing strike action. Would he become their legal adviser, taking the place of John Eber, now interned? Although young and untested in the field, Lee seemed a more promising alternative than right-wing lawyers such as

C.C. Tan and A.P. Rajah, who had other unions under their wing but to little effect.

Lee himself agrees that his first big break came from the postal strike of May 1952 and the way he saw it through. He was able to advise the union of its legal rights and duties. He drafted press statements and undertook to negotiate a settlement.

Given that no union was allowed to take strong action if the least suspicion of communist influence was attached to it, the postmen's strike marked a welcome return to industrial vigour. Lee described how it 'drew tremendous public interest and wide press coverage and sympathy'.[5] Mostly Malays, the postmen were able to achieve all their demands. The Colonial Government eventually gave in to them not wishing the situation to remain unnaturally quiet. 'I had been seen as a radical but effective spokesman for the workers and a successful negotiator for the Union.'[6]

Lee's personal prestige came into its own. He gained widespread public recognition. As a lawyer perceived to be left-wing, he took over the mantle of John Eber and Lim Kean Chye. As a union adviser his legal training gave him more to offer than men like Peter Williams and other Labour Party officials, so he could poach on their territory. Among the informal group of his like-minded peers he now had to be considered an activist, not merely a clever theoretician. Only a slight taste lingered in his mouth when the postal unionists claimed for years to come that they had helped launch the future Prime Minister's career.

In the wake of the strike, a number of people turned their attention seriously to Lee. Alex Josey was a good friend of Rajaratnam, with a background in intelligence work. By then, he was a journalist and an avowed social democrat. He began to cultivate the young lawyer. No doubt his were interests legitimate in someone of his profession and political leanings, but his MI6 training may also have spurred him to seek inside knowledge of this new political hopeful's calibre and outlook.

Another person who had more than one reason to deal with Lee was Othman Wok, a journalist with *Utusan Melayu*. They met in the course of the postal strike, and when shortly afterwards Lee became adviser to the union of which Othman was general secretary, they were thrown together frequently. Othman, an accomplished and gregarious man, was educated at Raffles Institution two years behind Lee and spent 1950 in England doing a diploma in journalism. He proved a reliable subordinate within the People's Action Party once it was formed, being a Cabinet Minister and its principal Malay figurehead for many years, and he weathered regular attacks from other Malays for accepting the PAP's brand of multiracialism.

A young man who added significantly to the momentum of 1952 was James Puthucheary. Detained in the Anti-British League raids of January 1951, he was released along with fellows student Abdullah Majid on 23 June 1952. It was not long before he met Lee and company at Rajaratnam's house. Puthucheary was a capable organiser with outspoken views. He provided a springboard for Lee and the others into the University undergraduate world and its small and faction-ridden radical coterie. They were fully informed about the months of discussions that led to the formation of the Socialist Club in February 1953 and contributed money and articles to the club magazine, *Fajar*.

Help was forthcoming from elsewhere on campus. Tom Elliott and Charles Gamba were two expatriates among the few academics sympathetic to the labour movement. They offered Lee friendship and advice based on their experience, and encouraged suitable students to assist him in bringing industrial unions of non-English-speaking workers under his wing.

Lee's, Goh's and Byrne's endeavours climaxed in late 1952 with the establishment of the Council of Action. Lee described the Council as 'a blanket organisation of all the [government] unions . . . and professional associations . . . a united front for political change with better terms and conditions of service as the rallying call. The leaders . . . ranged from illiterate Chinese dialect-speaking and Tamil-speaking daily-rated labourers, to English-speaking clerks, to doctors, dentists, engineers, and administrators'.[7]

The number of unions calling on Lee's assistance continued to increase. 'In December 1952, ten thousand workers of the Naval Base Labour Union went on strike. They sought my services . . . The arbitration drew public and press attention. The findings of the arbitrator (flown specially from Scotland) . . . gave enough concessions for the award not to be rejected'.[8]

Lee soon used his prestige to manoeuvre the paid secretary of the Union, a Labour Party leader, out of the job and have Sandrasegaram (Sidney) Woodhull appointed instead. Lee's patronage of young graduates such as Woodhull and later Jamit Singh, whom he knew from the Socialist Club, gave him useful proxies for detailed organisation in the unions. Moreover, it corresponded to his instinctive desire to be a tutor, a teacher, in the school of politics.

So far, so good. Pressure was mounting from different sides to form a popular party and serious discussions were given fresh impetus by the Council of Action rally in Victoria Memorial Hall and its success in gaining family and other allowances hitherto reserved for expatriates.

The release of Samad Ismail and Devan Nair in April 1953 was a further fillip for Lee. Samad was his prize contact: a fascinating character, he became Devan's principal mentor and guide when P.V. Sharma had departed for exile in India and finally China.* Samad was, we have already noted, a man who knew the Malayan and Indonesian Left intimately. Lee spent a great deal of time with him, deferring to him, trying to match Samad's personal experience and involvement with radicals by recounting what he himself had gleaned from intelligence briefings. They was no denying the sense of intrigue, of covert power and debonair grace, that Lee could derive from him.

In his seminal study of developments from 1945 to 1955, political historian Yeo Kim Wah claims that, through Samad Ismail and Devan Nair, Lee's group was able to negotiate with the MCP for a united front.[9] This is too precise a claim. Nevertheless, Samad and Devan between them provided inside knowledge and acted as brokers, not without reservations, expediting contact across the whole spectrum of English-educated and Chinese-speaking anti-colonialists.

> Sometimes weekly, most times fortnightly, a group—Goh Keng Swee, Toh Chin Chye, S. Rajaratnam, K.M. Byrne, Samad Ismail (a self-asserting communist ...) and I—met in the basement dining room of my home at 38 Oxley Road. The group discussed the policies of a political party which would make a broad appeal to nationalists and those with radical political views ... Our primary concern was how to muster a mass following. How did a group of English-educated nationalists—graduates of British universities—with no experience of either the hurly-burly of politics or the conspiracies of revolution, move people whose many languages they did not speak and whose problems and hardships they shared only intellectually?[10]

No exertion was needed now to keep the heat on the British colonial authorities. Even Sir John Nicoll, the Governor, was pressing the reactionary PP members elected to the Legislative

---

* P.V. Sharma, born 1917 in India, was a teacher trained at Raffles College. He was a key member of the Malayan Democratic Union (MDU) and of the Singapore Teachers' Union, through which connection he coached Devan Nair in Marxism.

Council to take advantage of the lull in communist activity and to broaden their base. To this end, the British convened the Rendel Constitutional Commission.

At the same time, Lee and his colleagues entered into discussion with David Marshall, a leading and high-minded Colony lawyer on friendly terms with Rajaratnam and Josey, and some of his associates. The purpose was ostensibly to form a new, united left-wing party to oppose the PP. Negotiations were strung out by the Lee group, and came to nothing: having decided that Marshall's proposed Democratic Labour Party was an election party with little future, they played a delaying game, probably in order to weaken its potential following.

The crucial problem was yet to be tackled—how to mobilise the Chinese masses. Lee had some union openings, and his new-found friends and acquaintances offered some promising connections and expertise. But he had no direct influence over what happened at ground level. His Malayan Forum speech in 1950 had barely reckoned with this obstacle to power.

The decisive year: 1954

> Then one day in 1954, we came into contact with the Chinese-educated world. The Chinese middle school students were in revolt against national service and they were beaten down. Riots took place, charges were preferred in court. Through devious ways they came into contact with us.
>
> We bridged the gap to the Chinese-educated world—a world teeming with vitality, dynamism and revolution, a world in which the communists had been working for over the last thirty years with considerable success.

Lee Kuan Yew, *The Battle for Merger*, 1961, p. 16

The events of 1954 proved a windfall for Lee and his colleagues, but only because they had the inner determination, particularly Lee, to respond to the challenge and to capitalise on the opportunities provided.

The Socialist Club was becoming a significant force at the University and from it was spawned the Federation of Pan-Malayan Students to cover the various tertiary education institutions. Among the fluent Chinese speakers in this umbrella body existed or came to exist close ties with the Chinese middle school pupils whose leading lights were often a few years older than average and had a history of involvement in Anti-British League cells.

When it was announced that several thousand youths would be called up for military training, the Chinese middle schools were organised to protest. On 13 May, 900 students demonstrated near the Governor's house, and forty-eight were arrested for unlawful assembly and rioting. The tertiary student leaders condemned the police and provided financial help to the Chinese school students.

In the midst of all this, the University Socialist Club itself got into trouble. The May issue of *Fajar* contained an editorial that attacked the newly formed Southeast Asia Treaty Organisation (SEATO) and described Malaya as 'a police state'. In the early hours of 28 May, eight students were arrested, their rooms searched and all material relating to the Socialist Club or *Fajar* was confiscated. Charges of sedition were laid and the students were released on bail for trial in August. Lee had been on a cruise to Hong Kong in May, but on his return he joined his colleagues in giving maximum support to the Socialist Club students; through the good offices of John Eber, now exiled in London, Rajaratnam and Lee obtained the services of D.N. Pritt, QC, a socialist barrister. One of the students on trial recalled Lee's dedication in preparing the brief;[11] at that stage he was admired on campus for his sincere anti-colonialism (as a liberal, not a radical) rather than for any obvious leadership qualities or gifts as an orator.

The period from May to August saw significant growth in relationships between the Lee group and the students. When the Chinese middle school leaders approached their Socialist Club friends to recommend a sympathetic lawyer, they were guided straight to Lee.

The result was that Pritt led for the defence in both cases, assisted by Harry Lee as his supporting counsel and Tann Wee Tiong, another lawyer Lee had suggested. The sedition charges in the *Fajar* trial of late August were quashed, but the Chinese middle school students lost their case six weeks later.

In a way the outcome of the two trials symbolised the emerging political forces and the British reaction to them. The *Fajar* students could be allowed some latitude because the English-educated posed a manageable challenge, neither widespread nor intense. By contrast, the Chinese middle school students drew on wellsprings of chauvinism frightening and intolerable to the colonial authorities. An indulgent response was out of the question.

The shift in Singapore's mood was dramatic. The calm of early 1952 had given way to turbulence, even volatility, as far as elements in the non-English-speaking Chinese majority were concerned. Passions previously subdued came to a head: witness the agitation among school students, the moves to establish a Chinese-language university, the revival of mass unions. As was obvious, the Malayan Communist Party stood to gain most from this reawakening.

At the centre of the revival were two men. One was Lim Chin Siong, steeled by training in Anti-British League cell work, gifted with fire to kindle others' hearts through his oratory in Mandarin, Hokkien and other dialects, set apart by a self-effacing dedication and a winsome boyishness. The other was Lee Kuan Yew, fast acquiring a reputation beyond the confines of his own language stream for his legal skills.

Few individuals could be effective in mobilising both the worlds these two men represented, but Devan Nair and Samad Ismail had broad credibility as anti-colonialist activists and radicals. Their seal of approval was enough to overcome suspicion of Lee and effect his introduction to Lim and company. With the two trials also linking forces hitherto separate, the time was judged ripe for a mutual Socialist Club friend to bring Lim Chin Siong to Lee's house one Sunday morning. Thus the MCP confirmed its re-entry on a phase of co-operation with open political movements, and Lee reached the turning point of his career.

'Lim Chin Siong is not the beginning nor the end of Communism. He is only one of their disciplined open-front workers. When the Emergency started in 1948, he was only a young school boy about fifteen or sixteen years old in the Chinese High School.'[12] Lee's words out of context appear to underrate Lim's importance, to himself and to the MCP. Although some authorities have cast doubt on Lim's MCP membership,[13] he was better able than any other person to rally the Chinese masses around issues of the MCP's choice. Within a few years of the Party being rendered headless, Lim Chin Siong and fellow leaders were able to train and recruit supporters at both general and cadre levels in the Chinese middle schools, in the cultural associations and among the dialect-speaking workers. The psychological basis of appeal was twofold: pride in the new China and insecurity at being stateless and receiving no serious or positive consideration from the colonial government.

Lee's excitement at gaining access to this vital but alien Chinese world shines through his words of seven years later which are quoted above. In 1979 the memory was still vivid.

> Did we, an English-educated, bourgeois group, with no organisation, and little ability to communicate with the Chinese dialect-speaking ... masses or the Mandarin-speaking educa-

ted elite, believe we could cope with Chinese pride ... in a period of intense resurgence, and stand up to the MCP, the protege of the CCP? In all honesty we did not think in those terms; we wanted the British out; we believed nationalism to be a more potent force than communism; we pressed on regardless of the horrendous risks because our visceral urges were stronger than our cerebral inhibitions.[14]

The contrast was electric. Apart from the language barriers, Lee and his comrades had the natural instincts and aspirations of a bourgeoisie favoured by colonial authority. Their time of relative hardship—the Occupation or student days overseas—was over. Now they were meeting intensely committed, disciplined students and youngsters wise far beyond their years, with a burning hatred of all that colonial master and local stooge stood for. The returned student would find no easygoing deference from this quarter. As a letter in the *Straits Times* from a teacher at Chung Cheng High School put it, 'the critical acumen and reasoned judgments' of his own pupils bore no comparison with the 'subservient and obsequious attitude of the Government English schoolboy'.[15]

Lee realised that, however energetic and well-connected he was for his purposes to that point, he was a latecomer in the world he had now encountered. That year, he started to learn Mandarin in earnest. His instincts were not towards the dialect-speaking proletariat but to those better equipped intellectually and to the China connection; so he moved to establish respectable credentials, or a footing at least, in the milieu dominated by the likes of Lim Chin Siong. He also began to re-assess his way of life and ponder the benefits of being less self-indulgent. As he recalled in Parliament years later (23 February 1977), 'They denigrated me. They said I had an air-conditioned office and I slept in an air-conditioned room. I was a bourgeois ... We learnt how they operated ... They are active. They are working with social democrats or democratic socialists. The social democrat likes his glass of beer, likes to have fun, so he leaves the meeting early. When all the chaps have left, they take the vote at two o'clock in the morning and carry the union. So, in the PAP, we used to squat till three or four o'clock in the morning.'

In 1954, events overtook Harry Lee Kuan Yew on his journey to power. His few contacts with the extreme Left burgeoned, and through the students, through Lim Chin Siong and Lim's lieutenant Fong Swee Suan, he was in touch with the leadership of the Chinese. He found himself mounting the pro-communist tiger for a ride into a united front quite different from what he had envisaged in London almost six years earlier. His assessment of the forces at work in Malaya had been correct, but he had not been prepared for the verve of the masses. Besides, diagnosis of reality was one thing, management another.

He sought advice from those, mainly expatriates, whom he believed would assist him cope with his predicament. For example, Richard Harris of *The Times* arrived in Singapore in late 1954, with experience of China and able to speak Chinese. Lee met him and asked Harris how to deal with the militant pro-communists in the People's Action Party, admitting he did not understand the problem himself. According to Harris, 'Lee's political formation was that of any other Englishman—he was on the left-wing of the Labour Party.'[16]

'Independence was far enough away for differences to be sunk.'[17] These words of Lee hint at the only major advantage he saw in British rule continuing for the time being: there would be no question of riding the tiger unprotected. By the mid-1950s the Special Branch had a keen ear to the ground and liaison between the police and military was planned ahead in minute detail for any crisis.

Meanwhile, the Rendel Commission was in progress. It received submissions from Singapore organisations. In November 1953 the Council for Joint Action, representing 'the largest organised body of opinion in the Colony',[18] produced a memorandum demanding full internal self-government and calling for appropriate means of tapping popular energy. The Commission brought down its report in February 1954, and the constitution it offered was accepted by the British Government. This paved the way for elections to be held by 1955, involving a vastly enlarged register of voters and the transfer of some powers to local legislators.

But Lee was understandably fearful that the British had severed Singapore from Malaya to keep the island indefinitely in bondage. The Rendel Constitution might be a ploy to buy off the people with a show of self-government. Lee's calculation was that a broad nationalist front could force the British to re-open the door to full independence for Malaya, preferably with Singapore taking the lead over Kuala Lumpur.

Given the factors he now knew he had to reckon with—the Chinese students and workers' groups in no mood to be passive and the limited scope the British afforded for political growth—Lee did not slacken his efforts to develop his own base. He needed more leverage over the relevant power blocs, and no one else was as well placed to achieve it. By the end of 1954 he was adviser to more than 100 unions and associations across Singapore's spectrum of languages. His energy was phenomenal.

The date for the formal inauguration of the People's Action Party was set and announced: 21 November 1954, 9.30 am at the Victoria Memorial Hall. Planning was firmly in Lee's hands.

The formation of the People's Action Party

Lee's group made the decision to cast the net of their party Malaya-wide. It was a decision whose logic was consistent with their own scattered birthplaces, with the fervour of their nationalist perceptions and with their ambitions for a ruling role in united Malaya. Those who seriously wanted socialism knew that any kind of carefully planned and distributist economy integrating all its sectors would be unworkable without the hinterland of peninsular Malaya.

But this was not all. Singapore had a distinctive racial composition, a distinctive history as a metropolis and *entrepôt* port and a unique strategic role. These factors introduced tensions and ambiguities into links with Malaya, and they signalled danger. As the Emergency petered out in the Malayan jungles, the MCP was concentrating on Chinese Singapore as the launching pad for national liberation. Equally, the growing disparity between modern Singapore and backward Malaya would raise the stakes in a multi-communal power game.

So in projecting pan-Malayan thinking from the outset, Lee's group would not only be following their instincts; they would try to outwit reactionary and communist alike. They could hope to discredit the former, appealing for radical changes with a groundswell of support. The British would ensure that the latter be kept in check. At the right moment Whitehall's obduracy could be tackled and Malaya reunited.

Thus it was that Tunku Abdul Rahman (UMNO) and Tan Cheng Lock (Malayan Chinese Association) were invited to share the platform at the Party's inauguration. Many of the Party's left-wing supporters were distressed that two such men were asked to give their blessing, but Lee and his fellow planners were determined. With the failure of multiracial parties such as Dato Onn's IMP, the only way for a Singapore party to keep a pan-Malayan perspective and ambition alive was to court the favour of Malaya's two major communal leaders.

A small sign of the move's importance to Lee emerged when the Tunku was about to visit him at home and discuss the inauguration.

Lee was frantic, and, to make a good impression, he importuned Samad Ismail for stories of the Tunku's anti-Japanese activities in the Kedah political association, *Sebrakas*.

The other major factor to be weighed was the press. Lee recalled, 'It was the age before the advent of television. Even the radio was a luxury found in few homes. Without Chinese, English and Malay press coverage, we could not have got off to a quick start.'[19]

Direct and favourable communication with the masses was vital. Not so much the English language press—the hostility of the *Straits Times* could be expected, even welcomed, given its British ownership. 'The Chinese press was on the whole friendly . . . This made it impossible for the English-language press to ignore the PAP, which it at first tried to do . . . The Malay press, the *Utusan Melayu* . . . was consistently friendly until 1964, by which time Yusof had sold out his control to UMNO.'[20]

The PAP's name was chosen 'mainly because this political party was meant for the people'.[21] 'Action' harked back to the Council for Joint Action. The emblem was to be a red bolt of lightning (*petir* in Malay), symbolising action, piercing a blue circle of solidarity, on a white background denoting purity. Its motto was 'Unity and Honesty in Action'.

At the launching, Lee sat centre stage because by then he was the best known of the group. There were fourteen convenors—two lawyers, two journalists, two teachers, one university lecturer and seven trade unionists. Notable absentees from the platform were Goh Keng Swee, K.M. Byrne and Lim Chin Siong. Goh had returned to London by October 1954 for doctoral studies, Byrne was prevented by civil service regulations from participating openly. Lim was content for Fong Swee Suan to be up front: he might have been reserving judgment about the Party while concentrating on union work, but he denies that his earlier detention in prison—the explanation Lee claims Lim had offered—was the reason.

The hall was full. The Tunku's most vivid memory of the occasion was the smell of toddy, the working Indian's drink.[22] Men far outnumbered women. Unionists and academics, rich and poor, were present together. Chairs were reserved on the platform with 'Special Branch' labels.

Lee delivered a vitriolic attack on the Progressive Party, the Labour Party, the new Malayan constitutional proposals and the Emergency Regulations. He summarised the new Party's objectives: to end colonialism and establish a democratic government for all Malaya, including Singapore, with universal adult suffrage; to entrench the right to work and its full rewards in the economic order; to abolish unjust inequalities of wealth and opportunity; to guarantee social security to those unable to work; and to infuse a spirit of endeavour, national unity, self-respect and self-reliance.

Speeches in Malay, Tamil and Mandarin followed, then half an hour of questions from the floor. The programme nearly encroached on an afternoon concert because Tan Cheng Lock spoke well beyond his allotted time. Temporary office bearers were elected in anticipation of an annual conference before June 1955.

'The Party was to be consciously radical and anti-colonial', according to Lee.[23] Anti-colonial, yes. How radical? At its founding there was no explicit commitment to socialism, nor in the manifesto that appeared.[24]

> The drawing up of the manifesto for the new Party was by no means an easy task, particularly when individuals in the group had different views and interpretations of terms such as 'democracy' and 'socialism'.[25]

Lee and his colleagues were nationalists first. Freedom must precede any economic or social restructuring. Their views of socialism clustered conveniently within the British Fabian tradition: let a socialist society evolve gradually; in the meantime take the initiative where possible to adopt positive measures such as welfare for the sick and aged or income redistribution or government-controlled industrialisation.

By avoiding the term 'socialism', Lee's group broadened the scope of their appeal for anti-colonial solidarity. They also served notice to any budding member who might be a doctrinaire socialist or worse that the PAP was their creation and its policy decisions lay in their hands.

One further consideration: the events of 1954 had impressed on Lee the absolute necessity of speaking Chinese in Singapore. Socialist rhetoric in English was not the way to reach the masses. As he said, admonishing J.B. Jeyaretnam of the Workers' Party some twenty-two years later, 'if he is really serious, I suggest to him instead of reading more Fabian Society tracts, better start learning a little bit of Hokkien and Mandarin'.[26]

The Rendel elections and 1955

There was agreement on all sides that the PAP would not be an 'election party', the charge levelled at the various Labour Party offshoots. It would be a mass party, functioning constitutionally.

The Colonial Government was well prepared to foil any violent bid for power.

Just as they had deplored flirtation with UMNO and MCA politicians, some of the radical elements in the Party argued against participation in the Rendel elections scheduled for 1955. The 'moderates' agreed that their hands would be tied behind their backs if they formed a government under Rendel. Anyway, they were too inexperienced for an electoral campaign on that scale. But, they asserted, a 'party committed to constitutional methods of change would be signing its death warrant if it stood outside the constitutional arena and merely protested with words and rude gestures'.[27] Their argument prevailed.

Four candidates were put up: Lee Kuan Yew, Goh Chew Chua, Lim Chin Siong and Devan Nair. Devan Nair was brought in to replace two others who were 'not qualified' and the balance was kept between 'moderates' and 'pro-communists'. A fifth PAP supporter, Ahmad Ibrahim, Vice-President of the Naval Base Labour Union, stood as an independent for Sembawang: the Indians and Malays were uneasy about the PAP's alleged extremism, and since their vote would be vital in that constituency, it was better for Ahmad to stand on his own merits.

Lee nominated for the seat of Tanjong Pagar because several unions for whom he had been a successful adviser had their headquarters there. Although his legal abilities brought him kudos, he was not blessed with a manner that attracted strong personal networks of support. So he was obliged to rely on others to help set up branches and organise workers. Moreover, he had not yet overcome the language barrier, and his first campaign speech in Mandarin was a tentative effort, based on a single page prepared for him by a Chinese-educated journalist and PAP cadre, Jek Yeun Thong.

The election was something new for Singapore. Automatic registration enlarged the electorate more than fourfold to 300,000 voters and over half of them actually voted, as against one-third who had done so in 1951. Indians no longer dominated electoral politics and the potential rural and female vote rose sharply. Six party groupings contested the election. The Progressive Party, dating from 1947, appealed to those not keen to see the British leave. The Democratic Party (DP) was set up by the Chinese Chamber of Commerce in February 1955 specifically for the elections; its appeal was to traditional Chinese loyalties. The Labour Front (LF) was in part a reconstruction of Singapore Labour Party fragments, and was modelled on the British Labour Party. Its base was the Trade Unions Congress, made up of English-or

Malay-speaking unionists. The Alliance in Singapore was dominated by the UMNO and the Singapore Malay Union: the local Chinese Association had been discredited and dissolved in 1953. With the Labour Front and the Alliance the PAP had a loose understanding—being independence parties, they would avoid contesting the same electorates. Lee Kuan Yew and the Tunku campaigned for each other's parties and the PAP offered diligent Chinese students to canvass for the LF and Alliance.

Unionist and student involvement meant that the strength of the Left could be tested without the experimental liability of an all-out bid for PAP victory. The results were fascinating, and repaid close examination. Twenty-five seats were at stake. The right-wing vote of 45 per cent was split between the PP and DP, who both put up candidates almost everywhere. They picked up 6 seats. In the Malay-dominated electorates, the Alliance polled well. The Labour Front won 10 out of 17 seats with 27.5 per cent of the vote. The PAP won 3 out of its 4 seats contested and polled the highest party vote in any one seat. Two left-wing independents, including Ahmad Ibrahim, and one right-winger made up the balance.

To his surprise Marshall was asked to form a government, and this he did in conjunction with the three Alliance members, *ex officio* members and nominated non-officials, making 18 out of the 32 in the Assembly. Almost immediately, infighting flared up.

Marshall's was the unenviable task of holding his government together and risking the label of 'stooge' if repressive measures were taken. He was given little help by the colonial officials. The prudence of the PAP was amply vindicated. In the Assembly it had a new platform; it had an entrée to policy discussion without the burden of responsibility if things went awry and it had time to consolidate its mass base.

The British authorities were obliged to do some recalculation after the 1955 elections. They had an unstable minority government on their hands, by contrast with the overwhelming mandate given to the Alliance in Malaya the same year. The groundswell of Chinese demands grew daily through the LF and PAP and through the associations, legal or not, that seemed to bubble up spontaneously among workers, rural dwellers and students. There could be no peace until much more substantial autonomy was granted. But they still had room to manoeuvre—given their perfected security control and the ambiguous election results—until a suitable succession emerged.

With David Marshall unexpectedly Chief Minister in a Labour Front government, the PAP moderates realised they would have to appear more radical than they had anticipated. This would play into the hands of more extreme Party members. From 1955 onwards socialism appeared as an objective of the Party; even Marshall claimed to represent 'dynamic socialism'. The shift was acceptable to the moderates because it was still offset by the 'pan-Malayan' and 'constitutional methods' clauses in the PAP charter.

The year 1955 was one of phenomenal growth in the trade union movement, among the Chinese especially. Marshall's democratic instincts obliged the colonial authorities to allow more latitude. The Singapore Factory and Shop Workers' Union and the Singapore Bus Workers' Union had been established or taken over by Lim Chin Siong and Fong Swee Suan the previous year, and allied with the middle school students they made most of the running in strike action and demonstrations. Ironically, it was Devan Nair who counselled militancy and who attacked Lee and his English-educated colleagues for being bourgeois. Lim and Fong were more inclined to temper any hopes of revolution and acknowledge Singapore's *entrepôt* constraints. The waters of union planning must sometimes have been very muddy indeed, what with the pressure of events, input from both MCP command and from freelance extremists such as Devan, and the need to gauge British reaction, not to forget divided public opinion, varying levels of union consciousness and the role of Special Branch plants.

The following catalogue gives some hint of the raised political temperature: a bus strike at Paya Lebar in February; a huge student demonstration on the eve of the elections to press for registration of the Chinese Middle School Students' Union; the notorious Hock Lee bus strike in April–May, which led to riots and bloodshed between strikers, students, secret society gangsters and police; a protest in mid-June at the detention of six Factory and Shop Workers' Union leaders who had wisely called off a strike in sympathy with the Harbour Board Staff Association's failure to win a long-standing log of claims; the October campaign for the abolition of the Emergency Regulations and not their replacement by a Preservation of Public Security Ordinance (PPSO).

Lee was nominal adviser to all the key unions involved, but he was often out of his depth. He begged Samad to rein Devan in. He sought to moderate unionists' demands and methods and had limited success, for example, in the middle stages of the Hock Lee strike. He was absent on holiday in the Cameron Highlands for the June disturbance. In fact, throughout 1955 his behaviour was like that of a moth, drawn to the spotlight, yet much bothered by its heat. Privately he repeated on numerous occasions the words that embarrassed him when an Australian journalist reported them publicly in early May: 'The Communists are certain to win and nothing and no one can stop them. Any man in Singapore who wants to carry the Chinese-speaking people with him cannot afford to be anti-Communist'.[28]

All Lee and his associates could do was take preventive action where they still had opportunity to do so. In May they released a statement clarifying the PAP's fundamental objective: 'an independent, democratic, non-Communist Malaya'. Before the Second Party Conference in June, Lee did a deal. In return for freedom to orchestrate the union movement, whilst maintaining a united front, certain militants would either step down from the Party's Central Executive Committee (Devan Nair and Fong Swee Suan, for instance) or not stand for the new Committee (Lim Chin Siong, for instance). Given Marshall's relatively gentle treatment of protest and industrial action, both PAP factions must have realised they were buying time against some sort of showdown. Demagoguery by Lim would only have so long to succeed or be put down.

Meanwhile the Legislative Assembly was galvanised into life by the oratory of David Marshall and Lee Kuan Yew. Crowds thronged the gallery to enjoy the cut and thrust of debate and interjection. There was a certain splendid luxury about Lee's Assembly performance over the next four-year period while its business was conducted solely in English. For the record he was able to set out the policy of his group, which stood as long as he retained command of the Party CEC. He could distance the PAP from the unconstitutional actions and words of individual members.[29] He could espouse a democratic non-communist future. On the other hand, he opposed the Emergency Regulations[30] and later the PPSO.[31] He attacked the 'useless, spineless lot'[32] who had sat on the Rendel Commission: the PAP would not be able to co-operate with the Governor to work the Constitution, but would support David Marshall to let him try.[33]

The battles that won a popular following for the PAP were being joined in the unions, the schools, the associations and out on the hustings. In those settings, Lee and his group were at an obvious disadvantage. James Puthucheary, who handled PAP propaganda and publicity for the elections, recalled the first PAP rally he attended in a totally Chinese village. 'Toh Chin Chye spoke first, in English! No response from the crowd. Ong Eng Guan was next, in Hokkien but not very good. The crowd was restless.' Puthucheary began to have a feeling of utter failure. 'Then Lim Chin Siong got up. He was brilliant, and the crowd was spellbound.'[34]

Lim's speeches in the Legislative Assembly were ghosted by Puthucheary and Devan Nair for him to memorise. He spoke infrequently and his eloquence was shrouded by an alien language. His last appearance in the Assembly (before his own detention) was on 4 October 1956 to second Lee's motion of concern at the arrests of trade union and civic leaders and the dissolution of two societies. In rebutting the Education Minister's assertion that those students engaged in *hsueh hsi* (study) method were practising communism, Lim said, 'Harry Lee also drives an American car. Therefore, Harry Lee is an American!'[35]

For a while in 1955, Marshall's Labour Front appeared to be gaining ground. A constitutional crisis in July had brought a ruling favourable to Marshall's wishes from the Colonial Secretary, Alan Lennox-Boyd, and the promise of internal self-government talks in April 1956. Marshall convened a Malayanisation Commission to localise the public service in August. The All-Party Committee he had set up on education was in full swing. The Chief Minister had stood between students and unionists and the colonial authorities, and he could not be dismissed as a stooge. In December he took part in the Tunku's talks with the legendary communist leader Chin Peng at Baling.

The Labour Front even seemed to be attracting party members much faster than the PAP. In November 1955, at the First Anniversary Conference, Toh Chin Chye proposed 'that political parties should sink their differences and unite under a single national convention to fight for independence'.[36] Marshall replied, 'I will have no truck with those who are playing footie footie with Communism'.[37] No doubt memories of previous negotiations with the PAP were also in the Chief Minister's mind.

MAY 1954

We do but merely ask
No more, no less, this much:
That you white man,
Boasting of many parts
Some talk of Alexander, some of Hercules
Some broken not long ago
By little yellow soldiers
Out of the Rising Sun . . .
We ask you see
The bitter, curving tide of history,
See well enough, relinquish,
Restore this place, this sun
To us . . . and the waiting generations.
Depart white man.
Your minions riot among
Our young in Penang Road
Their officers, un-Britannic,
Full of service, look
Angry and short of breath.
You whored on milk and honey
Tried our spirit, spent our muscle,
Extracted from our earth;
Gave yourselves superior ways
At our expense, in our midst.
Depart:
You knew when to come;
Surely know when to go.
Do not ignore, dismiss,
Pretending we are foolish;
Harbour contempt in eloquence.
We know your language.
My father felt his master's voice,
Obeyed but hid his grievous, wounded self.
I have learnt:
There is an Asian tide
That sings such power
Into my dreaming side:
My father's anger turns my cause.
Depart Tom, Dick and Harry.
Gently, with ceremony;
We may still be friends,
Even love you . . . from a distance

EDWIN THUMBOO

4

Preparing for Self-Government

> Soon there were back-seat drivers and conductors who had different views on reaching a common destination. In the years ahead the PAP was like an overloaded bus travelling down winding mountain roads, teetering sometimes on the brink of disaster into the political chasm below.
>
> TOH CHIN CHYE,
> *Petir*, Singapore, 1979, pp. 16–17

Constant vigilance was the price Lee's group had to pay for control of the PAP during those early years. Several times they suggested publicly or privately a coalition with the Labour Front and Alliance, not to form a government under the Rendel Constitution, but to precipitate a crisis for the Constitution through a political or economic standstill and gain from the colonial authorities a programme of new elections and greater independence in tandem with Malaya.

Two basic operational problems needed to be faced if the challenges ahead were to be met on their terms. They had to rely for much of the Party's delicate organisational work and outreach on trusted assistants. The lesson of Lee's patronage even of young English-educated graduates such as Woodhull and Jamit Singh in the unions was already clear: it was risky. They had a mind and outlook of their own. Fortunately, there were a few like Ong Pang Boon and Jek Yeun Thong who came from a Chinese-educated background but were willing to accept Lee's direction in the name of Party loyalty.* The other problem was that by 1955 Lee and his circle were stretched to the limit. Goh Keng Swee, ever the razor-

---

* Ong Pang Boon had graduated from the University of Malaya in Singapore, having been in the Socialist Club and deemed a 'hostile witness', at the time of the *Fajar* trial (Chapter 3). Jek Yeun Thong was a journalist with Marxist cell experience, detained briefly, he was the Prime Minister's Political Secretary 1959–63. Both men became Ministers in PAP governments.

sharp realist and political gamesman, was in London. The rest held down jobs where they were not completely their own masters. But Lee was now in a position to leave Laycock and Ong and set up his own law firm, Lee and Lee, in partnership with his wife and his recently qualified younger brother, Dennis Lee Kim Yew. This gave him more time for political pursuits. It also allowed more freedom to choose the areas of law he would practise. Although his prestige as an advocate and adviser had given his political career its greatest boost, Lee often said later that he had felt disturbed or disgusted by many of the victories he won for his clients. Examples he cited were Malays in the Hertogh riots,[1] student at the Pritt trials,[2] murderers,[3] *chap-ji-kee** operators[4] and tax evaders.[5] His experience strengthened his resolve to abolish trial by jury.†

The constitutional talks

As well as this, Lee had the extra responsibilities of being *de facto* Opposition Leader. He had to make sure that he was not outflanked by David Marshall, the Chief Minister. A major test, away from home but on familiar territory and of great importance, came in April and May of 1956. It arose as a result of the growing pressure of expectations that Marshall's tenure of office had generated.

For several weeks a thirteen-man All-Party Mission negotiated terms for *merdeka* (freedom) with the British Government in London. The Chief Minister led the Mission, and Lee Kuan Yew and Lim Chin Siong were its PAP delegates. Even before it left Singapore, Lee reckoned the Mission was divided and bargaining from a position of weakness, so he undertook initiatives of his own. He held private discussions with Alan Lennox-Boyd, the Colonial Secretary, and urged him to tie Singapore up with the Federation. When the Mission talks were stalemated by the British on the question of their veto rights in a joint Singapore–United Kingdom Defence and Security Council, Lee played a major part in framing two compromise proposals. He then procured a telegram from his Party in Singapore, authorising acceptance of the terms being offered by the British for transitional *merdeka*. All this with Lim beside him!

---

* *chap-ji-kee* A popular and illegal game of chance involving the selection of two out of twelve numbers in a specific order.
† Trial by jury was abolished in two stages—for non-capital crimes in 1959 and for capital crimes in 1969.

Preparing for Self-Government

However, Marshall forced his hand by insisting that through voting against the proposals he would be seen as more radical than Lee. Lee capitulated and the talks broke down, with nine votes against and the four conservatives (Liberal Socialists)* abstaining.

Tunku Abdul Rahman then issued a public invitation to David Marshall to bring Singapore into Malaya as a unit, like Penang. That was unacceptable, but Marshall did seek some other basis for reopening the talks—he had promised to resign if unsuccessful. The British approached the Liberal Socialists in case a more compliant Singapore government might be formed and negotiations resumed. Lee exposed this move to frustrate it and there was no alternative but to go home empty-handed. Marshall was upset at what he perceived to be Lee's disloyalty and machinations, and the latter rubbed salt in the wound by mimicking the Mission participants at a student forum in London. By the time Marshall returned home, he was so angry he ordered Lee out of his airport press conference.

While in London Lee had spent as much time as he could with Goh Keng Swee, just as Lim Chin Siong had with the exiled leftists John Eber and Lim Hong Bee. A good omen was the Goh had managed, between his PhD studies and his recreation, to recapture the Malayan Forum from the other two, whom he regarded as out-and-out Marxists with undesirable influence on the students from Malaya and Singapore.

The atmosphere at the following year's talks was quite different. Lim Yew Hock was the Labour Front Chief Minister, much more reliant on the British than Marshall. By then, Lim Chin Siong was in gaol and the Labour Front was managing subversion on British terms. The Federation of Malaya would soon be independent, and the Tunku had ruled out merger.

Lee again played a dominating role, this time being the sole representative of his Party and having more or less a free hand. The bulk of the agreements picked up what had been rejected in 1956, but with a refinement—the Internal Security Council (ISC). Membership would consist of three British nominees, the UK High Commissioner acting as Chairman, three Singapore Government nominees and a Federation of Malaya appointee with a casting vote. This arrangement was acceptable both to Lim Yew Hock and Lee Kuan Yew, who were courting the Tunku separately and assiduously. With elections possibly only a year away, Lee played a tactical master stroke. He requested the Colonial Secretary to insert

---

* The Liberal Socialists were an amalgamation of the right-wing Progressive Party and Democratic Party Assemblymen.

a clause preventing those who had been detained for subversion from standing for the Assembly.[6] He and the delegation were then able to take the happy position of accepting the Constitutional Agreement as a whole and protesting that the particular subversive candidate clause was 'against normal democratic practice', while they stood to benefit from the clause and knew full well it would remain. Moreover, argument over the subversive clause could distract attention from the ISC provisions.

One more round of talks was held in March 1958, to complete planning and legislative detail so that Singapore could move towards elections and internal self-government. Lennox-Boyd advised Lim Yew Hock that no further stalling was possible and that he was not the man of the future. Lee took advantage of his own emerging status with the British to insist that the three senior police officers—Chief, Deputy, and Head of Special Branch—should be appointed by the Singapore Government's Public Service Commission (PSC) with one right of challenge by the ISC before confirmation. This ploy reflected his preoccupation with local and personal control of the police, and was partly aimed at getting rid of Khaw Kai Boh, a Malayan intelligence operative groomed for high police office and at that stage in Special Branch. Lee loathed him, and the feeling was mutual: Khaw was paranoid about flirtation with the Left.

The Party reorganisation

Lee's experience of the vitality of the Chinese pro-communists and his tenuous bond with his more extreme English-educated colleagues must have made the development of a mass party none too relaxing for him. It was one thing for him to use the clenched fist and the slogans picked up from his radical comrades, legitimate enough in rallying popular support. But how could he stave off erosion of power within the Party?

By the time of the second Annual Party Conference in July 1956, the leftists were apprehensive enough of Lee's intentions and confident enough of their dominance at branch level to chance their arm. They nominated for five positions on the Executive, and succeeded in gaining four; Lim Chin Siong topped the vote. James Puthucheary was one of those then appointed to a subcommittee to revise the constitution, and he proposed that branches have greater power and that their committees nominate CEC members direct. This was not acceptable to Lee's group. In September and October, the Lim Yew Hock Government detained all the leftist CEC members and other cadres who were involved in union disturbances, including Puthucheary, Lim Chin Siong and Devan. Lee Kuan Yew was absent in the Cameron Highlands at the time.

At the next Annual Conference (August 1957) six leftists were elected to the Central Executive Committee. Lee later alleged that the radicals had stacked the Conference with non-members by giving them admission cards posted out to union premises. Although Lee demanded and won support for a motion to make the Party officially 'non-Communist' there was an atmosphere of foreboding and conflict. His group decided on a showdown, and he and the other five 'non-Communists' refused to stand for office in the new CEC. Ten days later, five out of the six 'radicals' were detained.

It has not been possible to establish once and for all Lee's role in the arrests. There is a strong likelihood that he had more than an inkling of what would happen, as he probably did with the previous year's arrests. By 1957 he was close to William Goode, the Chief Secretary, as well as to Richard Corridon of Special Branch. Goode, 'very sharp and deep, a politician to the fingertips',[7] would have matched his own observations with the views of Corridon and men like F.W. Dalley, a British unionist sent out to assist the local movement, who had spent much time advising Lee. Goode took the calculated risk of letting Lee come up. That meant restraining Lim Yew Hock, who increasingly wanted not only the PAP extremists but the Party itself and Lee curbed or even eliminated, and who had support to that end from top local Special Branch officers such as Khaw Kai Boh.

As the years he was Chief Minister went by, Lim had a doubly galling time. He plotted with Lee: in 1959 he told the Assembly, 'I did so many things for the good of the PAP after discussions with the PAP'.[8] Meanwhile he tried to outmanoeuvre Lee. On both counts he was foiled: Lee was too smart and had the *de facto* backing of the British who kept their preferred protégé informed.

Josey says of the arrests that it was 'a matter of bitter regret to Lee that he could only assume leadership again after the British, through an acquiescent Chief Minister, had jailed the culprits'.[9] Granted, to be helped by the British or the Chief Minister was to invite the odium attaching to a stooge or a weakling. The result might be worth it, but there was quite a high price to pay.

Who else knew of Lee's contact with Goode, Corridon, other British officers, or Lim Yew Hock? and, if anyone did, who knew what transpired?

The oft-repeated boast—'we gave no hostages to fortune' —requires that as few people as possible be in the know. It was only Lim's extreme frustration that led to his outburst in the Assembly on 4 March 1959. Otherwise the public slate might have remained clean, or at least only rumoured to be unclean.

Suspicions among the radical PAP camp of Lee's collaboration in security sweeps had been strong from 1955 onwards: Despite his disclaimer in the Assembly,[10] Lee has clear convictions about who was who in the PAP. 'When you meet a union leader,' he said in 1961, reflecting on the 1950s,

> You will quickly have to decide which side he is on and whether or not he is a Communist. You can find out by the language he uses, and his behaviour, whether or not he is in the inner circle which makes the decisions. These are things from which you determine whether he is an outsider or an insider in the Communist underworld.[11]

There was more to it than that.

Lee's friendship, first with Samad Ismail and then with Devan Nair who was strongly influenced by Samad, provided a grid to as certain allegiances. By 1956, Samad had fallen out with Lee and drifted away from the PAP, but not before he had arranged contacts and opened Lee's eyes to what was happening behind the scenes in Singapore. Devan began his transition to Lee's group late in 1956, frustrated to the point of tears and depression at his re-internment, realising the racial implications of mobilising the Chinese masses as he had insisted around chauvinist issues, and coming under the influence of Francis Thomas (a former colleague from St Andrew's School and currently a Labour Front Minister), Richard Corridon and Lee himself. Having been Lim Chin Siong's guide, he was able to confirm the young Chinese leader's dedication to Marxism and the slim prospects of a change of heart. Lee's analysis, based on Special Branch reports as well as his own observation and deduction, was again vindicated. 'Lim was the most important open front leader the MCP had built up. By 1955 he knew that I knew this.'[12]

> I came to know dozens of them ... Many of them are prepared to pay the price for the Communist cause in terms of personal freedom and sacrifice. They know they run the risk of detention if they are found out and caught. Often my colleagues and I disagreed with them and intense fights took place, all concealed from the outside world because they were

Communists working in one united anti-colonial front with us against the common enemy and it would not do to betray them.
Eventually many of them landed in jail in the purges of 1956 and 1957. I used to see them there, arguing their appeals, reading their captured documents and the Special Branch precis of the cases against them.
I had the singular advantage of not only knowing them well by having worked at close quarters with them in a united front against the British, but I also saw the official version in reports on them.
Many were banished to China. Some were my personal friends. They knew that I knew that they were Communists, for between us there was no pretence. They believed that I should join them.[13]

Lee prided himself on not betraying his 'Communist' friends and contacts. Unlike them, he would not ruthlessly abandon former associates when the parting of the ways occurred. Rather, he wanted to argue them round to an acceptance of Malaya's communal realities. His 'friends', however, might not have endorsed his pride so warmly. Whilst it is true that the teacher in Lee wanted to persuade the recalcitrants to come to heel, he was too much of a loner to be a credible storm-weather friend and too vindictive always to resist the punitive urge. Besides, his colleague, Goh Keng Swee, had not the least hesitation about leaping to judgment and decisive action.

The labelling of opponents as 'Communist' or 'pro-Communist'* was an easy option, either tactically or out of fear. Reinforced by the evidence of revolutionary activity and by the certainty that anyone more determined than they must be a Marxist, Lee and Goh became experts at reaching a verdict on an individual after passing sentence, like the Queen in *Alice in Wonderland:* 'Off with his head!' On one occasion, K.M. Byrne was summoned urgently to Goh's father's house to learn from Goh and Lee that Rajaratnam was a communist. Questioning revealed that the accusation was provoked by Raja's 'sinister' green eyes.

The other fundamental barrier to fairness was Lee's confidence that he knew more than anyone else. He had access to 'facts' and details from too many quarters, he deduced too much, for his honour to remain intact. But unfairness could be justified as a chess

---

* The reader may have noticed all documentation in the book originating from PAP or British sources uses capitals for 'Communist' and 'Communism'.

move to anticipate and check an opponent, not for Lee's sake but for the Party's and Singapore's.

So it was that after August 1957 the PAP was reorganised according to what Thomas Bellows calls 'the iron law of oligarchy'.[14] Lee and Toh worked out the details. Only cadres could attend the Party Conference. The cadres would be chosen by the majority vote of the CEC. Lee described it thus: 'The Pope chooses the Cardinals, and the Cardinals choose the Pope.'[15] The CEC reserved the right to suspend, demote or expel cadres or ordinary members. In March 1958 there was a re-registration exercise. Cadres would be drawn from the new register with the stipulation that they must be Singapore citizens (an easy way of excluding many extremists), over twenty-one and literate. A selection panel was set up to promote and appoint in the Party. Just after the elections in 1959 but before the release of the PAP detainees, the CEC was appointed for two years and all non-CEC and Legislative Assembly cadres were put on a temporary footing for a year.

Even such drastic measures did not prevent the crisis of 1961. But they signalled clearly to the membership whose Party it was. Their other advantage was that they did not cause many ripples among supporters outside the Party. Too much was happening on the public stage. And Lee's group, by dint of style and language barriers, was not the main focus of popular allegiance. Identification with the second level of leadership was the 'relevant and decisive affiliation'.[16]

Events on the public stage: 1956-59

Once the MCP decided to mobilise the people to the brink of revolution, working through the PAP, the unions, the Chinese students and the cultural associations, the Government could react in one of only two ways. One was short-term suppression, with weapons ranging from selective detention to all the panoply of state. The other was more constructive—executing social and economic measures to deny the Left any obvious monopoly of concern for justice.

The Labour Front Government of Lim Yew Hock showed itself suitably stern in purges and detentions. But, as Lee remarked later for all to hear, Lim and his colleagues had little idea how to tackle the reconstruction needed. The British and the newly enfranchised electorate would have to look elsewhere for that.

With the spectacular opening of Nanyang University in March 1956 came a new outlet for Chinese chauvinism and communist agitation. The All-Party Committee on Chinese Education had brought down its long-awaited report in February. It was received favourably in English-speaking circles as a statement of existing and future problems and solutions, but it called for categorical prohibition of all political activity among students other than discussion. Two PAP policy committee members were signatories to a statement of the English Teachers' Union (Chinese Schools) attacking the report as 'a shameless piece of colonial prudery!'.[17] Their objections were the tip of the Chinese iceberg, not least in the PAP where the factions struggled for power and whose Secretary-General (Lee) had been one of the most influential members of the nine-man All-Party Committee.

The Chinese education issue must have seemed a decisive one for the MCP. Certainly hopes soared as 1956 progressed. In September and early October the situation became explosive.

Lim Yew Hock's Government dissolved several 'front' organisations, including the Middle School Students' Union, detained five student leaders on or after China's National Day and ordered a large number to be expelled from two schools. A sit-in was staged by 4000 students at the schools, which the Government then ordered closed. Busmen brought in food, and Lim Chin Siong formed a Civil Rights Convention to rally the public. Things came to a head when the Government ordered parents to take their children from the schools by 8 pm on 25 October before they were forcibly removed. The police and army cleared the schools the next morning at 6 am. Planned mass actions were frustrated and contained. That night, over 200 people were detained in a series of security swoops. Lim Chin Siong was one of them: he was expecting arrest and had made preparations by salting away his union's funds. Further trouble spots were kept under control. Fifteen people were killed and more than one hundred injured.

The MCP had lost ground badly and its leaders were bitterly disappointed. What better issue to muster support against a colonial government, an English-educated Council of Ministers, a predominantly Malay police force and non-Chinese army! The fatal weakness was that although the MCP had developed an excellent open or semi-secret chain of command, it had been robbed of its planning brains by previous Special Branch action. Lim Chin Siong did not have the resources or skills of a tactician and he was too doctrinaire, as he admitted later to the British ex-communist Douglas Hyde.[18] Only a few of the Chinese-speaking were self-consciously communists, however proud most of them might be of China. They eschewed violence. After all, many had come to Singapore to find a new life and they wanted freedom, not only from exploitation but also from disaster.

Lee and his group learned the lessons of October 1956. Publicly Lee protested at Government provocation, whilst acknowledging that force was necessary to deal with mobs. He realised that the Government had been foolish not to purge the ringleaders earlier instead of having to flush out thousands of non-communist students from the school sit-in, thereby assisting the portrayal of Lim Yew Hock as the enemy of Chinese education. He also formed the opinion that show of force—tanks, bayonets, rifles, and so on—was often the best way to nip disturbance in the bud, a view held even more strongly by Goh Keng Swee.

The year 1956 gave the principal actors and parties in Singapore an idea of where they stood and how far they could go. To quote Richard Clutterbuck's analysis: 'Above all, the success and consequent prestige of the police kept the battle off the streets for the next seven years, enabling Lee Kuan Yew to establish his political position and conduct the political struggle with his rivals in the Assembly, in Party Committees and in private meetings without coercion by mob violence.'[19]

In retrospect 1957 was an easier year for Lee's group. Goh Keng Swee came home from London with a PhD and returned to the Civil Service. The renewed constitutional talks went well, the CEC under Toh Chin Chye resisted left-wing politicking during Lee's absence and Lee was able to make good use of Marshall's resignation challenge on his return to conduct a by-election campaign on the Internal Security Council and merger.

Despite the arrests of the previous year, the MCP network still flourished and by mid-1957 a new central union, the National Union of General Workers, had built up. Picnics became a major rallying technique with simple propaganda for all and careful ideological study for the faithful who stayed late. Plans were made to bid for control of the Labour Front's union base, the Trade Union Congress. The PAP was under pressure during the first three-quarters of the year. For a short while a Chinese language *Action Express* appeared, with anti-government material, but it was stopped. And the bid for CEC power was foiled.

The big event of the year was the proclamation of Malaya's independence (31 August 1957). Unfortunately it meant the Tunku had a head start on Lee in the pan-Malayan stakes. Lee, however, was not about to abandon the race and applied whatever heat he could. He warned the UMNO leaders that once the young Malay intelligentsia subjected them to critical scrutiny they might lose support.[20] He advised the Assembly that some of his colleagues detained in Changi had said to him, 'It's time to pack up before we do damage to the country.'[21] MCP guns used after 31 August would be seen by the Malayan people as killing the guardians of their freedom. The detainees sent him letters (as he had requested) to the same effect. The security tie between Singapore and the Federation came to the fore in November when four trade union leaders were detained in Malaya and accused of being under Singapore left-wing leaders' influence.

Fresh City Council elections were scheduled for December. This time almost all Singapore's adults were eligible to vote for what was to be a multilingual Council of thirty-two members. Previously commercial interests of a Liberal Socialist ilk had been dominant, but these elections presented something of a dummy run for the general elections due late in 1958. The PAP, although now more firmly in Lee's control, was in no position to fight all the seats, given its internal troubles. But it prepared a platform and organised elaborately, putting up a slate of fourteen candidates headed by Ong Eng Guan who was being groomed as the PAP's populist Chinese speaker—using Hokkien, the principal dialect of Singapore—to replace Lim Chin Siong. Some of the left-wingers and others dissatisfied with the PAP's leadership and its tactics rallied behind David Marshall, who came out of retirement to form the Workers' Party for the occasion.

The turnout for the elections was poor, and the 'upper middle class' was rebuked for not participating—the results should be a 'warning' to them. Lee Kuan Yew had been 'so indelicate' as to suggest that the PAP's electoral understanding with the Labour Front was reluctantly arrived at to save them from the Liberal Socialists, and 'in return perhaps for the LF saving the PAP from the Communists'.[22] The PAP won 13 seats and sought to make a pact with UMNO which had won 2 seats. This was rejected as 'unimaginable' by the Kuala Lumpur secretariat, but the UMNO members were allowed to vote with the PAP. A split resulted in Singapore UMNO, and some went across to the PAP in 1958.

Lee had thrown himself into the campaign with such nervous energy that his smoking got the better of him. He lost his voice when trying to thank Party workers after the elections. There and then, he resolved to give up the habit. In the ensuing years he developed a complete physical and psychological allergy to it.

With a plurality but not majority of councillors, Ong Eng Guan was elected Mayor. Melodramatic politics followed. A sort of PAP Huey Long, 'Baby' Ong was deemed by David Marshall to deserve, 'My God, the Mayor!' instead of the usual respectful address.[23] The Melbourne-trained accountant kept the anti-colonial kettle on the boil by sacking expatriates and seeking to take over an exclusive golf club for public picnic space (Harry Lee 'happened' to belong to it). He directed a host of campaigns, concessions and services pitched at people such as the hawkers, the small traders and the taxi drivers and their families. It was reported that pandemonium and chaos prevailed in the Council Chamber, whose galleries were often packed with spectators. Ong was re-elected Mayor when opposition moves to oust him after his first term backfired. But in March 1959 the Government responded to further troubles by taking over some of the City Council's functions. The PAP announced that if it came to power the Council would be scrapped.

From a long-term point of view, the Lim Yew Hock Government presided over significant developments. The Public Service Commission (PSC), established in 1955, gained executive powers in 1957 and Malayanisation of the civil service proceeded apace. The Education Ordinance of late 1957 set the foundation for Singapore's four-language-stream, bilingual policy which remained in force for twenty years or more. Many schools were built and opened, and language, technical and commercial education programmes initiated for adults. A Citizenship Ordinance in 1957 enfranchised most of the foreign-born Chinese under easy conditions.

But at a more popular level the Government's reputation was further tarnished during 1958–59, not only as a British stooge but for its use of secret society and gangster elements. The known favour of the Federation Government and UMNO was no public bonus, either. Commissions of inquiry into several by-elections produced sordid evidence of venality. In November 1958, Lim formed the Singapore People's Alliance Party as a 'new broom' for the coming elections: it was too late.

By 1959, the PAP leadership must have been relieved that their renewed overtures to the LF early in 1958 for a coalition government had been rebuffed. They were, nevertheless, cautious about forming a government in their own right. They knew that despite their best endeavours and personal British backing they could not be sure of how 'clean' and therefore how viable the Party was.

In March 1958, according to Lee, something happened to raise the stakes in his group's calculations. He met a man he nicknamed the *'Plen'* (from 'plenipotentiary'), Chinese-educated, 'several years younger than myself—an able and determined person,'[24] who purported to represent the top leadership of the MCP. As a proof of authenticity, Lee asked the *Plen* to withdraw Chang Yuen Tong, whom he claimed was an open-front communist cadre, from the City Council and the executive of the Workers' Party. Several weeks later, Chang resigned.[25] Lee says he and the *Plen* had three further meetings to discuss a united MCP and PAP anti-colonial front. According to writer Arnold Brackman's 'unimpeachable sources', a deal was made: the 'unassimilated' Chinese community would be rallied by the MCP behind the PAP, and Marshall would be dropped; in return, the detainees would be released and would thereafter be appointed political secretaries in Lee's government.[26] Lee's 'staunch denial' of the deal was hardly necessary: if there was an arrangement, it was lopsided in Lee's favour and shows the naiveté or desperation of the MCP leaders. And the deal did not involve the PAP, which was the essence of Lee's denial.*

'Towards the end of 1958 I began to discuss with Lim [Chin Siong], Devan and the other six in Changi camp the question of whether the PAP should fight to win the next general elections.'[27]

One of Lee's reservations was over what Lim and the forces he led would do if the PAP won the elections. Lim was anxious that the Party fight to win, and offered to go away to Indonesia to study. Lee replied that the MCP would be active with or without Lim.

However, in the meantime events developed with considerable rapidity outside the camp in Singapore ... 'There was considerable bitterness in the wrangles in the City Council between the PAP and the SPA.'[28]

Morale in the civil service was falling, with a government that was losing its grip the more beleaguered it became. The running-down of the administration was something Goh in particular could not contemplate. Then a local tax official contacted K.M. Byrne and revealed that a huge sum had been paid into the account of the Education Minister, Chew Swee Kee, from overseas. Toh Chin Chye duly announced the fact, and the former Labour Front minister, Francis Thomas, resigned from the government. Lee said, 'We decided that we had to fight to win because to lose would mean that a bunch of rogues would form the government and ruin the country and also fix the PAP. So in the end we had no choice but to win.'[29]

---

* Talking to students in London, Lee floated the possibility—not a serious one—that the PAP might call special by-elections for the detainees once they were released (*Singapore Standard*, 23 May 1958). Political secretaryships were a relatively harmless option.

The momentum was inexorable. In February 1959 the PAP began its lead-up to the elections in earnest. It released *The Tasks Ahead*, two collections of speeches declaring party policy on key matters. Various commissions of inquiry regarding the Chew Swee Kee case, the leak of tax information and the City Council were skilfully dominated by Lee through his cross-examining and he was able to reveal that some of the Chew Swee Kee money from overseas had gone into tin mining shares for the UMNO–SPA Deputy Chief Minister's wife. The Alliance was in turmoil and the Liberal Socialists withdrew from it. The Federation UMNO was warned by the PAP to avoid saying things which would be regretted later in dealing with a PAP government.

The PAP candidates, dressed in shining white, could be seen to lead the charge against corruption. There were fifty-one of them, one for every seat, and they were chosen by the CEC with a confidence that veered from well-founded to wishful. Many came from the recent intake of membership and were either acquaintances of Lee's group or people of limited experience (and therefore limited exposure to the Left). They had to sign an agreement to pay a monthly tithe to the Party and to resign from the Assembly if they should quit the PAP for any reason.

Once the heat was on, Lee stifled any qualms he had. He knew that Lim Yew Hock was desperate for an excuse to demand that Governor Goode close down the PAP.* So he had to be implacable in the fight for victory. There is an exceptional instance of this boots-and-all approach, where the PAP was widely suspected of playing dirty, yet managed to avoid serious damage. On oath for the Commission of Inquiry before Mr Justice Buttrose, K.M. Byrne said that a 'European' voice had telephoned him from the tax office with information about Chew Swee Kee's windfall. Neither the judge nor anyone else was going to believe a European would do any such thing to help the PAP. But an Australian tax official had died since the telephone call: what more convenient scapegoat? Surely in a crisis the good of the Party might justifiably require the compromise not only of a foreigner but of one of its own? Whoever devised this ruse, in the court proceedings Lee was able to distance himself from Byrne and watch the inquiry judge lambaste his colleague for lying and besmirching a dead man's reputation. Meanwhile, the political benefit to the PAP was sheeted

---

* It has been revealed recently that Lim took David Marshall on a cloak-and-dagger rendezvous down into a bank vault and begged him to refrain from comment while the PAP was destroyed!

home by Lee in the separate inquiry about the destination of the money itself.

But there were also moments when he threw in his towel. Despite confidence that wealthy business friends of Goh Keng Swee would put up the $500 deposit for each of the fifty-one electoral candidates, no money was forthcoming just before the deadline had to be met. Lee's reaction to the setback was to want to go off for drinks. It was Byrne who persevered and canvassed friends of less ample means for the required funds until they were found.

In the last stages of the elections Lee began to say publicly that the real fight would begin after the elections.

> The ultimate contestants would be the PAP and the MCP—the PAP for a democratic, non-Communist, socialist Malaya, and the MCP for a Soviet Republic of Malaya. It is a battle that cannot be won by just bayonets and bullets. It is a battle of ideals and ideas. And the side that recruits more ability and talent will be the side that wins.
>
> I further said that PAP would not adopt the behaviour of David Marshall or that of Lim Yew Hock in combatting the Communists because Marshall was vacillating, pushed from pillar to post and retreating in the face of each demonstration and because Tun Lim Yew Hock only used the big 'stick and the gun' as the answer till finally the GOC Singapore Base District and his helicopters took over. The PAP would not fall into either of these errors.[30]

His words might have had an immediate intention: to capture some of the right-wing vote. There was little risk of losing the Left. Voting was compulsory this time, and last-minute speeches would not disturb a well-settled image among those who depended upon press formulation of issues.

But, over and above that, Lee was setting out some of the prospects he and his colleagues discerned for Malaya's future. In the Legislative Assembly on 22 April 1958, he said, 'whoever forms the next government should give this bouquet to the departing Labour Front Government. They charted a minefield. We now know where the booby traps are, and have a fair idea where a few more might be. They got hurt in the process ... We hope that when our turn comes we will not be so badly hurt.' Or, as he said on 19 March 1959 in a slightly muddled metaphor 'We saw Pandora's box opened one by one till the smallest and last box, and we are moving forward into position to take over because we have no choice.'

Whatever the ultimate contest might be beyond the elections, 'the greatest immediate danger facing the people of Singapore was communalism and not Communism'. Lee accused the other parties of playing with fire by appealing to people on a communal basis.[31]

At the last session of the Assembly (19 March 1959) before the elections, Lee put his cards on the table. (A summary of his speech follows, together with direct quotes.) The PAP had no choice but to fight and win the elections, he said. The alternative was victory to 'a collection of scallywags, rogues and vagabonds'. That would spell the end of the democratic experiment. Communal violence and hostility would erupt. The temptation for Kuala Lumpur to take over*—the British being intolerably placed to do so—would be irresistible. 'Then, of course, the British are no longer responsible for internal security. Then we are all in the bag.'

'The fight here in Singapore and in the Federation is a fight to preserve the democratic system. On that we are agreed.' The British 'understand that if they snuff us out, then the one decent group that has been able to muster and rally support and recruits will go over. If not us, those who follow us would go over and join the Communists and bang the system'. 'That is the reason why we survive.'

Lee said he and his Committee had considered the possibility that their 'left-wing democratic movement' might be extinguished by the British or dragged down the 'slippery slope' towards a 'bloodbath' by the 'dirty tactics' of 'dangerous characters' associated with the SPA leaders. He was optimistic that 'international repercussions' would curb the former and that his warnings might encourage the Chief Minister to put the brakes on. But whether facing life or death, the PAP was ready.

Provided the election was followed by 'stable and sober conditions', the PAP would try to recruit the 'able people coming out from your Chinese middle schools, from Nan Ta,† even from the University of Malaya'. Lee and his colleagues would co-operate with the Tunku who, 'despite his shortcomings',[32] was not enslaved to money and not therefore prepared to use his power position ruthlessly to maintain the 'democratic' system and suppress the communists (unlike another American client, Syngman Rhee). 'We would, if we have to go down after five years for holding the gun with the Tunku and his troops in the north, the Communists on the

---

* with American backing?
† Nan Ta = Nantah = Nanyang University.

Preparing for Self-Government

ground, the British squatting over us, we would do so honourably, we will not yelp.'

There was no question of the PAP being out to grab power. 'If we were given the choice we would have preferred to work on the ground for many more years to build the movement up, because he who runs the country and holds the gun is at a disadvantage.'

The mood of Lee's thinking revealed in this and contemporary speeches is very different from his youthful confidence nine years earlier at the Malayan Forum. No longer was politics a matter of self-protection for the returned student. He and his small band, drawn from diverse backgrounds, had found common cause within a heroic succession. 'I will be the first to admit that when the PAP wins, it is not because of the strength and organisation of the PAP alone. Behind it lies the whole history of the struggle against the British and now a struggle for the destiny of this country.'

Gone was the homely prospect of Britain graciously abandoning an untenable colonial position after a little firm prodding. The pearl of Singapore had now to be quickly prised out of British hands and restored to its Malayan setting before the separate arrangement became fixed or another setting imposed.

A political leadership was poised to do the right thing by the people, grudgingly approved by the British. But could it hope to contend with the hysterical fanaticism of Islam (seen in the Hertogh riots) or the more calculating but intense determination of the MCP (seen in the Hock Lee riots)?[33] The Malays had to be given priority and special help so they could 'catch up with the others'.[34] The Tunku would be useful for the time being: his concern for a happy Malaya would predispose him to contain any tendency to run amok. Then as the PAP created more just social conditions, there would be less reliance on the gun to combat the challenge of communism.

Lee reckoned he and his friends had about ten to fifteen years before the ultimate contest. The haunting spectre of communal violence, however, could make a mockery of rational reckoning. So it had to be referred to softly, for fear of arousing it.

He was very impatient with the mud-slinging (though not above it himself) and the personality politics of Singapore. 'It is not Lee Kuan Yew whom they have to fight,' he said. He had found, or so it seemed, a few men to share his vision and form a team around it. They had already been tested and were prepared for trial by fire. Destiny had given this little group an integral role in the transformation of Malaya: from imperialism, from superstition, from feudalism, from racial and political divisions, to a just, modern, secular, multiracial, democratic and independent nation, reunited and flourishing.

On the brink of returning home in 1950, Lee had looked ahead to a post-colonial Malaya, achieved by a programme and a personal contribution not yet specific as to method and content. On the brink of office in Singapore, he was much more clear-headed about the way forward and the desired end result. All his energy and intellect, his nerve and discipline, would be required. This was to be a personal project on a grand but realistic scale.

MY COUNTRY AND MY PEOPLE

My country and my people
are neither here nor there, nor
in the comfort of my preferences,
if I could ever choose.
At any rate, to fancy is to cheat;
and, worse than being alien or
subversive without cause,
is being a patriot
of the will.

I came in the boom of babies, not guns,
a 'daughter of a better age';
I held a pencil in a school
while the 'age' was quelling riots
in the street, or cutting down
those foreign 'devils',
(whose books I was being taught to read).
Thus privileged I entered early
the Lion City's jaws.
But they sent me back as fast
to my shy, forbearing family.

So I stayed in my parents' house,
and had only household cares.
The city remained a distant way,
but I had no land to till;
only a duck that would not lay,
and a runt of a papaya tree,
which also turned out to be male.

Then I learnt to drive instead
and praise the highways till
I saw them chop the great trees down,
and plant the little ones;
impound the hungry buffalo
(the big ones and the little ones)
because the cars could not be curbed.

Nor could the population.
They built milli-mini-flats
for a multi-mini-society.
The chiselled profile in the sky
took on a lofty attitude,
but modestly, at any rate,
it made the tourist feel 'at home'.

My country and my people
I never understood.
I grew up in China's mighty shadow,
with my gentle, brown-skinned neighbours;
but I keep diaries in English.
I sought to grow
in humanity's rich soil,
and started digging on the banks, then saw
life carrying my friends downstream.
Yet, careful tending of the human heart
may make a hundred flowers bloom;
and perhaps, fence-sitting neighbour,
I claim citizenship in your recognition
of our kind.
My people, and my country,
are you, and you my home.

LEE TZU PHENG

5

Preparing for Merger

At 4 pm this afternoon my Ministers and I formally took office. The control of Singapore's internal affairs was formally transferred to the elected representatives of the people.

Each and every one of my Ministers is acutely conscious of the heavy responsibility and great burdens with which we have been entrusted. We have taken office because we believe that the PAP is the party most capable of discharging the duties and responsibilities of the government. We are the best organised and most coherent political leadership in Singapore. Every one of my Ministers has gone through years of political struggle before we reached this position. If we were weak or insincere, we would not have survived the stresses and strains of the political struggle that we underwent. The business of a government is to govern and to make firm decisions, so that there shall be certainty and stability in the affairs of our people. We shall do our best to give you not only a firm and stable government, but one which will carry with it the support and co-operation of the majority of the people.

LEE KUAN YEW,
broadcast, 5 June 1959

In Office

A little fudging is allowable at such a high point in Singapore's history and Lee Kuan Yew's career. The PAP had attained government with 53 per cent of the vote and 43 out of 51 seats. It was no mean feat. On the other hand, being fit and ready for office would not be enough. The political leadership of the PAP might be the best and most coherent on offer, but it had its weak links. Some Ministers had struggled a good deal less arduously than others. The real testing was yet to come.

Any elation Lee felt on becoming Prime Minister must have been short-lived. How would he and his colleagues make the transition from electioneering to administering? When would the inevitable showdown occur between his group and his opponents within the Party, especially the hard-core pro-communists? Would it be possible to win over some of the 40 per cent of voters supporting the Right, many of them English-educated, under pressure from their peers and from institutions such as the Roman Catholic Church? How would the PAP woo the Federation into merger? And how to establish a political network throughout the peninsula?*

There were undeniable risks in building a mass party, especially when its architect was a man who was unable or unwilling to curry favour with supporters.† Lee had few natural affinities with the different classes and groups that made up Singapore in 1959. He and several of his closest colleagues were quite atypical. Numerically the PAP membership was dominated by those who wanted the redress of their chauvinist or industrial grievances from the colonial era and by those who had come or been invited in on the crest of electoral enthusiasm. Loyalty to Lee's vision was by no means a foregone conclusion.

Over the six days between the PAP's election and the swearing-in of his Cabinet, Lee had moved with great skill. Although, as ever, things refused to turn out exactly as planned, he kept the initiative. Symbolic politics was becoming his forte: substantial achievement and the winning of hearts and minds would take a little longer. A major Party conference was set down for 31 May, to elect a CEC for two years without the benefit of the PAP detainees' participation and impact on their comrades. On the evening of 3 June a mass rally was held in the Padang to celebrate the PAP victory—again, before the detainees' release so that no one could be deflected from recognising the true engineers of that victory. Even the release itself was played very much along the lines that it was Lee's condition for assuming office, a concession he alone could prise out of the British.

Nevertheless, there was a rival rising star who epitomised Lee's problems inside and outside the Party: Ong Eng Guan. However

---

* Lee had expressed a low opinion of peninsular left-wing leaders. In his view their electoral standing owed more to dissatisfaction with the Alliance than to their own merits.

† K.M. Byrne's words: 'All of us know that the Prime Minister never tries to gain support from any of us by offering us bribes. That is against his very nature and make-up. He does not expect from us a personal bond of loyalty to him,' (Legislative Assembly, 4 August 1960).

justifiable Lee's disdain and suspicion of popularity, there was no doubting that the vacuum created by the purge of the Left in 1956–57 and afterwards had been filled by the demagogic figure of Singapore's PAP Mayor. Rajaratnam had put forward Ong's name to Toh Chin Chye in 1954 as Treasurer because of his accounting background, and he came into the Party well after the groundwork for its formation had been laid. He was groomed to be Lee's answer to (later, replacement for) Lim Chin Siong, because of his fluency in Hokkien.* The plan worked all too well. At the Party conference on 31 May, Ong gained the top vote in the CEC elections, just as he had done the day before in the people's poll. The CEC then met to choose the Prime Minister, and only Toh Chin Chye's casting vote won the day for Lee against Ong. Fong Sip Chee in his memoirs recalls the occasion somewhat cryptically: 'What took place on that day had a telling effect on Ong Eng Guan in his attempt to challenge the Party's leadership in the following years.'[1]

A few days after this upset, eight of the leading detainees were released on the Governor's orders. They went straight to a meeting with the CEC. Lee knew that at least one of them, Devan Nair, was on his side and had been for some years. He hoped that most of the others were by now persuaded of the MCP's folly in pressing for armed revolution. Only Lim Chin Siong was an uncertainty. Here were brains and organising ability the PAP could use: they were 'dynamos' and Lee wanted to 'put them where we can see how they bounce'.[2] The eight were not accorded citizenship papers or made PAP cadre members. 'They were given no access to secret matters. And Lim Chin Siong was specially put in the Ministry of Finance where he could do no harm'.[3] Of the others Lee was to lavish a lot of time on Fong Swee Suan. The Prime Minister's patronage caused embarrassment for Fong, and he was snubbed in some union circles. He was given the most sensitive of the political jobs and his later defection back to his old school friend, Lim Chin Siong, undoubtedly rankled with Lee.

In the decision over the detainees and in many other matters, Lee had sympathetic assistance from Sir William Goode, Singapore's last Governor and first Head of State. Lee admired him as a 'toughie', admitting that he owed him much.[4] But it would be foolish to exaggerate Goode's influence. Lee's statement in the Legislative Assembly on 8 October 1958: 'We were created by

---

* About 40 per cent of Singapore's Chinese at that time were classified as Hokkien (originally from Fujian Province in China). A much higher proportion of Chinese and people of other races understood or spoke Hokkien.

ambitions, not by special agents', is a pointed corrective to the idea that he was an involuntary puppet of any of the British, including Goode.

With whatever mixture of apprehension and zeal, the Cabinet lost no time in getting down to work. Lee drove his own Mercedes-Benz to the City Hall on his first Monday in power (8 June). He took over the former mayoral section and supervised its security and communication arrangements.

Almost immediately a film was produced for general release, introducing the Cabinet and setting out Lee's philosophy of democratic government. 'Ours is the more difficult task of governing, wisely and justly, with the support of the people. It is a twofold task, for not only must we make a success of the Government, but we must also let you know what we are doing in order to carry you with us' (14 June 1959).

He set himself to talk often to the people. His public speeches over the remainder of 1959 mixed careful analysis of Singapore's current situation with exhortation or reproof, pleading or contempt, depending on his assessment of each audience's needs. There was no doubt that the 35-year-old Prime Minister was on his way to making a virtue out of the necessity of walking a tightrope.

He was 'sure' the public sector unions would understand cuts in their variable allowances (21 June 1959). He told a trade union rally in the Badminton Hall that it was imperative for the movement to be imbued with the same democratic, non-communist, socialist ideals as the PAP itself and the union heroes recently released (shriven of their Marxism) from gaol (28 June 1959). He put the English-educated in their place at a University of Malaya Society dinner: 'Let us never forget that we, the English-educated elite, merit our place in society so long as we are able to do a service to that society.' He drew attention to the willingness of PAP leaders to sacrifice all personal advantage for a cause, though 'I hate to believe that when I am still alive my colleagues and I should be emulated' (25 July 1959). He was 'happy' to hear of the Chinese Chamber of Commerce's new-found enthusiasm for freedom from their former colonial protectors, and confirmed that the socialism they dreaded would come but only after the slightly less dreaded merger had been secured (8 August 1959). In opening the Civil Service Study Centre, he bade the civil servants learn the new political realities and become instruments of efficient administration (15 August 1959). He stigmatised the English-educated as 'devitalised, almost emasculated', although praising their survival skills in the open competition of Occupation days, and instructed the English-medium journalists to lay before their readers, even despite the newspaper owners, the prospect of being replaced by a breed which would not be 'deculturised' (16 August 1959). He attacked Chinese chauvinists, whether pro-Taipei or pro-Peking, in a speech to the Chinese Union of Journalists (1 September 1959).

'There is no such thing as an indigenous culture,' the Prime Minister proclaimed at an exhibition of Indian art; conspicuous by its absence from his description of Malayan culture and its roots in Indian, Chinese and European civilisations was any reference to Islam (6 September 1959). When he talked to the Muslim community a few days later, he described religious tolerance as an 'arresting' feature of Malayan life and warned against religion being dragged into the political arena or being used 'as a cloak for political ambitions' (17 September 1959). He reminded foreign correspondents that communalism posed a greater threat to Malaya's immediate future than communism (16 September 1959).

The Preservation of Public Security Ordinance was kept on, amended to exclude a role for the judiciary and to allow restrictions of residence, employment and activities to be imposed on suspects prior to or even instead of detention. Lee reaffirmed its relevance to merger, but again he insisted that the Government would clamp down on subversion from the Right no less than from the Left, and that it was better to improve social conditions than to rely on repressive laws in combating communism (Legislative Assembly, 14 October 1959).

He promised graduate employment openings in government service in a speech to Nanyang University; at the same time he emphasised the University's context—Southeast Asia, Malaya (28 October 1959).

He issued another more conciliatory call for close co-operation between civil servants and the political leaders. The former should instruct the latter how to implement the PAP's revolutionary programme. The political leaders, for their part, must guide the Government's assessment of priorities; they must not terrify the innocent civil servants and create an atmosphere of fear and character assassination (29 October 1959).

Lawyers were reminded that they had an important role in a democracy where laws were ascertainable and interpreted by an independent judiciary. They should aim for honourable esteem in Singapore, placing the law quickly and cheaply at the people's disposal (14 November 1959).

The Prime Minister nominated teachers to be the most influential group in youthful Singapore, able through language training and their own ideals to integrate the different streams and make even trilingual education effective (23 November 1959).

He reminded the Singapore Traction Company Employees' Union of their pioneering role in union struggles, in making a stand against the 'squeezing' of passengers, in agreeing to arbitration by tribunal and in building multiracial solidarity (15 December 1959).

To the people as a whole, Lee sang the praises of science and human ingenuity (26 September 1959). He talked in a radio broadcast of the change of status—immigrant to permanent resident—that had overtaken the people of Singapore. He explained the PAP's emphasis on hard work, but allowed the need for relaxing and rejoicing in a publicly responsible way (3 December 1959). A few days later he affirmed that radio could edify the people: 'Entertainment need not be spicy and sexy and degenerate before they [sic] can hold a mass audience' (7 December 1959).

The swearing-in of a local Head of State (*Yang di-pertuan Negara*), Yusof bin Ishak, 'to symbolise all of us'—collective leadership being too abstract to 'invoke mass enthusiasm and loyalties'—was also the occasion for Lee to proclaim the new flag, coat-of-arms and anthem for Singapore and to launch Loyalty Week (3 December 1959). At its close, Lee talked of a 'spiritual experience' issuing in closeness, coherence and loyalty—'an unforgettable event in our lives' (9 December 1959).

The densely packed analysis, the instinctive resort to sarcasm in approaching so many groups, the inflated nationalistic rhetoric, all showed the gulf between Lee and popular or sectional sentiments. The first few months in office look frantic in retrospect, short on solid accomplishment and long on flailing about. K.M. Byrne announced measures to 'improve' the union movement, which sounded soothing enough from his lips but decidedly threatening when Lee or Goh took them up. So-called 'yellow culture' was attacked. In July, Ong Eng Guan announced a 'Lungs for Singapore' campaign, relying on voluntary labour corps. The Government's anti-colonial intentions were more a spectre in the imagination of those who took capital out of Singapore to Kuala Lumpur or elsewhere, although Lee did dress down various expatriate individuals or organisations,* and the foreign community remained a convenient whipping boy for some time; Raffles' statue was almost removed.

---

* He condemned for example, the British general who made casual criticisms of the PAP to foreign pressmen; and he frequently attacked the *Straits Times*.

Strenuous efforts were made to cultivate Malayan and Indonesian leaders, especially the former. But during 1959 and 1960, Singapore could make little headway with Kuala Lumpur on merger proposals. As regards Indonesia, the PAP Government clipped the wings of CIA-assisted regional rebel movements using Singapore as a base against the Jakarta Government. Lee paid a visit there early in 1960. Unfortunately, he had queered his pitch somewhat by a New Year speech that mentioned his forthcoming host country among a list of nations with sagging standards, lacking the discipline 'to bring to reality the brave new world we all so ardently want to build for ourselves and our children'. He had also often referred to the problems of the Chinese in Indonesia. So it was not surprising that his endorsement of Jakarta's claims to Dutch New Guinea brought Singapore no reward of increased trade with her giant neighbour.

The prospects for mobilising the people were bleak. The population was growing at a rate of more than 4 per cent per annum. Unemployment was rife. The Chinese entrepreneurs were not committed to industrialisation as the secure base for economic growth. Many unionists and PAP members through whose hard work the Party had come to power were opposed to co-operation with foreign and local capitalists. Yet without rapid economic growth fuelled by investment, urgent social measures such as housing could not be undertaken and completed. The only major group keen on merger with Malaya was the Malays, and that was for the wrong reasons.

Given the PAP's continuing need for public support, it was decided to revive an initiative taken by David Marshall and the Labour Front and practised by the former PAP City Councillors. A directive went out from the Party that all members of the Legislative Assembly should conduct weekly meet-the-people sessions, to tackle individuals' problems and to clarify Government policy.

The primary rationale for seeking power in 1959 had been the need to halt the rundown of the administration. The thought that they might face an 'empty kitty' horrified Lee and his colleagues, and their grasp on the reins of power, the instruments of state, must have seemed ironic compensation.

It remained for Rajaratnam, the Minister for Culture, to reiterate the grim scenario that could always excuse Singapore's indifferent socialism. The PAP, he said, had gone as far left as possible. If the PAP failed, there would perhaps be an interval of 'rule by racialists and generals', then Singapore would go communist.[5]

The Ong Eng Guan Affair

>In 1959, towards the end of '59 and about five or six months after we took office, I had an uneasy feeling that one of my Ministers was 'going off his rocker'.
>
>LEE KUAN YEW, *Public Utilities Board Pasir Panjang power station opening, 15 October 1965*

>Lim Chin Siong one day came to my house and mentioned the trouble Ong Eng Guan was causing in the Government and Party and offered his help. I told him there was no big trouble and his help was not required. At the next Cabinet meeting I reported this overture to all my colleagues, including Ong Eng Guan.
>
>Lee Kuan Yew, *The Battle for Merger* 1961, p. 34

Ong Eng Guan's failure to perform in his portfolio of National Development might have stemmed from his intrinsic weakness as an administrator. This in turn might have stemmed from his character. But it is also true that Lee quite deliberately gave him 'enough rope to hang himself'.[6] Some months after putting his rival into a strenuous and unglamorous ministry, the Prime Minister compounded Ong's frustration by removing certain of his ministerial responsibilities.

From the moment that Ong brought his cause into the public arena with the sixteen resolutions for Party reform presented at a PAP conference on 18 June 1960, Lee recalled, the 'whole business of suspension and expulsion was allowed to run its full course'. The hope was that 'weak points in the Party and threats from outside could be brought into the open' (Legislative Assembly, 3 August 1960). Chairman Toh Chin Chye treated the resolutions as a challenge to the collective leadership of the PAP and so was able to isolate Ong: the Conference gave the CEC a mandate to consider his expulsion.

Clearly the rest of the leadership was well prepared. Only two PAP Assemblymen supported him.* If Ong was attempting to pick off Lee—and the charges of lack of intra-party democracy were aimed specifically at the Prime Minister—he failed; likewise any

---

* They were expelled, although one rejoined the PAP in its hour of need in August 1962 (see p. 109). Ong Eng Guan and these two formed the United People's Party (UPP).

plan of Ong's to win left-wing backing came to naught. He was too compromised himself to get away with most of his accusations. To say that Lee was under the thumb of three expatriates was patently out of character with the Prime Minister (although the relationships were important and followed on from Goode's day)* and rang hollow from a man who had close links with foreigners himself. Ong's claim that Lee had issued cards to non-members in August 1957 to have him ousted from the CEC was fobbed off when Lee produced a letter from Lim Chin Joo acknowledging the 'Leftist adventurer' childishness and unscrupulous ways that had led to the stacking of the Conference. Ong's espousal of the detainees still in gaol was easily discredited: Lee noted that Ong, whilst on the Internal Security Council, had not contested the veto against their release.

However 'sad and painful' it was for Lee Kuan Yew to denounce an ex-colleague, the Prime Minister rose to the occasion.[7] Ong resigned from Parliament in December 1960 and Lee appeared personally in the Commission of Inquiry before Justice Chua early in 1961. The Commission dismissed Ong's charges made in the Assembly of nepotism on the part of Lee and K.M. Byrne.† It was the Prime Minister's personal contribution to demolish the character of Ong Eng Guan in every respect. Lee was believed to have had the Special Branch working round the clock to nose out dirt.

There is evidence to support the view of the *Plebeian* newspaper that Ong was a useful scapegoat on whom to lay the blame for the antagonism towards the PAP of the Civil Service and the English-educated in general. For example, Lee's speeches in 1960 to these two groups were more conciliatory than before.

The by-election for Ong's seat of Hong Lim was set for 29 April 1961. It was preceded by seven weeks of intense door-to-door campaigning. The PAP put up Jek Yeun Thong, Lee's Political Secretary and a former detainee.

The result was 73 per cent of the vote to Ong. Lee Kuan Yew's reported despondency at the loss was understandable. The PAP

---

* The three were G.G. Thomson, Director of Information Services and Lim Yew Hock's speechwriter until 1959 (then director of the Political Study Centre and finally Professor of Political Science at Nanyang University), P.H. Meadows (banished by Ong to the Rural Board from the Ministry of Local Government—Ong alleged him to be M15), and A. Blades, Police and former Special Branch Chief.

† The charge that Lee and Byrne had made appointments on the basis of kinship, friendship and previous working acquaintance, and not on the basis of merit alone, was too subjective an argument to sustain.

was paying the price for its Secretary-General's un-Chinese behaviour—a bitter frontal attack on Ong. Moreover, Lee said, 'We saw no resolution to our economic problems after the defeat in Hong Lim because the Federation was not eager either for merger or common market. We wanted to resign and have fresh elections rather than carry on without a visible solution to our basic problems.'[8]

The threat of resignation, however, quickly became tactical. The Hong Lim result showed those with eyes to see that much of the support for the Left derived from Chinese chauvinism, not the other way round. Those blinded by fear of the MCP and international communism would not recognise such a simple truth. Hong Lim was a victory for Ong as the Chinese-speaking underdog. Its lessons, once learned, quickly led to action: a stocktaking of the PAP; a rejigging of its ground apparatus; fresh overtures to the Tunku; and Lee's decision to learn Hokkien.

Two days after the election Lee threw down the gauntlet. In his May Day speech, he 'clearly explained that the Government was not there just to be made use of by all and sundry, including the Communists. We were in office for the purpose of resolving the basic economic and social problems of the people. If we could not do this, then it was our duty to resign.'[9]

Towards the end of the Hong Lim campaign, the young Malay MLA for Anson died. The Anson by-election, held on 15 July 1961 was used to precipitate a split in the PAP between those who were loyal to Lee, his colleagues and his political line, and those who were not.

The Tunku's proposal, another by-election, and the PAP split

From a British point of view, both formal and informal, Singapore had long been the centrepiece in the colonial holdings of Southeast Asia. The idea of the regional British territories uniting—Singapore, Malaya, North Borneo, Sarawak and Brunei—had been put forward as early as 1887. By the 1950s and 1960s, however, other points of view had asserted themselves. The various North Borneo peoples might look to London, to a local centre or even perhaps to Singapore to be their focus of political loyalty, but not to Kuala Lumpur or Jakarta. On the other hand the peninsular Malays, conscious of Malay dominance of the archipelago, and despite the British bases remaining on the island, could never accept Singapore as their capital city. If was too Chinese. Distance, diversity and the nearness of Indonesia added further difficulties to any plan for integrating all the territories.

Lee Kuan Yew had already come to a clear if distasteful recognition that there would be a struggle to recapture Singapore's centrality in Malaya. He was not, however, left without bargaining counters. One was the risk of Singapore becoming a Yenan, or more aptly a Cuba, for the launching of communist revolution onto the mainland once the jungle-based MCP operation had failed. Another was the urgency of achieving some sort of racial harmony now that Whitehall had relinquished overt political and military control. Then again, if Singapore was part of Malaya, it could provide an inbuilt economic clearing-house to help the Alliance leaders improve the Malayan people's livelihood.

A point of concern for the British, Lee's group and those Malay leaders like the Tunku who were still pro-British was the likely role of Indonesia. Claims to Dutch New Guinea begged the uneasy question: why not North Borneo next? The rise of the mercurial Soekarno and the role of the Communist Party of Indonesia (PKI) were serious destabilising factors: as economic development lagged further and further behind population increase, the scope for external adventurism and internal revolution would grow, affecting the neighbouring British-related territories.

Partly for domestic consumption and partly with an eye to history, Lee took every opportunity to insist that he and his colleagues were the main instigators of Malaysia. True, he had been petitioning the Tunku since the early 1950s and Whitehall since at least 1956 for a tie-up between Singapore and Malaya. But so had David Marshall and Lim Yew Hock, both of whom would have been more likely than Lee to receive a favourable response from the Tunku.

Judging from Sopiee's careful account in Chapter 6 of his book *From Malayan Union to Singapore Separation*, the Tunku's thinking in late 1960 and early 1961 was affected most directly by discussions with British government leaders. Their view of their role in the region and its costs was changing, especially after the Suez crisis, which made the sea route to Australia via Singapore less vital. Moreover, Britain was looking towards Europe and planning her entry into the Common Market. They had shifted from their position—Singapore a separate colony—because the island's politics had become too volatile. Now their pressure was for merger between Malaya and Singapore.* For the same reason the Tunku,

---

* Britain was due to renegotiate Singapore's position by 1963–64; it would not be possible with the advent of self-government to hold on to the island indefinitely. Lee deflected attention from the British change of heart by 'hazarding a guess' (which he well knew to be wrong) that 'if tomorrow a Federation Government said it wanted Singapore, the British would be the most unhappy and unwilling people in the world' (speech for United Nations Day, 6 November 1960).

however, tended to fight shy of any arrangement with Singapore alone. He was responsive only to talk of a Greater Malaya or Greater Federation to embrace the Borneo colonies.

One other very awkward problem permeated the thinking of all parties to the negotiations. It was the ambiguous character of the British bases in Singapore. They obviously contributed to Malaya's defence against the internal and external 'enemies'. But they were also vital to the fulfilment of Britain's Southeast Asia Treaty Organisation (SEATO) obligations. To mention SEATO openly would be for the Tunku—and Lee—to touch a raw political nerve domestically. So planning proceeded with minimal public reference to it.

There is an element of romance mixed with truth in Lee's speech to the Singapore Assembly on 30 July 1963. He conjured up vivid pictures of intense discussion at the poker table, at meals, at golf. 'Slowly the unpleasant facts were placed before the Federation Government. What had been publicly known was that Malaya was vital to Singapore. But what we did not emphasise, lest we offend our friends across the Causeway, was that Singapore was vital to their survival.' The PAP leaders certainly went a long way towards winning the Tunku's acceptance. By the beginning of 1961 he could state in the *Dewan* (the Malayan Parliament): 'The PAP Government is as good a Malayan government as the Alliance is.'[10] Singapore had a Malay head of state, Malay was the national language, and a firm line was being taken against Chinese chauvinism.

What influence Lee had on the British and vice versa are matters for conjecture. He paid a visit to North Borneo in September 1960 and some type of Malaysia scheme was discussed with his friend Sir William Goode, now the Governor there. It appears also that Lee showed PAP cadres a British document proposing Malaysia, and reported to them concerns he had discussed with Lord Selkirk, Commissioner-General for Southeast Asia.* By the latter part of that year new bargaining counters were put forward and incorporated in PAP policy. Lee welcomed the idea of a political association between Singapore, Sabah, Sarawak and Brunei: his purpose was to arouse Malayan UMNO anxieties and hasten momentum for Kuala Lumpur to come in on the deal and clinch the real merger he wanted. From the British side the ploy seems to have been to dangle the Borneo territories before Kuala Lumpur like bait just out of reach and tempt the Tunku into swallowing Singapore.

---

* Lee denied having done so (Legislative Assembly, 29 January 1962).

It was in the period March to May 1961 that Lee's manoeuvrings paid off. The decisive factor for the Tunku was the Hong Lim by-election, whose result was interpreted to him by Lee as a warning that Kuala Lumpur would soon have to step in. 'We are not playing to a Singapore audience but we have to play to a pan-Malayan audience,' Lee had said before the Anson by-election.[11] So it was that on 27 May 1961 at a luncheon for foreign correspondents—with all the PAP Cabinet there—the Tunku went public, departing from his prepared speech with these words: 'Sooner or later she [Malaya] should have an understanding with Britain and the peoples of Singapore, North Borneo, Sarawak and Brunei . . . it is inevitable that we should look ahead to this objective and think of a plan whereby these territories can be brought together in political and economic co-operation.'

Sopiee points out that the Tunku's remarks were 'not so much a statement of policy as a trial balloon to test Malayan and Borneo opinion'.[12] There was suspicion of Singapore in Malaya and of Malaya in Borneo, and it surfaced strongly in the following period. According to Sopiee, the Tunku 'confided that Lee Kuan Yew was very excited over the proposal', but most of the other responses were hesitant and unenthusiastic.[13] There were still many obstacles to overcome before the formation of Malaysia could be realised.

Lee says that on 11 May he had discussed with the *Plen* the prospects for merger. Lee told him, 'there was no immediate likelihood of it, but that I was hoping for common market arrangements with the Federation'.[14] The *Plen* urged Lee to 'agree to the abolition of the Internal Security Council as the immediate target for the 1963 constitutional talks while deferring the question of independence for Singapore alone or through merger with the Federation.[15] Lee said, 'The *Plen* must have thought that I lied to him'[16] once the news broke of the Tunku's 27 May speech. The outcome, as Lee claims he anticipated, was that pressure was applied through its open-front leaders by the MCP to frustrate merger.*

Not that after 27 May merger was by any means a foregone conclusion. Although Lee's Government had won a measure of trust from the Tunku, the PAP and Singapore as a whole were

---

* Lee had discovered the *Plen's* identity (Fang Chuang Pi), so he says, from Special Branch files in October 1959—without telling Special Branch[17] Alex Josey in his 1974 book on Lee (pp. 170–71) asserts that the Tunku brought up the idea of Malaysia, presumably in private, on 2 March 1961. If this is correct, Lee did lie to the *Plen*, but more importantly, his behaviour over the period March to May 1961 was extremely tricky.

harbouring dangerous elements. The Tunku's speech did, however, give the green light for negotiations to commence openly. From Lee's standpoint the position could not have been better. He could not accept Singapore's isolation, but it would be no gain to rejoin Malaya simply as one of her units or states. Complete merger would undermine his pan-Malayan programme and put too much power in Kuala Lumpur's hands. Now at last there was a breakthrough—a merger involving a trade-off. Singapore would surrender some of her autonomy, but the stigma of dealing with her leftists would be shared. In addition, there would be concessions to her political and economic integrity, and thereby to Lee's wider designs.

Lee prepared for a Party showdown. The risks were high. Losing another by-election would not by itself destroy the PAP's command of the Assembly and government, but it would foment unrest and clamour for new general elections. This in turn would combine with strong currents of antipathy to Lee—and Goh—and push many PAP members, including Assemblymen, to the stage of regrouping. On the other hand Lee's strengths were the Tunku's approval, the 'fixed political objectives' of the PAP (to seek independence through merger) and his diminished need of the Party's lower echelons, given his growing command of the administration and of direct links to the public.

On 2 June Lim Chin Siong and his friends announced conditional support for the PAP in the forthcoming Anson by-election. They took more or less the MCP line Lee later alleged he had heard from the *Plen*. Events then gathered momentum rapidly. No effort was made by the leadership to contain the divisions thus revealed in the Party and the union movement; in fact they were sharpened, particularly by Toh Chin Chye, Devan Nair and Lee.

In the ensuing confusion, Anson was narrowly lost by the PAP's Malay Trade Union Congress candidate to David Marshall. Over 1500 abstained from voting on the day, 15 July 1961. Despite indications beforehand that the Anson result would be taken more seriously than Hong Lim because it represented 'Singapore in miniature', Lee announced 'We will govern'. There was none of the despair that had followed Hong Lim. A few days later, after the publication of pre-election letters from Lee offering to resign if Anson was lost, and Toh refusing to accept, the Prime Minister spoke out;

'The one compelling reason why I have to carry on is that I have been asked to continue and not to do so would be to abscond when trouble brews up. In some measure I have been responsible for bringing the party into office and I must see it through and never allow the power entrusted to us to be perverted by an aspiring junta.'[18]

An emergency session of the Assembly was convened for 20 July and Lee called for a vote of confidence. The whip was withdrawn. Thirteen PAP members abstained from voting after an all-night debate: it was known before the by-election that at least eight had defected. The Government now held 26 out of 51 seats in the Assembly.

It transpired that Lim Chin Siong, James Puthucheary, Fong Swee Suan and Sandra Woodhull had sought out Lord Selkirk, the UK Commissioner-General. What would the British do if Lee was voted out of office and yet the 'rebel' faction could command sufficient numbers of PAP Assemblymen to constitute a majority? The British response gave them heart to bid for a takeover of the PAP. Lee lashed out at the 'perfidy of perfidious Albion'[19] when he disclosed the 'Eden Hall tea party' in the Assembly. 'The plot, counter-plot and sub-plots would make an Oppenheimer thriller read like a simple comic strip cartoon.'

At the time it was alleged that Lee was furious because Selkirk had conferred first with the rebels on returning from London. But Selkirk did have dinner with the Prime Minister before he met Lim and company. So this was not the reason. If historian Mary Turnbull's account can be believed, Lord Selkirk entertained the possibility of not interfering should Lee lose office.[20] There was not the same bond between the two as there had been between Goode and Lee. Selkirk had wider territorial responsibilities than Goode and, moreover, he shared a common British conservative attitude of sympathy for the Malay position. We may surmise that he was not specially committed to Lee's survival. The British by now wanted to push the Tunku into absorbing Singapore without waiting for the Borneo territories and before they were forced to reimpose a colonial situation in Singapore. The PAP under Lee was expendable: consider his reluctance to purge the Left just then (for obvious domestic reasons), the trouble his pan-Malayan pretensions would cause, and his precarious grasp on the rudder. With Lee removed, it would then be up to the Federation to decide whether to allow Singapore to fester or to move in and take over.

Some at the time believed that Lee was play-acting 'a fairy tale of British lions and Communist bears', that he and Selkirk were in league. More likely his anger was real enough. He was well aware he was still walking a tightrope; he needed no extra pressures, least of all from the British. General elections in Singapore in mid-1961 could have produced an ungovernable situation. If the Left took over by intra-party coup, the Tunku's hand would be forced and the inter-communal prospects would be terrifying. Either way, Lee's group would have lost the fragile thread that connected it to power and sufficient popular support to implement its, 'rational' policies for Malaya.

Other assumptions have distorted analysis, one being that the British officials involved with Singapore had a single viewpoint throughout the period of Lee's 'battle for merger'. It could well be that some officials under the Commissioner-General disagreed with his methods of hastening merger or applying the constitution. Either through habitual commitment to Lee or conviction that Lee's combination of open argument and selective force should prevail, they might have decided to leak information that would undermine Selkirk's strategy and keep Lee's options open. It is reliably asserted that MI5 was passing intelligence to Singapore's Special Branch at the time.

The effect of the split on the PAP was, in Goh Keng Swee's phrase, 'a technical knockout'.[21] Reacting to the spate of sackings Lee's group had engineered—three political secretaries, five parliamentary secretaries and eight other Assemblymen—the base and infrastructure of the Party nearly collapsed. Pang Cheng Lian in her study of the PAP estimates that about 80 per cent of the members resigned, were expelled or allowed their subscriptions to lapse.[22] More seriously, the branch committees and organisers were decimated. Lee had handpicked thirty-one organising secretaries between 1958 and 1961; twenty-eight defected. Of the fifty-one branches, Goh Keng Swee recalled that only his and Ong Pang Boon's remained intact. The bulk of the People's Association and Work Brigade officers defected—supposedly neutral quasi-government workers, they were in fact party stalwarts selected by Lee to be a counterweight to dissident PAP branch workers.

Goh was sure that the speed of the disaster had only one cause: 'It took less than a week for the Communist United Front leaders to achieve this!' It was Toh Chin Chye, Goh went on to say, who stiffened his comrades' resolve to return to the fray.

Place: My office in Fullerton Building. I was sitting not at my desk but in one of the armchairs used to receive guests. I was looking at the ceiling, wondering what had hit us.

Toh Chin Chye entered the room and the following conversation took place.

Dr Toh: Why are you staring at the ceiling?
Myself: Do sit down, Chin Chye, we are all busted; the party secretaries, the PA, the organising secretaries, the Works Brigade. I knew the communists were much stronger than us. But I did not expect us smashed up like this in just one week.
Dr Toh: I've just come from Harry's office. He was staring at the ceiling just like you did. You should snap out of this mood. The fight has only just begun. It is going to be long and nasty. But if we keep on wringing our hands in anguish we are sure to lose. We should start thinking immediately of our next moves—how to rebuild the Party, rally the loyal Party members and how to carry the fight into the enemy camp.
Comment: I will never forget the occasion. What Dr Toh said made sense. I recovered my spirits quickly. This was fortunate as the pro-communists, intoxicated by their spectacular successes, underrated our ability to fight back and made mistakes which gave us an opening for a counter-attack, which eventually succeeded. But, as Dr Toh predicted on that day, it was a long and nasty fight.[23]

The truth of the matter was not so black and white. The decisive enemy behind the scenes or up front was never just a disciplined band of Marxists. No one believed at the time that all those who left the Party in 1961 were communists or fellow-travellers. But neither should they all be written off as opportunists abandoning what looked like a losing team.

There was an outrageous streak in the behaviour of Lee and Goh. Granted, they could not help the clarity of their convictions about the political and economic battle lines. But the magnifying glass of the two men's calculating and authoritarian personalities made the clarity white hot. Baiting, contempt, smear and secrecy were weapons that destroyed others' trust apace.

Moreover, the Government had failed as yet to deliver on promises and raised expectations; and Lee's and Goh's fear of communism, always genuine, sometimes exaggerated for reasons of propaganda and politicking (and self-motivation?) might well have been a self-fulfilling prophecy. Last but not least, there was bound to be a reaction from the PAP rank and file: Ong Eng Guan's fight with the leadership had already highlighted Lee's and Goh's affinity to the civil service manderinate; and more and more their elitist style of decision-making rendered critical and self-respecting Party membership impossible.

A quarter of a century later, there is a prevailing wisdom about the PAP split. Lee Kuan Yew and Goh Keng Swee are its determined custodians and it has been virtually enshrined as sacrosanct truth. Books have been commissioned, edited, rejected in a bid to entrench the correct interpretation. In the recent spate of writing on Singapore there has been no substantial dissenting scholarship. Ironically, and to the dismay of the ageing first-generation leaders, it is not alternative views that threaten the memory of their heroic fight against 'Communism' and 'Communists': it is citizens' boredom.

Out of the split emerged a new party, the Barisan Sosialis (Socialist Front). Untimely born, it was doomed to enfeeblement from the start. Some of its principal figures such as Lee Siew Choh and Sheng Nam Chin, both medical men, had been known to Lee and Goh and were persuaded by them to join the PAP in 1958, to give the Party respectability and cultural antennae unaligned with Lim Chin Siong or Ong Eng Guan. These men, Dr Lee in particular, turned out to be woeful leaders of the Barisan and could not have suited the PAP better if they had been planted.

There would be times when the Barisan would muster a significant following around the emotive issues of Chinese education, detention without trial or trade union discontent. But, quite apart from the trump cards held by the PAP or reserved by the Federation and British governments, there was no consensus within the Barisan about how to play its own hand. Internal disunity constantly expressed itself in personal bickering and ideological zigzagging, ably assisted by Special Branch and free-lance subversion. The MCP underground never established a satisfactory hierarchy or network to shape tactics or carry them through to fruition. Many of the Barisan's cadres were inexperienced at higher level political organising. Among several legacies from the PAP, the most extraordinary was the framing of the Barisan's constitution more or less to reproduce its parent body's.

In the long run it turned out to be self-defeating that the Barisan and its backers (including the MCP) set about building a new party from the fragments thrown out of the PAP. There was not enough unity of purpose. From a communist perspective, Singapore's proletarian consciousness might have been growing, but it was still tied to Chinese chauvinism, was relatively unformed and nowhere near ripe for harvest. The PAP parliamentary dissidents would have had more devastating effect had they resigned their seats in accordance with Party rules and forced multiple by-elections or even general elections. The resulting instability might have been used as an excuse for outside intervention, but it would have destroyed the PAP leadership's credibility.

Speculation aside, the Barisan was to suffer a further crippling blow that no amount of forethought could have avoided. During 1963 its best leaders were detained in two security sweeps. Thereupon its condition became terminal.

No elections—but a Referendum

For Lee there was not a moment to lose. The people who went on to form the Barisan had drained the PAP and formerly loyal secondary associations. They had substantial trade union experience and strength. Support for the renegades could be expected not only from the University of Malaya Socialist Club and from across the board in Nanyang University, but from the population at large. So he announced that he, Ahmad Ibrahim and Ong Pang Boon would temporarily relieve themselves of administrative duties 'to get the feel of the ground'.[24]

At the height of the crisis, parliamentary delegations from the suggested Malaysian states met in Singapore and merger was approved in principle. Lee called for a frank discussion of the fears delegate entertained regarding Malaysia and the interests they believed must be safeguarded. He urged them to set the pace and terms, not to let the British do so.[25]

Lee and the Tunku became the two principal champions of the new Malaysia proposal. They conferred in August and reached a formal agreement. They applied pressure to the British, nominating control of the Singapore bases as the lever by which resistance to simultaneous incorporation of the Borneo territories and Singapore would be overcome. Although it was by now clear that the Tunku would have precedence in the negotiations, Lee knew that his was the more thorough planning. So it remained realistic for him to hope that eventually the PAP would be the dominant force in Malaysia. The racial balance that the Tunku wanted Malaysia to represent, between Malays/indigenes and Chinese, seemed ill thought-out especially given that Sabah, Sarawak and Brunei were across the sea and relatively far away from the peninsula. No one disputed that the dominance of UMNO would have been damaged in a merger purely of Malaya and Singapore, but the Tunku must have appeared naive and paternalistic if he expected his party to have any easier a time of it in North Borneo. Lee's visits and relationships there—and the Chinese connection and long-standing status of Singapore—were more substantial factors than racial or political pipe dreams by Kuala Lumpur.

In September 1961, Dr Goh Keng Swee mooted a referendum to gauge Singapore opinion on merger and Malaysia. General elections were chancy and avoidable for the time being, but a well conducted referendum would provide a precise rallying point for the Government. There was no constitutional provision for such a device, evidence that the PAP leaders were pursuing legitimacy without risking too much. Originally advocated 'for the people to decide whether to accept or reject merger',[26] it was soon reduced to a choice between different merger proposals. The PAP could and did defend this shift on the grounds that all parliamentary parties in Singapore had accepted the principle of merger.

The Referendum was not actually held until 1 September 1962, but Lee and his colleagues invested enormous effort in preparing for it. The results of negotiations with Malayan and British officials were publicised piecemeal, wherever possible to suit a PAP timetable. Radio was used to saturation point—the 'Battle for Merger' series in September and October, forums and so on. Alleged pro-communist manipulation of various unions* and of several campaigns to protect Chinese education was revealed, as was contact between the Barisan leaders and the Communist Party of Indonesia (PKI); and the PAP delegation staged a noisy walkout from a socialist conference of Malayan, Singaporean and North Borneo parties in Kuala Lumpur, charging that it was stacked.

Lee travelled early in 1962 to Afro-Asian countries and mobilised fraternal socialist support. He and Goh Keng Swee appeared before the United Nations Committee on Colonialism to counter the arguments against the Referendum that David Marshall put on behalf of the Barisan Sosialis, his own Workers' Party and Ong Eng Guan's UPP.

In the Assembly the situation remained very tense. After a series of defections back and forth[27] and then the death of the PAP's

---

* Following the PAP split, the Trade Union Congress had been dissolved. The National Trade Unions Congress (NTUC) and the Singapore Association of Trade Unions (SATU) took its place. The NTUC was pro-PAP; SATU was pro-Barisan Sosialis.

Preparing for Merger

Ahmad Ibrahim following a prolonged illness, the state of the parties was 25–all. The British suggested to Lee that he form a coalition with the Right. Instead, much more cleverly, an approach was made to the top leadership of the Singapore Alliance seeking a guarantee in the 'national interest' that the Government's merger proposals would not be defeated on the floor of the Assembly. Consent was given with reluctance, it being rightly perceived as an act of political suicide.

'Without the slightest sense of moral embarrassment', Lee said later, 'we were meeting cardsharpers and we were not going in like spring chickens'.[28] It was announced in July that blank votes would be counted for whichever of the proposals on the Referendum form received the most votes.

Following Lee's 'coup' over citizenship for Singaporeans in Malaysia, and on his return in August from talks in London, the date was set for the Referendum. It was an emotionally charged time. Here was a fierce if contrived contest for supremacy, with the Government controlling information flow to the public and daring the limits of its parliamentary power. Ahmad Ibrahim's death eleven days before the Referendum robbed Lee of a treasured comrade-in-arms, a Malay party stalwart: it symbolised how chancy the situation was. It was no wonder that both then and when the result of the Referendum was announced, Lee broke down and wept.

Lee's victory showed how much ground he had gained from the Right; the Left, though polarised, was controllable. The Tunku had helped by threatening dire consequences—closing the Causeway and by implication shutting off the water supply, too—if Singapore rejected merger. Politicians of all hues, such as Lim Yew Hock, David Marshall, Lee Siew Choh and Lim Chin Siong, were seen to have chopped and changed, partly because the Singapore side of the merger process was carefully kept in Lee's hands and they were therefore obliged to react.

It was vital to Lee's purpose that the appearance of open argument and democratic rights be maintained. Yet again, however, the stakes were so high that contingency plans were made in case things turned out badly. A poll had been taken in Tanjong Pagar (Lee's constituency) by University Socialist Club students in July 1962, recording 80 per cent opposition to the merger plans. To stave off a similar result in the Referendum, rumours were put about that there were ways of checking who had voted how. In another plan, a small group around Lee apparently decided to take an early sample of the results: if they were unfavourable, an incident or two could be created to simulate leftist duress and so discredit and nullify the Referendum results.

The outcome—70 per cent in favour of the PAP's proposal — made such contingencies unnecessary. It also tided the Government over until general elections could be held to suit the leadership. No by-election was called for Ahmad Ibrahim's seat of Sembawang.

BUKIT TIMAH, SINGAPORE

This highway I know,
the only way into the city
where the muddy canal goes.
These are the sides of coarse grasses
where the schoolboys stumble in early morning
wet-staining their white shoes.

This is the way the city is fed
men, machines
flushed out of their short dreams
and suburban holes
to churn down this waiting gullet;
they flow endlessly this way
from dawn, before sky opens,
to the narrow glare of noon
and evening's slow closing.

Under the steaming morning
ambition flashes by in a new car;
the reluctant salesman faced
with another day of selling his pride
hunches over the lambretta, swerving
from old farmer with fruit-heavy basket.

The women back from market
remark that this monsoon will be bad
for the price of vegetables;
their loitering children, too small for school,
learn the value of five- and ten-cents
from hunger and these market days.

All morning the tired buses whine
their monotonous route, drag
from stop to stop,
disgorge schoolchildren, pale-faced clerks,
long-suffering civil servants,
pretty office-girls, to feed
the megalopolitan appetite.

This highway I know,
the only way out of the city:
the same highway under the moon,
the same people under the sea-green
of lamps newly turned on at evening.

One day there will be tall buildings
here, where the green trees reach
for the narrow canal.
The holes where the restless sleepers are
will be neat, boxed up in ten-stories.
Life will be orderly, comfortable,
exciting, occasionally, at the new nightclubs.
I wonder what that old farmer would say
if he lived to come this way.

LEE TZU PHENG

6

Into Malaysia

> The calculated risk is now over. The people have declared their will... Before 1 September our firmness could have been misrepresented as Fascist repression of a so-called colonial liberation movement. After 1 September I am sure you will want my colleagues and me to do what is right for the security and well-being of all in Singapore and Malaysia...
>
> LEE KUAN YEW,
> broadcast, Singapore, 4 September 1962

The Referendum marked an important step forward for Lee. His appeal to the Right, both openly and behind the scenes, had paid off. He had divided and confused those who for a variety of reasons supported the Barisan Sosialis and the Left. Above all, he had gained muscle and stature for bargaining with federal Alliance leaders and with British government officials.

From Referendum to elections

PAP ambitions had embraced Malaya from the beginning. In 1960 the Party extended its reach to the North Borneo territories. One of its purposes was made quite explicit during a radio forum before the Referendum. To Barisan fears of Singapore being controlled by two different parliaments Rajaratnam responded with a prediction of cold comfort: if the PAP won elections in other Malaysian territories it could control the central Parliament as well.

Lee plainly found many aspects of his dealings with Kuala Lumpur irritating. They were to be endured only because 'we are straining every nerve and fibre in our being to bring about this merger to give a secure basis for our society'.[1] The Tunku was desirable not for his 'charm' but his 'durability'.[2] He was 'quite a sentimental man',[3] yielding to pressures from the region's 'Malays' and postponing the date of Malaysia from June 1963 to 31 August. (Malaya had become independent on 31 August 1957.) The Tunku's suggestion that Lee might go to the United Nations as

Ambassador was rejected by the PAP, but it must have annoyed Lee to know he was regarded as a troublesome general to be removed by promotion to command an outer province. His brief visit to Moscow en route from London in September provoked the Tunku's rebuke, whilst Lee declared he was 'not contaminated'[4] when he reached home. However, when it came to dealing with the Malayan Chinese Association (MCA), neither side made any attempt to veil insults.*

Lee also worked up annoyance at the 'dawdling' of the British over Borneo and the bases, which provided him with a safety valve in the frustration of dealing with Kuala Lumpur. His (and the Tunku's) rhetoric over the UK's military bases in Singapore and who controlled them was valuable as domestic propaganda or in calling the British bluff. But no one would seriously suggest that Lee was anxious for the British to withdraw.

As momentum gathered towards Malaysia, one of the main sticking points was the clear intention of the PAP leadership to retain the nomenclature of Prime Minister and Cabinet. In August 1962 the Tunku indicated that, unlike Borneo's case, there would be no Cabinet posts for Singapore representatives since they were already of 'the same rank'. This was accepted by Lee but he looked forward to the day when Singapore members in the Federal Parliament could seek a place in Cabinet on the basis of a majority of House support. Attempts have been made then and later to view the use of the title 'Prime Minister' as an index of Lee's personal ambition. In his 1965 New Zealand tour Lee said, somewhat disingenuously, 'I expect the terminology of Prime Minister just stayed on in the constitution.'[5] The truth is likely to be more complex. Given the incompetence, *naiveté* and corruptibility he attributed to his federal counterparts, Lee probably wanted to pose the PAP and himself in Singapore as the alternative government. When the future unfolded and proved too daunting for the Alliance, Singapore would be ready and waiting to resume its rightful place, at the centre of Malaysia and the region. It was a piece of symbolic politics. There were to be occasions when Lee asserted openly this view of the rightful place of Singapore: 'Calculate any way you like, a peaceful happy prosperous Malaysia is only possible if we keep Singapore the centre of Malaysia.'[6]

---

* Goh Keng Swee's wealthy cousin Tan Siew Sin (Federal Finance Minister and son of Tan Cheng Lock, one of the grand old men of Malaya and the MCA) was quickly to become the MCA's chief participant in the contest of vitriol with the PAP.

Lee was not foolish enough in his joy at the Referendum result to believe there was a general enthusiasm for merger. He studied the figures for each constituency and began allocating resources and planning candidates for the elections that must come. He undertook a tour of all the constituencies, starting in earnest during November 1962. He emphasised that his Government would safeguard the rights of Singapore and pointed to the role of Singapore as pacemaker in commerce, in scholarship, in urbanisation, in housing policy, in industrial expansion. Even when he addressed the problems—Malay reluctance to break social ties for the sake of settlement in high-rise flats or the slowness of implementing birth control measures, for example—he did not stress unilateral solutions from the Government. It was again a phase of carrying the people by persuasion.

Behind the scenes a different line was being followed. In the wake of the Referendum and before the final countdown to Malaysia, political leaders and Special Branch officers with British assistance, drew up hit lists. These were discussed at the tripartite Internal Security Council meetings. Several times a stalemate was reached after the Tunku urged Lee to lock up his 'communists' and Lee countered with the names of people in Malaya he wanted out of the way (e.g. Lim Kean Chye, Samad Ismail): neither cared for the respective stigmas the other's moves would have entailed. Lord Selkirk also exercised a moderating influence to keep the distinction alive between political and security risks.

Late in 1962 and early in the new year there was a marked deterioration in regional security. Troubles simmered at Nanyang University. The industrial arm of the Barisan Sosialis, the Singapore Association of Trade Unions (SATU), was active; one of its top unionists was accused of siphoning off funds for subversive purposes and was tried for criminal breach of trust. A quiet coalition developed between certain leftists in Singapore and the Federation and the leader of Brunei's abortive uprising, Sheikh Azahari. Indonesia's opposition to Malaysia was growing louder and was being expressed in the tangible forms of psychological and practical assistance to dissidents.

In response, the Internal Security Council ordered a definitive mop-up of suspects. It came in the early hours of 2 February 1963—the notorious Operation Cold Store. According to Goh Keng Swee, Malaya said, 'Come in clean'.[7] One hundred and eleven people were detained in Malaya and Singapore, including Lim Chin Siong, Fong Swee Suan, the Puthucheary brothers and many other key figures in the Barisan Sosialis, SATU and allied student and civic groups.

Lee attempted to put some distance between his Government and the operation. At an airport press conference on his return from the ISC meeting, he said, 'We would never have contemplated it. It would not have been necessary because we could have carried on until August 31.'[8] He was attacked by Lim Yew Hock and federal Alliance leaders for his reported words, but claimed he had been misunderstood—Singapore did stand by the ISC decision. However, he did offer Lim Chin Siong safe conduct to any foreign country.

As often in the past, Lee quickly redoubled his efforts to offset any political advantage to his opponents, in this case the martyr value of the detentions. He was aided by the erratic behaviour of Lee Siew Choh and other Barisan Sosialis leaders, now deprived of their principal advisers. The constituency tours were resumed in March. The fears of communist or Barisan takeover, publicised in the English-speaking press, helped Singapore win concessions from London or Kuala Lumpur.

A march on the Prime Minister's office on 22 April led to the arrest of twelve Barisan Sosialis leaders. Their trial did not take place until late August, and what with preliminary hearings and preparation of defence briefs, precious energy was diverted from the Barisan's campaigning. Elwyn Jones, a British QC brought in for the trial, remarked, 'This is a case which has wholly failed as a criminal proceeding. It is a case which has much to do with politics but very little to do with criminal law.'[9]

Television transmission began in February 1963 and offered new scope for putting across the Government line using the different languages and dialects of Singapore. The fitful achievements of the last few years could be dressed up and presented to advantage while people were still hypnotised by the new medium. A set was placed in every community centre—the PAP had built more than 100 since 1959.

Not all that had happened under PAP auspices after 1959 was merely telegenic. The main advance was in the quality and scope of administration. There was some social gain, giving women a 'better' deal. Few of the measures, for example in housing and education, were immediately popular with their supposed beneficiaries, especially those who were poorer or more bound up with Chinese tradition and culture. There was some soft-pedalling with respect to the Malays. But Lee's stress on order as preceding law—justifying action against secret society gangsters as well as political dissidents—not only paid economic dividents in attracting investment capital, but helped recapture the votes of those whose allegiance lay to the Right. He also turned some potentially volatile forces to good account, as in his 1963 decision to allow the clamour for Occupation blood-debt payment just enough outlet to defuse its threat of hindering Japanese industrial assistance. Before the biggest crowd ever seen in Singapore he declared: 'Humiliation and degradation by foreign European powers is bad enough. It was worse at the hands of a conquering Asian nation like Japan—and it will be even worse if it should be by a neighbouring power in Southeast Asia' (25 August 1963). The persistent strength of anti-Japanese sentiment could perhaps be converted to fear of Indonesia, or of a Malaya in the wrong hands. (Lee was aware that the rally at which he was attempting this *tour de force* might turn nasty, and he carried a revolver in his pocket.)

It was Lee's and Goh's skill in negotiating Singapore's place in Malaysia that tided the PAP over 1963 and enhanced respect for the Prime Minister. Battles with the MCA or the British were portrayed, when successful, as vindication of the PAP (not least as bearer of Chinese hopes in and beyond Singapore) and, when not, as defeat graciously borne for the sake of Malaysia. The Tunku was courted assiduously until the new nation was assured. The concessions made in London during final settlement of terms were 'through regard for the Tunku': if British Commowealth and Colonial Secretary Duncan Sandys alone had been involved, Lee declared, he 'would have brought him to his knees'.[10] In May, Lee accused the MCA of wanting a collision between him and the Tunku. The insults flowed back and forth.

When Malayan, Filipino and Indonesian representatives met in Manila mid-1963 and proposed an axis between the Malay peoples, *Maphilindo*, Lee gave the suggestion an alarming—if usefully alarming—prominence. Little Singapore would fight to her last drop of blood to protect her territorial integrity, he had said in September 1962. Now, during the last debate on Malaysia in Singapore's Assembly, he raised the possibility of Singapore overwhelming the Federation—'not a possibility to be altogether dismissed' (30 July 1963).

Lee's final master stroke in the lead-up to the Singapore elections was played when the Tunku again postponed Malaysia Day. He declared Singapore independent on 31 August 1963 and took over foreign affairs and defence 'on trust' until Malaysia was inaugurated. He persuaded Sabah and Sarawak to do the same, perhaps trading on the suspicions of Kuala Lumpur; it was nevertheless an accomplishment since his own posture towards the territories swung from patronising beneficence to impatient counsel to barely concealed indifference.

This unilateral declaration of independence forced the British and Federation Governments to make some last-minute concessions to Singapore. Duncan Sandys was again singled out as responsible for resolving Malaysia's problems: Lee gave him until 12 September to do so or else 'face the consequences' of Singapore's *de facto* independence.[11]

Once Malaysia was guaranteed to Lee's satisfaction, it was time to advance the grander plans of his group. Domestic elections should be held as close to merger as possible in order to reap the publicity benefits of Singapore's attainments and 'before the Malaysian Central Government had time to take over and exercise firm power over the police to have any significant influence on the conduct of the elections'.[12] If the plan worked, the PAP would be seen as a movement encompassing all but the communists and a few Malay extremists and therefore fit to govern Malaysia and her peoples. It might take decades to achieve, but the elections would mark the public launch of PAP ascendancy.

The plan worked like a charm. Radio and Television Singapore were used unashamedly to favour the PAP: Lee even interrupted the moderator of one forum to say that it was only his graciousness that allowed radio and TV time for all 'and I am Prime Minister until the next Government is formed after the 21st'.[13] Former detainees were physically prevented from nominating in the one hour available for their personal presentation of papers. The election was called with minimum notice and the campaign period of nine days included the holidays and festivities associated with Malaysia's inauguration. Sites and permits for rallies were hard to come by. Printing facilities for opposition parties were almost unobtainable. Notice was given of the deregistration of seven leftist unions and SATU funds were frozen at the eleventh hour to prevent their being spent for electoral purposes.

Lee's public exposition of all the negotiations for Malaysia and a common market had had intrinsic propaganda value. It had also been a lure to industrial peace in disputes before the elections, and it gave him and his party great kudos. On the hustings he was well received, despite booing and jeering from hooded youths at different campaign stops and one incident in which Lee was pushed into a monsoon drain (to the Tunku's great amusement). Searchlights were used to show up dissenters in the crowd. Even hostility produced tough talk to the gallery from the Prime

Minister: 'You are all like parrots', 'Stop using your hands on me', 'I have done unarmed combat and know how to look after myself', 'They are toughs and you've got to be tough with them'.[14]

By the end of the campaign, Lee was exhausted. He kept himself buoyed up with drugs. His tactics had demonstrated a fierce determination, sustained for months and punctuated by private outbursts of tears and rage. Having brought his people to reluctant endorsement of merger on PAP terms in the 1962 Referendum, he had had to barnstorm ceaselessly to extract favourable terms, or at least the appearance of favourable terms. He had used all the resources and instrumentalities of the state both to seduce those who might have looked to Kuala Lumpur and to paralyse those who were fearful of merger (the extreme leftists or Chinese chauvinists). He portrayed himself and his Government as practitioners of the open argument. He claimed responsibility for the ISC not proscribing the Barisan: 'To have obliterated their symbol before the elections would have been to help build up this myth of Communist invulnerability—a myth we cracked in the Referendum last year.'[15] The PAP had rebutted the colourfully expressed accusation of Tan Lark Sye* and Barisan sympathisers from Nanyang University that the Government was 'damaging the education of the races' by alleging that a vote for the Barisan meant a vote for merger with Indonesia and its well known anti-Chinese stance.

Lee reserved a choice line of contempt for the Singapore Alliance, declaring it was effete, under the thumb of Kuala Lumpur, 'a hotchpotch of bank *compradores*, unsavoury and corrupt politicians from the former Labour Front Government, agents for airport contractors and airplane firms [Lim Yew Hock], touts who hope to get commissions from social welfare lottery tickets, friends of gangsters and others who hope to loot and plunder Singapore'.[16]

Despite explicit denials from the Tunku, Lee and other pro-PAP elements maintained that the Constitution would be suspended if an extremist government came to power in Singapore. This threat would have affected some wavering leftists, perhaps, but more to the point, it was aimed at discrediting the MCA in Malaya. 'The MCA are smarting from the humiliation in London on 9 July and again in Kuala Lumpur on 11 September when they were overruled because we stood firm on the rights of Singapore, and they would have shown quite clearly since they have no chance of winning they

---

* Tan Lark Sye was one of Singapore's best known *towkays*.

prefer to see the Barisan Sosialis win.' Singapore would then be taken over with a proclamation of Emergency, so this scenario ran, 'controlled and emasculated from the centre'.[17]

'If I tried to undermine the Tunku's government, then I expect him to lock me up', Lee had said more than seven weeks earlier.[18] Perhaps his words were a challenge. They came at a period when he was his most provocative self: the unilateral declaration of independence; the side play with Sabah and Sarawak; his scorn at the Tunku's easy journey to independence and love of pomp and ceremony; his allegation that the Tunku would readily intervene in Singapore; the bitter criticism of the MCA; and the offer to take over the Singapore Alliance as President.

The election could not have turned out better. To compensate for the transfer of votes to the Barisan, there was a solid defection of Malay and right-wing support to the PAP. With 46.5 per cent of the count, the PAP gained 37 out of 51 seats, winning 7 of them on a split left-wing vote. Lee spelt out part of the meaning of the results when they were announced (Victoria Memorial Hall, 22 September 1963). Malaysia's towns, even 'lost' cities such as Singapore, must be governed by consent, not force. His original plan to have the fifteen Singapore members elected for the Federal Parliament before he called general domestic elections—so he could test MCP impact in each constituency—had been frustrated and confused by the MCA. Now he had his revenge. He paid tribute to the leading PAP candidates who were unsuccessful, including K.M. Byrne, who had been moved 'sacrificially' to stand against the Barisan's S.T. Bani. He thanked the public servants whose constructive efforts had provided visible evidence to back the open argument.

Lee's desire to present Singapore as a model of dealing with communism by building a better society and his urge to hasten a PAP type of politics Malaysia-wide were sometimes, sufficiently dominant for him to brush aside loyalty to the Tunku. But having won this victory he was able to resume a more gracious position. He expressed regret that the central Government had seen fit to reiterate its ultimate authority and went on to acknowledge that for the next decade or two the Prime Minister of Malaysia must be a Malay. He stated at least twice that the PAP would hold back and not contest the forthcoming mainland elections to show that even so the MCA would 'still lose'.[19] He asked the Tunku to nominate one of the two Singapore senators and promised that the PAP would be a loyal Opposition in the lower house of the Federal Parliament, the Dewan Ra'ayat.

Relatively speaking, the first few months of Malaysia were calm. Lee's irritation stayed close to the surface but did not burst out more than to underscore his distinctive viewpoint here and there. He concentrated his wrath on Singapore miscreants—the Barisan Sosialis, the unions related to SATU, and the fifth columnists trained by the Indonesians. Further detentions occurred in October, and when the Assembly sat only eight of its Barisan legislators were present; three had been detained and two had disappeared. The troublesome magnate Tan Lark Sye's citizenship was revoked.

What had been said of the Referendum was true also of the 1963 elections. The Referendum had turned out to be 'a textbook lesson for old and new cadres'.[20] The PAP Government had won out, despite inferior ground organisation. By contrast the 1961 by-elections had been lost when the PAP branches and structure were fully operational. For the elections a comprehensive range of techniques, now including television, had been employed to mobilise and master the ground. Lee claimed in justification of the more dubious methods that they were no worse than those his opponents would have used if in power.

It was clear that Party organisation was no longer as important as it had once seemed. In the months after September 1963, direct access from Government to people was upgraded, and the formation of Citizens' Consultative Committees was mooted.

Federal elections 1964

With Singapore in good shape, it did not take long for Lee to revise his strategy for Malaysia. Well into 1963 he had held out against Alliance criticism for maintaining good relations with Indonesia: in September he termed the destruction of the British Embassy in Jakarta 'a twentieth-century ritual of showing disapproval'.[21] But by the end of the year he was admitting 'the fight was on, no holds barred'.[22] Blame for terrorist activity since late September had been sheeted home to Indonesia. He seems to have reached the conclusion that efforts must urgently be redoubled to advance the PAP and Singapore in Malaysia. One reason was the loss of trade with Indonesia, but there was also the spectre of a resurgent Malay culture. A powerful and successful Indonesia, he said in the national Parliament on 21 December 1963, would be an attractive 'larger whole' to provide refuge if the indigenous stock of Malaysia felt that all other guarantees of their position were lost except the Constitution. There would only be ten years at the outside to make the fragile formula for progress work—the immigrant stock generating economic growth, the benefits going to the Malay mass base to keep them happy. Lee alloyed whatever truth lay in his analysis with pointed insult. It was no solution to create Malay 'haves', he said. And while he acknowledged that it would not be possible for an immigrant political force 'to wield the mechanics and sinews of power in Malaysia' and 'foolish for anyone in Singapore to hold himself out as the oracle of any part of Malaya or the Borneo territories', he also asserted, 'I do not think there is a Malayan leader today who can proclaim himself as the undisputed Malaysian leader'. In so many words: if Lee could not realistically claim leadership in Malaysia, neither could the Tunku. Neither the rural nor the urban sector was being helped by the central Government to congeal and integrate and it was only a matter of time before the Malays and the Chinese woke up to the fact.

Much has been made of Toh Chin Chye's announcement on 1 March 1964 that the PAP would contest the forthcoming mainland elections. At the time Lee was leading a delegation from Singapore, Sabah and Sarawak on a tour of seventeen African states promoting his version of Malaysia. When greeted with the news on his return home, he expressed horrified amazement to his aides. In years to come, he repeatedly emphasised that the decision to 'have a go' was made while he was away. Apparently the CEC felt free to disregard Lee's undertakings to Alliance leaders because they had not been made after consultation with the PAP and were therefore not binding.[23] It looked like the Prime Minister's most signal defeat thus far.

Nevertheless, there was more to it than met the eye. The decision to contest the elections was hinted at by Rajaratnam before Lee left on his trip: 'The PAP must start operating as a pan-Malaysian party on a pan-Malaysian basis to help build a prosperous, independent and peaceful Malaysia.'[24] Whatever misgivings Lee had about the decision vis-à-vis its tactical value or the Tunku's future trust in his word, it is very unlikely he did not endorse the fears of Singapore's isolation 'with a City Council-like mentality', 'cornered like a rat'.* The most likely reconstruction of the episode is that, before his departure, Lee stated for his colleagues' and his

---

* He was also angry that Devan Nair had been disqualified by the central Government's last-minute change of rules from standing at the 1963 Singapore Assembly elections; by birth, however, Devan automatically became a Malaysian citizen, and could therefore be put up at the 1964 Federal elections as a symbol of personal and Party revenge.

own benefit that he would not be party to any decision and did not want to know about it during his absence. So the timing of the announcement would have been intended to deflect responsibility from Lee, a difficult task given the presumption, by now fairly well founded, that he was at the bottom of almost everything the Singapore Government did.

In looking back on the events that led to August 1965, the Tunku stated that Lee was 'not sincere': 'I said to him once, "Kuan Yew, I can never trust you as a politician".'[25] To note his opinion is not to endorse it but to observe the gap between the two men: the Tunku fatherly, tolerant in a nepotistic way, gradualist; Lee not wanting the Tunku's fatherliness, intolerant of personal favour, urgent for reform. The Tunku believed he was in tune with local history; Lee wished to reshape it. Lee had worked very hard to bridge the gap; now the announcement of PAP involvement in the mainland elections undid all his work. It confirmed the Alliance's perception of a wilful and aggressive edge to PAP hopes of mastery, an edge already displayed more legitimately in the Singapore elections.

The 1964 elections were called earlier than legally necessary, a pre-emptive move to gather the Malaysian people behind the central Government in the face of Confrontation and to discredit the opposition parties who had not wanted Malaysia for one reason or another. But the PAP could expect to be disadvantaged, too. With pressure being applied from Kuala Lumpur and of course from Jakarta, it would be much harder to construct an alternative Malaysia and succeed to power in the long term. Vigilance was vital if the Alliance was to be matched and, ultimately, outclassed. Lee might have been addressing Kuala Lumpur when he remarked in another context, 'If you lack subtlety, the Government will find it that much more difficult to leave the fight in your hands.'[26]

Lee was to concede after the elections that the PAP approach had been 'too subtle'.[27] He and the PAP had purported to support the Tunku and UMNO. Theirs was a token participation simply to register that the urban population now aspired to a more equal society. Yet in the same breath that Lee denied offering a Chinese-language criticism of the Tunku's calibre 'one of the elementary principles to observe before one can lead public opinion is never to contradict one's basic stand', he also told a rally at Kluang, West Malaysia, on 29 March 1964 that the Tunku needed to be saved from his friends, particularly those of the MCA. He stated that military and economic pressure from Indonesia could be withstood; the communalistic basis of politics was the permanent and greatest danger. He noted that 20 per cent of Malaysia's Malays had direct connections with Indonesia.[28] He bemoaned the inability of same Malays in government to distinguish between communists and Chinese chauvinists.[29] The PAP aspired to take the place of the MCA or Socialist Front in representing the urban population, but Lee's prescription also involved drastic changes in rural policy to prevent religious 'obscurantists' from holding sway. 'UMNO needs to learn from the PAP,' he said.'[30]

One fact should dispel any doubt that the PAP decision to contest the April 1964 elections was fraught with a strain of paranoid urgency. The Party did not have anything like an adequate organisation on the ground in Malaya. This made the resort to instant appeal—claiming to represent the urban Chinese or Indians, which really negated the PAP's avowed non-communal intentions—all the more tempting. The frequent talk by Lee of a 1969 bid for office in coalition with the brighter young Malays, some in the PAP and others now being drafted into UMNO, was hardly flattering to the Malays, least of all to those in the central Government. No doubt the strongest insults were hurled at MCA personalities, but he attacked the Government and UMNO many times regarding election tactics and strategy.

The PAP received a disproportionate amount of attention; Lee in particular drew large crowds. It turned into a field day for attacking the Singapore leader. His old enemies from the Left said he was 'more like a Hitler or a Mussolini but with less polish and skill',[31] whereas Tan Siew Sin of the MCA described him as reminiscent of 'a chameleon, a remarkable creature which can adjust its colour to its surroundings'.[32] From the MCA also: 'Lee Kuan Yew's political power has always been built over the dead bodies of his friends and allies.'[33] Reference was made to the Singapore Government's low interest payments on employees' provident fund contributions. Singapore's high-rise flats were described as 'skyscraper slums'. Several Malay politicians used vivid language to denigrate Lee—a 'bee', a 'hungry dog'. 'Fists' might have to be used to teach the PAP the meaning of democracy.[34] Above all, Tunku Abdul Rahman established his own position early in the campaign. 'The PAP wants to teach us what is good for us. We know what is good for us, and what is bad. They say they want to join the UMNO, but we don't want them.'[35]

Lee displayed an amazing confidence—given the events of the last few years culminating in the PAP's election about-face and the ensuing campaign—that it was irrelevant whether the Tunku liked him or not. 'If all the nine win, an agonising reappraisal will have to be made.'[36]

Only one PAP candidate won: Devan Nair. The Alliance gained 89 out of 104 seats, a staggering result. 'The MCA, pronounced dead by the PAP, won 27 seats.'[37] Lee's insistence afterwards that his analysis had been vindicated could only ring hollow. It may be that the Chinese were persuaded to stay with the Alliance not out of regard for the MCA but for their own protection against the Indonesians. The fact remains that the PAP could not win on its chosen battlegrounds.

The temperature rises

When the Dewan Ra'ayat met in May, Lee was at his patronising and didactic best. His congratulations on the Tunku's victory died the death of a thousand qualifications. The PAP was put forward as the harbinger of loyal but critical opposition, of knowledge how to administer a modern state properly, of confidence in the tide of history and the push towards equal opportunity. 'We deem it our duty to ease the way forward to a more just, equal society.' 'We want the democratic system to endure, even if it means that for many years we shall be denied an opportunity of office' (21 May 1964).

The effect of this relatively young man, so unlike other Malayan Chinese, pontificating on Malaysia and the world, was galvanic. One moment he seemed to accept a subordinate role; the next he was champing at the bit to save Malaysia. His performance in and outside the Parliament demanded a response. A Malaysian Cabinet Minister, Khir Johari, said later that 'his daily routine was reduced to getting up in the morning, reading the statements of PAP leaders in the newspapers and spending the rest of the day thinking of a reply'.[38]

From late 1963 to the day of Singapore's separation from Malaysia there was no stopping the deterioration of relations between Lee and the Tunku and their respective confidants. Careful research makes it hard to avoid laying much of the blame at Lee's feet, and for several reasons. The first is Lee's constant pretension to objective judgment without the least hint of irony. He said, addressing the national Parliament on 21 May 1964, 'One of the reasons, Sir, why Western-style democracy has not taken roots in the newly independent countries of Asia and Africa is because the governments in power do not contemplate with equanimity the thought that power could pass to an opposition and also because the opposition opposes merely to bring the government down, regardless of the harm inflicted on the country.'

The second factor is the PAP's lack of a mass base to give effect to the 'enlightened self-interest' of its policies for urban–rural harmony. This was only a little less true in Singapore than in Malaya. Attempts to press for the resolution of class struggle rather than race divisions came curiously from a man who was principally supported by the Chinese urban bourgeoisie of Singapore and its recent additions, including few Malays. It was also somewhat naive to assert the PAP's capacity to demand high standards of administration as safeguard against the pendulum swing first to a dictatorship of the Right and thence to the Indonesian extreme Left. The PAP was not the party of national government; Singapore was not the capital of Malaysia; there could be no question of transposing the particular administration of Singapore to Malaysia as a whole.

Above all, the pressure that the PAP leadership put on Kuala Lumpur was unrelenting. In retrospect, the Tunku described the situation thus: 'It appeared that as soon as one issue was resolved another cropped up; where a patch was made here a tear appeared elsewhere; and when one hole was plugged other leaks appeared.' (Dewan Ra'ayat 9 August 1965)

Whether in the planned common market in which Singapore had an obvious stake, rural policy in peninsular Malaysia or Malaysia's foreign posture, where Kuala Lumpur clearly had to be in command, Lee and his colleagues intervened with indiscriminate passion. Singapore had not previously been acceptable to Malaya under congenial leadership; Singapore under Lee became intolerable. According to the Tunku, 'We dreamt of Singapore in connection with Malaya as what New York is to America, but little did we realise what the leaders of the PAP had in mind was a share in the running of Malaysia. This was considered as unacceptable, since the Alliance is strong enough to run the country on its own ... We must not be pushed around by a State Government if this Federation is to have any meaning. Singapore came into the Federation with her eyes wide open and they came in on their own accord and because Malaysia was born the PAP was returned to power. Now having joined the Federation, the party in power in Singapore must try to make Malaysia workable.'[39]

The sheer magnitude of Lee's self-appointed task within Malaysia and the haste with which he pursued it can only be characterised as extraordinary. The events that led to Separation arose either from his superhuman energy or from his opponents' reaction, their certainty that he was bent on demonic purposes.

DO NOT SAY

do not say my people are lazy
because you do not know.
you are only a critic, an onlooker.
you cannot know or judge,
passing the *kampong* in your car,
staring at economic data.

do not think my people are weak
because they are gentle,
because they do not build skyscrapers.
have you ever worked in a *ladang,*
or danced the *ronggeng?*
can you sing the *dondang sayang?*
do not think that we have only music
because we love life.

do not write that we have no literature, culture.
have you ever listened to the *sajak* or *pantun*
stayed a night at the *bangsawan?*
have you read the epic *shairs*
or the theological theses?
how many times have you wondered about history in the blade
and ancestry in the handle of the *keris.*
or felt the pattern of the *songket?*
have you lived in a *kampong?*

do not condemn us as poor
because we have very few banks.
see, here the richness of our people,
the brimful hearts that do not grab or grapple.
we collect humanity from sun and rain and man,
transcending the business and the money.

do not tell us how to live
or organise such nice associations and bodies.
our society was an entity
before the advent of political philosophy.

do not say —
because you do not know.

MOHAMAD HAJI SALLEH

Glossary

kampong village; *ladang* a clearing for non-irrigated farming; *ronggeng* a dance for couples; *dondang sayang* a musical dialogue and serenade between a couple; *sajak* modern Malay poetry, free-form; *bangsawan* Malay opera; *shairs* literary form incorporating rhythm and rhyme; *songket* hand-woven cloth, shot with gold or silver thread; *keris* traditional dagger (often ornamented for ceremonial use)

7

Out of Malaysia

> After the riots, I told my colleagues that even if we died, that was the least we could do. But never give in. We demanded that Malaysia stood by the agreed documents of the constitution. We stuck our necks out.
>
> LEE KUAN YEW,
> election speech, 29 August 1972

Malaysia's first major crisis occurred in the middle of 1964. Riots broke out between Malays and Chinese in Singapore on 21 July, the Prophet Mohammed's Birthday. At least twenty-two people were killed and hundreds injured.

From riots to separation

The trigger was a discreet attempt by Lee to confer with Singapore's Malay civic leaders and keep them on side; he wanted the Malays to understand the constraints on the PAP Government, especially in housing, which lay behind certain decisions affecting their welfare. His efforts were attacked and brought into the public arena by the local UMNO, guided by Syed Ja'afar Albar and others from Kuala Lumpur.

Ja'afar Albar was one of many Malays who had developed respect for Lee as an unusually frank and forceful realist, only to become progressively disenchanted with him during the lead-up to Malaysia's inauguration. He and others felt Lee had won too many concessions from the Tunku and had tricked the latter into promoting a Malaysia quite different from the UMNO mandate's provisions agreed to in 1961. In particular their suspicions had been aroused by Lee's unilateral declaration of independence on 31 August 1963. They were determined to put Singapore in its place.

There was also the matter of revenge for the PAP's defeat of UMNO candidates in Singapore's 1963 elections. The time seemed ripe (in the *Guardian's* words describing the situation) 'to squeeze Mr Lee in his home ground' (28 April 1964), after the PAP failure in the mainland elections and with Malay disaffection on the increase. Singapore's UMNO was purged of 'traitors' and attempts were made to buy off or discredit the PAP's Malays: Haji Ya'acob was offered ten years' salary and Rahmat Kenap was branded a *kaffir* (infidel).

Lee was deeply angered by this interference. Years later, during an election speech on 29 August 1972, he said

> After the riots, I told my colleagues that even if we died, that was the least we could do. But never give in. We demanded that Malaysia stood by the agreed documents of the constitution. We stuck our necks out.

In subsequent weeks the PAP called publicly for the 'smacking down' of the 'ultras' (the word Lee used to describe the Malay extremists), the suppression of newspapers featuring inflammatory articles and a commission of inquiry into the race riots. Lee offered the PAP's help to subdue the extremists. Privately, he had orchestrated the suggestion of British Prime Minister Sir Alec Douglas-Home, made to the Tunku who was in London during the riots, that the Alliance form a coalition with the PAP. For a brief time Lee adopted a conciliatory attitude towards Malay rights.

Singapore was shaken by riots again early in September. The Tunku acknowledged the role of Indonesian *agents provocateurs*, as he had in July, but he stated even more bluntly than before that . . . 'it needed only a little incitement to start off trouble'[1] because of the Singapore Government's treatment of its Malays. This time Lee was in London and speculation was rife about his lobbying activity there, without need for telephone or intermediary. He was known to be very frustrated at delays in setting up the Commission of Inquiry and, far more importantly, at his helplessness, given that Singapore's police and army were controlled by Kuala Lumpur.

Sopiee makes the cogent point that the PAP's public demands for action against 'ultras' all but guaranteed that none would be taken.[2] And when it could be suspected with some justice that the PAP was behind Commonwealth press or government pressures for a coalition, that idea was squashed forthwith.

A round table conference was held late in September with six of the top Alliance and PAP leaders. Afterwards Dr Toh announced a truce for the next two years—sensitive communal issues would be avoided and party politicking minimised.

Sopiee contends that the PAP still hoped for a coalition with the Alliance as late as the tenth anniversary of its founding in November 1964.[3] The evidence suggests rather that the September meeting induced a more sober realism. This mood was possibly what gave rise to the false rumours in October that Singapore would secede. Late that month all bets were off: Khir Johari foreshadowed a reshuffle in the Singapore Alliance to enhance prospects for victory there in 1967. The PAP regretted that the truce had been violated and announced it would reorient and reorganise itself 'so that we can get at Malaya'.[4]

What emerged from the National Theatre rally that climaxed the tenth anniversary celebrations on 22 November 1964 was a clear call for democratic socialists in Malaysia to 'bring the country together, isolate the enemy and build that climate of opinion on which they could mount a movement comprised of all the have nots in Malaysia, regardless of race, religion and language, to bring about a more equal and just society'. The line was that nothing could stop the triumph of the democratic socialists once their message got through to the 'have nots'. Hence the last-ditch efforts of Alliance and other reactionaries to undermine it.

Lee's apparent belief that the technocratic PAP would be a convincing medium for the message of hope to the 'have nots' was demonstrably absurd. In reminding his faithful audience that the PAP had resisted the blandishments of a capitalist system seeking to buy off individual politicians, he proclaimed that an idealistic drive for justice still burned in PAP hearts. His words might have provoked derision had they been spoken to the people of a *kampong*, a rubber plantation or a tin mining settlement.

More significant at the time was the return to ideological purity. From then on, there would be no sullying compromise with the Alliance. What was needed was a united opposition front to promote a true Malaysia, combining democratic socialism and parliamentary democracy. Open political debate would be the method.

Events before and since make it easy to be cynical about the PAP's commitment to open argument and democratic socialist ideals. The usefulness of these principles was certainly rhetorical in part, aimed at the international scene generally and at Britain and her newly returned Labour Government specifically. But Lee and most of his close colleagues still placed themselves in the British Fabian succession, and to honour its slogans, whether in the breach or the observance, was to find renewed moral justification for seeking power and fighting when prudence might advise holding back.

So it was that Lee and his ministers entered the fray when Tun Tan Siew Sin brought down his second Malaysian Budget on 25 November. Unfortunately it was not easy to stir the public's and have nots' resentment at payroll and turnover tax. Moreover, Tan was mischievous enough to suggest that the PAP attack on joint tax assessment of husband and wife income might be 'because a number of members of the Singapore Cabinet had wives with substantial professional earnings' (Dewan Ra'ayat, 3 December 1964). Other Alliance members quickly pointed out the incongruity of Lee and the PAP championing the have nots' cause from a position of luxury. They assailed their Singapore opponents' two-faced and power-hungry tendencies, and mocked at old enemies becoming political friends.

A few days later in Singapore the Tunku spoke out unequivocally: 'If the politicians of various colours and tinges and flashes in Singapore disagree with me, the only solution is a breakaway, but what a calamity that would be for Singapore and Malaysia!' (*Straits Times*, 10 December 1964).

Lee backtracked. He adopted a more favourable overall assessment of the Budget. But animosity soon flared up again and clashes in the Dewan Ra'ayat drew from him a memorable speech on 18 December, raising fundamental questions about Malaysia. Could men 'preach ideas—novel, unorthodox heresies to established churches and established governments, where there is a constant contest for men's hearts and minds on the basis of what is right, of what is just, of what is in the national interests?' Or was it a closed society where by mass media 'men's minds are fed with a constant drone of support for a particular orthodox political philosophy'? Whatever the faults of the colonial system, it had generated 'the open mind, the inquiring mind'. The Malaysian people were bound to ask why Malaysia existed, and they would find their own answers.

In a sense, the radical aspect of Lee's philosophy was enshrined in this speech. He had attained political superiority by standing outside most of the conventions and ethnic loyalties of his compatriots. Now, in a moment of passion, he was modelling his nonconformity for Malaysians to emulate. What was left unstated was the darker side of his behaviour: antagonism to an open society that dissented from his views. His speech was a classic case of the pot calling the kettle black.

Talk of new, looser arrangements, even of secession, began to circulate in PAP and Alliance quarters, apparently a way of toying with alternative contingencies or calling opponents' bluff, but all the same evidence that the unthinkable was being thought. Goh Keng Swee, for one, was convinced by December 1964 that remaining in Malaysia would only retard Singapore's economic development.

With the Cabinet divided among those who shared Goh's view

and those who were determined to promote the PAP as Malaysia's vanguard, Lee was playing a pivotal role. He was perhaps the only one who felt the full weight of arguments on both sides. He began 1965 in a statesmanlike vein. 'Fifteen months of Malaysia should have taught the leaderships of the different territories the risks of collision,' he said, 'We can make or mar our future; make it by accommodation and tolerance, or mar it by throwing a tantrum every time we do not get our way.' (New Year message, 1965). It was not long, however, before a mass rally heard him almost gloating over the dangers ahead; he noted that the *Utusan Melayu* was now attacking the MCA, thereby laying bare divisions within the Alliance (24 January 1965). Two days later Rajaratnam sounded the alarm: silence 'far from sobering (Malay) extremists, will be a stimulant'. The Tunku responded immediately and heatedly to politicians 'whose minds are obviously distorted, polluted'.[5]

Lee spoke in Kuala Lumpur late in February and declared that the Tunku's response was a 'turning point in Malaysia'. The Alliance had written off Singapore and other sophisticated urban areas in Malaysia. 'Its primary interest now was to hold on to its rural base in Malaya.'[6] This perverse and wilful deduction highlighted the incompatibility between Lee's 'direct' method of building a multiracial society and the Alliance's 'indirect' two-stage method. Before departing for Australia and New Zealand, Lee went further on the offensive with two speeches in key peninsular towns. He emphasised the fallacies in the Alliance argument that Malaysia's races should attain internal unity before uniting with each other. He accused secondary leaders in UMNO and the Alliance of attempting, especially in Sabah and Singapore, to consolidate Malay supremacy outside peninsular Malaysia. 'This campaign has altered and accelerated the realignment of political forces within Malaysia" (Malacca, 3 March 1965).

Lee then became all too present in his absence. Not only did daily cables report his many relevant speeches in Australasia, but the Singapore Government submitted its memorandum to the dilatory Commission of Inquiry into the 1964 race riots. The memorandum, after careful although selective recital of facts, attributed motives.

> The riots were willed by irresponsible and reckless propaganda based on falsehoods and distortions of facts. Their purpose was principally to re-establish the political influence of UMNO among the Malays in Singapore. An even more important objective was to use the Malays in Singapore as pawns to consolidate Malay support for UMNO in Malaya (Singapore Government memorandum, March 1965).

The period from late January to August 1965 is marked by an exceptional abrasiveness on the part of Lee and certain others in the PAP leadership, notably Toh Chin Chye and Rajaratnam. It seems that the latter decided to go for broke, while Lee himself became trapped in a self-fulfilling prophecy, a kind of death wish. Every poisonous outpouring from *Utusan Melayu* or some similar source was dutifully translated—with help from Lee's twelve-year-old son, Hsien Loong, who had been schooled to proficiency in Jawi (the Arabic script form of Malay)—and laid by the Singapore Government before the public of all races and ages—through ministerial speeches, through its news digest, *Malaysian Mirror*, which was even sent to Malayan schools. Alliance policies and statements were caricatured and then knocked down. Cracks in the Alliance were spotlighted. The Malays' catchcries, for example that they were the indigenous people, were analysed critically. What of the newcomers who made up one-third of the Malays, men like Syed Ja'afar Albar? Had not the Chinese been in and out of the archipelago for more than six hundred years? Again, as Lee said at the University of Western Australia on 1 April 1965, the 'exclusive use of Malay language by 1967 would leave a few federal Ministers deaf and dumb in Parliament'.

Before Lee left for overseas he announced the composition of the opposition front that the PAP was assembling; it was to include two Malayan parties and parties from Sabah and Sarawak. He also launched the slogan 'Malaysian Malaysia'. The net result of the PAP verbal assault led by Lee was to cause the Alliance to close ranks. 'Young men in a hurry must be resisted.'[7] The third annual Malaysian Alliance Convention in April saw the coalescence of the separate territories' parties into a National Alliance.

Lee returned home mid-April. He had been well received in Australasian government circles and by the press. He was known to have won an extended hearing from Australian Prime Minister Menzies. 'Nobody is better fitted to put Malaysia's case' stated the *Sydney Morning Herald* editorial of 18 March 1965, soon reprinted in the *Malaysian Mirror*. The Tunku had been apprehensive before Lee's departure: 'Seemingly their intention is to create an impression, especially to the outside world, that things are not going well in this country because they are not in control of affairs.'[8] Reports from the High Commissioner in Canberra, Lee's *bête noire* of 1956–63, Tun Lim Yew Hock, and from the Malaysian Minister of Commerce and Industry who visited Australia immediately after Lee, relayed Lee's critical comments and fuelled the Tunku's apprehension further. So Lee sought out the Tunku to give a personal assurance that he had been loyal throughout his tour, and still was. However, he could not forbear from suggesting constitutional changes, which the Tunku angrily refused to discuss. Shortly afterwards he filed two libel suits against Ja'afar Albar. On the same day, Toh Chin Chye announced a forthcoming convention to consolidate a united opposition front.

With the drama hurtling towards some kind of *dénouement*, the next three months witnessed little self-restraint. On 1 May 1965 Lee called for patience and forbearance, but seemed unable to open his mouth without being provocative. In the *Straits Times* of 29 April, he said, 'Special privileges will help only a small group of Malay bourgeoisie to become capitalists, who will later exploit the poorer section of the people of all races.' Having accepted hitherto that the Malays by and large were the indigenous people or *bumiputras* [literally 'sons of the soil'] he began to assert that none of the three main Malaysian races was more native than the others.

Lee was out of the country for the middle two weeks of May, addressing a socialist youth conference in Bombay and visiting Cambodia and Laos. His intelligence network had homed in on the scheming of some Alliance leaders to arrest him and, he surmised, arrange a prison 'accident' to dispose of him. Through British High Commissioner Lord Head, Harold Wilson, the new British Prime Minister, was alerted and sternly warned the Tunku against any such move. In Phnom Penh Lee held contingency talks with his friend Prince Sihanouk to arrange a base where Rajaratnam could head a government-in-exile should Lee (and possibly Toh) be detained.

Meanwhile, back home, Toh Chin Chye released the finalised plans for the formation of the Malaysia Solidarity Convention (MSC). The announcement came just before the eighteenth UMNO General Assembly was due to begin, and so the potential of the MSC to enrich democracy was overtaken by its threat value. The UMNO leadership had an uphill battle to defeat a resolution from the floor calling for Lee's detention, it being assumed that Toh spoke with Lee's voice in the latter's absence. There were calls also for Radio and Television Singapore to be taken over. The Tunku and Dr Ismail successfully counselled against UMNO playing into Lee's hands or dignifying his terms.

On 21 May Lee returned to Singapore and immediately issued a challenge in the *Straits Times* that drew fresh fire onto himself: 'If we must have trouble, let us have it now instead of waiting for another five or ten years. If we find Malaysia cannot work now, then we can make alternative arrangements.' He laboured the

Solidarity Convention's desire to have the concept of 'Malaysian Malaysia'—a concept at best meaningless to Malays, at worst suggestive of Chinese takeover—written into the Constitution. He denied that the reservation of special rights to Malays was a fundamental provision of the Constitution. He temporarily abandoned the claim that socialism must triumph: before deciding whether capitalism or socialism was appropriate for Malaysia, there were now very basic questions to be resolved—who owns, who belongs to Malaysia? Again, 'if it is necessary to have a Malaysian Malaysia through such a group of parties making an effort to win the majority of seats in Malaysia to form the Government, well, so be it. It has to be done' (*Straits Times* 25 May).

The blatant if reactive communalism of Lee's rhetoric began to stand out. In Australia and New Zealand, he had spoken coolly, cynically, of his optimism for the future because of the easygoing, undisciplined indigenous peoples of Southeast Asia. Now he spoke in heat: 'Let us be quite frank. Why should we go back to old Singapore and once again reduce the non-Malays in Malaya to a minority?'

The Speech from the Throne launched the second session of the Second Malaysian Parliament on 26 May 1965, and things went from bad to worse. An ambiguous reference in the *Agong's* (King's) Speech to 'enemies within' produced a torrent of 'verbal garbage' from all sides, and an unprecedented amendment from Lee to the motion of thanks. Dr Mahathir bin Mohamad led off for the Alliance and left no one in doubt over whom he regarded as internal enemies, cataloguing examples of the PAP's anti-Malay character and of Lee's personal ambition. 'They have never known Malay rule and couldn't bear the idea.' The Socialist Front politician, Tan Chee Khoon, accused the PAP of 'bum-sucking' the UMNO. 'But', he said, 'the love affair between Tunku Abdul Rahman and Lee Kuan Yew has turned sour.' Lee's 'blatant making eyes' at the Government benches less than a year before had ceased.

When Lee rose the next day (27 May), he declared that a new chapter had been reached in the drama of Malaysia. There was a worrying drift in Alliance policy—against legitimate labour concerns, against legitimate public meetings, in postponement of local government elections. If the Tunku 'would say to us publicly what I had the advantage of discussing with him privately two days ago, then I think a lot of fears will be allayed'. Lee insisted that Singapore would not secede—that would be to betray like-minded comrades in Sabah, Sarawak and Malaya (Penang, Malacca, even Johore) into the clutches of 'extremists' such as Ja'afar Albar. With people like Mahathir to hand, what lay ahead for Malaysia? It was not feasible to govern East and West Malaysia using local military forces. Alternative arrangements would be possible. 'I have got certificates to prove . . . that my father and my grandfather before me were born there in Singapore and their labours helped build this little place from the marshland it was, and I have not the slightest intention of allowing it to go back to marshland. Forwards, never backwards! Forwards to a Malaysian Malaysia, never backwards to secession and an isolated and a contained Singapore. That is not progress.' The PAP would demonstrate that it could do as much, if not more, for the Malays and indigenous people. 'We tried to help UMNO members privately, but they wouldn't listen.' 'In ten years we will breed a generation of Malays with educated minds.' There could be no change to Malaysia without state government agreement. Let there be an open contest for Singapore in the next elections. 'We love it; we relish the prospect of a meeting of minds, a conflict of ideas, not of force. We are gentle people who believe very firmly in ideas.' Because the PAP was sufficiently confident that 'the weight on the ground is such that eventually it must emerge', it always 'finds that it pays to play the rules and be loyal'.

Lee's speech was less aggressive than some he had given. It was in fact a committee effort. But the patronising tone of having a 'monopoly of wisdom' conveyed itself and provoked strong reaction, compounded with outrage at PAP hypocrisy. Of the many speeches in Malay and English that followed, Dr Ismail's was the most devastating because he was an independent-minded man not given to public insult.* The PAP, he said, after wooing the Alliance and flirting with the Opposition, had contracted a marriage of expediency with the latter. 'When the time comes, I am sure the PAP will have no compunction to annul the marriage, if we can judge from past experience.' Attempts to impose non-communalism straight away arose from a failure to understand ordinary people's consciousness—they could not forget their race. The PAP method treated everyone like chemicals in a crucible. Singapore's experience of virtual homogeneity disqualified her from pretending to be the measure of Malaysia. Witness the half-hearted support the PAP gave to Malay rights and its stinginess in helping the development of Sabah and Sarawak, despite rhetoric about honouring the Constitution and knowing best how to uplift the Malays and indigenes. Like Dr Jekyll and Mr Hyde, the split personality of

---

* Dr Ismail was the Alliance Government's Minister for Home Affairs and Internal Security at the time.

the PAP could not be concealed for long. 'The public now knows, and the world will soon know, that the PAP is a party whch shouts "Fire! Fire!" while committing arson.' 'Like medieval men, it is easier for them to destroy than to understand a phenomenon which is strange to them' (Dewan Ra'ayat, 31 May 1965).

Lee sought special leave to speak again and produce proof that Alliance extremists wanted Malay dominance of Malaysia. He was promised but not given forty-five minutes by the Speaker. In frustration he summoned a press conference on 3 June and detailed the evidence. The thrust of his remarks was that the UMNO, not only through its 'very high frequency' outlets but even through its so-called moderate leaders, was worsening the 'real danger'— 'Malaysia's own internal weakness'. 'Any regret or vacillation at the cost of upholding Malaysia's integrity against Indonesian aggression would bring catastrophic results for all of us,' he said: 'absorption or conquest by a third power,* 'supremacy of one community over the others in Malaysia' or 'a drift towards . . . the partition of Malaysia'. 'All three have gruesome implications.' The only reasonable alternative was enshrined in PAP/MSC policy, which was not bound up with leadership or election struggles but commended itself by its multiracial, socio-economic logic. 'We are here to protect Malaysians and we intend to do just that.' Lee alleged that he had become the foremost object of attack only because he had the courage to speak the truth openly.

The Tunku remained silent throughout the debate, but not, as the PAP leaders claimed, because he disapproved of the views of his own UMNO extremists. It was left to Tun Razak to say that Lee was not the enemy—yet. Razak appealed to Lee's 'dedicated' colleagues to realise the dangers of the road along which their leader was taking them. He 'is expert at creating a situation which does not exist'. To prove he alone could rule Singapore, he was joining with men he despised to stir up division believing the Tunku would maintain harmony. If trouble broke out 'we must hold him fully responsible'. The Government could cope with him democratically and constitutionally, provided he and his colleagues behaved in the same manner (Dewan Ra'ayat, 3 June 1965).

The cry again went up for drastic action to detain Lee or eject Singapore from Malaysia. Many favoured the former course

---

* Lee explicitly stated he did not necessarily mean Indonesia when he referred to a 'third power'. Who then? The USA? Britain and the Commonwealth? An Asian power?

because of their concern for Singapore's Malays. The Tunku acknowledged how disturbed he was. Just before he left for London and the Prime Ministers' Conference he expressed willingness to deal with Lee's problems, then added, 'I wish I had not listened to all that persuasive talk before ... Then Malaya would still be a very happy Malaya—no confrontation, nothing.'[9] Lee saw him off at the airport in Singapore and later claimed the Tunku was embarrassed by the farewell because he had been entertaining proposals for the Singapore leader's detention.

A few days after the Tunku had left, Ong Eng Guan resigned his seat of Hong Lim and renounced politics. Lee said later he suspected there were 'some very good reasons of a cogent and probably attractive character' why Ong had resigned. He 'believed that the plot was to bring about a PAP defeat by the Communists'.[10] The absence of an Alliance candidate in the ensuing by-elections certainly made it look that way, as did the Alliance and *Utusan Melayu* support for the Barisan candidate Ong Cheng Sam. The truth may rather be that the newly reorganised Alliance hoped to win the seat itself but was prevented from fielding a candidate because the Singapore Registrar of Societies did not register the party in time. The point of then giving support to the Barisan would have been to retaliate for being outwitted, as well as to put the PAP in a vulnerable position. A PAP defeat could justify repressive measures against Singapore, or against her leaders, at the very least.

Late in June the Tunku was admitted to a London clinic, to receive treatment for shingles. On his sick bed he drew up a balance sheet for and against Malaysia retaining Singapore. 'Every movement caused grinding pain, but the mind was alive and active; so as I laid [*sic*] there I was thinking of Mr Lee Kuan Yew. The more pain I got the more I directed my anger on him ...'[11] Lee was making all the Tunku's plans for Malaysia unworkable. The heady mix of Islam and Malay consciousness was no longer under his moderating control, and it was beginning to radicalise UMNO. Every time some attempt, however low key, was made to unite the Malays, Lee would draw attention to it and demand that it be stopped. Even the definition of Sabah and Sarawak indigenes as Malays—which might have allowed the Tunku to weaken the nexus between 'Malay' and 'Muslim'—was held up to ridicule by Lee as a naive mistake, as bad arithmetic. The genial and benevolent partnership of Malay aristocrat, Chinese *compradore* and British capitalist was under premature siege by Lee's appeal to the 'have nots' of all races on the basis of a socialism not even proven in urban Singapore. Ostensibly Lee had accepted the Tunku's leadership for the time being, yet he continued to apply pressure directly or through the British Government (to many of whose members and local diplomatic representatives he was known to be close) to secure a direct role for himself in the nation's management. A happy Malaya, or Malaysia embracing the Borneo territories with their economic and cultural advantages, and with their disagreeable aspects minimised by the intervening sea, was being threatened by this impatient and ambitious young man. The only beneficiaries would be the communists or the fanatics, both of whom were waiting eagerly for their main chance.

The arrest and replacement of Lee, the military and economic subjugation of Singapore or its expulsion, were three solutions that had been proposed at different times. The first two were distasteful, not only in themselves but because they admitted defeat on the part of the Alliance Party and could prove costly and counter-productive sooner or later. The third would certainly solve one set of problems, but might well create another—for example, the status of the British bases; apparent abandonment of the island's Malays; loss of control over what was perceived as a centre of communist subversion whilst being equally an economic powerhouse.

The Tunku reached a tentative decision on or about 29 June. It corresponded to what had been his instinct all along. He had put his concern to Lim Kim San, a PAP minister in his London delegation. He wrote to Razak and asked him to discuss separation with the Cabinet seniors. Coincidentally Razak and Lee met that same day at the latter's request, but reached a stalemate.

The Singapore Cabinet had been looking at separation as one possibility for many months. Clearly it was more agreeable to some than to others. Goh Keng Swee and Lim Kim San enjoyed friendly personal links with their federal counterparts but were hardliners against accommodation with the Alliance, especially on the common market and Singapore's contribution to federal revenues. They drew up contingency plans for Singapore's survival as an independent economic and political entity. On the other hand, Toh Chin Chye and Rajaratnam were all for using any leverage, domestic or international, to prevent Singapore and the PAP being rendered inoperative within Malaysia. Lee was torn in two. He strove to explore every avenue of pressure or negotiation, only to frustrate success by reasserting his own terms. He sent emissaries to Razak, sought direct meetings with him: then laid down defiant conditions or dealt out blanket condemnations of 'them', the other side.

Out of Malaysia

During the Hong Lim campaign Lee's confidant and press agent, Alex Josey, was given fourteen days to leave. Rajaratnam described the move as *makan kechil* (*hors d'oeuvres*) 'to whet the appetite of the extremists for the main dish—the arrest of Mr Lee'.[12] The Bank of China in Singapore was also ordered closed. Tunku Abdul Rahman defended these actions taken in his absence, and denied that a case was being made for Lee's arrest.

The Hong Lim result on 10 July showed the PAP firmly in command, having gained 60 per cent of the vote. But it was a Pyrrhic victory for Lee as regards Kuala Lumpur. His plea of 1961—'take Singapore in before the situation becomes uncontrollable'—had been exaggerated for effect. Now it was groundless.

It appears that further conciliatory approaches were made by the British Government through Lord Head. One such was to include acceptable PAP leaders in the central government while Lee went off as Malaysian Ambassador to the United Nations. Josey says none of the approaches was 'ever seriously considered by the Alliance Government—or by Lee Kuan Yew':[13] certainly true of the former, since Lord Head's close association and frequent dining with Lee destroyed the credibility of a would-be disinterested negotiator.

The final days

The Tunku returned home through Singapore on 5 August. He had set the machinery for separation in train—though not irreversibly—eleven days earlier, having weighed up the Josey affair and the lack of official British fuss over it, the Hong Lim results, and finally Razak's letter expressing senior Cabinet members' agreement that Singapore go its own way. On Friday 6 August he, Razak and three colleagues resolved to proceed. Goh Keng Swee, already in Kuala Lumpur, was informed, and he telephoned Lee.

Lee was with his family in the Cameron Highlands: in his words 'even a submarine has got to surface and breathe'. He had gone there, as always, for refuge, feeling the pressure and fearing the inevitable. Now, on Goh's summons, he drove at breakneck speed to the capital. The time was over for pretending to others—and to himself?—that Malaysia could hold together indefinitely, that Singapore, or at least he, could triumph within Malaysia against all odds. This would be the showdown, and the Tunku must be faced calmly.

The Singapore Cabinet was hastily assembled and arrived at the Tunku's official residence on Saturday morning. The others must shoulder collective responsibility with their leader for immediate decisions and consequences. Agreement would be difficult. Goh had already accepted the necessity of separation; several of the others had not. Lee reckoned that there were still ways of holding on and reducing communal tensions. But his bargaining position was not only fragile; it was solitary.

As they waited, talked in a desultory fashion, made notes, their counterparts in the inner Federal Cabinet arrived to meet with the Tunku. Only one of them acknowledged Lee: Dr Ismail saw that the Singapore leader, unusually vulnerable, had picked up a golf putter and was toying with it, so he went over and the two men putted in turn for a few minutes.

Around midday Lee was summoned into private session with the Tunku. He put forward his proposals. They were rejected as too late. 'I knew from what he said—and he has an intuition about these matters—that we would all be in for big communal trouble if Singapore, or if I and my colleagues, insisted on going on with Malaysia as it is.'[14] The argument that 'blood will flow', used often to tame the MCA by UMNO leaders in the past and derided by Lee only two months previously, apparently convinced him this time. However, a number of his colleagues felt very strongly against separation; since the Tunku was unwilling to meet them, Lee extracted from him a note to Toh Chin Chye. Lee saw the Tunku again on Sunday 8 August, with Toh Chin Chye's reply and the signed separation agreement, and explained, probably as a last-ditch plea, how unhappy some of his colleagues were. Just before he signed the agreement himself, following his Saturday meeting with the Tunku, Lee told Tan Siew Sin, 'Today is the day of your victory, the day of my defeat; but five or ten years later, you certainly will feel sad about it.'[15]

On Sunday 8 August the Alliance National Council and the Government Ministers and State Chief Ministers were informed. News leaked to the British High Commissioner and he and his Australian counterpart Tom Critchley (who was much closer to the Tunku than Lord Head was) made unsuccessful bids that day, that night (at a party), and the next morning to have the separation postponed at least. On Monday 9 August the Tunku in the Dewan and Lee at Singapore's City Hall simultaneously announced the break, and the two houses of Federal Parliament processed the necessary three readings of the legislation without delay or opposition.*

---

* Devan Nair expressed regret; Syed Ja'afar Albar was warned by Dr Ismail beforehand just outside the chamber not to go and speak against Separation (he resigned forthwith as UMNO Secretary General).

During the morning, firecrackers were let off in Singapore's Chinatown. At noon, Lee gave a press conference. He was on the verge of tears as he called for calm. He recalled the events immediately preceding separation, and went on, 'Every time we look back on this moment when we signed the agreement which severed Singapore from Malaysia, it will be a moment of anguish. For me it is a moment of anguish . . . It broke everything we stood for.' At this point 'Mr Lee broke down. Tears rolled down his cheeks. For a moment he buried his face in his hands. He started to speak, then broke down again. Apologetically he said he was far too angry to go on with the subject' (*Straits Times*, 10 August 1965).

Singapore was independent. It was some kind of release for all the principals concerned and for most Singaporeans after the years of tension and bickering. It was a release for Lee too, but not of a kind he welcomed. Whatever advantages good fortune or management could wring from Separation lay only in the future. The notion that Lee was secretly pleased about events at the time is completely wrong.[16]

Reaction

> 'Chinese believe that tears are not mere manifestations of uncontrollable emotion. They are, legitimately, the recognised expression of patriotism, loyalty or filial piety . . . At the press conference, Lee Kuan Yew . . . broke down and wept so bitterly that proceedings had to be suspended for some twenty minutes. Lee's grief was sincere enough. Human defence mechanisms are traitors, however, and he was in danger of facing the press with a quite deceptive and unbecoming composure if he failed to give way. But it was meet that he should weep, and the tears were there, requiring no bidding.'[17]

Josey quotes these words of Dennis Bloodworth but adds, 'After the Conference, Lee Kuan Yew said he had wept for the Chinese left behind in Malaysia.'[18] The added sentence disarms Bloodworth's eagerness to explain Lee by the traditions of his race. There was far more to the Prime Minister's tears than ritual grief. Self-pity and rage were dominant, together with frustration at his helplessness.

For months afterwards, his colleagues recollected, it was impossible to calm Lee: even in public he would vent his feelings towards 'them', his adversaries. In the first days after Separation he could not hold back tears when he talked, very feelingly, of Devan Nair and his family and the hardships they would face as Devan carried a solitary torch for the PAP across the Causeway; when he made bitter allegations that his former Marxist friend, Samad Ismail, was up to mischief in Kuala Lumpur amongst UMNO leaders. Toh Chin Chye was obliged to cancel press conferences and take on extra responsibilities to minimise embarrassment all round.

Separation opened the floodgates that Lee had kept shut or almost shut for years. Over that period his doctor had prescribed drugs to calm him down, drugs to pick him up. Some in Lee's circle, including other medical men, felt that commonsense advice had been neglected because of a pharmaceutical bias to his doctor's training. The drugs had an innocuous enough effect when Lee could see his way through situations, but under the enormous strain of recent events their impact was curious and unpredictable. One moment Lee could be smiling, offering the Tunku a brittle picture of acceptance, even some sort of pleasure. The next moment when he was near people with whom he could allow himself to relax—colleagues, selected foreign journalists, subordinates—he would burst into tears or pour forth a torrent of emotion-laden words, recollections, predictions.

Malaysia had begun belatedly in 1963, on Lee's birthday, 16 September, a coincidence on which he remarked. And now, against all natural law, Singapore had been cast out after less than two years. Even though restraint might be prescribed to help both Malaysia and Singapore survive in a hostile environment, Lee dropped his guard over and over again. If Singapore could have been governed by the gun indefinitely without breaking whoever tried to do it, he said, 'I think it would have been tried' by the British, 'or I think by us', or by the central government.[19] 'We will trade with the devil'[20] in the event of no economic co-operation between Malaysia and Singapore. 'I don't want to speak about Devan Nair because I feel too strongly about him'.[21] The Tunku has had it . . . we want him—not because I like him . . . I was even prepared to serve under Dr Toh.[22] 'You know, I am deadly scared of assassination.'[*,23]

Although he could no longer help Malaysia to progress, he still believed himself responsible for two million people directly and nine million indirectly. Under the strain, his normal self-control failed all too obviously. 'Anger does not help,' he said in the midst

---

[*] Security arrangements for Lee were quickly stepped up after Separation—he was aware of an intermediary being used to organise a 'kerfuffle'. He also alleged that communists had tried to assassinate him.

of a tirade against the Malaysian leaders; 'silence is golden' was another unlikely motto he set himself. He even revealed some of his methods of handling stubborn or lackadaisical Singaporeans.

Reluctantly he admitted that he was for the moment the 'exchange' with all the 'lines open'. He was first among equals, 'probably because I was born and bred in Singapore'.[24] 'I am a common man, a small man,' he said on another occasion.[25] Yet despite his protestations he could not deny or escape the reality of his position. Everything flowed through him.

Apart from Devan Nair, Lee pointed to no one else who was bearing the burden of Separation as he was. Some of his colleagues were almost *blasé* about it. Perhaps this is why he noted caustically that 'Hitler was a corporal' like Goh Keng Swee.[26] Others who had resisted, such as Toh Chin Chye, had needed admonition to bring them to their senses. Could they not see, as he saw with terrible clarity, the likely scenario if Separation were not accepted? It would mean incarceration of the PAP leadership, popular pressure for their release, elections and PAP victory, incarceration again, denial of further ballots and imposition of martial law—leaving no alternative to Singapore, without bullets or PAP organisation, but to go in with the communists.[27] What of Ja'afar Albar's more extreme plan: to suspend the constitution and rule Singapore directly, imprisoning Lee? This would precipitate establishment of a government-in-exile from Phnom Penh, as arranged with Sihanouk, and all hell breaking loose if any Chinese were killed.[28]

By rights Singapore should have been able to advance economically and politically to a dominant position in Malaysia. Lee had played every card he had. He had retained the nomenclature, instruments and style of an alternative central government, even developing a distinctive foreign policy. He had worked on British friends and courted international attention. He had primed his intelligence network: his brother, Freddy, was put in charge of airport police; his 'bodyguards' were made available to visiting Malayan VIPs; Special Branch, MI5 and other informants kept him briefed on Alliance moves beyond his official due. He had rallied and manipulated key leaders in East and West Malaysia. He had relied on the Tunku as 'a long stop and a contrast':[29] he and his Government had made significant strides in organising Singapore whilst claiming liberality in handling unions or dissidents compared with Kuala Lumpur.

Not all of Lee's ploys had worked: for example, the arrangement of television camera shots to show the Tunku to disadvantage when they made joint appearances was a little too subliminal. Again, the

Singapore NTUC held a rally in April 1965 to attack the PAP Government's delay in meeting union claims, it was supposed to counter accusations of NTUC servility, but only provoked scorn and louder accusations. The most blatant example occurred when Lee pressed Dr Ismail repeatedly to introduce a Suitability Certificate for university entrants, then pretended in the Dewan debate on the measure to accept it half-heartedly. During the parliamentary lunch break Ismail threatened to tell all unless Lee gave him full backing.

But the more basic problem was the insuperable weakness in Singapore's position. Dependence on water from Johore meant that 'we cannot destroy the position of the Malaysian Government'; conversely, quitting Malaysia only increased dependence. Staying in meant no Singapore Government control of police or army, and Tan Siew Sin's threatened foreclosure on the Bank of China would have jeopardised the precious flow of cheap goods that upheld the living standards of Singapore's Chinese masses.

Another consideration aroused Lee to fury. What role was the United States of America playing? On 30 August he launched his famous attack on the Americans and their lack of civilisation. During a press conference, he cited three incidents from his own experience. The first was a CIA attempt to bribe a Singapore Special Branch officer some years earlier and the Kennedy Administration's subsequent efforts to buy reparation. The second was the failure of State Department officials to offer him and Dr Goh the courtesies of protocol at US airports when they flew in to defend Singapore's merger proposals before the United Nations. Lastly he condemned the 'impudence and impertinence' of American specialists expecting someone very close to him (his wife) to fly to Switzerland or the US for (gynaecological) treatment.

He did say later, 'My personal bitterness is irrelevant in matters of national policy.'[30] Surely such an outright claim could only be considered self-deluding in a man whose political judgment was so manifestly coloured by his own experience and reactions. Yet personal bitterness has rarely been a sufficient explanation of Lee's public behaviour. In this case he was deeply worried that the Americans' growing closeness to the Tunku's government might lead irresistibly to them filling the vacuum if the British became disillusioned and withdrew. The assessment of an Australian academic, K.G. Tregonning, who talked with Lee on his birthday (16 September 1965) may be closer to the mark. 'Mr Lee's criticisms of American maladroitness in his personal affairs were calculated sops, to save America's face from the unpalatable truth that, in his estimation, if it intervened it would make any situation in Malaysia far worse than it was.'

His son's *Reader's Digest*, 'in simple language for simple Americans', stated that the ultimate objective of the US presence in Vietnam was to control the Straits of Malacca.[31] Lee accused the Americans of buying and selling leaders in Korea and Vietnam;[32] and 'if they go in and help the racist groups there [Malaysia] and brutalise the country . . . we cannot stand by and do absolutely nothing and sit idly watching. We are one people'.[33] Two years later he mused on the strangeness of US policy—supporting the Israelis in the Middle East and Muslims in Southeast Asia.[34]

It is hard to ascertain Lee's explanation of Malaysia's break-up. At first he said the smacking down of six people only, the 'mad mullahs' would have been sufficient to preserve the nation. He spoke of a closed, traditional society envying and, worse, fearing the honest, effective and open Singapore administration. He labelled as critical the failure of Australia and Britain to heed his urgent pleas. Later he looked for more conspiratorial theories. Lim Kim San contended in 1976 that Singapore was expelled because it had thwarted the Tunku's plan: there was one spare point of the Malaysian star in the national flag, waiting for a chastened Singapore to return.[35] Lee made the same contention some months later on 23 February 1977 in Parliament: 'And the expectation was that in two to three years we would be so down on our knees and crawling that we would have to go back on any terms. No autonomy . . . Maybe if they were kind, like Penang and Malacca.' What was the Tunku's plan supposed to be? Economic exploitation of Singapore? Forcible assimilation?

In 1969, after the notorious Malaysian 'May 13th' riots, Lee told the boys of his old school that Malaysia 'was not workable, not for reasons of personality, conflict of leadership, but for fundamental reasons'.[36] By 1981 he was apportioning some blame to the PAP for precipitating the crisis that culminated in Separation. He referred to two CEC decisions made while he was out of Singapore: to contest the mainland elections of 1964 and to forge the Malaysian Solidarity Convention. 'These two decisions were momentous. I did not take part in either of them. I made discreet enquiries—Chin Chye and Rajaratnam led the CEC in taking them. Inevitably, though none of us knew then, they led to one Saturday on the 7th of August at Temasek [Singapore Government residence], Kuala Lumpur.'[37] Technically Lee is right about the decisions. It must be recalled, however, that neither of them was made without debate long beforehand, debate in which Lee participated or which he knew about.

He adds, 'It is not possible for us the participants to weigh objectively the contribution of each other and of so many others to the sum total result'.[38] Objectively or not, it is clear he has held on to one absolute conviction throughout—that he was the wounded one, that he bore no responsibility at all for what had gone wrong. History had been cruel, skewing merger negotiations to the advantage of the peninsula through the postwar division of Singapore and Malaya, and through Kuala Lumpur coming up the straight to win autonomy before Singapore.

This evidence of this and many other examples suggests that whenever Lee anticipated an embarrassing or distressing outcome, he tried to walk away from the trigger decision. With the prospect looming of a flashpoint for Malaysia, not only was he absent in Africa, Australasia, elsewhere in Asia, and lastly in the Cameron Highlands, but he wanted it believed that he had nothing to do with what might have been about to happen.

Four points of interest will serve to round off this review of the Malaysia period.

Firstly, the paradoxical contrast of the leadership ensembles in Kuala Lumpur and Singapore. The Alliance Cabinet was united in personal loyalty to the Tunku, yet had no co-ordinated programme for tackling the problems of inter-communal rivalry and consequent intra-communal tension. Increasingly UMNO became polarised and the MCA weakened. (Lee had contributed to these tendencies.) On the other hand the PAP Cabinet, whilst not united by personal affection or loyalty towards Lee, could not be cracked open. Either in hope of some future re-merger or in relief that the pressure was off, its members recognised that 'the PAP Government could henceforth concentrate its energies on the economic and social problems that beset Singapore'.[39] Lee's secret was not his popularity but his ability to absorb colleagues' economic or political agenda within his larger designs and in the name of a PAP that must resist both communalism and communism.

The second observation is linked to the first. The initiative for Malaysia was commandeered by Lee. But he acted almost always in concert with his team. The Tunku, once he decided to run with the ball, often left his colleagues and his mandate far behind. This personalising of the leadership had worse long-term effects on Malaysia than on Singapore, on the Tunku, Tun Razak and Tan Siew Sin than on Lee.

The other two points both relate to the secrecy of the Separation moves. Lee said in August 1966 there had been no time for consultation and consensus-seeking over such a fateful decision. The Cabinet had been 'gradually embroiled in something which we half suspected but never quite admitted was possible'. Henceforth they would adopt the esoteric role of prophets talking in parables.[40] But a precedent was set, however unavoidable at the time (given fears of racial trouble), for fundamental policy to be decided and enacted without seeking a popular mandate. The Malaysian Government has not been loath to fall back on the precedent, and the Singapore Government has perfected the use of elections to endorse decisions already made. In both countries democracy suffered a body blow.

At the crucial last stage, the British and other friendly powers had been excluded from resolving the conflict. The Tunku did not want more pressure for an accommodation with Lee, nor was Lee for his part about to knuckle under because of British urging. Was the withdrawal of British forces from Southeast Asia hastened by Separation—since the Singapore bases no longer guaranteed Britain a watertight excuse to intervene in local and regional politics for reasons of self-interest under the guise of altruism?

The date of 9 August 1965 marked the beginning of a new era. Singapore's strategic importance was, if anything, enhanced by Separation. It would be a serious mistake for anyone to mock at the island's enforced return to the indignity of smallness and isolation. Lee Kuan Yew might have led his people energetically down a blind alley, but after the initial shock of such a reverse his imagination would be rekindled to seek and open up more promising paths to glory.

9TH OF AUGUST

I

A proclamation, gently colonial:
Singapore shall forever be ...
We think he sought alternatives
But failed against those minds.
They had been fingered through
By a hoard of words, spumed
Across the *Ra'ayat:*
Their call became a prayer
In firm ancestral beckoning.

Some say his clever tongue
That bruised so painfully,
Made it difficult;
Others that he merely rummaged through
Such bigotry,
While holding forth that we were merely firm.

And now we are more silent
Harder on ourselves
Waiting for the years to bring back
Commonsense.

II

He sought alternatives, for us;
But how could he against
Minds that had been fingered through
By a hoard of words, spumed
Across the *Ra'ayat*
Till their call became a prayer
In firm ancestral beckoning.

They kicked us out ...

One laughed, and called for coffee,
Another didn't turn a hair.
Many quoted him, picked a word, a gesture
Suitable to their history .... their mood ...
Forgetting his crying eyes meant much.

For us what then?
Make strangers out of friends
To face each other till the bitter end.

EDWIN THUMBOO

8
A Place in the Sun

> I have decided that we shall make and build and never give way.
>
> LEE KUAN YEW,
> 27 December 1966

Only well into 1966 could Lee Kuan Yew begin to talk calmly of the future. Apart from any instability on the regional front, he had a personal prejudice to overcome, one long shared by the PAP leadership, that the idea of a small island nation was a political joke.

Not that there was any shortage of instability. The future of Sabah and Sarawak was placed in doubt by Singapore's eviction from Malaysia, and for a time their secession seemed a definite possibility. Other problems loomed large; what would become of the Malays in Singapore and the Chinese in West Malaysia? Which way would the Americans move, not only in Vietnam, but with regard to Malaysia, Singapore and Indonesia?

Indonesia's turmoil was the immediate concern. A coup attempt and counter-coup occurred less than two months after Separation—the September 30th Movement and its aftermath—and, while the heat was taken from Confrontation, the prospects for future relations were uncertain. Kuala Lumpur warned that Singapore would have to choose between Malaysia and Indonesia in establishing diplomatic ties. Meanwhile, the Malaysian Government was holding secret talks with the Indonesians to rebuild Malay brotherhood.

The lines were drawn across the Causeway. Tariff restrictions were applied; all prospect of a common market or economic union disappeared. The Singapore Government announced its determination to pursue barter trade with Indonesia. Threats of work permits and double taxation were bandied about.

From time to time, insults and querulous diplomatic notes passed back and forth. A major potential blow-up was averted at the last minute in February 1966. Singapore troops coming home from border duty in Borneo expected to resume their own barracks, which were still occupied by Malaysians. A foreign journalist pieced together scraps of information and deduced that trouble was at hand. He gained an interview with the Prime Minister and, after running the gauntlet of Lee's anger and accusations that he was a Malaysian *agent provocateur*, he agreed not to file the story for publication unless it became clear that someone else was about to do so. Hurried activity behind the scenes followed, forcing the British High Commissioner to leave his sick bed. Within a few days the Tunku announced that the British would kindly make quarters available to resolve the problem. The journalist lost his story.[1]

Despite the Tunku's optimistic prediction that absence would make the two nations' hearts grow fonder, the bitterness of the leaders, Lee and Tan Siew Sin in particular, simmered on and sometimes boiled over, preventing any calm discussion. The manifest relief of the majority races of Singapore and West Malaysia at being free of each other provided no counterthrust towards reunification.

A new identity

Singapore again became, and this time quite avowedly, an enclave in Southeast Asia. Lee computed the perils of the situation. 'If *Utusan Melayu* and the extremists get the Muslims in the region worked up, we may grow from two million to seven million: we would have to throw out a life line,' he told civil servants on 30 September 1965.

He persisted in this theme well after the first flush of rage at Separation. 'If you insist on treating a person as a political liability on the basis of race, then eventually he must coalesce in self-defence,' he said, alleging that Chinese from Malaysia, Australia, New Zealand and South Africa had gathered in Singapore because they had not been happy in these other countries.[2]

Lee has never rejoiced in the thought of a vast influx of Chinese into Singapore. He categorically refused to open the island to Chinese fleeing Indonesia. He told the Tamil community in February 1966 that he could not allow more Indian immigration, or he would have to permit entry to Chinese too. He set his face resolutely against soft-headedness in the matter of Indo-Chinese refugees: Singapore has resisted what he has spoken of as Vietnam's cynical attempt to destabilise the region by expelling indiscriminate numbers of Chinese into it. 'We either grow calluses or we will die of bleeding hearts.'[3]

A Place in the Sun

The danger and promise of being an enclave have dominated Lee's thinking from August 1965. The images he first summoned for independent Singapore—linchpin, sparking-plug, eye, oasis, yeast—all communicated the importance, the vitality, the intensity of the little island in contrast to its 'peripheral regions'. According to his New Year message for 1966, 'We are building a sane, stable, tolerant and prosperous society' despite the surrounding *milieu* of poverty, intolerance and xenophobia. But the images also reached for a context, a larger whole, in which Singapore could be a shining centrepiece.

Singapore has discovered a kind of economic and spiritual hinterland through becoming a global city. However, this has not solved the specific problems of living within a tight girdle imposed by immediate neighbours. One of Lee's major frustrations was at the sudden curtailment of the space he needed to build a new civilisation.

'This is the southernmost tip of Asia and we are linked with that continent by that causeway and it cannot be destroyed,' he said to civil servants on 30 September 1965. '*Half of it belongs to us. Even if the other half they want to destroy, our half will remain our half. We are at once in a most commanding and, at the same time, a most hazardous position*' [italics added].

For a time he talked openly of his continuing responsibility to all Malaysians, of Singapore's need to 'come up tough'[4] and to negotiate re-merger with Kuala Lumpur from a much stronger position Referring both to his neighbours and to the wider world, he predicted graphically that Singapore would become a poisonous shrimp making things very unpleasant for any bigger fish trying to swallow her.

At all costs, however, some way had to be found of ensuring that there would be a future. It was too awful to contemplate Singapore being engulfed. Lee turned the atmosphere of brinkmanship and crisis to unusual effect. He took to calculating how far he wanted to raise the stakes for those more distant nations that claimed to be players at the table. His approach to their governments was nothing if not frank and frontal; he seemed almost to be daring them *not* to come to Singapore's aid.

For instance, one proposal floated by Goh and Lee was that Australia should become a raw materials base, sending partly processed products to be finished in Singapore for regional export and marketing. The tie-up would have jeopardised Australia's friendly relations with the government in Kuala Lumpur and linked her more closely to Singapore than to New Zealand. Moreover, the practical problems posed for Australia by such a plan would have been insuperable in view of existing trade and aid arrangements. When it was firmly rejected, Lee and Goh displayed no qualms about mocking and berating successive Australian governments for every sin imaginable. Revenge was doubly sweet when they could win concessions from their failed partner.

Again, the result of Lee's virulent post-Separation attack on the American, was not only to stay the British and Commonwealth hand but to provoke a revised US strategic view of Singapore that took greater account of the region's racial tensions and the island's potential advantages. It was not long before Lee was being courted by the Americans, from President Johnson downwards, and being praised as Southeast Asia's most dynamic leader. His trenchant criticisms of US immaturity and gaucheness reaped remarkably handsome rewards.

The history of Singapore's bases is yet another case in point. Britain's moves to disengage east of Suez, prompted both by a hard-learned and more realistic sense of proportion about her global role and by the desire for substantial savings, had been looming for some time, particularly in Labour circles. Lee's rhetorical flourishes, asserting that the whip hand was his, and Singapore's ejection from Malaysia played their part in hastening withdrawal. Yet when timetables for closing the bases were announced in 1967 and foreshortened in early 1968 following the devaluation of sterling, Lee blustered away and was able to wring astounding and untypical concessions, delays and compensation from both Labour and Tory governments. By the end of 1971, Singapore emerged from the fracas relatively unscathed and probably much stronger.

With the passing years, Lee's desire for space has appeared in more subdued form. The change of heart was signalled when he threw his weight behind the Association of Southeast Asian Nations (ASEAN) in the mid-1970s. ASEAN is by no means a surrogate for peninsular Malaysia, but if properly handled and if fortune is kind, it can provide an attractive setting in which the jewel of Singapore can radiate or refract light to the Pacific basin and the world.

An important distinction needs to be made at this point. Lee is rightly uneasy about being cast as leader of the overseas Chinese. His primary stated concern is with his island's advancement and prosperity, originally through merger and now alone. Any judgment, particularly by regional groups, that Singapore is purely a Chinese phenomenon is not only belittling but dangerous. As far as Lee is concerned, the island's success and influence are not measured by the cynical or misguided recognition they receive, but by their intrinsic merits.

In passing, it is worth speculating on Singapore's reaction to the worst that could happen to her from outside. (A communist uprising from within is unthinkable; anyway, it would provoke intervention from Malaysia and Indonesia.) Given their Israeli-style orientation, what would the island republic's armed forces do? What if the communists were able to advance through Thailand and then into the north of the peninsula or come across the South China Sea as the Japanese and the refugees did? How would Singapore respond if Kuala Lumpur called for help to meet such a threat?

What if racial war erupted on the other side of the Causeway? For a long time, suspicion was voiced in Malaysia of Singapore training troops for jungle warfare (using facilities in Brunei, Taiwan and Thailand), requesting permanent air space rights or suggesting duplication of the Causeway. Would Singapore attempt to sequester the southern portion of the peninsula? How would her own Malays fare? There is a troubling ambiguity about Singapore's position that limits open discussion, for fear of making things worse. The only prediction that can be confidently made is that Indonesia and the superpowers would not be detached spectators in the event of trouble.

Singapore and her Malay neighbours

Lee Kuan Yew found it hard to put behind him the trauma of the Malaysia years. To be sure, the tasks of building a new and viable Singapore claimed much of his energy. It was a relief not to have to worry about the rural sector. But the outrage remained—all that money and effort wasted, all those political opportunities lost, the endless stupidity of his opponents—and, sharpened by fear, it spurred him on more than ever to beat the odds against survival.

The course of relations between the governments of Malaysia and Singapore has taken many a twist and turn over the two decades since Separation. At first there was the pronounced worsening noted above. The logic of the chief actors' words and deeds, their intense competition to determine the future, had to work itself out before a more co-operative style was possible. Aided by close colleagues and by valiant self-discipline, Lee achieved a measure of insulation from the cut and thrust of abuse. There were occasional spectacular lapses: on 17 October 1965 he addressed a Singapore union gathering and attacked Malaysia for being a medieval feudal society. But he vented most of his spleen in private. By 1968 it was possible for him to demote Jek Yeun Thong from the Ministry of Labour on the grounds that Jek had bungled the plan to introduce permits for Malaysian workers, provoking undue controversy and forcing Singapore to back down.

The relationship entered a stand-off period from 1968 to 1976. Although each side had its token value to the other as a whipping boy, the most provocative incident probably occurred when the hair of three Malay youths was cut while they were visiting Singapore in 1970. The disastrous Malaysian race riots of May 1969 could not be attributed simply to Singapore's interference, even though the Democratic Action Party (DAP) was successor to the PAP and its celebration of electoral gains did fan the fires. The most that could fairly be said was that Lee was stirring the pot from a distance—he had the sense to be overseas—and that he had a previous record of inflaming racial tensions. Conversely, the Tunku's clumsy handling of the communal and religious issues that surfaced so often after Malaysia's formation and his unilateral ejection of Singapore established two trends: Lee became a saviour figure in the eyes of many Chinese Malaysians when they realised they no longer had effective political representation from the partnership of the MCA and the Tunku; and the Tunku and UMNO lost ground among the Malays for not affording them sufficient protection and advancement. Needless to say, the Tunku made vigorous efforts before the elections to implicate Lee, charging massive infusion of funds, training and counsel. But the distressing aftermath of the 'May 13th' flare-up had far more plausible explanations and required such urgent attention that attempts to blame Singapore receded into the background.

Visits on both sides, mostly unofficial, and obligatory rounds of golf helped prevent the channels of communication from closing, although irritation and provocation were never far from the supposedly businesslike surface of the negotiating table. The two nations institutionalised their separation by various measures affecting currency and stock market arrangements, by breaking down Malaysia Singapore Airlines into two new entities and by rationalising immigration procedures. Malaysia undertook to provide many more tertiary training opportunities: one of Lee's continuing complaints was that Malaysian students were always among the ringleaders of dissent in Singapore's colleges of higher learning; besides, it was in the interests of the Malaysian Government to have control of its own education system.

The two governments could never draw close while their leading figures viewed each other so negatively. For his part Lee was agitated by what he perceived as the ineptitude of the Malaysians. He feared that 1969's May 13th riots and bloodshed would pave the communists' way to power; it was hard for him to credit Kuala Lumpur with the common sense to take countermeasures. In fact, the armed forces were built up very rapidly and weapons were supplied to selected civilian areas. Far from being allowed to exploit the situation, the communists themselves split into two factions. When talking among his associates Lee consistently failed to accord due recognition to Tun Abdul Razak, who took over the day-to-day running of the country after the May 1969 crisis and succeeded the Tunku as Prime Minister in September 1970. Less biased commentators would want to praise Razak for acting with such aplomb—in a real sense he saved the nation and set it on a new course, broadening the Alliance to incorporate non-racially based parties into a new Barisan Nasional [National Front]—but Lee was apt to say that his Malaysian counterpart was not up to handling leftists and extremists at home, let alone the leaders of the non-aligned movement or the *politburos* of Moscow and Beijing, with all of whom Razak established contact. Lee ridiculed the Malaysian proposal for a Zone of Peace, Friendship and Neutrality (ZOPFAN); he repeatedly alleged that, at the instigation of the MCA and other Malaysian groups, adventurers were attempting 'black operations' to destabilise Singapore and that Kuala Lumpur was failing to hold them in check.

On the Malaysian side; the early 1960s had seen the Tunku go out on a limb partly in pursuit of his own agenda and partly because Lee had been such a plausible advocate of merger with Singapore. The unfolding of events had damaged the Tunku's standing as the nation's 'father' caring for all races, and his popularity reached its nadir in 1969: there was, therefore, a certain poetic justice when he tried to blame Lee for making trouble during the lead-up to the May elections.

The passing years had not given the Tunku's deputy and successor, Tun Razak, any reason to stop worrying and start to love Lee. Although, theoretically, he should have understood Lee—having known him since 1939—the latter unnerved him, and Razak was inclined to take Dr Ismail's advice: 'Don't talk to that fellow too long—he'll persuade you of anything!' Whilst not yielding to blandishment, demand or threat from Singapore or elsewhere, Razak was not as adept as Lee at manipulating the foreign press, and he tended to give the appearance of not being fully in control. Some have suggested that it was not for their left-wing credentials that Razak appointed aides and advisers but for their unwavering hostility to Lee. The reality is that Razak was far less mesmerised by Lee than the latter might have cared to suppose. The Malaysian Prime Minister implemented national reconstruction, rural development, economic planning and foreign policy with a degree of attention to socialist orthodoxy alien to the Tunku and beyond Lee's reach.

Nonetheless it is true that of that generation—the Tunku, Razak, Tan Siew Sin, and so on—only Tun Ismail was relatively relaxed in handling the Singapore premier; accordingly, he was often called on to negotiate. Even the younger, more technocratic leaders were flummoxed by Lee's style; Tengku Razaleigh, Finance Minister for some years, could not believe his eyes when he saw how Lee and Goh steam-rollered British, Malaysian and Singaporean participants in the *débâcle* of the 1975 takeover of the giant Haw Par conglomerate by Slater Walker.

With Ismail's death, and then Razak's in early 1976, the whole tenor of relations changed. A key figure who influenced the change was Ghazali Shafie, a Malay civil servant with British secret service and Emergency security experience who rose to political prominence in the UMNO shake-up that followed the events of 1965 to 1969 (Mahathir and Musa Hitam were two of its more celebrated but short-lived victims). Ghazali Shafie was indebted to Lee and admired him. Datuk Hussein Onn[*], a lawyer and of a prominent Johore family, became the new Prime Minister; and through Ghazali Shafie's offices as Minister of Home Affairs Lee was at last able to convince the Malaysian Government to take action against the journalist Samad Ismail. Lee was sure that Samad had been instrumental in souring relations and whipping up Malay hostility through the press. More than any other Malay, Samad Ismail (even if Lee had preferred to think of him as a Javanese) seemed to have grasped Lee's mindset with uncanny intuition: in that regard Lee's suspicion was quite justified. Lee had confided in him, and where there is trust there is conscious vulnerability. Ghazali Shafie (more than likely with domestic axes to grind) alerted Hussein Onn forcefully to Samad Ismail's Marxist and subversive record, painting a grim picture of the rising tide of Malay and Islamic susceptibility to communism that Samad symbolised. Only weeks after

---

[*] Now Tun Hussein Onn. The honorific Datuk (below the rank of Tun) was formerly spelt Dato.

receiving a prized Malaysian cultural award, Samad was detained, later making more than one television confession.*

Hussein Onn was inclined to take Lee at face value. An obstinate, incorruptible man, his five-and-a-half years at the helm of government eased Singapore–Malaysia relations into a new phase. He did not appear to envy Singapore's formidable economic success and so be inclined to react with a pale imitation. He had not been privy to all the independence and merger negotiations—he had not joined UMNO until 1968—and like his father Dato Onn bin Jaffar, he was a nationalist before he was a communalist.

It was fortunate that Hussein did not allow an incident that occurred early in the piece to do much harm to his relations with the Singapore Prime Minister. Malaysia got hold of at least one copy of a tape onto which Derek Davies, editor of the *Far Eastern Economic Review*, retailed the gist of an interview he had just been given off the record by Lee Kuan Yew. Among several extraordinary assertions, Lee was supposed to have expressed a preference for populist Malay politicians because they were buyable: he thought the new Malaysian Prime Minister altogether too naive and upright.

Ghazali Shafie also managed to please the Singapore premier by tarring those of Razak's courtiers who were hostile to Lee with the leftist brush. Some of them were detained, all were dropped from advisory councils. In both West Malaysia and Singapore, 1976 marked a renewed emphasis on the communist threat and the need for its elimination among Malay and Chinese alike. Plots and their perpetrators were uncovered; television confessions and sensational headlines abounded. We shall shortly discuss one of the high points, the Socialist International episode.

This joint crackdown reflected Hussein's desire to deal with Singapore dispassionately and to accommodate Lee if it was the right thing to do. Although he was criticised for letting Lee outflank him, Hussein promoted steady improvements to their working relationship, culminating in the agreement of 1980 with its excellent provision of an inter-governmental committee to facilitate contact at many levels of the two administrations. However, he did not hesitate to argue against Lee, notably at the Commonwealth Heads of Government Regional Meeting in Sydney (May 1978).

The current phase began when Dr Mahathir bin Mohamad succeeded Hussein Onn, who stepped down in 1981 on the

---

* At least one of the confessions was written for him in English. He translated it into Rhiau Malay, not his own idiom, so that the discerning listener would realise the contrived nature of his admissions.

grounds of ill-health (he had told Lee of his heart condition). Mahathir had never been afraid to speak out: he challenged the Tunku publicly in speech and letter over the Prime Minister's handling of the 'May 13th' disaster and as a result was expelled from the UMNO Executive Council. He immediately became a cult figure in exile, with prominent Malays beating a path to his door. He compounded his transgression by writing a controversial book, *The Malay Dilemma,* in which, among other things, he attacked UMNO and the Prime Minister for allowing the Chinese to exploit the Malays economically. The Tunku had already lost credibility among the Malays and Mahathir crystallised their disenchantment with him. The danger was that, without firm leadership, the potent combination of race and religion would channel Mahathir's quarrel with the Tunku into an uncontrollable force that would overtake both them and the nation. In the nick of time Razak valiantly managed to turn the tide, leaving Hussein Onn with an easier and more conciliatory path to follow. Hussein prided himself on being his own man and he charted a steady course towards modernisation, choosing Mahathir as his deputy and therefore successor.

Mahathir and Lee made an almost rapturous beginning. They were after all, birds of a feather—opportunistic, eugenicist, racially competitive, untroubled by traditional courtesies, both modernisers with a more or less secular worldview and nationalists who needed to define the object of their loyalty. Lee publicly celebrated the fact that he was dealing for the first time with a Malaysian leader who was 'non-U',[5] whose life experience gave him a compatible outlook. The same could be said of Musa Hitam, Mahathir's deputy. Both had been through the University of Malaya in Singapore, both had been put out to pasture because of conflict with the aristocratic establishment, both had made a remarkable comeback. The advantages of Malaysia and Singapore to each other might thereafter be exploited on the basis of unashamed self-interest.

There are problems, nevertheless. Malaysia and Singapore are vastly different societies, quite apart from the political fractures inflicted on them after World War II and in August 1965. Singapore's character, despite all modifications and foreign influences, has been shaped by her predominantly Chinese population. Malaysia has been experiencing an Islamic revival, triggered partly by the conflicts of the 1960s to which Lee contributed, but owing its present direction to the growth of worldwide fundamentalism and the consequent fervour that enables Muslim societies to put their own stamp on a process of modernisation otherwise wholly borrowed from the West. The Malaysian governments of the last two decades have also been much more susceptible than Singapore to pressures from the grass roots or from vested interests.

Whether Mahathir can ride, let alone tame, the Islamic tiger remains to be seen. It is most unlikely that his own astuteness—shown in the co-opting of important Muslim figures onto his caravan—will overcome the popular perception that he is a political eccentric, albeit a determined and ruthless one. He himself is reported to be willing to push his programmes ahead, despite criticism and unpopularity, and then return to private life—his medical practice, or, more likely, a business career—when his path is finally blocked. Apart from religious extremism, there have been many obstacles so far, such as the refusal of the sultans to allow Mahathir to lessen the constitutional power vested in the *Agong* (King), who is elected for a five-year term from their number; the *Bank Bumiputra* scandal whose taint continues to hover all too near the Prime Minister and his second Finance Minister, Daim Zainuddin, and the clash between the central Government and the Sabah Government elected in 1985, which has brought racial and religious issues to the fore and once more raised the spectre of secession.

Judging from past form, Lee is not about to lock Singapore into the fortunes of Mahathir or his deputy, Musa Hitam. The PAP Law Minister, E.W. Barker, is close to the present *Agong*, the Sultan of Johore. Singapore's High Commissioner in Kuala Lumpur, Maurice Baker*, knows many highly placed Malaysians. Networks of individual contacts and business acquaintances can be marshalled to supplement the leaders' relationship or to compensate for changed circumstances.

Bearing these provisos in mind, observers acknowledge the strengthening of links between the two countries over the last few years. The focus no longer need be placed quite so relentlessly on whether Lee is at peace with whoever is Malaysia's Prime Minister. Middle and upper echelons of both governments meet regularly. Complementarity has been achieved, however tentatively, in a number of areas: labour-intensive industries have been relocated from Singapore to Malaysia; there have been joint air, sea and land defence exercises, even without British or Australasian involve-

---

* Baker, a Eurasian academic (Professor of English at the University of Singapore), helped found the Malayan Forum in London 1949–50, together with Goh Keng Swee, Tun Abdul Razak and other prominent Malayan students of the time.

ment; conditional plans are afoot for the piping of natural gas and more water to Singapore, for the widening of the Causeway, for joint tourist promotion and co-ordinated air services, and various long-standing disputes have been settled. The Malaysians are now able to accept Singapore's exemplary value in urban development without having to copy her slavishly and furtively.

If relations with Malaysia have somehow stabilised and become more constructive, despite the barriers of communication between such diverse patterns of culture and political leadership, the same may be affirmed of Singapore and Indonesia.

Traditional dislike for the middleman, especially when he is Chinese, has always coloured the attitude of the giant archipelago nation to its own Chinese population, as well as to its tiny island neighbour. The army's massacre of Chinese in Indonesia after Sukarno's downfall, on the pretext of eliminating communists, is one of the worst blots on its escutcheon. As Lee remarked when criticising the United States for supplying offensive weapons to Jakarta, 'I sincerely hope that the Chinese communist looks so very different from the Chinese Indonesian national ... in the Indonesian soldier's gun sights.'[6]

Lee Kuan Yew's government was placed in the infinitely delicate position of having to cope with Malaysia, while a far bigger and more volatile Malay neighbour defined and pursued its own regional interests. With Confrontation over, luck had it that fraternal strains did not disappear; they have persisted to this day. But the risk has always been that Jakarta and Kuala Lumpur may close ranks to threaten Singapore's sovereignty and very existence.

It might therefore have seemed surprising that Lee personally insisted on the execution of two Indonesian marines captured during Confrontation in 1965 and convicted of bombing a lift in downtown Singapore. Although they were not hanged until 1967, the Prime Minister, who was in Tokyo at the time, refused to advise clemency, despite pleas via every conceivable channel and a last-minute personal letter of appeal from President Suharto himself. When the marines' bodies were received in Jakarta, there was rioting, the Singapore embassy was raided and its flag burned.

Coming on top of Singapore's links with Israel and her proudly Chinese image, this incident affronted Suharto and his new government. The President was particularly incensed because he had tried to dissuade his predecessor, Sukarno, from pursuing the policy of Confrontation and to encourage positive contact with Malaysia and Singapore. Not until March 1973 was there any substantial improvement in the atmosphere; only then, after considerable diplomacy and explanation behind the scenes, did Lee go to Jakarta. Fortunately he overcame his scruples and agreed to the suggestion of Singapore's Malay-speaking Ambassador, Lee Khoon Choy, that he put flowers on the marines' grave. The Indonesians were delighted by this and by other unexpected signs of adaptability—Lee wore a *batik* shirt for the first time, for instance (although he was adamant that an unforeseen incident in which he had to attempt folk dancing would be the last, some instincts could not be retrained).[7] The rewards have outweighed the sacrifices. Now Lee has regular 'four eyes' meetings with Suharto. In 1985 the Indonesians even received him with a traditional Bugis ceremony, presenting to him gifts normally reserved for a king. Short of supposing irony on the Indonesians' part, the gesture can be taken to show how far the two leaders have come.

Needless to say, it has not all been plain sailing. There was consternation on Singapore's side when the Indonesian military gave advance notice that they were planning to annex East Timor. For some years afterwards Singapore broke ranks with Indonesia in regional forums and in the United Nations itself before extending acceptance of the *fait accompli*. Fears for her own future and possibly for Brunei's dictated this nervous response. (The irritation she caused Indonesia, however, was mercifully minor compared to the animosity provoked by the Australian media's, critical reports.) Singapore has also voiced a firm commitment to international shipping's rights of passage through the Straits of Malacca, a stance at odds with both Indonesia's and Malaysia's territorial claims but not unduly disruptive, considering the major powers' support for it.

On the Indonesian side, misgivings have surfaced at several levels, including government circles and the press. The former and present Foreign Ministers, Rajaratnam and Dhanabalan, have been criticised for aggressive and unilateral foreign policy initiatives. Singapore's economic rhetoric often glosses over her profit at others' expense. For instance, the complementarity principle by which the Association of Southeast Asian Nations (ASEAN) promotes bilateral economic co-operation casts Indonesia in a role similar to that of nineteenth-century Portugal towards England—producing wine for the market of an industrial society.[8] Singapore's proposal of multilateral or bilateral defence projects has aroused the suspicion that one of her main underlying motives is a desire for profit from the sale of military hardware.

Indonesia's reserve about current governmental relations despite a generally mature and positive atmosphere appears to have two causes: she wants to bypass Singapore in oil refining and trading and reduce the flow of her capital there by way of investment or tourism, and she has developed a healthy scepticism towards the Singapore leadership, qualified only in some quarters by a respect for Lee Kuan Yew that is tinged with Javanese mysticism.

Developing a foreign policy

For the rest, there is a seasoned rationality about much of Singapore's foreign policy and behaviour. Whatever external elements are taken into account and whatever personal factors are operative, Singapore's decision makers have long since acquired and mastered habits of calculating forward moves and discerning the grand design.

As we have already seen, Singapore's independence, although traumatic, did not catch her leadership unprepared in the area of foreign policy. Before and during the Malaysia period, Lee, Goh, Toh and Rajaratnam and their colleagues all had gained experience of forays overseas to explain or negotiate policies and to promote the island's international profile. Having built on and enlarged a network of contacts and having formulated a global perspective themselves, they spoke with open scorn of the Malaysian Government's performance in diplomacy and foreign affairs.

The transition to a fully fledged foreign service had to go ahead, although Lee begrudged the expense and doubted the benefits in some cases. It was not a difficult transition; in fact, it was a matter of high priority, given the urgency of consolidating economic links, strengthening or redrafting military and intelligence connections, advertising Singapore's charms and gaining international recognition. The core group in Cabinet was able to continue its policy formulation while creating a technical elite at home and abroad that would provide briefing and advice and execute decisions. Diplomats were by no means the only ones involved: the Government established agencies such as the International Trading Company (INTRACO) to help Singaporeans deal with centrally planned economies and to assist investment in foreign countries according to local conditions; the Economic Development Board (EDB) and the Tourist Promotion Board set up offices in major cities. The Government had overall supervision, most of which could be exercised through the Public Service Commission, ministers of state or parliamentary secretaries. Only certain tasks—the choosing of ambassadors and heads of mission—were reserved for the Foreign Minister and Prime Minister.

Much of the day-to-day expression and outworking of guidelines has been left to those deputed to do so. For instance, Tommy Koh, who was Singapore's Ambassador to the United Nations for many years, rarely had his proposals overruled or was sent direct orders concerning a vote or negotiating tactics. The prerequisite for faithful discharge of policy is a clear understanding of it, which means diligent and regular perusal of official thinking.

The roll call of foreign mission heads would suggest an intriguing range of selection criteria. They have generally been chosen from the ranks of politicians, academics, businessmen, journalists and lawyers. Besides factors intrinsic to the posting—including appropriate linguistic skills, previous standing or first-hand experience in the country concerned—domestic political judgments and agenda are brought to bear. For some leading party cadres, putting out to pasture or 'sending to Siberia' has been perceived by the recipient as a major consideration. Co-opting independents, perhaps with an expectation of neutralising them, is another ploy. Appointments and secondments may serve yet other purposes: testing and extending the ambitious, placing the weak on probation, deploying loyal hatchet men at the price of frustrating their domestic career and effectiveness. It would be invidious to name names, but many Singaporeans would find it easy to match individuals to these categories.

Career diplomats are only now beginning to receive key postings. They have been chosen for their good academic records and trained to move up the ladder with little expectation of attaining the highest levels, so flair and ambition have not been their hallmarks. There are obvious exceptions, such as Kishore Mahbubani, Singapore's current Ambassador to the United Nations. It is interesting to note that Indians have been over-represented and Malays under-represented in the upper levels of the foreign service: lack of tertiary qualifications may not be the only reason for this.

The less public side of Singapore's foreign policy, from its information-gathering stages to its implementation, deserves a few remarks before the policy itself is discussed.

The government has exceptional access to the West's military and civilian intelligence, not only because Singapore is a major listening post and clearing house. The British connection formed the original basis of access, which has been augmented primarily through Lee's, Goh's and Rajaratnam's personal familiarity with significant officials and operatives from the agencies and front organisations that exist in the United States, Australia, Canada, Malaysia and other ASEAN countries. In addition, the overseas Chinese business community has its own antennae, into the signals of which Lee can tap. Because of their clan and commercial connections, many Singaporeans are unsurpassed founts of practical knowledge about almost any country in the world.

Singapore and the world

Singapore is governed on the basis of a globally oriented strategy which is, in Rajaratnam's words, 'a judicious mixture of well-trained and well-equipped defence forces, friendly alliances, wise foreign policy, and giving as many countries as possible a tangible stake in the security, prosperity and integrity of Singapore.'[9] The bottom line is survival, but fear of sinking to the bottom line has spurred the nation to accomplish and project a great deal above it.

The aim articulated by the leadership after Separation was to fashion a new role for Singapore that would be consoling to herself, attractive to the wider civilised world, but problematic to her immediate neighbours. Defiance has sometimes been evident in Singapore's self-advancement, and it has tended to undermine programmes of regional co-operation. Moreover, it has locked domestic politics into a course that brooks no opposition and claims to be scientifically independent of the special interests of those who are in power for the time being.

What are the premises on which foreign policy has been based? Lee Kuan Yew has described them thus: 'We want to be ourselves. Those who want to thwart us and prevent us from being ourselves would necessarily be non-friends. Therefore, our policy is to seek the maximum number of friends with the maximum capacity to uphold what our friends and ourselves have decided to uphold. That is the beginning and the end of any foreign policy for a situation like Singapore's.' Friendship is never to be taken for granted. 'We must always offer to the rest of the world a continuing interest in the type of society we project.'[10] It is essential for Singapore to consolidate her strategic or economic value to more than one major power, preferably to more than two. Eternal vigilance and a resilient nervous system are required for a small nation to manage on such terms. As Lee put it, 'A multi-polar world theoretically means a diffusion of power centres. In reality, it makes for greater anxiety because nobody is in total control.'[11] The global balance is forever changing and 'one must always recognise who are likely to be friends for a long time and who are likely to be friends for just a short while'.[12]

Another central feature of Singapore's global attitude is the realisation that 'the world does not owe us a living'. Every grain of rice, every bit of raw material, has to be imported and paid for, as the Prime Minister has often reminded citizens. Markets have to be found, investment courted, trading links maintained; goods and services of increasing sophistication and diversity have to be produced. Being at a strategic maritime 'choke point', Singapore has gone into fields such as petrochemical refining and production, shipbuilding and repairs, oil exploration and drilling. High-technology specialisation gives Singapore an edge in weapons and armaments and other forms of manufacturing, in medicine, banking, communications and more.

For international consumption, Singapore has claimed to be a developing country, part of the Third World. In the 1950s and 1960s, identification with the mass of new nations lessened the risk of becoming a pawn. The claim has been harder to justify in recent years, even discounting the contribution made by the foreign presence in Singapore. By any standards, the island has experienced remarkable rates of economic growth. One sign that the claim is a case of prudent image-making rather than conviction is that there is not a serious commitment to development studies in the university curriculum.

The search for a safe brand of independence and an advantageous type of liaison with Malaysia and Indonesia must mean a low profile on Singapore's part. The tendencies to assert herself and to play on tensions between her bigger neighbours have created contradictory pulls, reflected in periodic fluctuations in the regional perception of Singapore. The Prime Minister believes the situation to be natural. 'Your nearest neighbours are hardly ever your best friends.'

The leaders have formulated and refined their own system of statecraft, which begins and ends on an international canvas and depends on long-range forecasting. Their approach owes a great deal to their professional training, their emergence during the dying stages of colonialism when many experiments in independence were failing or had already failed, their experience of partnership and conflict with communists, their absorption of the very communist methods they feared, their commitment to the envisaging, implementing and propagandising of a modern state. Lee would also claim to have rediscovered his Asian roots in facing up to the world as he finds it.

Observers, whether in criticism or admiration, have detected the influence of thinkers and strategists as diverse as Plato, Machiavelli, the unknown author of the classic Chinese text, *Three Kingdoms*,

Confucius and Mao. The observers are probably right, but the influence confirms existing impulses and does not create them.

'Know yourself. Know your enemy. A hundred battles. A hundred victories.' This ancient advice from Xun Zi has been the deliberate slogan of Singapore's foreign policymakers weighing up the people and governments with whom they deal. A thumbnail sketch will illustrate what Lee and his colleagues have achieved with the passage of the years.

Consider the new nation's first experiment at forging a new context, signalled by Lee's declaration. 'We are natural Afro-Asians.'[13] Feelers were quickly put out in search of recognition from the United Nations and symbolically suitable countries. Toh Chin Chye and Rajaratnam were soon despatched on a goodwill mission to nine African states, Yugoslavia, the Soviet Union, India and Cambodia. (Toh found the going hard, because Lee's previous African tour had left a legacy of resentment at critical and insulting remarks the Prime Minister had made about the states and their leaders.[14]) Lee wrote to Nasser of Egypt and Shastri of India for assistance in military training; their refusal gave him a good excuse to press on with the Israelis who came to his aid under the designation 'Mexican agricultural advisers'. In April 1966 Lee himself went off on a demanding mission to Eastern and Western Europe, Cambodia, Thailand and Egypt. He wanted to dispel any suspicion that Singapore might be under Britain's thumb (because of her bases) or turning to the Right. He was able to thank Sihanouk personally for support given in the final days of Malaysia and to profess admiration for Cambodia's model of non-alignment. In Sweden he identified with a socialism that was able to industrialise a backward rural society less wastefully and slowly than capitalism: a piece of grandstanding for the leader of urbanised Singapore.

The tangible result of these moves and travels was generally disappointing. On his return home, Lee said, 'It is my duty to see that Singapore is not isolated. What else do you think I have been travelling for?'[15] Having made the effort to find rapport with the non-aligned movement, only to convince himself that its strength no longer existed beyond the level of rhetoric—the spirit of the 1955 Bandung Conference had dissipated—Lee's consolation was that his pitching of an Afro–Asian line was forcing Britain, Australia and New Zealand to consider his needs as well as their own. The ending of Confrontation and the rift between Malaysia and Singapore put quite a different complexion on the five-power defence agreement. It is important to bear this factor in mind when assessing Lee's contribution to the September 1966 Commonwealth Prime Ministers' Conference in London. He played a tricky game of being intransigent when speaking in public on behalf of the blacks, yet conciliatory in private discussion as the Conference mulled over the Rhodesia question.[16] Years later he was to say that Singapore had concerned herself with southern Africa in order to earn the Commonwealth's interest in Southeast Asia.[17]

Lee was not slow to perfect a deft and sure touch for handling Britain, Australia and New Zealand. 'Competitive', 'dismissive' and 'kindly' are three adjectives that would begin to sum up his respective attitudes to each nation and its successive governments.

Through the media he has publicly challenged the British and exhibited towards them a blend of resentment (at his own and Singapore's frequent brushes with arrogant officials or businessmen), admiration (for the English language and for the benefit to his Singapore of secretive and hierarchical law-and-order apparatus and the acumen of certain political, administrative and military leaders) and regret (that loss of the entrepreneurial spirit and of the will to work has sapped the United Kingdom's potential to continue her historically inventive contribution to civilisation's future). Political defections to the Right from the ranks of the Left, particularly if they have been among Lee's extensive network of acquaintances, have received his approval, and he has sometimes called on the British to recapture their former glory by forswearing, the welfare state, the 'adversary' mentality of trade unionism and the slogans of the open society. Today's run-down cities with their ethnic ghettoes and inadequate amenities are a forceful reminder to Lee that there is a growing gulf between the privileged world into which he entered by pure merit and the economic and cultural degradation of the British community at large.

Lee has given every indication of believing that he has the exact measure of Australia and Australians. Despite having professed respect for certain individuals such as Sir Robert Menzies (who served as Prime Minister from 1949 to 1966), and although Singapore has milked Australia for a wide variety of specialists, facilities and programmes, he has delighted in pointing out the many failings of his southern neighbours, not least poor leadership. Some other instances include Lee's observation of the Australian troops who 'packed up and refused to fight' when the Japanese advanced upon Singapore in 1942; the reluctance of Canberra to take his warnings seriously during the dark days of Malaysia, and the seeming preference of senior Australian diplomats and officials for Malaysia over Singapore; the size ('those are a large people' he once told the Legislative Assembly) and the lack of civilised attractions ('my eldest son ... rather liked it, as a place for a holiday' Lee said in 1971); the bastardising of the English language; the combination of high protectionism, low value-adding resource development and union power that makes Australians the 'dole bludgers of the South Pacific', undeservedly prosperous now and with little prospect of relevance to the region's future.

Towards New Zealand, a country whose population numbers are much the same as his own, Lee has expressed his people's special regard and warmth of feeling. A strong economic relationship has been cemented by New Zealand's military assistance against communism, her welcoming treatment of Singapore students, and her aid in animal husbandry, agriculture and food processing.

A splendid example of Lee's calculated play on what he saw as these three nations' susceptibilities came to light when the British military withdrawal from Singapore was running its course. Determined that there would not be a vacuum, he obtained the promise of a low-level but credible replacement defence force under the acronym ANZUK (Australia, New Zealand and the United Kingdom). From his point of view, ANZUK could, while it lasted, underwrite regional security and, what is more, the Australians could pay for their previous favouritism by keeping Malaysia from carrying out any dishonourable intentions towards Singapore.

Once he had extracted whatever international mileage he could from promoting an independent Singapore, and having effected a credible renewal of existing alliances, Lee could turn his attention to an accommodation with the USA on terms he was willing to contemplate. Having shocked Washington into taking him seriously, he let it be known that he looked to the Americans to take the lead, with Japan and Western Europe, in propelling Southeast Asia's and Singapore's economies quickly forward. The intensification of the Vietnam conflict was already playing an unintentional part and proving a blessing to Singapore. Lee took the opportunity of an extended visit to North America to air his conviction that precipitate disengagement from Indo-China would be disastrous. Having previously addressed himself to the folly of the US involvement in the first place, he could not strictly be accused of changing his tune—only of singing a different portion of it.

Those who vilify Lee for selling out to the Americans have perhaps failed to detect his cleverness. Quite rightly, he once boasted: 'I am the only chap in the whole of Southeast Asia that is not on the American payroll.'[18] It could be argued that he is one of the few leaders to have outwitted the blunderbuss-wielding giant that is the world's most powerful nation. Singapore has no US military installations on her soil; the only American troops to come her way have merely been short-term visitors on rest and recreation leave. She has no treaty that obliges her to make facilities available on demand, whatever her qualms. On the other hand, she has acquired sophisticated capability in areas of her choice, many of them explicitly geared or readily converted to her own military use.

Taking the argument further, it is worth observing that a veritable cornucopia of benefits has descended upon Singapore in repayment for years of friendly insults. Lee has assailed the American way, the American psyche, the media's fickle manipulation of voters and legislators alike, the counterculture and the peace movement, and he devoted all but the last months of Jimmy Carter's presidency to criticising America's aimlessness and loss of credibility, saying that her friends were turning pessimistic, her enemies adventurist. Singapore has been rewarded for Lee's blunt advice to Washington, too: he has called for a global strategy reliant on trade and investment, on air and sea power rather than on land forces; he has recommended enlarging the fleet to cover the Indian and Pacific oceans simultaneously; he has urged the Americans to be cautious about selling arms to China or allowing China undue weight in an East Asian balance of power, he has offered a regular diagnosis or forecast of the American economy, and in October 1985 even addressed Congress on the strategic dangers of US protectionism. Every word is spoken by a man who calmly recognises that he and his island are theoretically too small to deserve a hearing.

Who else but Lee has received so much—the fêting of the CIA and of successive administrations, preferential rights to personnel training and equipment, high multinational corporate rating and input—for so little? Under the circumstances, he can afford to put up with American vulgarity and boorishness. Time will decide whether Lee's successors will continue the relationship on the same basis, merely ironing out the wrinkles.

Newly sovereign Singapore's regional associations multiplied on paper; but it was some time before they had much substance. The Association of Southeast Asian Nations (ASEAN) is the most important of them, created at a Bangkok meeting in August 1967 between representatives of Indonesia, Malaysia, the Philippines, Singapore and Thailand. (Since 1984 Brunei has also been a member.) Singapore was not positively attracted to the Association, believing it would be of benefit mainly to the weaker member states. However, there was something to be said for inhibiting development of a pan-Malay brotherhood and muting political differences in the region. It was only as the member countries' economies grew, as the world economy was hit by a quadrupling of the oil price after October 1973, and (in Singapore's case) as Lee's attitude softened, that correct if distant relations developed between ASEAN governments and their leaders.

Over the intervening years, each member country has brought a different furrow to Lee's brow. He has often been worried enough about the Thais—their corrupt or inflexible generals and leaders, their unstable experiment with democracy—to pay them an urgent visit or to offer unsolicited counsel for fear that the line would not be held against communist advances from Indo-China (and at some stages from within Thailand) or against the beguiling overtures of China. The Philippines are far enough away not to be a preoccupation, so long as the US bases are not threatened and the internal situation does not get out of hand. President Marcos' professions of admiration, like all flattery, have done little for Lee's estimation of him. The sickness of the Filipino economy and the inroads of the New People's Army have made recent times more worrying. Has Marcos lost his grip on reality? Why has he not groomed a proper successor? Might there be another desperate exodus of refugees? Where would the Chinese among them go? Singapore's role in the Aquino assassination of August 1983—providing intelligence to the Manila authorities about the senator's homecoming movements—is one of a number of incidents that has aroused speculation about the extent of liaison behind the scenes.

For various reasons there have been tensions between Thailand, the Philippines and Brunei, on the one hand and Malaysia and Indonesia on the other. To some extent the tensions have allowed Singapore to play a mediating role within ASEAN.

There are advantages to her on bilateral fronts, too. Thailand, the Philippines and Brunei provide cheap resources and market or investment openings; as well, they have sites suited to basic anti-guerrilla and conventional jungle warfare training. Access to the US facilities in the Philippines brings higher skills to Singaporeans without the stigma of direct presence.

Between 1967 and 1975, Lee and Rajaratnam reminded themselves and their neighbours that Southeast Asia could have a greater hold upon its own fate only when constituent nations had more advanced economies. The gap between ASEAN planning and reality was recorded in tedious detail and there was a characteristic teacher's tone to the Singaporeans' advice that leaders should steer clear of proposals that were bilaterally good but regionally harmful.

The second half of this period, from 1971 onwards, saw Singapore increase her active commitment to ASEAN; Lee paid courtesy calls on all his counterparts, tax incentives were offered to Singaporeans investing in ASEAN and there were exchange visits by every kind of delegation. On his fiftieth birthday, the Prime Minister was in gracious vein saying, 'Indeed, where co-operation is possible, we should help advance their interests as we advance our own.'[19] For the first time, there was a conscious attempt to reconcile global and regional interests.

Having coped well with the 'therapeutic crisis' of the British withdrawal, Singapore had to readjust to the 1970s' skyrocketting oil prices. Relations with Middle Eastern ('West Asian' in Singapore parlance) states were upgraded and Singapore's 'neutral' diplomatic posture towards Arabs and Israelis—in practice pro-Israeli because of existing links and because of Lee's spiritual affinity to the artificially re-created Jewish nation—was revised to lend more vocal support to Arab rights. The changes were designed both to protect access to oil supplies and to align Singapore more closely with Malaysian and Indonesian thinking. As well as sending goodwill and trade missions to them, Singapore offered Middle Eastern countries her expertise in managing port facilities, urban development and free trade zones and her financial and commercial services to encourage the investment of 'petrodollars' in Southeast Asia. Lee appeared to get on particularly well with one Middle Eastern head of state, the Shah of Iran, and praised him fulsomely while visiting Teheran in September 1975.

The years 1975 and 1976 marked a watershed for Singapore and Lee. The two years encompassed the 'fall' of Indo-China to the communists, the deaths of Zhou Enlai and Razak, the attack by the Dutch Labour Party on Singapore's integrity within the Socialist International, and Jimmy Carter's election as President of the USA. All galvanised Lee into seizing initiatives and making moves that both head and heart had long been prompting but that circumstances or inertia had inclined him to resist.

Well aware that the Americans would be licking their wounds for some time, he went among his ASEAN partners orchestrating a new prominence for the regional association. Singapore would, as far as possible, stay in the background, persuading other member countries and their leaders to dominate the play out front. This style, it was hoped, would minimise the friction and irritation of a small nation asserting itself. The plan was to attract a quantum increase in American (and other) economic commitment to the region, and to claim whatever morsels or even crumbs could be gleaned from the US military table. Lee was at his old last, not only anticipating problems and defying adversity but responding positively to the challenges of the moment. 'I believe my best course is to take an intermediate view of events. I have no apocalyptic predictions. Nor will my views tranquillise opinion that all is and will be well, for that way I shall surely lose my credibility and reputation,' he told the Asia Society in New York.[20]

The Bali summit of February 1976 brought the ASEAN heads of government together for the first time and symbolised a new commitment to economic and social co-operation. Political and military cohesion might lie further down the track. Lee gave his blessing: 'If we are able to combine our individual fortes, whether it is national resilience in Indonesia, *Rukunegara* [national fundamentals] of Malaysia, the New Society of the Philippines, the traditions of monarchy and Buddhism of Thailand, or Singapore's matter-of-fact habit of facing up to the realities of life, together, we can do what we individually cannot do as well.'[21] This was a more positive attitude than he and Rajaratnam had previously been accustomed to express. Whether there was a parallel change in his underlying view of the ASEAN societies and their leaders is another matter.

Allusion has already been made to the impact of Tun Abdul Razak's passing; Lee's condolence message described him as a 'close friend from student days'.[22] The other death that occurred in early 1976, that of Zhou Enlai, heralded the impending close of the Chinese communist giants' era. Lee was lucky enough to arrange a visit to Beijing in May of that year, only months before Mao Zedong also died. Although disabled by a stroke, the ailing Chairman of the People's Republic, received Lee, for whom China thereby took on a human face. The hard work, the new vocabulary, above all the enormous internal problems that characterised modern China disarmed the immediate anxieties and pronounced defensiveness with which Lee approached his ancestral homeland. Possibly Zhou's absence from the scene—given the low opinion of Lee he had expressed—made the trip a little more comfortable. From then on, the psychological barrier of fear that China still exerted a pull of ethnic loyalty over Singaporeans could be breached in a bid for the benefits that an affluent, highly organised little society could hope to garner from freer contact with its spiritual mother. Lee pointed triumphantly to the superior standards of living enjoyed in Singapore and forecast that his citizens would want to kiss the ground when they returned home. So confident has he become of having the measure of today's China that he can both joke with the Chinese leadership and challenge them publicly to withhold support from Southeast Asian insurgency movements. He visualises Singapore as the 'transformer' from the West to China and he was tickled by the image Zhao Ziyang proposed of Singapore as the eyes and mouth for China's stomach. On Goh Keng Swee's retirement, the former Deputy Prime Minister accepted the invitation of Beijing to undertake a major freewheeling consultancy and has been helping to fulfil the images. Lee is not so sanguine about China in the long term.

The PAP's resignation from the Socialist International (which it had been invited to join in 1966) pre-empted a Dutch Labour Party motion to have it expelled. Lee mounted a major campaign to justify Singapore's unique brand of socialism, and Devan Nair put together a book, *Socialism that Works* (Singapore: Federal Publication, 1976), for quick release on the domestic market. Every charge of undemocratic practice was rebutted, or explained where necessary, whether the suppression of trade unions or the treatment of political detainees. Singapore's big guns were wheeled out to do duty. Rajaratnam wrote, in rather manic vein, 'An Epistle to the Synod of the Socialist Orthodox Church' and Devan Nair flew to London to present Singapore's defence by attack. It was a hurtful time for Lee. In letters to the Chairman and General Secretary of the Socialist International, he claimed that the Dutch presentation was full of distortions or errors and he lashed out at the young socialists who 'feel they have a civilising mission among the backward nations of Asia' and 'hide their arrogance behind a smokescreen of liberal intellectualism'.[23]

(The year 1976 was one of dramatic revelations—terrorist plots were foiled and an international ring of subversives uncovered. Shortly after the Socialist International moves. Samad Ismail's detention in Malaysia was coupled with arrests of Malay journalists in Singapore allegedly under his influence. Several individuals were detained or banished at around the same time. Although Lee acknowledged that there was no serious threat to Singapore, he did not want the potential and the patterns of subversion forgotten.)

A probable consequence of the Socialist International episode was that Lee soon kicked over the traces of any but the most old-fashioned and unideological socialism 'Equality of opportunity' was the one shibboleth he could still bring himself to utter. In one sense, honesty and realism prevailed, as they almost always did with him: without an indigenous and self-sufficient economic base, nationalisation of any magnitude would spell stifling inefficiency, ruinous for a country the size of Singapore. The abandonment of irrelevant battle cries, whatever their appeal and resonances for old comrades in arms, was inevitable.

Lee's crossing of the China threshold completed his orientation towards East Asia. Hong Kong was already a congenial watering place, being another stimulating Anglo–Chinese mix, and Lee had wide and deep connections there. It has been invaluable to be able to funnel Hong Kong's reserves of talent and capital into Singapore when they are flighty and, in turn, to draw on them when Singapore needs them.

By 1972 Taiwan, which had once figured in the PAP's official mythology as a corrupt right-wing bogeyman, had overtaken the People's Republic of China in volume of trade with Singapore. Some years after Separation, Lee began regular visits to the island for high-level consultations, and during the first half of the 1970s Singapore's armed forces periodically flew in troops on jungle training. Mystery surrounds the purpose of Lee's visits, which are usually described as private, and rumours abound—one of the less frivolous being that he has sought technical advice on the most suitable ways of meeting Singapore's specialised energy requirements.*

Singapore's relationship with North and South Korea neatly illustrates a cardinal principle of her foreign policy: deal with both sides when nations are internally divided or externally at loggerheads. Other examples have been the two Vietnams, the two Germanies, China and Taiwan, Israel and the Arab states, and the bloc of the United States and her NATO allies versus the USSR and the Warsaw Pact countries. In practice, South Korea is much more to the fore through trade and the construction industry. A similar lopsidedness is evident in the other examples cited.

Japan has provided Lee with the most inspiration and food for thought over the last decade. Having been glad to see the 'humiliation of the small warriors' in 1945, his attitudes have turned around. Perhaps it is a case of mastering one's former masters. Besides, he pointed out as long ago as 1967, 'I think it is unrealistic to believe that a thrusting nation like Japan will forever be penitent for its misdemeanours in the last war and just produce transistors and scooters and little cars for the rest of Southeast Asia'.[24] Investment and two-way trade are not his only desires. Social

---

* A feasibility study argued against the proposal of a nuclear reactor and power station on Singapore territory (Pulau Tekong being the most likely site).

values, work patterns and high technology represent the commodities he would like to import, and in the early 1980s he willingly drew flak for encouraging the 'aping' of Japan. He expressed the hope that companies would take over some of the state's burden and make lifelong provision for workers, with loyalty, productivity and quality improvement in return. The Japanese themselves became uncomfortable at Lee's ardour but it was not long before others pointed out that he was being unrealistic in idealising a society that many in Southeast Asia still loathed.[25] What the Japanese could add was that their employer–worker arrangements came from consensus, not by prime ministerial *fiat*.

Lee has also changed his position about Japanese militarism. He used to be fearful that Japan would rearm on a grand scale and opt for nuclear weapons. When his fears were not realised, and in fact were disappointed, he started to press for an upgrading of Japan's military preparedness so she could share more of the US burden, help check the growing Soviet presence around the western Pacific, including vital sea lanes to the Middle East's oil, and preserve the slowly changing balance of power with China.

Because of Lee's ambiguity about the other ASEAN countries, much of Singapore's diplomacy has been left to Rajaratnam and Dhanabalan. Lee's own initiatives have been limited. He promoted a consultative process between ASEAN and Australasia, Japan, the USA and the European Economic Community (EEC), to maximise the region's economic and security options. He lashed out at the Vietnamese when they invaded Cambodia and installed a tame government there and when the refugee exodus was at its height: Vietnam, he said, was 'drunk with hubris'.[26] He repeated a Malaysian accusation that Western countries were creaming off skilled and professionally trained refugees, leaving ASEAN with 'the rubbish in the garden'.[27] Knowing Prince Sihanouk well, Lee was needed in the delicate and unpredictable business of cobbling together an alternative Kampuchean government from three politically irreconcilable and militarily and numerically unequal factions, including the dreaded Khmer Rouge; he seemed to justify these probably fruitless endeavours on the grounds that they would divert Vietnam's and China's energy.

One or two incidents have suggested some dissent on Lee's part from the zeal with which his colleagues in foreign affairs pursue such tasks as procuring Hanoi's withdrawal from Cambodia. At the New Delhi Commonwealth Heads of Government regional meeting in 1980 he told Australian journalists that the question of the Kampuchean coalition's seat in the United Nations did not bother him greatly (a position more congenial to the then Australian Foreign Minister, Andrew Peacock, for whom Lee had an affectionate regard, than to the Prime Minister, Malcolm Fraser). En route home afterwards aboard the Australian government Boeing 707 there was a shouting match and Lee allowed himself to be 'persuaded' by Fraser (in exchange for military benefits to Singapore) back to the hard official ASEAN line. The next day Rajaratnam issued a statement reaffirming Singapore's unwavering stand on the matter.

Dhanabalan has proved himself as strident or urbane, depending on the occasion, as Rajaratnam. He led the attack on Australia for its International Civil Aviation Policy agreement which discriminated against ASEAN, particularly Singapore. Lee clearly backed him then, surprised and pleased at Malaysia's support. But he was apparently quite happy when Dhanabalan received his comeuppance from Foreign Minister Hayden and Prime Minister Hawke after accusing Canberra of 'trying to bend over backwards to please Vietnam, thinking thereby that Australia will have a role to play'.[28]

Knowledge within ASEAN of these little nuances among Singapore's leaders take some of the sting from her self-appointed role as back seat driver. To the outside world a picture of unity is presented and differences are not generally aired, but Singapore tends to be the odd nation out or to find only one other to agree with her. Resentment wells up occasionally at instances of feet-dragging, hypocrisy or special pleading, such as when Singapore was reluctant to take her alphabetical turn at appointing a Secretary-General for ASEAN and her eventual appointee, Chan Kai Yau, made no secret of his reluctance about accepting; when Hanoi slyly advertised how much trade was going on between Vietnam and Singapore, despite the latter's hard line on Indo-China, or when Lee floated a novel definition of ASEAN 'consensus' (five minus one agreeing on a proposal).

There has been a similar division of labour in other areas of foreign affairs. Rajaratnam (succeeded by Dhanabalan) took on the United Nations and the non-aligned movement (NAM), and has given every appearance of enjoying the opportunity for straight talking and aggressive pamphleteering. Once communism lost its air of invincibility and was visibly racked by divisions, Rajaratnam took special delight in debunking the myths he had half believed himself in the distant past. His attack on Cuba's partisan chairmanship of NAM was one of his more colourful; members of the movement would judge whether 'the New Delhi summit has merely blessed the self-degradation at Havana or rescued it from the brothel area into which it had wandered'.[29]

Lee has been a faithful supporter of the Commonwealth, and in 1970 he was rewarded for his and Singapore's achievements when he was made a Companion of Honour by Queen Elizabeth II. He has felt free to criticise many of the Commonwealth heads of government and the nations they lead, or to give them advice. Sometimes he has been repaid in kind; at the Ottawa Conference, Gough Whitlam of Australia lambasted Singapore for her selfishness. Lee's interventions and views have continued to command some respect because they are cogently argued and come from a heady global perspective. Newcomers to the club such as David Lange of New Zealand tend to be very impressed on their first encounter with him. The 1971 Commonwealth Conference was hosted by Singapore, and not a few delegates reacted with a mixture of admiration, wry amusement and irritation to Lee's chairmanship; he tried to be tactful but kept playing the schoolmaster, steering sessions and working conference members for long hours. Whatever sentimental attachment he still has to Britain, his stated reason for staying with the Commonwealth is that it exerts a counter-gravitational pull to the USA and the USSR and offers a sane forum in which problems can be discussed, faced and solved. He believes that its track record has been surprisingly good, better than other similar international organisations. The shared experience of being English-speaking and having a history of British administration and enterprise is not a reason to look back, rather to draw on a common memory bank and to expedite decisions for the future.

Apart from all the relationships that occur within the framework of dialogue between nations and governments, Singapore's leaders have cultivated captains of industry and commerce, right-thinking academics and corporate planners with a strategic bent. Experts have been consulted or invited to Singapore. Lee is sceptical about the benefits of 'think tanks' and conference-going, but not sufficiently so to avoid them at all costs. They provide attractive opportunity to gather fresh data and argue viewpoints—and to present Singapore to the transnational world.

A global philosophy

Lee wants Singapore to be in the vanguard of historymakers. All things being equal, the future should belong to an international elite in disinterested possession of the discoveries of science and of the necessary financial resources to set up a new world order. The tiny handful at the top (0.1 per cent) would derive their satisfaction from hard work and creative genius, and apart from requiring a support workforce (1 per cent) for security and maintenance could allow the other 98.9 per cent of the population to pursue leisure activities such as painting, fishing, yachting, scuba diving, skiing or hunting.

All things are not equal, however. Lee suffers from periodic bouts of electrifying fear that his careful construction work will be destroyed. 'It is a fallacy to believe that we are relentlessly to progress to an ideal state of world harmony,' he has said.[30] Corruption and stupidity must be nipped in the bud, democracy must be tempered by economic reality and by strict control of the irrational forces of religious and racial bigotry.

Behind these has lurked the threat of communism. Lee believes that he understands its changing nature better than most. According to him, he 'dabbled' with Marxism as a student. 'But the practice of Leninism and Maoism by the MCP is completely different from the theoretical ideals of Marxism. It is a heartless organisation—a framework designed for the seizure of power by stealth, by force, by every means. The degradation of all human values, the destruction of all humane relationships, are all justified by men who initially must have believed in the sanctity of human life to have had the dedication to want to uplift the human being from the misery of poverty and exploitation of the old colonial society.'[31]

He knows what it is like to share a united front with communists or fellow-travellers. Had Britain not handed over power when and as she did, had there been a shoot-out, he believes he would have gone over to their side.

Fortunately, his personal experience of supping with the devil was cut short. On the assumption that his picture of the MCP is correct, it is fair to ask whether his spoon was long enough for him to avoid being affected. His cynicism about the MCP exercise of power has not made him self-critical; only more pessimistic about the future.

The communism of the mid-1980s may no longer be monolithic, may no longer be destined to triumph, may not pose an immediate internal challenge to any ASEAN country (except the Philippines); yet is still has the capacity to wreak havoc on the global scene either on its own account or if connected to other, smaller sources of conflict.

Lee has professed himself greatly impressed by the communist countries' ability to convert human societies into the weapons and muscles of war, but not the sinews of economic growth. He believes that communism is the enigma of our era—gaining in military size and strength yet proving very inefficient in satisfying the needs of its own people and allies. China has taken halting steps along the capitalist road—helped by Singapore—but because her leaders are so old, it is too soon to predict whether she will persevere or revert to another period of revolutionary ferment. The USSR is too heavily committed to maintaining its dominance for genuine détente to be possible. Moreover, neither hostility nor unity within the communist camp presents a soothing scenario.

The free world is endangered on different fronts. Out-and-out nuclear war is the most catastrophic. Another is more pertinent to daily affairs: the need to go on increasing defence expenditure so that communism may be checked. The threat here lies, at the very lowest, in inhibiting transfers of capital and technology from 'North' to 'South', a process jeopardised by the absurd burden of debt on the South nations. Lee has appealed to the North's governments to cancel the debt, but he doubts the capacity of Western democracies to act out of enlightened self-interest. His more subtle and quietly spoken answer to communism has been the concept of an arc of encirclement in the Asian region, stretching south from Japan to Australasia and the Pacific, through ASEAN, tying in Bangladesh, Sri Lanka and Pakistan. The proposal is infinitely more supple than the rigid anti-communist treaties of the past (SEATO and the Asian Pacific Council); Singapore for one trades with Vietnam, the Comecon countries and China, and sells them a variety of goods and services. The nexus Singapore has demonstrated between economic progress and political security is worth reproducing elsewhere, and she has gambled on helping several countries in the invisible arc—such as Sri Lanka, Bangladesh and the Pacific islands—without being able to weigh all the costs and benefits in the balance. Lee would be the first to acknowledge flaws in his proposal, and he has pointed them out: the instability of the Philippines, Sri Lanka and Bangladesh; New Zealand playing fast and loose with ANZUS; Japan and Australia not outward-looking and unselfish enough; ASEAN bedevilled by economic nationalism; India pursuing the foolish and irrevocable tack of a centrally planned democracy and flirting with the Soviets; Burma's failed socialism and ethnic tensions and many other uncertainties in the wider world. But if it could succeed, Lee's proposal would create a grid of alliances based on economic growth; he has always been sure that communism can ultimately be defeated or combated only by societies more visibly just and prosperous. His other hope for the arc of encirclement would be that his island republic would be guaranteed a pivotal and better earthed position in the grid for many generations to come.

Strengths and weaknesses

No sketch of Singapore's place in the sun would be complete without an assessment of its strengths and weaknesses. Lee Kuan Yew's contribution needs to be seen under both headings.

Much of Singapore's global and domestic policymaking is shaped by an acceptance that she is too peripheral to alter the ground rules of the international economy. Such phenomena as the wide range of salary and wage levels among Singaporeans, the pressures for ever-rising productivity and quality, the constant invasion of the island by expatriates—whether for business or tourism—must be justified in terms of dancing to the tune of the global market place that Singapore firmly wishes to frequent.

She has exploited and advertised her great strengths to the world—her strategic position on the east–west and north–south axes; her adaptable and well-heeled workforce with its fluency in English, Mandarin and Malay; her superb infrastructure of port and communications; and her excellent working conditions (accommodation, food, ease of travel, diversions near to hand).

Coupled with these is the advantage smallness brings. It is not difficult for resourceful economic managers to find nooks and crannies for Singapore enterprise to fill, or to adapt quickly to a promising development in technology or marketing. (This demands the close co-operation of public and private sectors and a failure of imagination, skill or nerve on either side can have a serious impact.)

On the other hand persistent recession would leave little Singapore terribly vulnerable; her enormous foreign reserves could only cushion the impact for a time. The same two-edged fate applies to her extensive worldwide investments.

It is the sword of political realities, sharpened to an unusual degree by Singapore's Prime Minister, that hangs above the island's future. In the light of his well-settled convictions about race and intelligence, democracy and excellence, and given his pervasive influence on policy, Lee must be counted a lucky man to have survived unscathed for so long. More importantly, Singapore has not yet been penalised to any appreciable extent for her leader's imperfectly concealed prejudices.

There have been times, when neighbours have objected to Singapore's connections with Israel on the one hand, Vietnam on the other. There have been times when reports and rumours reached neighbours of Lee's latest attack on lesser breeds, soft cultures or corrupt politicians; his speech in Parliament on 22 March 1985, stating that although he was nominally the highest paid leader in the region he was in fact the lowest paid, was not a model of tact towards Marcos, Suharto and Mahathir. There have been times when liberal opinion has condemned Singapore's domestic practices, her trade with South Africa or her arms sales to Africa and Central America.

Nevertheless, Singapore remains too valuable to the real policy makers of the region and the world, too admirable in the eyes of self-styled military and economic realists, for upset and condemnation to be more than safety valves. Even current moves by Indonesia and Malaysia to set up their own ports, to bypass Singapore in trade and foreign dealings, may merely provide psychological satisfaction without doing her undue harm.

Credit should be given to Lee since Separation for accepting and practising as much restraint as he has in the expression of his more controversial views. Were it not for his certainty that history will vindicate them and were it not for the sheet length of time he has been on stage, he might well have avoided communicating them to anyone outside his inner circle. The statesman in him, too, has made many a moderating contribution to debates at home and abroad.

His more than a quarter of a century in office has helped in other ways. He has had time to undo mistakes and to repair damage caused by *ad hoc* reaction and overreaction. Freed by Singapore's success, he has roamed the globe and taken lengthy periods of leave. He has become familiar with many of the world's most 'powerful' people. Knowing the strains of leadership, he can surmount misgivings he might entertain about fellow heads of government to offer them sympathy in their time of need. Indira Gandhi found Lee to be one of the few who made a point of contacting her while she was in the political wilderness. The names of retired leaders who have been visited or welcomed by Lee are too numerous to list here. It is all part of the protocol proper to those who are at home in the world's penthouses, juggling top-secret reports, worrying about downturns, border build-ups and personal needs, and trying to make some sense of them all.

Being a small island, Singapore has tried to blend into the global political and economic map that others have drawn, not wanting to be either too obtrusive or too negligible. As a result her leader's excesses have gone unnoticed or caused a pinprick of irritation. Sometimes, however, she has been singled out for the Aunt Sally treatment. Lee and his team do not take kindly to their republic being caricatured and then criticised, and they quickly respond with the charge of hypocrisy.

We may presume that Lee is not bothered by his people's lack of interest in foreign affairs. He has said that people of the other ASEAN states will take ten to fifteen years to catch up with their leaders' insights into Singapore, and there is no good reason for supposing that his people will return the compliment very much faster. One can hardly doubt that Singaporeans are being affected by his policies, not only the individuals who participate in ASEAN exchanges or who study and travel abroad, but the population at large. Yet for the most part Parliament and the other public institutions of review are devoid of any substantive debate over broader global matters. By contrast, in almost every utterance he makes, the Prime Minister himself puts forward a position, an arguable point of view about the world. How much is he speaking into a void? How long will the respect that accrues to him in Singapore for his international performance be based on reverent media reports or unthinking pride? Do Singaporeans wish to adopt the same outlook on the world as their Prime Minister, or do they wish others to assume that they do? If the time comes that a Singapore government decides or is compelled to adjust and perhaps even to overturn the island's international posture and linkage, Lee Kuan Yew may no longer be there to call the changes and see them through. Singapore's attainment of a special place in the sun represents his most enduring and inimitable achievement; another leader would have to negotiate with the outside world on the basis of a new set of ground rules and a different style of relationship.

Biographies

GOH CHOK TONG

Goh was born in Singapore in 1941. He was educated at Raffles Institution and the University of Singapore, and obtained his Master of Arts in development economics from Williams College in the USA. He served as a junior administrator until he was transferred to the new national shipping line, Neptune Orient Lines, in 1969, rising within four years to be its Managing Director. Elected to the Marine Parade constituency in the 1976 general elections, he was appointed Senior Minister of State for Finance in September 1977. He was given experience in the Trade and Industry, Health and Defence portfolios, and became First Deputy Prime Minister (remaining Minister of Defence as well) after the December 1984 elections. His involvement with the PAP dates from long before his parliamentary career. He is married with two children.

TONY TAN KENG YAM

Born to a wealthy and well-connected Singapore family in February 1940, Tony Tan was educated at St Joseph's Institution and the University of Singapore, graduating in physics. He completed an MSc from the Massachusetts Institute of Technology and a PhD from the University of Adelaide. After lecturing in mathematics at the University of Singapore, he joined the Overseas-Chinese Banking Corporation in 1969, nine years later becoming its General Manager. He was elected to Parliament at the 1979 by-elections and represents the contituency of Sembawang. He has had ministerial experience in the fields of education, trade and industry (holding both portfolios at the time of writing) and finance, and was Vice-Chancellor of the National University of Singapore for some years. He is married and has two children. He is a practising Christian.

ONG TENG CHEONG

Appointed Second Deputy Prime Minister following the 1984 elections, Ong was born in Singapore in 1936. Educated at Chinese High School and the University of Adelaide, he graduated in architecture; subsequently he obtained a Master's degree in civic design from the University of Liverpool. In 1972 Ong was elected to represent Kim Keat constituency in Parliament. He has had ministerial experience in communications, culture and labour. He is Secretary-General of the National Trades Union Congress at the time of writing (with a successor likely to be appointed early in 1986). He was elected to the PAP CEC as Second Vice-Chairman in February 1979, and became Party Chairman in January 1981. He is married with two children.

Suppiah Dhanabalan

Born in 1937 in Singapore, Dhanabalan was educated at Victoria School and at the University of Malaya in Singapore, from which he graduated with an honours degree in economics. He joined the Singapore Administrative Service in 1960 and was seconded to the Economic Development Board, where he helped establish the Development Bank of Singapore, eventually becoming its Executive Vice President. Elected in 1976 to represent Kallang constituency, Dhanabalan resigned from the Bank in 1978 to take up appointment as Senior Minister of State for National Development. Since 1980 he has been Minister for Foreign Affairs, with concurrent responsibility for the culture portfolio and then its less ominous-sounding replacement, community development. He is married and has a daughter and son. He is a practising Christian.

9
More Than Survival

> I have come to the conclusion that each generation must learn its own lessons ... What we, the elders, can do is to save our young Singaporeans from unnecessary, self-inflicted wounds. The duty of leadership is to preserve the climate of confidence and discipline, without which Singapore will wither away and die.
>
> LEE KUAN YEW
> to PAP MPs after the Anson by-election loss, 17 November 1981

In August 1965, there was no one to save Lee from the wound of Separation. Singapore's Malays were the only group of citizens who felt it as a trauma, and they had concerns of a quite different order from their Prime Minister's. The Chinese and the Indians, together comprising 84 per cent of the population, stood poised to make something of their small island and its independence. Their relief was tempered less by worries about the future than by the thought of relatives across the Causeway.

If no other event had done so before, Separation put on ice the formation of class consciousness in Singapore. Right from the outset of modern times (1819) ethnic, linguistic, cultural and religious characteristics, no less than the measurement of relative prosperity, formed the perceived basis of individual identity and social belonging. Latterly, friction between the various races, increased by merger and Confrontation, had been a more obvious cause of strife than exploitation by colonial or local masters. To express it another way, the righting of economic injustice was a lower priority in 1965 for the majority of Singapore's people than escape from the hothouse of contact with the peninsular Malays' politics and the prospect of assimilation to their dominance.

The sudden shock of being free created a unique opportunity for the Prime Minister. Whatever Lee's emotional and mental state, he was in no mood to run away. To use Mao's vivid image, Singapore presented herself to him like a blank sheet of paper on which he could inscribe a beautiful blueprint. No one else was remotely fitted to the opportunity. Lee's principal opponent, Dr Lee Siew Choh of the Barisan Sosialis, had lost ground dramatically since the 1963 elections and, caught offguard by the turn of events, he dismissed Singapore's independence as bogus.

The paucity of alternative leadership allowed the PAP to claim a monopoly on national loyalty. The period after Separation was punctuated by student unrest in Chinese-medium colleges and schools. It was smacked down firmly by the Government and subversive instigation was alleged, in several incidents students themselves resisted disruption and intimidation by their more radical fellows. Moreover, when the army seized control of Indonesia from Sukarno, the Communist Party of Indonesia (PKI) was decimated, leading to the closure in late 1965 of one of the main support arms of opposition to the PAP, the communist Malayan National Liberation League headquarters in Jakarta. As for the Singapore UMNO, it was reduced to pathetic straits; never strong, it was now even more cut off from its parent body in Malaysia.

The blueprint of independence will occupy these two chapters. The problems of selection and interpretation of facts are nowhere more acute than at this stage of investigation. Relatively little is known of what lies behind the major domestic events of the last twenty years. Prior to 1965, and since then as far as Singapore's international dealings are concerned, alternative sources and records can be invoked to check and highlight the relevant parts of the official dossier and of the generally unprobing descriptions local academics and media have churned out.

So these chapters' painting of Lee and the changes in post-Separation Singapore will have to be impressionistic. There is the added risk of being wrong the closer we move to the present day and can more easily lose or mistake the pattern of meaning. What follows is in no way meant to be exhaustive or complete; it is one person's reading of a political saga that, while it cries out to be interpreted, withholds many of the details necessary to interpretation.

A changing political face

Lee's first need was to review his team's readiness to meet the challenge of mobilisation. Three Cabinet colleagues had been politically indispensable so far: Goh Keng Swee, Toh Chin Chye and S. Rajaratnam. Goh and Toh were independent types who invested themselves in economic planning and party management respectively. They disliked each other energetically and with a measure of grudging admiration. Rajaratnam lived in his own indestructible world of heady rhetoric, keen observation and fairly easy relationships. Now it was up to Lee to assess their particular skills and their reactions under the pressure of recent events, then determine the importance of each one to the Singapore of the future.

One other person outside Cabinet assumed a new prominence in Lee's calculations—Devan Nair. Devan's friendship was important and, on a more practical note, it was touch and go how long he could be spared from the day-to-day direction of Singapore's union movement.

In Lee's mind, the hour called for decisive action, to gear up the economy, build substantial new defence programmes and so embark upon full nationhood. If only by default, the people were ready and waiting. Ironically, there was a surge of enthusiasm for the PAP, boosting membership considerably just when the PAP machine was becoming less relevant. The fight against the MCP and its frontmen, against Kuala Lumpur and against chauvinists or opportunists was not yet over, but it had been overtaken by more pressing matters. Government performance was at a much higher premium than Party solidarity.

Over the first years after Separation, a number of the Prime Minister's moves revealed that his thinking was along these lines.

Goh Keng Swee was put in charge of defence, and alternated between that portfolio and finance with the less visionary but capable Lim Kim San (a friend from Raffles College days and a successful businessman before entering government service). Thus two crucial areas were firmly under his control. Dr Albert Winsemius, a Dutch economist who had impressed Goh and Lee with his part in the 1960 United Nations Development Plan for Singapore and who became thereafter a regular consultant and visitor to the island, was summoned urgently from his home in The Hague. His brief was to prepare a plan for the reorganising of Singapore as a global city.

Rajaratnam was put in charge of foreign affairs and given the task of building a diplomatic corps and a ministry to give effect to Singapore's international policy.

In early 1968, Toh Chin Chye was switched from the Deputy Premiership* and made Minister for Science and Technology and Vice-Chancellor of the University of Singapore. It was the first

---

* The post of Deputy Prime Minister was thereby abolished; it was restored some years later for Goh Keng Swee and then split into First and Second Deputy Prime Minister (initially Goh Keng Swee and S. Rajaratnam).

public mark of his declining usefulness to Lee's Government and doubtless owed something to his opposition to the wholesale introduction of national service and his real unhappiness at the Secretary-General's neglect of consultation within the PAP.

C.V. Devan Nair returned from Malaysia in mid-1969 to take over the National Trades Union Congress.

The People's Action Party

The inner cohesion of the PAP core group began to disintegrate in the absence of daily external attack. Loyalty to Lee had never been the basis of the group's cohesion, and loyalty to Singapore and the Party meant different things to different people. Now it became important to identify where one stood *vis-à-vis* the Prime Minister, either to adjust one's position to his or to calculate how long one could get away with disagreement before irrevocable breakdown of the relationship.

The disintegration was very slow. The first conclusive hint of it came to the fore late in 1978 when Toh Chin Chye was criticised by the normally bland *Straits Times* for his heated defence of the Health Ministry and its performance. At the beginning of 1981 he was demoted to the backbenches, and Ong Teng Cheong supplanted him in the chair of the PAP Central Executive Committee. Other signs of a shake-up tumbled into view. By September 1984 all the old guard except for Lee had left the CEC, and after the December 1984 elections only E.W. Barker remained out of the older second-echelon ministers in Cabinet. From 1981 to 1983 the Cabinet was like some sort of chrysalis into which the Party emptied its old form, re-emerging with a new identity but with the same name and the same Secretary-General.

The rationale for thorough blending of Party and Government has been stated frequently over the last decade. The PAP has become identified in the public mind, it is said, as the bearer of Singapore's destiny. It is the guiding star that has pointed the way forward out of conflict with communist and communalist alike. No other institution has taken the initiative to resolve the problems and dilemmas that faced a colony en route to self-government, on into merger with Malaysia, then out in the cold as an independent and sovereign nation. So it is quite proper for the executive bodies of Government and Party to coalesce so that they can be attuned to each other fully and efficiently.

Probing behind the rhetoric discloses a logic of development that is far from self-authenticating. At numerous points along the way, cadres in the Cabinet and in the Party at large have resisted such tendencies. Toh Chin Chye, Ong Pang Boon and the late Wong Lin Ken have been three of the more prominent. Lim Kim San, Kenny Byrne, Yong Nyuk Lin and Jek Yeun Thong are others who have drawn attention to the harm they believe has been done by making the PAP, its policy and decisionmaking, subordinate to the Government's priorities as defined by the prevailing power brokers.

Someone looking back through Darwinian spectacles might presume that only the fittest to rule have survived. Thus, Toh Chin Chye has fallen from power because his failure to adjust to changed circumstances has finally caught up with him; Ong Pang Boon has consigned himself to irrelevance by persisting with romantic notions of blue-collar workers, chauvinist notions of Chinese culture and sentimentality about the role he and his late wife (Chan Choy Siong) once played in organising the PAP. Long ago Jek Yeun Thong was useful to Lee; now he is not, so he may go off and sulk.

This hypothesis breaks down, however, when one asks: How is it, then, that so much politically inert material survived for so many years? With a better Opposition to scrutinise their performance, a whole array of Cabinet ministers and underlings would never have stayed the course as long as they did. Because of their family and 'old boy' connections, their symbolic value in terms of race and education stream or their total dependence on the leadership for viability—and notwithstanding their modest executive talents—they have been useful to plug various gaps in the government.

A spectrum shift has occurred between the policy, structure and personal relationships of the 1965 Cabinet and those of 1985. Today's team consists mostly of high-calibre technocrats being tested by Lee in the political hothouse where he reigns supreme; they have to cope with sometimes bewildering permutations and combinations of portfolios; they are well paid and the principal sacrifice they make is of their privacy. Twenty years ago there was less intellectual ability on display, but there was also a diversity of strongly held viewpoints—for instance, 'stay with Britain and the Commonwealth' versus 'go with Japan'—and at least a number of men had their own strong personal and party base. Rewards were deliberately pegged back. Then loyalty was to the Party platform, now it is to the Prime Minister, not in theory to Lee personally but to the office he happens to hold.

In its favour, the group of implants grafted into the Party or Government since 1976 seems to be 'taking' more successfully than previous attempts. The radical changes to CEC and Cabinet indicate as much.

At present, three men stand out among the nominal leaders who have been put through their paces at home and abroad: Goh Chok Tong, Tony Tan and Lee Hsien Loong.

Goh Chok Tong was the first of the trio to achieve a high profile. He drafted the Budget of 1979 and, after corrections were made by the Finance Minister and the Prime Minister, presented it to the Parliament. The following year he co-ordinated the by-election campaign for the Party and was allowed to announce a very important policy change—the planned Second Industrial Revolution, a scheme to upgrade the workforce rapidly for high-technology industry with corresponding wage increases and provision of retraining opportunities. He has had responsibility for subsequent elections, with their mixed results, and for setting in train the Government's 'total defence' programme. At first he adopted the tough abrasive style that Lee Kuan Yew originally reserved for recalcitrant sectional groups, but he was rebuffed by the public. Since then he and his colleagues have heeded the Prime Minister's call 'to translate' figures and hard-headed analyses of complex problems into warm, simple and human terms, terms which the ordinary people can understand.[1] It remains to be seen how well he has sized up each audience.

Tony Tan has been more consistent in personal manner; his caution enables him to exude an air of quiet and secure conviction. He has also presented the Budget on several occasions and the Prime Minister let it through with no corrections. Dr Tan is one of the few members of Singapore's *de facto* aristocracy to come forward in politically explicit service of the PAP vision. His strong Christian conscience adds both commitment and timeless standards to the working of a highly proficient mind. His background in university lecturing and banking has fitted him well for the portfolios he has been given—education, finance, trade and industry—and the revamping of Singapore's bus service was a managerial task demanding attention to grassroots needs. He is known locally as 'the smile on the face of the tiger' and has won approval for moderating unpopular policies.

Brigadier-General (Reservists) Lee Hsien Loong does not fall within any local class, being his father's son and a distinguished alumnus of Cambridge and Harvard universities in his own right. His systems ability, his wide reading and his military career have trained him to the long view. His rise within the armed forces was spectacular. He achieved public prominence when he was appointed to head an emergency rescue operation handling the Sentosa cable car disaster that occurred in January 1983. Shortly after his election to Teck Ghee constituency in December 1984, he was appointed to understudy Goh Chok Tong and Tony Tan in their ministries (defence, trade and industry) and to be Deputy Government Whip. His first major creative test—in progress at the time of writing—is the chairmanship of a twelve-man committee drawn from the public and private sectors to scrutinise Singapore's economy and prepare a new plan to suit the more sober mood of the second half of the 1980s.

Lee Hsien Loong's entry into politics at a time of severe downturn and after some years of military service may work to his advantage, provided he can mastermind a retrieval plan. Many expatriates and local businessmen blame the Second Industrial Revolution scheme (with which Goh Chok Tong is identified) for moving wages ahead too fast and assaying markets of unproven viability.

In any succession stakes, these three must be the current favourites. For the moment Goh Chok Tong is centre forwards and team spirit submerges other players' ambitions. But with it becoming a sacred truth that the leadership changeover must be smooth, Goh himself may have to surrender his position in the name of team spirit. When the time comes, the principal factors deciding each one's prospects will be performance, popular appeal and Lee Kuan Yew's support. By such criteria Lee Hsien Loong is likely to start odds-on. Goh Chok Tong has not shrunk from the possibility that he will not be Prime Minister. 'If Singapore will be better led by somebody else, if I'm just to warm the seat, so be it,' he has said.[2]

Goh also articulated an important condition: 'the General would have to convince the MPs as well as the people that he was best for the job.' The PAP has been directed by the Prime Minister for so long and has given the impression of being so supine that recent changes in its ethos easily escape notice. In fact, the party base of Goh Chok Tong—and of his former Cabinet colleague, Lim Chee Onn—is very strong and dates back to Youth Wing days. Since the shock of the October 1981 Anson by-election loss, the younger leaders have put a lot of effort into strengthening PAP fibre. Party stalwarts have not been as hostile towards Goh and his colleagues as they were to the sudden imports of the 1970s. Before undergoing the Prime Minister's scrutiny, policy proposals are discussed and thrashed out by cadres and younger ministers; this has helped to develop camaraderie and cohesion. In the matter of pre-selection, considerable initiative is now taken by the PAP machine. There have even been signs of Goh Chok Tong striking out on his own—he authorised the naming of a very able businessman, former journalist and detainee, Ho Kwon Ping, as a likely candidate for the December 1984 elections, but when he met with reluctance from a number of quarters, including from Ho himself, nothing more was done about it.

What will the Party do if it has to choose between Goh Chok Tong and Lee Hsien Loong? Will Lee Kuan Yew accept the decision if it conflicts with his own wishes? Will Tony Tan be a 'compromise' winner? It will be fascinating to see how the Party and the people of Singapore answer these questions.

Goh Chok Tong informed a PAP dinner gathering that Lee is fully 'aware of his omnipresence in Singapore. He himself told me ... that was the reason why he was determined to step down sooner than later.'[3] 1988 is the year most often designated as the deadline—when Lee Kuan Yew celebrates his sixty-fifth birthday. The pressure is building up for a fully trained new team to be ready to take over the present structure of government. It may be doubted that Lee Kuan Yew's omnipresence will be reduced if he remains as elected President or adviser extraordinary.

Of the two who were first to resign from the current batch of trainee leaders—Bernard Chen and Lim Chee Onn—the latter should not on any account be written off. He accepted his removal from the secretaryship of the NTUC in 1983 without recrimination, and took it upon himself to withdraw even further from the limelight than Lee had pushed him. In terms of current definitions of ability and ambition, he would seem to be a formidable figure for the medium- or longer term future. Having built a power base too quickly and suffered for it, he is not likely to make the same mistake again. The evidence is that Lee singled him out and pushed him into the driver's seat of the trade union movement, despite vigorous protest from Phey Yew Kok and others in the NTUC. Devan Nair agreed to this drastically changed style of union leadership, but requested that Lim be made a minister (which is what happened) so that the NTUC might have the compensation of a direct voice in Cabinet. Within two years Lee became alarmed at the extent of Lim's empire-building—almost a mini-government with its own team and its own high-powered financing proposals—and arranged for him to be dropped from the NTUC. Again, Devan Nair was called on to assist and to corral the older unionists (Devan was, reportedly, more reluctant this time round, having been bitten once and also because, now that he was President, he was supposed to be above such manoeuvres. But it was vital to Lee's purposes that Lim's ousting be portrayed as a union initiative.) Lim Chee Onn's return to Cabinet rank—as distinct from his backbencher appointment in 1985 to chair the parliamentary accounts committee—depends on the Prime Minister behaving uncharacteristically. Further down the track, he may be called on by Lee's successors. Of course, other paths are open to him.

The process of creating a new leadership nucleus has continued fitfully from 1966 onwards—'a conscious effort from 1970' according to Lee Kuan Yew[4]—and it may not yet be complete. The Prime Minister told the 1982 Party Conference, 'The yardstick is, who can best protect and advance the interests of Singaporeans? By asking this question, we shall get a good team together. They may not be as rounded, as multifaceted in their skills, as the original team. . . . Furthermore, the original team was solidly backed by a people who had suffered . . . The final handing on of the baton is not going to happen immediately. But it cannot be delayed beyond this decade.' The old guard's slowing down with age, the demands of a young electorate (some of which need resisting or tempering), the inherent smallness and vulnerability of Singapore, and the children who are this generation's hostages to fortune constitute compelling pressures to search out and train leaders who are problem solvers. 'When the younger team has weathered their first crisis on their own, you and I will breathe easier.'[5]

Lee was puzzled by the uneven results of his early attempts to find talent. Then it dawned on him that, as he said, 'the older generation of leadership had come from all over Southeast Asia. It took me a long time to discover the significance of that.'[6] They had formed a spontaneous and unrepeatable grouping, toughened by the Japanese Occupation, by their tussle to come out on top in a united front with the militant Left, and by the resilience that made independent Singapore succeed against the odds. Ordinary recruiting at a measured pace would only produce 'DC3 aircraft' calibre, not 'Boeing 707' or '747'. Recruits in the first part of the 1970s either could not make the grade (such as Tan Eng Liang, whom *Time* magazine once proclaimed to be an up-and-coming leader) or sought their own unacceptably high Party standing (such as Lee Chiaw Meng, who was rumoured to have a pact with the ever-popular Ong Pang Boon to form more than the 'bridge' leadership the Prime Minister had told the 1971 National Day rally was the best Ong could expect). According to Lee Kuan Yew, 'the urgency to test out MPs and ministers started from 1976'[7] probably when he realised that the renewal venture was not working, that the PAP was in quiet rebellion (against his overbearing ways) and that the old nucleus was breaking up. The surprising thing was that it took him so long to acknowledge that the forlorn state of PAP morale could not be glossed over by euphoric word pictures of the kind he offered to the 1971 Party Congress.

Few Singaporeans with the required attributes have offered themselves enthusiastically for a political career. The fear of being demoted or humiliated is not without justification, and even the ambitious would think twice about declaring their intentions. Lee was only stating the obvious when he said, 'The younger men in Cabinet are not here because they are my proteges, or because they have wormed their way into the hearts of Dr Goh, Rajaratnam or me. The MPs know me. I am impervious to flattery.'[8]

Lee has also taken note of instructive foreign examples. He believes Mao and Nehru both bequeathed a legacy of serious leadership problems. 'In both cases, by hanging on too long, a creator generation lost the chance to facilitate and to ease the way for their successors,* and thus to have more influence in determining the nature of their successors.'[9]

The selection of PAP candidates has turned from a somewhat haphazard affair into a highly conscious process. Relying on deliberate investigation, with some input from hearsay, talent is spotted at pre-university and tertiary level, within the armed forces, civic groups, the union movement, the administration and the private sector. Where are the natural leaders? Who has the intellectual equipment? Where is the evidence of sincere concern for community and nation? The next stage is usually an approach by one of the PAP new generation senior officials for a tea party chat (some special cases are undertaken directly by the Prime Minister or a colleague of his vintage). If interest is shown, a rigorous testing of psychological aptitude follows, then a thorough security check, a crash course in political history and a round of interviews in which, sooner or later, the Prime Minister meets prospective candidates. Weaknesses are exposed and probed remorselessly—such things as being a woman, wife and mother, or a sheltered and unassertive technocrat, or being monolingual.

To what extent suitability for a particular constituency and its needs overrides other criteria—eligibility for Cabinet, middle rank or just parliamentary backbench, the racial and religious equilibrium of Parliament, whether someone's political outlook is perceived to be self-generated or derived from the PAP—is not known. For the elections of the 1970s, the placement of particular

---

* Deng Xiaoping and Indira Gandhi, both of whom Lee had recently met.

candidates was kept a secret until nomination day. However, the ploy, intended to disconcert the Opposition, backfired when the Opposition parties also began to resort to it with their better prospects. Nowadays, fair indication is given beforehand.

It may be asked whether the Prime Minister accepted any responsibility for choosing Pang Kim Hin, a rather withdrawn systems engineer, to take Devan Nair's place as MP for Anson at the by-election of October 1981. What can be said is that, when J.B. Jeyaretnam won the seat, Lee heatedly defended the hapless Pang against the absurd charge of nepotism—he was Lim Kim San's nephew by marriage—and even promised that, braced by his baptism of fire, he would be fielded again, a promise that has yet to be fulfilled.

In 1984, the PAP unsuccessfully pitted two of its 'best' men, Ng Pock Too and Mah Bow Tan, against J.B. Jeyaretnam of the Workers Party and Chiam See Tong of the Social Democratic Party. The Prime Minister stressed how important it was to elect them, that he had plans for them.

It has become abundantly clear that the problems facing the PAP are not peculiar to the leaders of the younger generation. Recently Lee himself has shown that he too is no longer surefooted in negotiating the changed obstacle course of Singapore democracy.

The 'hard and unpleasant part' of the renewal process has been getting people to step aside. 'I have learned not to shirk it,' Lee once said.[10] Not all those stood down have recognised any prime ministerial sorrow. The turnover of parliamentarians has become less and less a function of normal attrition—loss of seat at election time, malfeasance, ill health or death. MPs have gone out to grass whether they liked it or not, whether their branch members liked it or not. Some have accepted their fate graciously, others have protested, but ultimately they have had no choice.

Lee's low regard for women MPs was the excuse for him to dispose of Chan Choy Siong in 1970. Many attested her to be an excellent, hardworking, dedicated member of Parliament and PAP cadre, but she had to go. Was it because she had cast her CEC vote for Ong Eng Guan in the 1959 selection of a Prime Minister,[11] or because she was Ong Pang Boon's wife and the influence they both enjoyed among the Chinese-educated needed dilution? (She died some years ago in a motor accident, her Party loyalty intact to the end.)

By contrast, some hacks have been allowed to outstay their effectiveness, and some of those deemed failures in higher positions and demoted from them have held onto their parliamentary seats if they so wished. Perhaps in these cases, considerations of kindness or of pension levels being proportionate to length of service prevailed with the Prime Minister.

The 1984 elections, however, saw about one-third of the candidates standing for the first time. This batch of replacements has been introduced with the same accelerated urgency as the reconstitution of the CEC. The deafening silence of the Party machine must mean its consent to the exercise of what is technically the Prime Minister's, i.e. the Secretary-General's, prerogative. If there is not consent but dismay, how will it come to the surface? And who is going to ask the question of questions: will Lee Kuan Yew recognise the right time for his own withdrawal?

Another sign of the PAP's transformation is the explicit redefining of its nature and objectives. In November 1982 the Party was declared to have become a national movement dedicated to the service of Singapore and to the advancement of the people's well-being. Its revised objectives are: to preserve nation and territory, to safeguard and advance Singapore through representative and democratic government, to infuse a sense of patriotism and identity by forging a multiracial society that is fair, just and tolerant to build a self-reliant, dynamic society that rewards citizens according to their performance and contribution and that also has compassion for the less fortunate, to achieve the optimum in economic development and in social and cultural fulfilment and to provide equal opportunities for all Singaporeans to achieve their maximum potential so that there will be a place and a role for them, whatever their contribution.[12]

It would be hard to quarrel with this platform and its 'motherhood and apple pie' provisions. Only when precise definitions and actual working content are supplied can there be a proper critique of it. A number of the early PAP leaders have demurred at the neglect or abandonment of aspects of the original charter and more particularly at the changes that have stolen over the ethos and direction of the Party. Toh Chin Chye and Ong Pang Boon have voiced their feelings publicly, and many others have done so privately during interviews or conversations. In turn they have been accused of sour grapes or of failing to accept the inevitable. After all, it is said, a stance of anti-colonialism, pro-merger and socialism has long lost its aptness to describe or prescribe Singapore's situation. Dhanabalan has gone so far as to demand that the older generation realise that the torch has passed from their hands (his strictures, of course, might have been directed to the Prime Minister). His peers have spoken more softly but said the same thing. Besides, the changes about which they have complained—the reduced autonomy of public institutions, the de-emphasising of direct governmental responsibility for the disadvantaged, the decline in accountability of leadership to Party and nation—may be construed as the price to be paid for overall improvement and growth.

The framework of democracy

The constraints of parliamentary democracy have been accepted since the PAP came to power in 1959, but the struts and joints of the framework have undergone significant pressure and alteration.

THE CONSTITUTION AND THE PRESIDENCY
The development of the Constitution bears the unmistakable marks of the Prime Minister's influence. Immediately after Separation, he announced that a panel of foreign jurists and chief justices would be called on to draft a new document incorporating existing provisions from the Malaysia or self-government periods of Singapore's history. The international project was abandoned, however, and a local Constitutional Commission was set up to look into the protection of minority rights; from it eventually came the Presidential Council that remains in attenuated form today. (David Marshall, first Chief Minister, resigned from the original body, protesting that its deliberations were subject to too many exemptions and that it was dominated by current government ministers.) Meanwhile, amendments were passed during the first Parliament of December 1965 to enshrine the independence thrust upon the island. In 1972, responding to what he alleged to be outside interference connived at by the Opposition, Lee introduced a major amendment preventing surrender of sovereignty (including armed forces and police) except with the specific agreement of two-thirds of the voters. Other changes are allowed if two-thirds of the Parliament pass them. In the second half of 1984 the President assented to amending legislation that permits up to three non-elected Opposition MPs to sit in the House.*

---

* The three non-elected MPs would be those Opposition candidates receiving the highest votes short of a plurality. With two elected Opposition MPs entering the House following the December 1984 elections, the Workers' Party chose not to take up the offer of another seat for its candidate who just missed out. As far back as 1972 other options were canvassed—e.g. seats for university staff—but nothing came of them.

By 1971, Lee had come to the conclusion that there was an unbeatable jinx on constitutional reform. Despite the advantages of having been tutored by the best experts at Cambridge and of having received advice from Britain's leading theoretician at the 1956 Constitutional Conference (and later in private) Lee claimed that the Tunku set him thinking along a more helpful tack. 'We had a chitchat once late in 1962 in his sitting room at the Residency. I looked at a beautiful leather-bound green-covered volume Constitution with some Arabic letters. I asked what this was. He said it was given to him by President Ayub Khan [of Pakistan]. His new Constitution. It looked splendid. He said, "But you know, Kuan Yew, they make very good constitutions. They have many brilliant lawyers and with every new leader they have to make a new one".' The final straw resulted from a request by Lee to the British High Commissioner in 1970, to pass the Constitution to experts for polishing. Back it came in elegant shape, and Lee's heart sank. He realised the more he looked at it that 'the experts just have no idea why we had made certain basic alterations'. His 'real-life, hands-on' experience compelled him to leave the Constitution in its existing, untidy form. He 'never regretted it'.[13]

The fact is that Singapore's Constitution is by no means sacrosanct. It is pliable to the touch of its proper guardian, Lee Kuan Yew, who knows the priority of good order over law and the difference between appropriate and inappropriate law. Just a few weeks after insisting that only minor amendments could be made, Lee foreshadowed a revamping of the presidency that would turn it into an elected office of greater importance, probably restricted in eligibility to former Cabinet ministers and giving the President right of veto over the spending of Singapore's reserves.

Lee has grumbled many times about the dangers, frailties and poor portability of the Westminster one-man, one-vote, two-party system. According to him, 'It didn't work in France, Germany, Italy, Canada, Australia, New Zealand' and is under grave stress now in Britain because the leaders of the Conservative and Labour parties no longer share the values derived from a common educational background. He also endorses Goh Keng Swee's view: 'Only the United States' fund of great wealth, robust strength and talent has prevented the collapse of democracy there.'[14]

To him, a redesigned presidency is a brainwave. Singapore's perseverance with democracy, principled but ambiguous, has complicated the search for good people to lead Singapore in future. Who will have Lee's authority to teach the people how to overcome their self-destructive tendencies and their shortsightedness? No other Prime Minister could conceivably fit his mould. Why not move into the presidency, on the theory that the new leadership team needs as much time as possible to take over the reins and establish credibility? The current indications are that a White Paper will be brought before Parliament in 1987 for debate and passage. If Opposition members are convinced that an outrage is being perpetrated, there may be a referendum.

The mood is a far cry from the days of Benjamin Sheares, the Eurasian obstetrician and gynaecologist who was President from 1970 until his death in 1981. (He attended Mrs Lee [Kwa Geok Choo] in Singapore when American specialists were wanting her to travel overseas for treatment.) Like Yusof Ishak, Singapore's first Head of State (1959–65) and then President (1965–70), and Devan Nair (1981–84), Sheares came of a minority race. But, unlike them, he had no known political interest or usefulness—Yusof was the Malay newspaper proprietor chosen to be Head of State before merger, pro-PAP, tied closely by kinship or friendship to politicians on the peninsula; Devan Nair was a founding father of the PAP and latterly guru of Singapore's trade unions with connections to the regional and international labour movement. Sheares maintained Yusof's quiet, dignified and impartial style.

Devan Nair was probably intended to be forerunner of a more distinctively political presidency. He had been plucked from management of the NTUC, brought into Parliament to oversee the younger generation's grassroots political training and elected President two years later. His premature resignation has complicated the transition to a popularly elected and more decisive Head of State, and could well mean that Lee himself, against his stated preference, will be the first candidate for the new office. (If the events culminating in Devan's resignation have tarnished the presidential image, blame cannot be apportioned to him alone.)

Singapore's fourth President, Wee Kim Wee, took up office on 3 September 1985. It was stated publicly that his tenure might not reach a full term. Although Chinese by race, Wee comes of a Malacca Straits-born family, is fluent in English and Malay, and represents (more affirmatively) the same background as the Prime Minister, to whom he is distantly related. While working for United Press International and then for the *Straits Times* after its head office was moved to Kuala Lumpur in 1959, he acquired considerable skill in dealing with expatriates and trouble-shooting with the Singapore Government. On Rajaratnam's recommendation, 1973 saw him appointed High Commissioner to Malaysia, where his manner and linguistic facility made him a great success.

He went on to serve as Ambassador to Japan and South Korea from 1980 until 1984, at which stage he was called upon once more to follow the ill-fated Wee Mon Cheng, his predecessor in Tokyo, as Chairman of the Singapore Broadcasting Corporation. Lee Kuan Yew, however slow he was to recognise Wee Kim Wee's worth, has clearly identified the new President as an unpretentious man of integrity who will restore the prestige of the office, keep a low profile and provide a contrast of role but precedent of race for the one who is to come.

THE COMMUNAL BASE

At the more visible level, Lee's supremacy over the political process, virtually unquestioned between 1968 and 1984, is reflected in his clever management of all Singapore's significant ethno-cultural groups. The 1963 elections at the birth of Malaysia enabled the PAP, rid of its Chinese chauvinists and extremists, to capture new middle ground, notably among the Malays and the English-educated. The effect of Separation was to retrieve support from the Chinese but put the Malays at a disadvantage. The latter's identity was threatened by the loss or feared loss of special privileges, by the forcible if gradual dispersion from their tightly knit rural and maritime communities into high-rise estates and by the disregard for their culture implied by the officially esteemed values. They were not called up for national service, so they missed out on the work training and jobs that went with it. Cut off from direct Malaysian political support, their voice was muted and the only channel left for their disgruntlement with the PAP and its Malay seniors was the ballot box. The September 1972 elections saw their vote for Party candidates reach its nadir, though the damage done in any one constituency was reduced because housing resettlement was well advanced. Lee claimed to have won back at least half of the Malay 'ground' by 1980, and has declared that any remaining problems are not serious. The Malays' doors of opportunity have been shut and opened, their councils and organisations founded or supplanted, according to Lee's perceptions and timetable. The only Malay currently a Cabinet Minister, Ahmad Mattar, is vividly aware of the stakes, having been caught in the race riots of July 1964; he appears to accept that the position of the Malays is as good as it can be under the circumstances. His Chinese colleagues of the same vintage recognise that it is an area in which they are somewhat at sea: Goh Chok Tong, for instance, to use his own words, 'told himself that he did not have the breadth or depth of knowledge of the complex subject [effective Malay participation in national development].' And if he had applied a logical and analytical mind to the subject, he risked offending the Malays with some 'cold conclusions'.[15]

The Indians of Singapore are better integrated into the political system. Lee's assessment is that they have been equally divided into those who support the PAP Government because they have benefited and 'those who would have an opposition because that is part of an Indian culture'.[16]

ELECTIONS AND OPPOSITION

When the main opposition group, the Barisan Sosialis, took its unequal struggle out of the constitutional arena, the PAP was left to dominate electoral politics. As well as by-elections, there have been five general elections since independence, all called before the five-year limit had elapsed and to suit the PAP. Each carried its own specific request for a mandate: April 1968 (58 seats, 7 contested) to ratify and allow tough Government measures in response to Britain's accelerated withdrawal from Singapore; September 1972 (65 seats, 57 contested) to introduce measures that would improve the people's quality of life; December 1976 (69 seats, 53 contested) to reaffirm the PAP's defence and security stand; December 1980 (75 seats, 38 contested) to confirm the current directions of policy and test the leadership succession and December 1984 (79 seats, 40 contested) to test further and redeploy the new leaders before an economic downturn. It is becoming less easy for the Government to presume on victory at the polls when short memories and the revolution of rising expectations combine to intensify immediate grievances at PAP inadequacy or arrogance.

Permission after the event is another ingredient lost from a once-foolproof electoral strategy. During the tame 1970s, Lee's words, spoken after the 1972 election, could have served as an unconsciously ironic motto: 'Singapore politics is like playing a Shakespearean tragedy without props.'[17]

The Opposition has begun the long haul back from the wilderness. Opposition parties have been badly bruised and mauled. The Prime Minister and Rajaratnam have ridiculed their activists and candidates, labelling them 'jokers' and 'opportunists'. They have been infiltrated by security and intelligence agents; they have been charged with receiving foreign funds and engaging in 'black operations'; defamation suits have been filed or threatened by PAP ministers to avenge or discourage alleged excesses. Unfortunately Lee's disdain for Opposition figures such as J.B. Jeyaretnam—even to the extent of using minions to purvey insults or reject requests—

has begun to be seen as a more general disdain. Each new example of persecution or discrimination, each episode of the PAP pack baying at one or two isolated figures, each litany of actionable offences, draws more ordinary Singaporeans to join or sympathise with Opposition parties. The crowning revelation came from Teh Cheang Wan, Minister for National Development, when he told Parliament that government services had been downgraded in the two constituencies that failed to elect a PAP representative.[18] It is quite another matter, however, whether any of the Opposition parties can build a genuine mass base comparable to the Barisan Sosialis or PAP in their heydays.

There is another kind of opposition whose emotional pull in Singapore is all but gone: the political detainee. According to Professor Jayakumar, Minister for Home Affairs, speaking in Parliament on 14 May 1985, there is only one person still held in this category,* Chia Thye Poh, former Barisan MP and assistant lecturer at Nanyang University. The drop in numbers is not a sign that the Government is more mellow or less vigilant; only that political 'subversion' is dormant and the battle for people's hearts and minds has no need at present for cannon fodder. The approach of the twentieth anniversary in February 1983 of the security mop-up, Operation Cold Store, might also have had something to do with it.

Apart from those who were banished or went into exile, hundreds of men and women on both sides of the Causeway have spent the best years of their adult lives in prisons or holding centres without trial. They were detained under internal security regulations dating back to colonial days. Despite the fact that people from all walks of life and racial groups have been locked up, the common charge they have all faced is that of subversion, predominantly communist subversion. The methods of interrogation are more restrained than in some countries, although still alienating and sadistic. Internal security operatives extract confessions not by extreme torture but by subjecting the detainee to solitary confinement and severe disorientation and then getting him or her to write and rewrite drafts until an acceptable version is produced. Release was formerly dependent on an admission of guilt and a written statement of future good intent; recently verbal undertakings have been sufficient.

---

* There are over 1600 held without trial, mostly under criminal law and immigration Acts. Some of them may be political detainees by an Amnesty International definition of the term.

The conditions of all prisoners were improved following a Commission of Inquiry set up by Lee in 1959 and chaired by Devan Nair. On a darker note, both officials and detainees have alleged that psychotropic drugs were used in specific cases, particularly after Operation Cold Store. The gathering of material for this book involved more than one harrowing interview with those on the executing or receiving end of detention. Yet in the nature of things neither side is likely to be able to substantiate its respective charge—of subversion or of maltreatment—in a court of law. (J.B. Jeyaretnam recently announced that the sole remaining 'political' detainee, Chia Thye Poh, was demanding a legal hearing, which may explain why he was still imprisoned at the time of writing.)

What have been the circumstances under which political detention has been practised in Singapore? The Republic has had sole responsibility for its internal security since Separation. Lee has ensured the fullest possible exercise of the responsibility. The paraphernalia of secret surveillance have fascinated him for years and he has had close personal connections with British, Malayan and Australian operatives and their organisations from at least the 1950s. In his anti-colonial heyday, he was able to mock the sinister results he had observed at first hand of the Special Branch's moral and logical slide into repression—his famous Assembly speech of 4 October 1956 on the subject is still quoted against him. Once in government, an instinct deeper than respect for democratic convention took over: power. Lee's preference was that the instinct be exercised within bounds unless the enemy's behaviour dictated otherwise. The trouble was, as he had remarked in the Assembly, that repression is a habit that grows addictive with time and practice. However interminable the chicken-and-egg argument may be, any investigator will be struck by a record bristling with instances of dissent being labelled subversion and thence communism, and will suspect that the authorities were not all incapable of making the distinction. One former detainee, although he now acknowledges that events have vindicated Lee's general policies, recalled that he had challenged the Prime Minister, to whom he had been quite close, for describing him in public as a communist while knowing full well that he was not. Apparently, Lee's reply was a lame 'You shouldn't be upset—that's politics'.

Over the years the Internal Security Department has developed an inimitable repertoire, including telephone tapping, mail interception, immigration checks, direct interrogation (which may be polite, brusque or insinuating in tone), personal shadowing and electronic surveillance. Its selective use—on newcomers to suspect groups, for example—not only creates a self-fulfilling ethos of conspiracy but is economical of resources, since it makes any suggestible recipient hold back in uncertainty and fear, thereby removing the need for observation round the clock. Informers, paid and unpaid, do their loyal work on campus or wherever else they are needed, even overseas. Some years ago Singapore's military and civilian intelligence services were merged to constitute a formidable network with global connections.

Criticism of these developments or unfavourable publicity from organisations such as Amnesty International rankles with Lee. He considers that praise is due to him for playing the game. The worst he has done to dissidents is gaol them and look after them, or, to be more precise, have them gaoled and looked after. He often remarks that if roles had been reversed no time would have been lost in eliminating him. Since Lee, Goh and Rajaratnam have reserved the right to define subversion, to charge them with inconsistency or to protest one's innocence of Marxism or of violent intentions (as almost every detainee has done) only serves to provoke their fury or their indignation.

Those who have suffered at the Government's hands have their own point of view. In the words of Dr Poh Soo Kai, a former detainee, 'While harsh measures and torture are being used by a government which is not exposed to any form of national emergency, the detention laws remain the central evil.'[19] The detainees' abiding problem is to persuade their compatriots of this truth. The passing of the years must have made their struggle seem painfully unreal and shadowy. When Said Zahari, the Malay journalist and ex-colleague of Samad Ismail, finally emerged from more than sixteen years' loss of liberty, he had conceded not an iota to the official version of his past. But he did concede that the future looked bland: 'There are no politics to go into in today's Singapore, in my opinion. So I have decided to remain a journalist and to become apolitical.'[20]

PARLIAMENT

For most of the period under review, Parliament was a pale shadow of the Assembly of 1961 to 1963. Being unicameral, and with no Opposition members in the House from 1966 to 1981, its legislation underwent little thorough scrutiny (except for those matters examined by the Presidential Council for Minority Rights). Sittings were kept to a minimum, the Prime Minister was often absent, and when he intervened he swamped the matter in hand. The quality of a member's contribution to debate suffered from the lurking thought that it made no difference to the outcome. PAP backbenchers were encouraged, sometimes orchestrated, to ask questions and even to play at being a loyal Opposition. But only a hardy soul would willingly risk the Prime Minister's or Dr Goh's wrath if he exceeded the bounds. The political scientist Robert Gamer rightly characterised the situation of the 1970s when he wrote, 'The criticism in Parliament serves more as a means of insulating the Cabinet from its critics than as an instrument for negotiating grievances.'[21]

The news of Jeyaretnam's advent to the Opposition benches drew a venomous reaction from Lee and Rajaratnam. (Goh Keng Swee laughed.) Every rule in the book has been thrown at the Workers' Party leader.* He has been fair game for all and sundry to attack him, while the Speaker has regularly acquiesced in demands that he be gagged. His fellow oppositionist, Chiam See Tong of the Social Democratic Party, came on the scene three years later and has escaped much of the fire; so far he has not provoked it by pointed or persistent questioning. Whatever Jeyaretnam's merits or faults—and Lee has occasionally admitted that he has his unwitting uses—Parliament is a far livelier place because of him; issues are debated more thoroughly and ramifications of government policy winkled out into the open. It is also a less seemly place because of PAP gang warfare, inspired by the Prime Minister's anger that Jeyaretnam presumes to treat him upon terms of equality.

The Westminster system of junior ministers and parliamentary secretaries has proved a mixed blessing—the incentive to perform well and hope for reward being offset by the threat of demotion, gently sideways or abruptly downwards.

Over and above that, the role of a Member of Parliament is due for serious examination. Some would contend that MPs have become office boys, carrying messages from the leadership to the people, requests from the people to the leaders. Others point out that they function as municipal clerks, assisting constituents to approach the correct department or interceding directly on their behalf and often having to transmit and justify messages of rejection. A new system of town councils has been foreshadowed that may affect MPs' grassroots contact placing them even more in the firing line between Government and citizens. The parliamentary

---

* During the 1970s and 1980s, Jeyaretnam has been involved in many protracted court cases with political overtones. At the time of writing he faces a threat to his legal career, if not his parliamentary position, as a result of minor criminal charges being pressed home by the Chief Justice despite their dismissal in a lower court.

committee system, too, is at the crossroads: will it regain its traditional capacity to offer bipartisan critique and counsel regarding policy matters? Much of MPs' responsibility is unrelated to their previous training or is mismatched with it, the latest example being the induction of PAP MPs as advisers to trade unions.

The PM now gives every impression of regarding Parliament and its procedures as barely tolerable forms with little to offer Singapore's political management. He and some of his deputies have been bemoaning the ease with which unsuitable Opposition candidates can proceed through selection to election and yet the uphill task that good, carefully chosen PAP candidates face if voters decide to be fickle. Exposing MPs to more and more demands and expectations is hardly a positive solution; it may well end up discrediting, intentionally or not, the whole system of representation out of which the existing laws require government leadership to be produced.

A goddess of many arms

Government control reaches far beyond the explicitly political. One of Singapore's most distinctive phenomena has been the progressive takeover of all forms of nation building.

THE CIVIL SERVICE

From his first day in office, Lee has set about ensuring a compliant and efficient administration. Its importance for political management had long been engraved upon his soul. Through the eyes of the public sector unions in which he served his apprenticeship, he observed the inertia of a civil service infected by indecision over such issues as Malayanisation and out of touch with the pressing political objectives of removing Singapore's colonial masters. Through Goh Keng Swee's eyes he pictured the results of poor economic stewardship. As he moved about, his own restless gaze lit upon example after example of personal or corporate incompetence and waste. The civil servants of whom he approved, Caucasians and locals both, showed the contrast in even less tolerable light. He decided to put the civil service on notice, cutting allowances, compelling attendance at political education lectures and even prescribing weekend sessions of public works such as beach cleaning.

The ensuing experience of government opened his eyes further. Tensions in the PAP and then the split of 1961 made it imperative to base credibility outside the Party so that programme targets could be fulfilled and advertised. Merger brought with it the need to demonstrate superiority. Sudden independence meant redoubled effort and planning.

(Although many Nanyang University graduates were absorbed by the PAP Government into the civil service, they did not have an easy time of it. Complaints about their calibre were fair game for a bureaucracy that remained thoroughly English-educated in nature and style of operation. High promotion of Nanyang graduates was generally restricted to those with a more technical bent or those with further qualifications gained at Western-type institutions.)

Those Lee has appointed to head the various civil service echelons and departments have almost all had one common virtue: toughness, and one common fate: a downturn in the master's approval. The bureaucracy has been effective because its tasks and their time frames have been clearly defined by the leadership within a unique context of subordination and political literacy. Internal lines of responsibility and specialisation have not been blurred. Very often Lee has followed up projects by calling for reports or doing spot checks himself.

To prevent standards from sagging, salaries and allowances have been raised to high levels. Committees have a specific mandate to identify talent in the private sector, in tertiary institutions and in comparable overseas settings (English-medium, culturally compatible). Newcomers are channelled into the appropriate ranks of the civil service or onto statutory boards and official bodies. Since Separation, Singapore has been run increasingly like a vast, interlocking series of corporations, with top civil servants exercising multiple directorships. The service has become a major pathway for political aspirants, where they can learn administrative and managerial skills before being obliged to come to terms with constituency work and parliamentary procedure. When Hon Sui Sen was brought into the Party and Government in 1970, reluctantly it seems, but yielding to the personal pleas of his old friend the Prime Minister, the precedent was set for a force-feeding process that has produced many of the current crop of leaders.

The endemic diseases of the bureaucracy flourish in Singapore. Power adds its own blight to the insensitivity of officialdom. Living off public funds and appropriations reduces the pressure to be efficient, businesslike and accountable. There is a high-handed lack of consultation about much of the planning and execution of policy which disregards those supposed to benefit from programmes and denies the possibility that they may be the best judges of their needs. Only one magic cure exists for the ills of the civil service, but the wand that conjures it up is not within the power of the people or their elected representatives to wave. From time to time Lee or Goh has done so—intervening to confront an offender directly, abolish an empire at the stroke of a pen (and perhaps create a new one), regroup particular units under the Prime Minister's Office, cut loose from a trend or fashion in policy and so undermine the 'mafia' that has flourished with its implementation. No one can presume himself immune from the disease or the remedy.

THE JUDICIARY

Yielding place of honour to the civil service is the judiciary. Although Lee has bemoaned the lack of draughtsmen and threatened to introduce expatriate judges, he has not made Singapore's legal service more dependent on foreign models. For many years the High Court bench remained unchanged from British days, and the judges' ageing caused them and the informed public some concern. In 1976 Lee told a Canberra parliamentary gathering: 'I fortunately have not appointed any judges since I came to office. So there can be no question of my having fixed the judiciary. They were there; I inherited them.'[22] This piece of relaxed insouciance does not reflect the true picture. Even before Lee was obliged to nominate several men to vacancies on the High Court, he had put a range of procedures in place to ensure that his understanding of the law prevailed. Many new minimum and mandatory sentences have been added to the books. All jury trials have been abolished. Subordinate court powers have been increased, and the right of appeal limited. Categories of admissible evidence have been extended. The promotion or removal of certain judges and magistrates appears to bear some relation to the pattern and nature of their previous verdicts. Probationary or short-term tenure represents an implicit method of alerting the judiciary to national needs. One other major obstacle to the attainment of the highest standards in the legal service is the gap between its remuneration and what a top lawyer can earn in the market place. Because it is not the premier service, Lee has been loath to aim for the same level of comparability with the private sector on which he insists for the civil service and the political leadership.

THE TRADE UNION MOVEMENT

Singapore's trade union movement has altered almost beyond recognition. At the peak of its political power in the mid-1950s, when the British colonial system was on notice, there were two virtually separate movements, one of non-communist unions made up mostly of government employees, the other of unions inspired or controlled by the communists and based on Chinese educational, social and proletarian self-protection. The PAP was the only party that could speak to both movements and invite them into an uneasy alliance; Lee was one of the few non-communists who bridged the gap between them. As we saw in Chapter 3, he began his rise to eminence via the former and then used his reputation for advocacy to gain access to the latter. Both ended up mobilising support for his cause rather than theirs.

The coalition could not and did not last. The non-communists were too small to form a mass party in their own right, and the communists would never have been allowed to do so. Once the PAP was in government, no formal union representation was possible in its councils because the two wings could never agree. Following the PAP split and the formation of the Barisan Sosialis, the union scene became factionalised and divided along party lines. Gradually the Barisan-backed Singapore Association of Trade Unions was crushed: its leaders were detained, member unions had funds frozen, were harassed and finally deregistered, and the weight of the PAP's achievements and the Malaysian years descended upon it. The Government-supported National Trade Unions Congress (NTUC) struggled to its feet, but its weakness was (and is) congenital: its capacity to act depends upon subordination to the PAP leaders' agenda.

From Lee's point of view it was strange and unacceptable that at the very time after Separation when he had most sections of the community behind him, the NTUC wanted to assert its traditional role. He made it clear that strikes and go-slows would be treated as high treason. Some of Lee's trade union friends, harking back to the 1952 postal strike, criticised him for forgetting what they had done to help him. Lee's reply was blunt: his involvement with trade unionism had been to mobilise an anti-colonial force, not to benefit the unions; or, as he put it to one leader boasting that Lee would not have come to power but for him, 'Do I require a stooge?'[23]

Lee must have been convinced by what he saw as insensitivity to past and present that he would need to reform the labour scene drastically. But if any hesitancy lingered it was swept away by Britain's decisions to withdraw from the Singapore bases. With a new mandate from the people and a new Minister for Labour, Sinnathamby Rajaratnam, the Government introduced tough laws to entrench the rights of management and reduce the scope for union action. At a broadly based union gathering, Lee appealed for support over the heads of the NTUC leadership to the rank and file. The Prime Minister presented a simple model of prosperity in which all workers would share, provided they co-operated with the

Government and concentrated on improving productivity instead of fighting for the sorts of rights their British cousins had won.[24]

Further relief came the Government's way in 1969 when Devan Nair resumed the reins of the NTUC from less adequate or appropriate hands. Devan's friendship with Lee and his own pedigree conferred on him alone the right and the ability to hold the NTUC together on track. However, there was a need for new and strong Chinese leadership to do what the Chinese leaders of 1964–69 had not done—tap the vast reservoir of workers not yet unionised or lost since the disintegration of the leftist unions. Phey Yew Kok was the man. From being secretary in one of the airlines' white collar unions, his consummate wheeler-dealer skills took him to the presidency of the NTUC, under Devan's approving eye.

By the time of Phey's downfall late in 1979 and his disappearance early in 1980,* the prospect of a much more drastic overhaul was being laid on the union movement. The NTUC had readjusted to being a major instrument of government policy, but had not surrendered its autonomy. Co-operatives and benefit schemes had been introduced under its auspices to offset the unions' weaker position in bargaining with employers. Lee decided that faster and more thorough changes were necessary to fit the workforce for what became known as Singapore's Second Industrial Revolution. Guided democracy must prevail to prevent out-of-hand behaviour, such as untimely union hostility to guest workers or expatriates. There must be no hangover of anti-colonialism coming to the surface in rebelliousness towards one's own government. The relationship between employers and workers must not be of the 'them and us' kind that prevailed in Britain. A desirable model for the Singapore worker would combine Japanese work attitudes, West German group morale and American individual initiative. Higher standards and output would depend on team spirit overcoming any tendency to cheat the employer. In reversal of its 1959 policy that portrayed small unions as easy victims for the bosses' exploitation, the Government insisted that house unions, with management participation to boot, would be the best ground structure for the NTUC. A substantially amended Trade Union

---

* He was charged with embezzling funds from his own unions—he was attempting to set up a cheaper alternative to the official NTUC supermarket chain, over which there had been some dispute. The story became even more peculiar when it emerged that Phey had retained his special Member of Parliament's passport and was therefore free to leave the country.

Act came into force in April 1983, giving legislative expression to these changed objectives.

Lee's eloquence was always in inverse ratio to the ease of his task of persuasion, and rarely was it more needed than when he advocated a technocrat-run NTUC. He argued that the old guard unionists would have their place, but it would be to help brief the scholars and professionals who were equipped by training and ambition, as he himself had been, to be the front men. This change was demanded by an environment in which highly qualified business and government leaders would tread underfoot those unionists unfamiliar with the jargon of economics and personnel management. The technocrat Lim Chee Onn, as well as Ong Teng Cheong who followed him, was appointed to the NTUC by the Government, and for the first time the 'symbiotic relationship' between Lee Kuan Yew and Devan Nair was depersonalised and became a formal liaison between the PAP and the NTUC (incidentally leaving Devan with his exit door).

In the current situation, the NTUC is dominated by officials and MP 'advisers' whose personal experience is far removed from the feelings and mentality of the ordinary worker. Yet they are the worker's spokesmen. They seek legitimacy for themselves by trying to increase the NTUC's membership, but it is a bleak thought that the non-unionised and guest workforce—the great majority—can choose only between them and being out in the cold, possibly further penalised.

THE LOCAL BUSINESS COMMUNITY

The response of Singapore's business community to the Government and its nation building has been varied. The old *towkays* (leading merchants) cannot dispute the political changes above and outside their sphere of influence. They cannot dispute the success of the Government's intervention in the economy. But there is resentment that so little thanks comes their way for their entrepreneurial skills, so little recognition of the personal networks into which Singapore plugs in the South Seas and beyond or of the stability that family, clan and company bring to the nation. It is not just the immigrant attitude dying hard. Some of the older ones knew Lee Kuan Yew and his family or Kwa Geok Choo and her family when there was no Prime Minister and no independent Singapore; for the sake of peace and survival they have made an accommodation with the Government. When Lee goes it will be a different story. Resentment has accumulated at being ruled by one who does not have a feel for times past or who does not know in himself what it is to be Chinese. The rest wriggle under the weight of restrictions, the thick layer of bureaucracy and the Government's apparent preference for Western and other foreign businessmen.

Politically, the men who control the Chinese Chamber of Commerce and Industry still represent the only homogeneous point of crystallisation for an alternative grouping in Singapore. Alone of the younger generation PAP leaders, Tony Tan has personal standing and connections in these circles.

THE ARMED FORCES AND POLICE

The history of Singapore's armed forces and defence capability provides fascinating windows into the mentality of the leadership. The first recruiting drive was held soon after Separation to augment the regular forces, and most of the applicants were Malays—unemployed, uneducated, but with a martial orientation from colonial days and from their own culture. When they were turned away, tempers frayed and there were nasty scuffles. Since it was precisely the Malays of Malaysia or Indonesia whom Lee saw as the frontline threat, embarrassment strengthened determination to militarise the Chinese majority and to exclude Singapore's Malays from all combat roles, as well as higher or more sensitive officer ranks. The importing of Israeli advisers accentuated the aggressive defence posture that a wronged PAP Government was committed to adopt.

'The more ready we are to fight, the less likely is it to be necessary'[25] was the Prime Minister's rationale looking back on the first few years of the new policy. Its implicit racial bias had passed a first and terrible test without there being a catastrophe: the Malaysian troubles of May 1969 did not spill over seriously into Singapore, and the armed Singaporean Chinese rookies did not run amok in the Malay areas of the island.

When the reorganisation and rapid expansion of the armed forces were undertaken, two problems had to be solved. The first was psychological: in the mind of Singapore's majority race the inherited picture and personal memories of soldiering from China's and Malaya's (and, very recently, Malaysia's) history were negative, so how could this new and alien demand be presented in a palatable way? Lee and Goh came up with the Japanese model, a foolhardy notion that might have passed muster simply because it was not advertised for what it was. The soldier would go off to battle with the blessing of neighbours, and eventually he (or his remains) would return to a home town reception covered in honour and glory.

The increasing drift to English education also gave scope for the evolution of new traditions and models with which to clothe militarisation. The Singapore Armed Forces' code of conduct was drafted, at Goh Keng Swee's request, by Father Terence Sheridan, an Irish priest with experience of Southeast Asia. Once Dr Goh explained what he wanted, Fr Sheridan produced six golden rules; they were accepted with little alteration.

The economic strain of a large standing army was avoided by coupling a small regular force with basic compulsory national service for males eighteen years of age. Job training and guaranteed employment were sweeteners for servicemen, and the pay-off was a large army of long-term reservists called up for annual retraining.

Interestingly, right from the first call-up in 1967, the structure of national service was closely tied to educational attainment. Commissioned officers were to be drawn exclusively from those who had completed their 'A levels' or those who were embarked upon tertiary studies. While some university students might have resented being ordered about by a sergeant with his 'O' levels or Senior Cambridge certificate, the overall effect has been a powerful reinforcement of Singapore's meritocracy. The leaders must be not only bright, but tough. (The instant laboratory of large numbers of other ranks has produced findings that had considerable impact on education policy.) Over the last few years the Government has facilitated a flow of planning methods, ideas, intelligence and personnel between the armed forces and the civil service, the PAP and the union movement. This military–administrative interchange already existed in the other ASEAN states, except for Malaysia, but Singapore has pushed it much further.

In the view of many older Singaporeans, national service is one of the two chief standard-bearers of a new docility, whatever other costs and benefits it brings. The political leaders have the unilateral right to define ally and enemy; they have fashioned the armed forces into a formidable weapon at their beck and call.

The other principal standard-bearer of control (also fed by national service induction) is the police. Lee formed close links with the colonial police and their Special Branch officers more than thirty years ago; he quickly learned to set great store by their capacity to supervise the population and maintain order, provided their deployment and functioning were kept firmly under the right political direction. However, even with the British in command during the 1950s, the racial balance caused problems for the composition and perceived fairness of the police force. The same issue arose when Singapore joined Malaysia and police were the responsibility of the central Government. (The availability of

British-trained Gurkhas to be personal bodyguards was a godsend for Lee when he felt threatened from the Chinese extreme Left, the MCA's 'hit men' and the Malay 'ultras'.)

Today's police force continues to be of paramount but understated importance; since Separation it has been progressively integrated with the overall ideology and apparatus of government. Salaries and conditions have been improved to levels on a par with the armed forces and civil service. The future upper echelons of officer ranks are recruited chiefly, if not entirely, from among undergraduates or graduates. The military and police intelligence branches have been combined. Training for specialised operations is often undertaken in the United States, Australia, East Asian countries or elsewhere overseas. Domestic operations are computerised, and international agreements link Singapore's police personnel and data banks to their Malaysian and other foreign counterparts. Japanese-style police posts have been introduced to the housing estates; together with neighbourhood watch schemes, boys' clubs and crime prevention committees, and reinforced by the deliberate distribution of police personnel and families in every residential block, they constitute a daily and ever-present reminder that Singapore will not stand for civilian law-breaking, disturbance or dissent.

The incidence of serious crime has decreased over recent years, although sophisticated white collar crime has flourished. Secret societies have lost much of the power they originally had as China-derived triads practising quasi-religious initiation ceremonies and engaged in protection rackets, abductions, political 'dirty tricks' and gang warfare. Petty crime and personal assault, often opportunistic and born of the moment, are the prevalent forms of crime, as well as illegal gambling, which remains an endemic and noisy part of Singapore's life. The smallness of the island enables patrolling to be very effective in creating an atmosphere of vigilance and self-regulation.

In a real sense the armed forces and police together constitute a modern equivalent of clergy who guard the faith. To them is entrusted the execution of the rituals of national security. The reputation, the sound and sight of sophisticated technology and of uniformed personnel create a glamorous and formidable mystique which needs only occasional reinforcement by rhetoric to produce the proper respect for authority.

GRASSROOTS ORGANISATIONS

Up until recently, the Prime Minister's Office has assumed direct responsibility for ensuring a favourable community response to the Government. Although the PAP has run kindergartens and creches and has also kept in touch through the MPs' meet-the-people sessions, it is the Government-sponsored organisations that have mobilised particular layers and cross-sections of the community. The Works Brigade was created in 1959 to channel youthful energies into projects. The People's Association came next, with its community centres and management committees. Citizens' Consultative Committees date back to 1965; they have linked the 'external' Government to existing clan associations and natural leaders of the Chinese-educated world. (Several interviewees spoke of the close rapport Ong Pang Boon and Lee Chiaw Meng had with these ground-level organisations. Is this the reason why the Prime Minister reacted against his two subordinates in the mid-1970s, thinking that they were empire-building?).

The latest grouping, which was started on a trial basis in 1977, has come quickly to the fore—Residents' Committees. These operate in the Government-built housing estates; they take into account the growing preponderance of English even among flat-dwellers. The Residents' Committees are made up of volunteers and invitees, and their method of operation permits a measure of local leadership to emerge through lobbying and co-ordinated action—although any contest between Residents' Committees and powerful bureaucracies such as the Housing and Development Board is hardly an equal one. Together with the careful placing of military and police personnel to monitor and protect the estates, a panoply of feedback and control mechanisms is now in place.

A weekend seminar held by the People's Association in 1982 voiced criticism of the Government for exercising too much control over the media and hindering political development by its retention of the Internal Security Act.[26] The criticism was partly a symptom of frustration that the Government was shuffling the Residents' Committees to the top of the pack and downgrading the other groups it had formed to work with the people.

Normally, each Member of Parliament spends considerable time with these grassroots organisations and has some rights in nominating their members—subject to veto by the Prime Minister's Office after security checks have been carried out and other factors (balanced representation, etc.) have been weighed. But the unique Singapore situation of Party-as-national-movement-as-Government has been deemed by Lee to mean that non-PAP MPs should not have anything to do with Residents' Committees and the like.

CAMPAIGNS

Popular support is also solicited by the scattergun technique of national social campaigns, which have become one of Singapore's most distinctive features. The first few of these were conducted by Lim Yew Hock's Government in 1958, against spitting, litter and pests. Their achievement was bound to be minimal while the different sections of Singapore society had little sense of the common good or the civic bond that made for a mutually dependent future. It was a time of spiritual tribalisms contending with one another.

But then, late in 1964, public morale was low. There had been two bouts of race riots. A distraction was needed, an edifying distraction. One day a lawyer (member of a scarce breed) was killed when his car collided with a buffalo ambling across the road. The Prime Minister resolved to act against such waste. Singapore was not to be a place where the squalid past impeded progress. Animals and beggars were to be kept off public thoroughfares and out of sight.

Before long, carefully planned and co-ordinated campaigns became quite common. Cabinet's ratification is needed for a particular cause to be promoted nationwide. The relevant Government minister launches the campaign and his colleagues back him up with prolific speechmaking. The media and the community centres are saturated with publicity—colourful displays featuring banners and logos, jingles, commercials, recorded telephone messages, educational programmes and competitions.

If the velvet glove fails, the iron fist can be brought to bear. Heavy fines, regulations and police enforcement leave no doubt that the leaders are serious about the inculcation of desirable social norms and limits.

With campaigns multiplying—over seventy between 1958 and 1985—it was only logical that someone should co-ordinate them and in 1979 the Prime Minister's Office undertook to do so. Schedules and protocols were drawn up.

Lee has said, 'Were Singapore a traditional and settled society with age-old customs and habits as in the towns and villages of China and India, I would not attempt a campaign to change behaviour by exhortation, argument and persuasion ... Fortunately, Singapore is a young community ... highly motivated. Immigrants or their children are keener and emotionally more ready to try out new ideas for better results ... The easier changes have been achieved ... The more difficult targets are higher education, better work attitudes, more considerate and co-operative conduct.'[27]

There is another way of seeing the campaigns. People acquire reserves of loyalty and goodwill from personal experience on the homely scale of the family or beneficial organisation to which they belong. Meritocracy increases individualism, under whose regime the transfer of these reserves to the wider nation is not likely to be automatic, but calculated and superficial. For the individual, the 'bonus' of fun or reward or expression of talent or momentary praise can easily be preferable to the point of the campaign. Human conscience is dulled by endless instruction, by having no choice but to do what is deemed 'good'. The risk run by official campaigns is that of vaccination. Could the administration of little doses ultimately increase Singaporeans' resistance to a whole range of virtues and prohibitions?

The younger leaders have joined the lists with their campaign for 'total defence'. Since there is ample provision to keep the internal security situation under control, they have announced part of the detailed planning that has been done to meet an external threat. All the same, it is an expression of trust in the people's reliability to act on command. The outcome of the December 1984 elections might have caused Lee and Rajaratnam to wince at the thought that this reliability is in doubt and the campaign premature.

THE MEDIA

The freedom of the fourth estate—the press and the media generally—is not absolute anywhere in the world. Among practising democracies, however, there is usually sufficient independence of ownership or dedication to profit for news and opinion to circulate without being unadorned amplifiers of government propaganda.

Ever since they met and began agitating and organising against colonialism, Singapore's leaders have been fully aware of the media. Sinnathamby Rajaratnam was a journalist who poured his fighting spirit into words; so was Samad Ismail, whose political friendship influenced Devan Nair and Harry Lee for a time. So were serviceable cadres such as Lee Khoon Choy, Othman Wok and others of all races whom the passing years have seen come and go. Among the attributes Alex Josey brought to Lee were his writing output and his contacts. The Prime Minister has frequently made himself available to selected foreign reporters and presenters; in return he gains a forum where his views are better disseminated.

Lee and his colleagues recognise that human beings rely on the media to shape the images and perceptions of a world that is outside their direct experience but that bears in upon them more and more. The media can support or destroy national identity. It would therefore be gross dereliction of duty to allow the communists or fellow-travellers to work the system in order to overthrow it. Equally, pedlars of any deeply held chauvinism or hucksters of the permissive society must not be tolerated. The media should present wholesome and truthful pictures of national life, based on the accepted values and on sensitive and objective feedback about public opinion.

There is no great difficulty about radio and television. Both are under government control. The former was an instrument of colonial propaganda and light entertainment. Television was rushed into operation by February 1963 (ahead of Malaya) to assist the PAP Government gain the upper ground as it approached elections and Malaysia.

After letting Radio and Television Singapore (RTS) find its own feet within the path he ordained, Lee became dissatisfied with its competence and its occasional lapses of taste. His first move was to give his press officer day-to-day supervision of programming. Then he decided to replace RTS with the Singapore Broadcasting Corporation (SBC), railroading an older colleague of his from the Occupation media unit (Domei), Wee Mon Cheng, recently retired as Ambassador to Japan, to be its Chairman. Lee wanted Wee's admiring knowledge of Japanese society to percolate down through the Corporation into its programmes. When Wee's term of office was cut short after charges of tax fraud were laid against him and his family, the man who had succeeded him as Ambassador was appointed to replace him—Wee Kim Wee (not a relative of Wee Mon Cheng).

Adequate description of the PAP's relations with the press would take more space than is appropriate here. All the Malay, Chinese and English newspapers have been under fire from the Prime Minister at one time or another. He and Goh will not tolerate anyone else ploughing, so to speak, with their heifer. Direct action has been threatened and taken often enough to make it clear that the Government means business. A list of incidents conveys none of their impact, but does indicate their scope: closure of newspapers (*Eastern Sun, Singapore Herald*); detention of editorial staff (*Nanyang Siang Pau, Berita Harian*); amalgamation for competition (*Nanyang Siang Pau* and *Sin Chew Jit Poh* with the fledgling *Monitor* group) and for rationalisation (the *Times* and *Monitor* groups in 1984). Foreign current affairs journals from the 'free world' have not been banned or censored, but there have been instances of their correspondents being forced to leave and their distributors being sued. Lee has hinted at or openly alleged CIA and KMT meddling through MCA and Malaysian operatives and of Chinese and Soviet communists controlling the purse strings in subtle efforts to 'sour up' the ground. In 1971 he gained notoriety for his views when he braved a meeting of the International Press Institute in Helsinki shortly after having forced the *Singapore Herald* out of existence.

The formation of Singapore Press Holdings from the *Times* and *Monitor* groups boosts the island republic's competitiveness in communications. It also heralds a new era for Singapore's world of print journalism. Several major foreign dailies and periodicals are now printed in Singapore simultaneously with their parent editions; their appearance has not had a stimulating effect on the local English-medium press. Already the struggling *Monitor* has ceased production. Homegrown journalists have good reason to be demoralised and to ponder the future of their craft as they watch imports from Hong Kong and Taiwan or the West produce what the Government wants.

Lee has never consciously sought servile compliance with his wishes. 'I don't want obsequious, inert, dull and stupid newspapers. I want lively and sensible newspapers. There is a lot of leeway for responsible journalism,' he has said.[28] But he has not hesitated to lambast offending reporters even down to cadet level. With self-censorship in force and with full command of the situation—since 1975, newspapers, publishers, chief editors and printing presses all require a licence—he still cannot stop himself from meeting head-on almost every infringement of his tolerance. The relatively bipartisan coverage of the Anson by-election in 1981 brought his wrath down upon the *Straits Times*, and several journalists were taken off political reporting.

The vehemence of Government reaction is instructive, whether it derives from Lee's fury at any hour of day or night, Goh's more private rage or Rajaratnam's sadness that the old professional's skill and instinct for limits have faded. Perhaps the reason for it is that Singapore's newspapers are the most temperamental part of the nervous system connecting the head to the body politic. Malfunctioning or momentary autonomy is not tolerable when the health of a whole organism is at risk.

An interesting sideline to the media story is that mass rallies have reappeared in Singapore's public life, not just at election time. Television took politics off the streets in the 1970s. But the media's failure to cover Opposition points of view fairly and accurately has driven voters to seek less filtered forms of contact. Something of the vigour of the 1950s and 1960s seems to have returned. The standards of oratory may not be high—the Prime Minister is the only PAP leader left who has a mastery of rally techniques—but the use of other languages and dialects as well as of English stirs a ready response from the crowds. It is a breakthrough for them to hear the issues that affect them being canvassed without put-down or promise of solutions to be imposed.

Nation building

> My basic guiding principle in nation building is to unite the majority and minority races in Singapore, to impart to them common values, and to make them committed to share good and bad times together.
> Lee Kuan Yew in an interview with Takuhito Tsuruta, 25 November 1981
>
> Sir Robert Menzies, in spite of three-year periods, won and stayed in office for twelve years [*sic*—actually seventeen]. But he knew that popular representative government means that sometimes even when 51 per cent (he once told me up to 55 per cent) are against you, if it is right, proceed. When it works out all right, they will swing back. But if you flinch, then that 55 per cent becomes 65 per cent and you are out ... The way to ensure your pension is to ensure good, stable, fair, just government which commands the trust and respect of the people.
> Lee Kuan Yew, Parliament, 23 February 1977

The results of human creativity tend to take on a life of their own. Composers are sometimes amazed that the music they are hearing comes from their brains and fingers. How much less predictable and more unwieldy is the art of the politician! Few democratically elected leaders seeking to shape the destiny of flesh-and-blood people have time to do more than paint hasty brush strokes on their chosen canvas in obedience to their own urges and the dictates of whatever sectional interest has captured them.

For almost twenty-seven years, Lee Kuan Yew's people have given him the opportunity to create and rework a complex design. Distracted briefly when his Malaysian hopes were dashed, he soon recovered poise. He has acquired a wisdom about nation building that flows into his every move. Singapore represents much more than survival; her Prime Minister can describe his achievement quite unselfconsciously in terms as bold and directive as 'uniting', 'imparting' and 'making'.

Over the last two years, there have been hints that some of the subjects of his handiwork are resisting or eluding his grasp, but he is proud that he has carried most of the people for most of the time. It would be worthwhile, then, to reflect on his practice of statecraft, drawing together thoughts that he and his colleagues have expressed to various audiences, so that we may understand both his accomplishment and Singaporeans' response to it.

Lee Hsien Loong communicated some of his father's insights when he spoke to a Singapore audience in April 1985. According to Brigadier-General (B-G) Lee, the Singapore political system rests on three pillars 'Firstly, there are no pressure groups dedicated to promoting the interests of its members, if necessary at the expense of the public at large.' The other two are that there are no ideological preconceptions and that, where emotions clash with logic and practicality, emotions usually give way. Although the metaphor of a pillar is not altogether valid, the message is clear enough: Singapore has strong leaders not beholden to anyone. They make decisions and weigh feasibility by considering a number of viewpoints over and above their own. 'The paradox of Singapore's success' so B-G Lee believes 'is that its policies are formulated almost cold-bloodedly, yet these policies work only because of emotions, the strong ties between the leaders and those being led. This is the formula which we must try to duplicate, in both parts, in the next generation.'[29]

There are other important characteristics of the leadership style—its resort to anecdotal observation or trial and error, its superhuman effort to embody prejudice in policy and make it come true. Singapore's success is due to more than the leaders' policies and their ties with the people. But Lee Hsien Loong's remarks still hold true.

Singapore has many strengths. Each of her leaders is dedicated to her well-being, and is possessed of 'a good constitution, strong nerves, a clear mind and iron resolve'.[30] Traditional Asian cultures and stern circumstances have made her people realistic and practical. There is energy and bounce compressed into a tight space. Singapore can function as a unit. As the Prime Minister told the 1984 National Day rally: 'I saw the Olympics trials, and a rider could not persuade his horse to go over. So he went over the top all by himself. And I thought to myself how lucky I was I got a horse. I said, come on, giddy-up, let's go. We can do it. The horse took a deep breath. Over the top.' The leaders have harnessed the people's individual purposes to national goals and have shown them how their self-interest and Singapore's security and prosperity can work to each other's advantage. The reliability and trustworthiness learned during the entrepôt era—the merchant's word his bond—

has enabled Singapore to do well in today's world. Unlike Japan, whose blind spot, Lee believes, is security, Singapore is willing to ward off expansionist and aggressive powers and to be ready to deal with sudden threats from insurgents, dissidents or extremists nearer to home.

In creating a new Singapore, Lee once said he needed 200 people at the top and 2000 at the grass roots who would form 'a hard core with reflexes attuned to the national interest'.[31] It is a theme he has often repeated with minor variations. Unlike the communists when in government elsewhere, the PAP did not and could not replace the existing administration with its own cadres when it came to office in 1959. Lee has made a virtue out of necessity by politicising the civil service and keeping it on its toes, by bringing civil servants into the Cabinet and thus renewing the PAP, if need be against the PAP's will. Even more, as this chapter has documented, the tentacles of government reach into most recesses of Singapore's life, to reform and reorder them. Lee has occasionally been lulled into overstating his success and proclaiming that Singapore was never better prepared—his speeches to the faithful in 1971, 1975 and 1980 are examples—only to find his best laid plans coming unstuck.

It should not be thought that Lee's wish is to bring everything under the Government's wing. He is vocal in opposition to state welfarism; by contrast with genetically comparable Hong Kong, he believes that Singapore has already grown soft and too accustomed to subsidies. His purpose is rather to guarantee a stable minimum (consisting of educational opportunity, basic medical services and housing for the poor), to deny exploiters and profiteers a blank cheque and to give all a sense of belonging. For the rest, the obligation passes both to companies to do as much as they wish for their employees and to individuals for themselves. Then the real achievers and innovators can surge forward and relentlessly push the horizons back.

A new Singapore is only possible by learning the lessons of history and of other advanced nations. Local-born talent informed by the right character and personality comes on stream too slowly, and must be supplemented by outside input. Lee looks for maturity in the willingness of his people to accept that expatriates can only be induced to stay and give of their best if they are better rewarded than Singaporeans.

Singapore has made it her business to keep abreast of world political and economic thinking. Being small and nimble, she is well placed to be in the vanguard of the future, ready to jump into what Lee has referred to as the *'telematique'* society. 'People can stay where they like and be plugged through computers into the centres of government, of industry, of social activities ... The arrangements for work, residence and recreation ... will be totally altered. There will be a change in the molecular structure of society.'[32]

Alongside the envisaging of a bright future, Lee does not forget the shadows. If he can convince the 'ablest' Singaporeans to share his vision and serve their fellows in a spirit of *noblesse oblige* (and the modern economy creates an elite, whether noble or not), the necessary condition for attaining excellence is fulfilled. But it is not enough. Security, like electricity, cannot be stored indefinitely. If the economy goes down, if the people lose faith or the young become impatient and trifle with their vote, Singapore cannot be sustained and defended for long. The island will revert to mudflats, the talented will go to richer pastures and the rest will become guest workers in developing countries.

Lee has often remarked that he, Goh, Rajaratnam and the other first-generation leaders could have gone off long ago to enjoy privacy and wealth. They chose to stay. A nation has come together around them. Time is yet to tell if these men's response to challenge has been contagious and the torch of their efforts able to kindle popular endorsement beyond their lifetime.

LEAVING HOME, MOTHER

But oh the demands you make
on us Singaporeans!
Since you didn't choose us
but we chose you
(most of us, at any rate
and we still have that choice)
your demands shall be commands.
They shall be observed:
the schools' daily litany
five mornings saluting
five stars and a crescent;
our young men shall bear arms
to deter unnamed enemies;
we shall accept as treasonable
strikes not in the national interest;
Southeast Asia's cleanest city
shall be Asia's cleanest city;
we shall enlarge the airport
for the Jumbos
and develop Sentosa
but only for the tourists;
our already low birthrate
shall further decline;
the world's second busiest port
shall become the world's busiest port;
we shall keep our hair short,
we shall continue to view Art
as an adjunct to Culture
serving Politics.

And me? Knowing you
Knowing you demand acts, not gestures,
I chose a medium not so cool
to spread your message hot
from the repetition and elaboration
of your likewise leaders.
After two years, hoarse with belief
reeling from the nearness of you
Supersonic Singapore
I thought it best to opt out awhile
the better to view you from afar.

ROBERT YEO

10
Less Than Paradise

> Everything sooner or later in 1966 will be ordered and organised.
>
> LESS KUAN YEW,
> Singapore, 24 February 1966

Recognising that, whatever else he might have been doing, Lee had been fighting for their benefit, the people did not express any concerted desire to seek leadership elsewhere once their island suddenly found itself alone in the world. They were willing to close ranks behind a man whom they might not be able to understand, but whose commitment to political survival and power were unmistakable. Their allegiance meant that, for the moment, Lee and his chief lieutenant, Goh Keng Swee, had no need to justify or excuse the running of Singapore as a tight ship.

A check was made of the world's small nations to determine suitable models. Switzerland and Israel reached the short list. Lee had been aware of both experiments for many years, dating back at least to his student days in England. During the early 1960s it dawned on him with new clarity how similar Singapore was to Israel, both migrant enclaves surrounded by Islamic nations and subject to resentment from disaffected Muslims within. With the emphasis on becoming indigestible, even offensive, to predators, Singapore was progressively militarised in the early years of independence and to that end, as we have noted, Israeli help was sought and obtained. Switzerland was relevant in a number of ways: a multilingual society, armed and mobilised to protect its neutrality; a national economy selectively industrialised and able to attract disposable immigrant labour for the less pleasant jobs, a people only too willing to prosper by serving the financial needs and whims of all comers with the help of superb infrastructure and facilities, and venturing out into the world without inhibitions except those dictated by efficiency and calculated self-interest.

Although many changes had already come to the face and workings of Singapore, they had not yet gone beyond the piecemeal stage and they were unfinished. A more thorough transformation could now be contemplated.

Chapter 8 studied the posture adopted by Singapore's leaders towards the outside world, and Chapter 9 examined the developments in domestic political institutions and leadership patterns. The other and, in a real sense, more fundamental endeavour of Lee Kuan Yew's Government has been to reform and reshape the society, somehow enthusing the people or carrying them by reward and punishment as it does so.

Lee's durability in office and his reputation for forcefulness have tended to enhance the plausibility of a three-headed myth: that he is behind every aspect of Singapore's social engineering, that he is the sole reason and motivating drive behind Singapore's modernisation and that nothing is left to chance.

Anyone who has delved into the facts will know that, from the outset and particularly since 1965, Goh Keng Swee has been Singapore's supreme ideas man, her visionary with a practical bent. His unusual perspective—the academic economist who, having been exposed to the incongruities and hardship of war, committed himself to measure academic knowledge against human reality and to research the historical causes of statistical trends—has resulted in many brainwaves and flashes of lateral thinking. Moreover, he has invited like-minded men to work with him and Lee. Albert Winsemius of the Netherlands, I.F. Tang, J.M. Pillay, Hon Sui Sen and, more recently, Tony Tan are examples of technocrats with the initiative and awareness to tackle problems from a variety of angles.

Admittedly, it is not always easy to discern whether Lee or Goh has been the ultimate inspiration of any particular scheme. Their reflexes, some instinctive, some learned, have been virtually identical. They are both rationalistic, elitist and oriented towards technical sophistication. Both are hard and cynical, yet able to care for society—*masse*. But of the two Lee is the less systematic in paying attention to detail. He is also the more moderate because he has taken into account what the people in their current political groupings can or cannot be persuaded to tolerate; for the same reason he has sometimes been more inclined to panic. Goh, by contrast, has been amazed at what he has got away with. He regards any reliance on exhortation as a counsel of despair.

A further facet of the myth to be debunked is that the leaders do not let up. When Lee escapes from Singapore or sidesteps problems temporarily, even for tactical reasons, and when he leaves his colleagues and subordinates to get on with their jobs (which is most of the time), the way is opened for them to misread or disregard, execute overzealously or plain bungle his orders and plans. Discovery unleashes the master's wrath, but not all damage is discovered. Some years ago at a university gathering the Prime Minister digressed from his topic to pour contempt on the social sciences (partially excepting economics), whereupon the Public Service Commission awarded no further scholarships in those areas. When he was petitioned to reverse the policy, he did not appear to know that there was one.

Another popular misconception is that every effort is made to exclude serendipity from Singapore. In fact, Goh and Lee have been all too aware that fate can play fast and loose with them. 'Barring unforeseen circumstances' is the ritual prayer that prefaces all Government predictions. The first five-year plan that the PAP devised was before taking office, and it was largely the work of James Puthucheary who defected in 1961 and helped form the Barisan Sosialis. Moreover, it went off course well before Malaysia's inauguration cut it short anyway. The next plan was undone by Separation! Longer term forecasting and programming do occur, but mostly behind closed doors (to avoid the stigmas of socialist central planning and rigidity) and on the basis of likely alternatives, allowing for different variables and different weighting to the variables. The secrecy of decisionmaking has also covered the many occasions when the Cabinet or committee concerned was not on top of the problems, could not spot a clear way through them or was simply flying blind.

It is true that for a large part of the time since independence the Prime Minister has been accustomed to operate with a minimum of normal democratic checks and balances. Interestingly, the poor state of his public relations during and after the 1984 election campaign has coincided with a greater clamour from sections of the community for a say in policy. Whether he manages to wrest back unquestioned supremacy or not, he will certainly try. Neither is Goh Keng Swee a spent force, although he has stepped down from Cabinet and Parliament and has relinquished much of the daily round of backroom meetings and interventions, the hallmarks of his political career.

At this stage, one more twist in the Lee–Goh partnership should be noticed. As long as some areas of social engineering were kept from Goh, either because they were deemed politically too hard or because they were not perceived to lie within his competence, the results in those areas were uneven, reflecting a mixture of planning and impetuosity. Goh Keng Swee, being more of a cool optimist than Lee, was willing to wait for the main chance. When eventually called on to solve intractable problems, he has often succeeded by sheer application and patience.

Many of the policies that this chapter describes predate Separation. Many of them were conceived during the days of colonial or Labour Front government. But whoever initiated them and however much they came about in pragmatic response to particular situations, it is a good working hypothesis that they bear the stamp of two men's minds. Where appropriate, some distinction will be made between Lee's and Goh's patronage. It would also seem fair to assume that each has announced or foreshadowed those policy directions and refinements that he wishes the public of Singapore to associate with him.

For the sake of the economy

The transition from immigrant to national economy was made a matter of urgency. A changing political environment and a growing population with nowhere else to go had shattered the comfortable belief of earlier migrants that Singapore, the capital of the British Empire in Southeast Asia, would shield and support any and every enterprise. The PAP had given fresh impetus to labour-intensive industrialisation when it came to power in 1959, to mop up some of the unemployment and to take the emphasis away from *entrepôt* trade. Now, with independence, the Government took the lead in offering an offshore haven to the booming economies of the developed world, pioneering and promoting activity in the secondary sector—manufacturing, utilities and construction. Simultaneously, it moved to improve the quality of transport, communications, financial and commercial services. The primary sector, never large, shrank even further. The nation would sink or swim in reliance on only two resources—its people and its location.

In day-to-day terms, according to Professor Lee Soo Ann, 'the form and extent of economic activity' was 'constantly . . . manipulated to preserve the political independence of Singapore'[1] and, it may be added, the supremacy of the Government. Goh and his old friend, Lim Kim San, the Minister for Finance, intervened wherever they considered it necessary to integrate planning, to fill gaps or to provide ginger to market mechanisms. Essential services were kept or brought under tight control.

Although privately owned land, that most precious of commodities for housing and industrial expansion, could have been prohibitively expensive, the Government was able to override opposition and continue to acquire it under legislation that provided compensation well below market levels. Massive reclamation projects were also undertaken to increase the area available. These complementary policies played a large part in enabling the Government to expedite economic growth.

The economy has been harnessed to three engines: the OECD countries, the region (Indian/Pacific rather than just ASEAN) and Singapore's own stewardship, productivity, savings and domestic market. Being a small unit—albeit with a big appetite—Singapore was not expected to require a great deal of energising by any one of the world's economies. With an eye to diplomatic effect, she could afford to state a prudent maxim for the 1970s and beyond: complementarity within ASEAN, competitiveness globally.

Without the long industrial development that Switzerland had experienced, the transnational corporations offered a speedy trade-off between their profits, access to a cheap workforce and tax concessions on the one hand and their transfer to Singapore of equipment, know-how, marketing techniques and outlets on the other.

For obvious domestic and international reasons, socialist goals were still espoused to begin with, but Lee and Goh never tired of pointing out that nationalisation was a futile exercise in Singapore. To their revised way of thinking, social equity must depend on economic growth, although Goh had probably never believed that a society open to international forces could do more than provide a basic minimum for all, and otherwise endure inequalities. By 1978 Lee felt moved to accept an invitation to visit the heartland of capitalism; as guest of honour at a convention in Orlando, Florida, he delivered a paean of praise to the forces of the market and free enterprise that had, again in a paradoxical, state-controlled way, liberated his people into the upper reaches of modernity.

Specific outside factors had powerful effect. Britain's accelerated withdrawal from her Singapore bases made the need for restructuring all the more pressing, although its impact on the economy was exaggerated for propaganda purposes. Other boons helped offset withdrawal: the escalating American presence in Indo-China and the region; resumption of trade with Indonesia as well as President Suharto's encouragement of oil prospecting, in reversal of his predecessor's policy; and the influx of Hong Kong capital, nervous at what the Cultural Revolution was doing to China. The oil crisis of the 1970s was a further jolt; it, too, was used to goad Singapore's workers to greater effort and to spell the end of the adversary model of trade unionism.

The blight of a large labour market resulting from the post-war 'baby boom' became a blessing in the late 1960s as employment opportunities expanded and the reservoir of potential workers among women was tapped. There was no shortage of takers for industries that needed semi-skilled process and production labour. Guest workers made up the complement (and will until 1992, although Lee's declaration that the workforce must be fully Singaporean by then is not likely to be adhered to). Malaysians and other 'hungry, lean, keen' Asians (from Thailand, Sri Lanka, India and Bangladesh, but not Indonesia) do the outdoor and menial jobs Singaporeans are reluctant to do, in construction, domestic service and so on. At the other end of the scale, there has been a contrived 'brain drain' into Singapore (mainly of Chinese) from Malaysia, Hong Kong, Indonesia and Taiwan, and from elsewhere if considered culturally compatible; this has more than compensated for the seepage of emigrant Singapore professionals.

By 1973 Singapore reached all but full employment, a remarkable management feat, to be assisted over the years by the slower birth rate. The Government battened down the hatches and kept wages low to stay competitive. To this end, and with the unions already under control, Dr Winsemius advocated the formation of a National Wages Council (NWC) to recommend an annual level of increase. (Originally made up of government, business and union representatives, the Council has now lost Government participation, and its role is limited to producing a report on the state of the economy.) A mood of 'hasten slowly' prevailed.

Then in 1979 Goh and Lee made the decision, again on the advice of Winsemius and others, to move upmarket. Mechanisation, automation and computerisation were to be encouraged. According to Lee, 'We gave our investors and managers three years notice of high wage increases, or a free labour market with no more immigrant workers.'[2] Education and training programmes were stepped up at every level to improve manpower performance.

Starting from a low baseline, Singapore has experienced her first twenty years' independence as growth by surge and lull. As far as possible, inflation rates and money supply have been reined in and budget deficits avoided. No one could deny the skill of Singapore's economic management under what Augustine Tan, a sharp-eyed economist and MP, called 'the invisible hand of Adam Goh'.[3] It has been Goh Keng Swee's habit to submit all proposals, in Dennis Bloodworth's witty description, 'to the cold, impersonal appraisal of a pawnbroker conning a seed pearl through his jeweller's glass'.[4] Nowadays Lee, his Cabinet and administration have to make do without daily access to Goh. The downturn of 1985 has been a real test of the mettle of Tony Tan, Lee Hsien Loong, Goh Chok Tong, Dhanabalan and the other younger leaders who have some claim to economic competence.

Before he stepped down from government, Goh did his best to set in place people, institutions and processes that would automatically follow his guidelines. His speeches and writings (and the books that reproduce them) present a lively dossier of practical action and reflection. His imprint is engraved upon all who have worked with him: the caustic or flippant tongue, the probing analysis, the poring over statistics or discarding them, the discussions in the penthouse or on the golf course or after tennis, the words of praise, the putdown of a supposed expert—even sometimes of himself, as a warning that colleagues should not succumb to an over-reverent complacency.

Few economists in the world have had the freedom and the expertise of a Goh Keng Swee to range across the landscape of economic planning and explore all avenues. Perhaps the greatest tribute to him is that, because of the skill and deliberation he brought to bear when opening Singapore up to the transnationals, the Republic has handled them with more finesse and retained a better semblance of partnership than far bigger and wealthier countries.

Goh's dealings with foreign governments and expatriate businessmen have been notoriously unapologetic. His brawls with Canberra and Whitehall have belied the gentlemanly tone of the final memoranda. His treatment of Jim Slater (mid-1970s) or the firm of Jardine Fleming (mid-1980s) caused considerable fluttering in the financiers' dovecotes. He once compared regulating bankers to 'frying fish. It must not be overdone.'[5]

He has insisted that government intervention in the market place be done on an efficient and strictly competitive basis: the dictates of national security or global strategy may require state ownership or participation, but these do not excuse slovenly management or corruption. The impact of any mistaken investment made despite best efforts to assess prospects prudently—for example, in petrochemical production and ship-building—can be cushioned by the maintenance of very high foreign reserves.

Over the years he has had many pet projects. Jurong, a swampy tract on the western side of the island that was converted into a vast industrial complex, was affectionately known as 'Goh's Folly'. With the help of Australia's Laurence Hartnett, he established a booming arms industry which caters not just for domestic needs but for specialised international demand.

The mobilisation of local capital through the compulsory savings of the Central Provident Fund (CPF)*, and to a much smaller extent the Post Office Savings Bank, has given enormous impetus to the economy. It has been the springboard for building up local industry and utilities, investing surplus funds at home and abroad and laying in massive reserves. Almost incidentally, it has enabled CPF contributors to start owning their flats and to put aside something for their retirement.

Goh took a keen interest in Singapore's housing stock well before the PAP came to government. Through his leadership, the Housing and Development Board was created; it was made sufficiently independent to be able to undertake land acquisition, approval of designs or contracts and oversight of planning, building and maintenance with a minimum of red tape.

The gradual taming of the informal sector has been another of his accomplishments. For instance, food hawkers have been brought into covered centres so that they pay rent to the Government and 'pirate' taxis have become a thing of the past. In return, the NTUC, with Goh's assistance, established supermarkets to sell essential goods at controlled prices and formed union co-operatives to run taxis and other services for the public.

There are always particular difficulties when one man presides so totally over economic policy. Goh set up the Monetary Authority of Singapore to keep a close watch on financial affairs. In its internal and external dealings it has had more than its fair share of conflict. Goh might have won most of the battles, heads might have rolled, but there has been a price to pay. Disagreements have been personalised, and however rational the Government's case, the suspicion of vendetta and bloody-mindedness has remained. The same could be said of a number of unpleasant conflicts that have soured relationships within the Cabinet or the highest echelons of the civil service. Goh has found it very hard to forgive or forget what he regards as stupid or imprudent decisions—the purchase by the Government-owned Keppel Shipyard of Straits Steamships was a case in point. Eyebrow-raising is a habit that has crept into the cocktail hour when bureaucrats and businessmen compare notes over the latest shuffling of directors in concerns where Government patronage applies. Goh's caution over the decision to proceed with

---

* At the time of writing, employees contribute 25 per cent of their nominated wages each month and employers another 25 per cent up to a ceiling amount. There was considerable controversy and electoral backlash in 1984 when some Government ministers suggested that the lower age limit for withdrawal of funds not already utilised for allowable purposes might be raised from fifty-five to sixty or sixty-five.

the Mass Rapid Transit scheme and the huge outlays that it entailed led to an uncharacteristically public period of dithering; dithering by itself could be admirable, but it made mock of the claim that the younger leaders were being given their head. Likewise the Government Investment Corporation, which Goh set up, is firmly in the hands of those he regards as older and wiser; he persuaded a reluctant Prime Minister to be its Chairman.

Population control

It was already the conviction of both Lee Kuan Yew and Goh Keng Swee at the outset of their political careers that various forms of population control were essential. The strain on Government to produce work, education, housing and other services must not be allowed to exceed realistic capabilities. But the existence of deep-seated traditional patterns and values, often reinforced by religious teachings, meant that the path to change looked rocky, sometimes impassable. One of the benefits sought in merger was the restoration of a natural hinterland to Singapore that might ease some of the politically sensitive population pressures.

When Singapore was thrown out of Malaysia, there was no question of waiting for a propitious climate of opinion or deferring to squeamishness. Changes already in the pipeline were pushed ahead. A White Paper on family planning was tabled on 27 September 1965, proposing a policy that would 'liberate our women from the burden of bearing and raising an unnecessarily large number of children and as a consequence ... increase human happiness for all'.[6] The Family Planning and Population Board was established four months later, solely to implement Government policy. Aided by legislative changes, the Board's approach was to offer free contraception to those who accepted the programmes and to encourage the belief that restricting family reproduction to two children would release more money for consumer durables, such as scooters and even cars, and improve the quality of child rearing. Incentives and penalties were gradually introduced.

Abortion and sterilisation became legal in 1970 and their availability was further liberalised in 1974. There was opposition to abortion from the usual quarters, particularly the Roman Cathlic Archbishop and his more influential laity. Free debate was allowed in Parliament and a Select Committee established to deliberate the issues; the Bill lay on the table for over a year before being passed in December 1969. Initially an 'environmental' clause provided the blanket cover for pregnancy to be terminated—family and financial circumstances of the woman—but now all that is needed is a request for abortion from a woman (accompanied by her written consent) to a registered practitioner. By the early 1980s there were between 15 000 and 16 000 abortions per annum. Legal voluntary sterilisation was introduced with less fuss at the same time as abortion and became progressively accessible without delays or stipulated minimum number of prior births. After peaking at over 10 700 in 1976,* the annual rate has been somewhat over 6000.

The Government has not made or called for a thorough investigation of the psychosocial consequences of these changes, which might be presumed to have drastic impact on the women who bear the brunt of them (one in fourteen of the sterilisations is performed on a man). An attempt to mount a cross-disciplinary study involving social workers and medical officers was nipped in the bud.

Separation induced a more vigorous sense of priorities in the Prime Minister, and although he has continued to pay lip service to the right of all to reproduce themselves, he has been perennially worried about the overbreeding of anaemic stock. Resources are too precious to be squandered on people who are genetically inferior and who, because of inadequate nurture, will not reach even their limited potential. From time to time his blend of eugenics and fostered elitism shows itself to the public; it has been unacceptable if entrenched in targeted measures (such as higher tax deductions and the ill-fated priority registration for children of tertiary-educated mothers). The matchmaking ventures of the Government, providing opportunity—through computer dating, subsidised cruises, holidays or dinner parties—for graduate women to meet males who are on an academic par or mildly inferior, and creating the right climate of opinion by panel discussions and lectures, have brought some results for their troubles and money, a precedent for pre-university and undergraduate students and a little tragi-comic relief to the community at large.

Public housing in Singapore symbolises the response to a number of concerns shared by Lee and Goh. Eighty per cent of the population now live in high-rise flats built under the auspices of the Government, and the majority are purchasing their housing (drawing on their CPF holdings) rather than renting it. The goal is full

---

* Many women would have delayed sterilisation until 1976; the lunar year corresponding to 1976 was under the Chinese zodiac sign of the dragon, the most propitious of the twelve signs for male births.

home ownership by 1999. The Housing and Development Board (HDB) had been set up by the PAP some months after coming to office and was gearing up for action when Bukit Ho Swee, a shanty town and hotbed of dissidents, burned down in mid-1961. Providentially timed, the fire was kind enough not to cause death, despite being fought with ineptitude. Overriding technical objections, Goh Keng Swee and his appointee as head of the HDB, Lim Kim San, decided to plan for high-rise units, ten storeys being the initial compromise. Goh considered that the smaller the area used for building flats and the greater their residential density, the slower the pace needed for the troublesome resettlement of those squatting on land scheduled for public housing.

The first units erected were one-roomed with tiny kitchen adjoining; communal toilets and washing facilities were provided for each floor. Improvements were made to each successive project, Queenstown after Bukit Ho Swee, Toa Payoh after Queenstown, and so on. (Toa Payoh illustrates Lee's unswerving resolve to urbanise Singapore and forget food self-sufficiency—it contained choice market gardening land.) Now new towns and estates are dotted over the island, and another statutory board, the Housing and Urban Development Corporation (HUDC), caters for the needs of the growing middle class. Designs have been improved; flats comprise one to five rooms with full facilities and with some scope for occupants to add their own extras. Most of the blocks rise well beyond ten storeys. In recent years far more attention has been paid to landscaping, shopping needs, public transport access and community amenities.

The visual impact of the estates can be breathtaking, especially at night and from the air, and therefore tends to distract the observer from assessing what they mean both to the Government and, above all, to those who live in them. It is also easy to forget that private housing takes up a disproportionate amount of space, especially the bungalows and gardens of the wealthy; moreover, few of the people who determine and oversee housing policy have to live with its consequences, because they do not reside in HDB or HUDC flats (the mind boggles at the thought of Lee doing so!).

Public housing is one of several imperatives under which the Prime Minister operates in order to control an immigrant society with no commonly accepted traditional leaders. The name of his game is not naked control, but control earned through the accomplishment of projects that, he claims, improve the social fabric and maintain the prospects of economic growth. The HDB has been Lee's effective instrument in altering the political demography of

Singapore—breaking up natural communities based on affinity of race, clan, religion, language and dialect or on generations of friendly contact and shared work, and transferring the fragments into compact areas that are easy to monitor and easy to isolate should the need arise. Only one attempt was made to put an existing community—a Malay settlement at Geylang Serai—holus-bolus into a block of HDB flats, and it was abandoned before completion.

Home ownership has given Singaporeans a stake in their country. It has softened the impact of changed location and changed lifestyle. Its funding through the CPF has also demanded that the people place a tremendous degree of dependence and trust in the Government to husband or release their savings with due care. The impetus for it came out of the race riots of 1964, and was recharged five years later by the Prime Minister: 'I saw something in 1969 which assured me no end and I decided we will up the stakes. We had riots in 1969, a spillover of the riots in Malaysia. With my own eyes, I saw them going down to the void deck [the open space on the ground floor of a block of flats] and carrying up their motorcycles. His is not insured and he knows it. That'll be the end of his motorcycle if someone tosses a match. I said, yes, why not give him a home quickly... When you are a house owner, you say, "Please, this is yours, this is mine. Live and let live."'[7]

The speed with which rehousing has proceeded has been breakneck, a sign both of conditioned public demand and of urgency in the planners' minds. Little attention has been given to alternative housing profiles and, in the earlier stages at least, human problems were not anticipated but dealt with only when they had erupted and could no longer be ignored. Lee himself referred to the strain of 'living in a pigeon-hole inside a beehive'[8] but went on to say that the Government would ease the strain by giving the estates an atmosphere of community. He has managed to curb practices that are incompatible with high-density living: after an accident during Chinese New Year celebrations in 1970, he ordered a ban on firecrackers and lamented the deaths of people who could have been productive for another twenty or thirty years.

Singaporeans' capacity to readjust to crowded, noisy and often impersonal surroundings has been amazing. The children have sometimes helped the process of social levelling and exposure; at other times they have become the symbols of failed neighbourliness—one thinks of the so-called 'latchkey' breed or of small eyes peering suspiciously between shutters. The Government has safely taken the initiative in forming Residents' Committees since few others have wanted, or been allowed, to do so.

Lee's concern with cleanliness is evident in the housing policy. The traditional *kampong* and shanty town, which are planned to be things of the past by 1992, are not only assertions of self-help community; Lee considers them breeding-grounds of dirt and germs. In this respect the new housing estates do not represent complete victory for him, for many of them have sordid public areas such as lifts, corridors and open ground space where litter, waste, graffiti and wilful or casual damage reflect the flaw of the whole concept.

As the housing programme draws nearer to fruition, the longer term questions are beginning to come into focus. Will the awakening of the desire for upward social mobility beget frustration when citizens are not satisfied with what is actually available to them? Will older estates be rebuilt to keep pace with consumer demand for bigger and better accommodation? Will the greying of Singapore and the Government's plea that filial care towards parents be expressed in domestic arrangements produce a political backlash?

Visitors to Singapore are impressed by the cleanliness and greenness of what they see. Rubbish is collected daily, and an army of workers is responsible for trimming verges, looking after plants and trees, sweeping paths and roadsides. The Singapore River and some of the canals have been cleaned up. The land reclamation programme has made former tracts of swamp and coast available; hills have been excavated to provide filler, and whole cemeteries have been exhumed and relocated in a smaller space. Growing need for water catchment and storage (to minimise dependence on supplies from West Malaysia) has added to the pressure on farmers, and the military compete with the civilian population for what land remains. Even the small islands around Singapore have been developed for a variety of purposes.

Lee and Goh have both taken a keen interest in all this. Lee's brother-in-law helped plan the planting and landscaping of many of Singapore's traffic islands and urban gardens. As the Prime Minister goes from his office with its magnificent outlook and moves about the island, he sits at the back of his air-conditioned car and notes down what can be improved.

His intervention is often crucial, as it was in the decision to abandon extensions to the Paya Lebar airport and start afresh at Changi. Every aspect of the city has changed almost beyond recognition in the twenty years of independence. Little is left standing of historic precincts such as Chinatown, despite advice from teams of United Nations consultants, and most of the monuments or homes that have been preserved have been spared demolition rather than been given financial assistance. The new city is a symbolic message to the world: here is a thrusting, cosmopolitan and thoroughly modern society. Its layout also encourages tourists to stay away from residential areas so that Singaporeans can be protected from undue moral contamination and invasion of privacy.

The balance between industrialisation and the protection of work environment and safety may tip a little toward the latter if the emphasis on high technology and brain services continues. Traffic problems have still not been solved, although the expensive MRT system is under construction. Costs associated with car and truck ownership have been raised to prohibitive levels. Obsolete vehicles must be scrapped. Access to the central business district is restricted. Yet the roads are often jammed and the pollution fearsome at peak hour. This is an example of modernisation going awry, one which has been repeated all over the world: the deliberate propagation of consumerism has been all too effective in weakening attachment to the getting and rearing of children and, as with excise on legal drugs, has been a source of revenue outweighed by social costs and curative expenditure—with governments alternately laughing and crying all the way to the bank, unwilling or unable to do anything substantial about it.

Provision of recreation and sports programmes was not a government priority in the first years of independence. But as Lee's consciousness of what would be needed for Singapore's transformation fanned out from its fixed and firm points of departure, he realised clearly that promotion of the 'rugged society' would not be enough. 'Gracious living' became the slogan of the late 1960s. Safety valves were needed from the rigours of each day: military service, hard work, odd school hours, heavy travelling and pressure-cooker home environments. Although there was a risk that certain sports would kindle a patriotism not directed towards Singapore—Lee noted with some dismay a couple of incidents during the 1970s when the Singapore crowds favoured a ping-pong team from China (on one occasion over their own team)—the promise of physical fitness and mental diversion was irresistible. The National Stadium was constructed on the site of the old Kallang airport and opened in 1973. One or two subsequent attempts to turn sports heroes into potential political leaders proved rather disastrous.

Reorganising a society leads to dislocation; dislocation breeds different forms of alienation, ranging from withdrawal and escapism to lawlessness. As change accelerated, the Government accordingly found it necessary to adopt a wide range of measures to preserve order. The tendency of rootless people to gamble and speculate was checked by establishing official lotteries, cracking down on illegal betting and keeping a careful watch on institutions such as the stock exchange and homegrown chit funds.

Lee has had no compunction about chastising and castigating people whom he believes to have forfeited their rights by behaving anti-socially. His attitude is one that Goh Keng Swee has supported to the hilt.

The record of Singapore's nationhood shows that a veritable spate of laws and regulations has come into force to deal with all sorts of offenders and criminals. The scope of capital punishment has been broadened considerably, and thrashing with a cane ('four feet long and half an inch thick')[9] according to the Director of Prisons) is used to 'deter' a wide variety of crimes. Lee has not hesitated to comment unfavourably on trial verdicts with which he has disagreed, although such comment has been infrequent of late. The strong objections of lawyers to the abolition of trial by jury and to the harshness of penalties have been disregarded or howled down contemptuously. Not all have found it possible to come to terms or to argue with the Prime Minister when he has defended these alterations at the movable bar of 'Asian values and mores'. He is, after all, one of the few Singaporeans who has not only mastered the British legal system but is free to adapt it to local conditions as he deems fit.

Since 1970, Lee has taken direct charge of the team prosecuting corruption. This ensures that the small unit gets every co-operation from relevant bodies and individuals. Information is gathered about offences committed inside or outside Singapore so that prompt action can be taken, even if it involves prosecution of someone in Government. There are other political advantages, too. Lee's or Rajaratnam's accusations of opponents' corruption have been a feature of most elections.

The one area in which Singapore has had to tread warily is that of international terrorism. Mercifully her experience of it so far, while very taxing for men used to decisive handling of their own wayward citizens, has been limited.

Identifying the nation

There is something strangely apt about the fact that the two men who have presided over the building of a multiracial Singapore are themselves *Babas*, Straits-born Chinese. Their roots are in a rich but rarefied culture all too easily overwhelmed by bigger groups and by the homogenising force of modernisation. It remains to be seen whether Baba customs can survive as more than objects of curiosity or fad; neither Lee Kuan Yew nor Goh Keng Swee shows any great enthusiasm for preserving the culture of his childhood.

Lee has become very aware, even self-conscious, about his own emergent chauvinism. He would claim that it is cast in genetic and ethical rather than ethnic and cultural terms, although he would not deny that his political pilgrimage has brought to the surface pride in his civilised forbears and a residual sense of racial superiority. 'I understand the Englishman,' he told Parliament on 23 February 1977. 'He knows deep in his heart that he is superior to the Welshman and the Scotsman. Deep here, I am a Chinaman. Yes, an uprooted Chinaman, transformed into a Singaporean.'

The content of his views about race and culture is more fully developed than most people realise. A number of those interviewed for this book were quite surprised when they first encountered the strength and range of their Prime Minister's convictions. While he has not disclosed all the sources that have influenced or reinforced his thinking, Lee appears to be familiar with a corpus of 'research' that has come out of the USA claiming to discern and evaluate 'scientifically' the different genetic endowments of various racial groups. Although he has limited his major public pronouncements to the debate 'nature versus nurture', a rough profile of his personal views can be assembled from all the references and allusions that have slipped out over the years.

Lee believes that the world's population can be separated into two main categories. Those of mixed race and culture, such as Americans and Australasians, bridge the two ends of the spectrum. On the one side are the groups that are soft, intuitive, pleasure-oriented and easygoing, except about issues of religion and custom. They are happy to live in small, self-sufficient rural settlements. Geographically, their origins may generally be pinpointed to the lowlands between the northern and southern tropics, and as a result they are better suited to the sprint and the short-distance haul, whether in athletics or any other field of endeavour. On the other side are the groups that are intense, calculating, disciplined, achievement-oriented and sceptical. Their genes have weathered more extreme climes, and so they are well able to adapt themselves for the protracted business of organising and modernising societies on a grand and complex scale. These divisions, into which the major races and cultures not only of Southeast Asia but of the whole world can be classified, should not be taken as completely static and immutable. Education, modern elite formation, physical environment and social context, adaptive or conservative, can blur them. Female and male characteristics do correspond to the divisions but may cut across what is otherwise substantially determined by a particular group's history and beginnings. The important point to recognise is that the fittest will survive; Lee is less and less patient with what he regards as the social democracies' excessive feather-bedding of the rest.

To his way of thinking, the advantage of the overseas Chinese is that they are uprooted, amenable to modernisation, while being robust and having cultural 'ballast'. Lee aims at engineering a transfer of the ordered values and literary riches of Chinese tradition, with their bestowal of identity under the mandate of heaven, into the more adaptable and technologically oriented mould of a modern English-language society. He believes that the overseas Chinese, unlike the Malays, have been able to jettison just enough of their inherited baggage to remain trim but stable for the voyage across the ocean towards the harbour of rationality.

Goh's views in this respect have not been declared; a reasonable guess would be that they are along similar lines but much less formed. His temperament inclines him not to classify too rigidly, and he is not as puritanical in intellectual or moral outlook as the Prime Minister.

It will come as no surprise to learn that Lee does not believe in racial intermarriage. As far as he is concerned, Singapore will not progress by assimilating or blending communities. His reason is partly that 'grandparents like to see grandchildren in their own likeness'.[10] So far there has not been a significant trend towards intermarriage, but it may not be long before the situation changes. A Singaporean consciousness has been growing, the linear successor of the Malayan consciousness among the English-educated perceived by Lee when he was a student in the United Kingdom. It gains strength where other loyalties and sources of identity break down. Custom and religious conviction may mean that Malays continue to marry only fellow Muslims or converts. Other faiths, especially Christianity, may provide enough common basis to draw more and more couples together across Chinese, Indian, Eurasian and Caucasian distinctions.

Related to this tendency is the imperious hold the English language has taken. 'Within ten or fifteen years, Lee Kuan Yew expects the Chinese language to be unimportant', wrote Alex Josey in 1974.[11] Written Chinese is cumbersome, specially for science, and occupies too much of the human memory bank. Allowing that the sentiment is accurately attributed to Lee, his mind has changed somewhat over the last decade, probably because of the new China connection. Even so, the prediction will come nearer to fulfilment than any Singaporean might have guessed. The linguistic transformation of Singapore is the single most dramatic index of the changes that the island's people have experienced since the Japanese departed, and more particularly since 1965. By 1987 English will be the undisputed 'first' language of education.

Had Singapore stayed in Malaysia, the character if not the outcome of language competition would have been quite different. Chinese chauvinism has been much more readily eroded by English than it could have been by Malay. When people think they are learning a language principally for its usefulness to them, their defences tend to be down. The switch to English happened, surreptitiously almost, as part of the logic of Singapore's position, colonial to begin with, then global. Parents voted with their children's feet. When he could restrain himself from reacting hastily to an immediate crisis in the educational system, Lee was able to stand back and watch the irreversible momentum of his own primary language as it became *the* language of Singapore.

There is still need for standards. On his instruction, BBC English is to be the model for speech. The result is that the newsreaders of SBC affect a clarity of diction and steadiness of modulation that border on the robotic or the constipated. (The edict from on high might have gone astray.) There is a local patois, nicknamed 'Singlish', whose survival is uncertain; but it is likely that attempts to eliminate all Singaporean idioms and inflections will fail. Living languages inevitably acquire dialect variations.

Traditional art forms of East and West are practised by a small number of Singaporeans and enjoyed by most. The dominance of English is, however, having the effect of standardising culture and reducing interest in specialised forms such as Chinese opera. Even the patterned inventiveness of conversation and the proverbial wisdom of Malay culture is under threat from the pervasive influence of television and mass-market leisure programmes.

English writing—poetry, plays and prose—has gone ahead by fits and starts. The best of it exhibits a sensibility that is deeply personal and wistful. Encouragement has come from local teachers and from exceptional figures such as D.J. Enright, who taught at the University of Singapore during the 1960s. (He fell foul of Rajaratnam after suggesting in his inaugural lecture that genuine culture could not flourish in the kind of antiseptic environment the Government seemed intent on creating. He was duly summoned to receive a rebuke and warning from the Minister for Labour, a Malay, while the Minister for Culture, Rajaratnam, stood by and translated. It was, as Enright observed in his autobiography, which he named in honour of the episode *Memoirs of a Mendicant Professor*, 'a case of the translation preceding the original'.)[12] Before his election to the presidency, Devan Nair took on the 'arty-crafty' University establishment and brought back vivid recollections of the Enright affair.

Lee likes to portray himself as a bit of a philistine. He and Goh have made no systematic attempt to contrive a single cultural pattern that pretends to capture the Singapore spirit. Journalism and popular writing are in ferment because of or, more often, despite the Government; there is a strong strain of self-mockery and sardonic wit, and the recovery of the political cartoon may be the next development to await.

LANGUAGE AND THE EDUCATION SYSTEM

Few combinations of topics animate the Prime Minister so much as language and education. His public treatment of them reveals the same kind of self-investment that shines through when he examines health matters. Part of the explanation lies with the political training goals he set himself. 'I am not a specialist in teaching' he said to principals at a seminar on 24 January 1979. 'But I am a specialist in learning, because I had to learn languages.'

Soon after his election to the Assembly, Lee became embroiled in educational policy debate. The All-Party Committee to which he was appointed was compelled by the pressure of events to take proper account of Chinese-medium education, hitherto operating with private funds on a shoestring budget. Guidelines were duly framed to trade financial assistance from the Government for a clamp by school authorities on student agitation.

Although the PAP introduced refinements when it came to office in 1959, the existing education system was retained, and was not changed drastically until the second half of the 1970s. Non-government schools were gradually brought into line; again, in return for funding the Government gained leverage over curricula and over the appointment of principals. The PAP's commitment to universal education and to equality for all four language streams entailed rapid expansion of building programmes and teacher training. Two sessions a day became the norm for primary and secondary schools. Technical and vocational education remained the Cinderella of the system but some upgrading of it was undertaken for the sake of industrialisation.

Hopes of merger with Malaya dictated that Malay should be designated the national language. Those who were pupils during the early 1960s bore a heavy load, often learning three languages at school while still speaking dialects at home or outside the classroom! Concurrently, the PAP attempted to break the stranglehold of the Chinese middle school and work towards an integrated education system; victory came only after stiff resistance.

Following Separation, bilingualism was adopted as the basic policy framework. Whatever each school's principal language of instruction, English was employed more and more for teaching technical subjects and the so-called 'mother' tongue, whether it was ever spoken at home or not, for courses such as Civics. The drift to enrolment in English-medium schools became a minor landslide.

One of Lee's abiding concerns was to harness the education system to nation-building, particularly the fostering of an elite. In the early 1960s he discussed with confidants a 'janissary' plan, by which five-year-olds might be taken from their homes and placed in special institutions that could prepare them for a lifetime of service to the state. The proposal was, of course, politically out of the question, so Lee was obliged to rethink it. At the same time, his more mature observation and experience of parenting began to convince him that stable family life could actually enhance patriotism. When he turned his attention specifically to the later stages of secondary education, his arguments for crack pre-university colleges proved more convincing. He made a point of doing some careful ideological homework, reading up on the subject and discussing it whenever the opportunity arose; he also visited Britain's Eton, some of its North American equivalents and even certain schools in Eastern Europe. The outcome was that Singapore's National Junior College opened in 1970 (Lee's elder son, Hsien Loong, was among its first intake of students). From 1974 onwards, similar ventures multiplied; in due course they took over the two-year pre-university field and developed their own pecking order.

In 1975 the Prime Minister moved from the planning headquarters to the battlefield; he 'started taking a personal interest in education after our more pressing problems had been surmounted.'[13] A decade of successful independence from Britain and Malaysia had provided valuable lessons: the experience of national service, the needs of the economy and the people's own expectations. It was time to take over the restructuring of an overburdened and anomalous educational system before it proved a total hindrance to Lee's national objectives.

Immediately, Dr Toh Chin Chye, who had hitherto shouldered responsibility for English-medium tertiary education, stepped down from his Vice-Chancellor's post. When he refused to be Minister of Education simply in a supervisory role, he left the field altogether and Chua Sian Chin took nominal charge of the portfolio. The University of Singapore's graduate and staff studies swung back to pure research and international publication from seven years of Toh's emphasis on public-oriented consultancy.

Previous Ministers of Education had not exactly triumphed in the portfolio, according to Lee. Yong Nyuk Lin 'took on the job where angels fear to tread'. Ong Pang Boon made little headway, despite being Chinese-educated; 'he, after seven years, got stale in education'.[14] A Chinese-educated engineer with a London PhD, Lee Chiaw Meng, followed, he only lasted three years before being sent in 1975 to tame Nanyang University and oversee the transition to English as the principal teaching medium.

A crisis point was reached when national service testing revealed that large numbers of English-educated youngsters who had not completed secondary schooling were functionally illiterate. The consequences of thinking only of the brightest students while forking out huge sums on the rest would have to be checked. Goh Keng Swee's sarcastic comment was, 'Most countries produce illiterates without spending any money.'[15]

The partnership of Lee and Goh set about educational reform with a vengeance. Lee was horrified at the rundown of the system: the Ministry was compartmentalised and under siege, struggling to react to each new problem. He weighed in with many initiatives and directives. By itself that was not enough. As the Goh Keng Swee Report on the Ministry later said, 'Because the Prime Minister has no formal contact with the ground level, he has to rely a lot on first principles. Furthermore, when policies come from the Prime Minister, there is a tendency for such policies to be immediately executed without thorough analysis.'[16] So Lee decided that an overall plan was essential; in August 1978 he called on Dr Goh to choose a team—systems engineers in the event—and produce one. To Lee's way of thinking, the objective was simple: 'To educate a child to bring out his greatest potential, so that he will grow up into a good man and a useful citizen'.[17]

While waiting for Goh's report, Lee proceeded with his own changes. He established the so-called Immersion Scheme that placed the brightest 8 per cent of students in nine selected schools to improve their bilingual skills. He came out of his Istana office frequently to conduct lengthy sessions with personnel throughout the educational field. There was no holding him back once some kind of correspondence between aims and performance was a real possibility. He reasoned, exhorted, probed and listened, not always with his usual impatience but sometimes asking his audience to rise to the occasion. 'I have actually come tonight to find out how to do my job better' he told a joint campus (Nanyang and Singapore universities) student meeting on 5 January 1979. 'Convention requires that I speak to you first.'

A few weeks later he addressed a seminar for school principals. 'I am trying to explain why this policy [the Immersion Scheme] is right. If you are convinced ... then I believe you will go back and implement it. The alternative is to ... weed out those who disagree ... and instal people who agree ... It will take time. But you know me, I do not lack perseverance.' With reference to the principal of Raffles Institution (his old school) he said, 'I am delighted that here is a principal with a commonsense approach and a willingness and courage to face the facts.' When Madam Liu, the principal of Whampoa Secondary School, demurred at the elitism of the Immersion Scheme, its demoralising effect on those schools, staff, pupils and parents not involved and its possibly faulty connection to the business of choosing future leaders, Lee launched out on a long and cutting reply that included these words, 'Psychologically, I think Madam Liu is representative of our problems ... There is always unhappiness for those adversely affected by change. I sympathise with them. But I cannot allow them to hold up the rescue operation.'[18]

In 1979 two reports were released, Goh's team submitting the major *Report on the Ministry of Education 1978* and spawning the *Report on Moral Education* which Ong Teng Cheong and a group of parliamentarians and bureaucrats prepared and presented some months later. Lee celebrated the lifting of constraints on structural reform when he wrote to Goh, 'I have reflected on your proposal that your letter and report be tabled in Parliament for discussion and debate. I accept it. [This] is a watershed in our history. A generation of Singaporeans is coming of age'.[19] Lee indicated his agreement with all but a few findings of the Report, and stated his belief that 'family-transmitted' cultural values and attitudes to learning had saved students from the shortcomings of the education system.

In turn, Goh Keng Swee accepted Ong Teng Cheong's Report: 'On the whole, your Committee has done a good job and I suggest that the report be published.' Goh did, however, dissent from the professionals' response to it. 'They take the approach of a cook preparing a dish. A list of ingredients is made out with quantities of each. The cooking time is then prescribed. To me moral beliefs form an integrated system of thought and does [sic] not consist of a conglomeration of bits and pieces.' He also sharpened the political and sociological implications of entrenching filial piety, he distinguished between tolerance of other cultures and tolerance of wrong conduct and he rejected the Report's recommendation that dangerous sports be avoided. 'We will not have a rugged and robust society if we discourage children from playing such games.' He expressed the hope that, with outside help, curriculum and teaching material could be developed.[20]

The new education system was duly introduced, not without an unusually lively debate in Parliament and among the public. It involved formalising the 'streaming' of children (begun by some ambitious parents at kindergarten level) with a Primary Three examination. Most would then proceed three years later via the Primary School Leaving Examination into secondary education; but for the duller pupils vocational training would be available after five further years of schooling and thereafter as they dropped out. Those who could reach the 'O' level General Certificate of Education would either go on to pre-university colleges or to the Polytechnic and job training, via National Service for the males.

At last there was some hope of meeting the two basic requirements of a sophisticated economy: pinpointing each person's place in the 'talent pyramid', 'our natural human resource, determined by our genetic pool' as Lee said at a National Day rally in 1979, and converting the talent pyramid to an 'expertise pyramid'. Lee believed that Japan had forged ahead of China and achieved maximum conversion not because of inherent superiority but because of better organised education and training facilities and a more adaptable social system. 'It is prudent to assume that our talent pyramid, as a society descended of immigrants of peasant stock, will not be as rich and creamy as that of Germans and Japanese.'[21] However, home motivation was there and a growing number of parents were themselves educated and industrially trained.

The problems of an ill-equipped workforce and an export-sensitive local manufacturing sector could be addressed directly. After a hard look at the economies of East and Southeast Asia, Lee and Goh cast caution to the winds. They pressed ahead with plans for what was modestly dubbed the 'Second Industrial Revolution'. Certain luxuries allowed before must be dispensed with. Lee declared, 'As we go up the technological ladder, we just cannot waste our time messing around repeating the same knowledge in different languages ... Let's move, and move swiftly, into our common working language.'[22]

Three unfinished edges required trimming and planing if the economy and the education system were to be dovetailed. They were the ubiquity of dialects, the quality of teachers and the state of Nanyang University.

On 7 September 1979, the Prime Minister launched a campaign to promote the use of Mandarin. Lee considered his argument compelling even in Chinese terms. Since the war two generations of students had not mastered to fluency what was supposed to be their principal language, Mandarin, because they reverted to dialect in their daily lives outside the classroom. The dialects themselves were turning, he said, into 'limited, pidgin-type patois' under the impact of Mandarin schooling. It was a stark choice—English–Mandarin or English–dialect. 'Logically the decision is obvious. Emotionally the choice is painful.'

The Government has taken whatever measures lie in its power to follow the campaign through. Cantonese television programmes from Hong Kong are dubbed into Mandarin. All arms of the administration are instructed to use Mandarin when Chinese-speaking clients are seeking assistance. Hokkien is being downgraded in the armed forces. Lee voiced his hopes thus: 'In ten years we should be able to get Mandarin established as the language of the coffee shop, of the hawker centre, of the shops, of course, together with English. And I think unavoidably also Malay, because Indonesian customers come in speaking Malay.'[23]

After some years of the new education system and as a result of the generally freer political climate, the Government has moved to head off criticisms. Tony Tan, the Minister, has handled the situation adroitly. He has insisted that parents have the final say when considering the 'streaming' options for their children. He has agreed that schools and principals are the best equipped to look after their own patch. But there are endemic problems of low morale, nowhere felt more keenly than by Singapore's teachers. With inadequate training and briefing, caught in the language transition, they carry the burden of delivering the Prime Minister's cherished dream of a well trained, civilised workforce whose members each know their place. Teachers face pressure from the

Government, the ministry, the principals and the parents. Their union is a prime target for closure if they step out of line. There is the disheartening prospect of standing in front of pupils who can afford no time for the fun and enjoyment of childhood and are locked into a cycle of routine schooling, extramural tuition, remedial classes and syllabus changes.

As things turned out, the third of the education problem areas, Nanyang University (NU), proved easy to smooth out. A joint campus arrangement was begun in 1978. 'At the time,' Lee said, I believed we could restart NU.'[24] The Nanyang Council, happy to share his belief, expressed hope for a new lease of life. But details and figures soon came to light that convinced Lee it was not possible. Armed with a report by a British expert on higher education who had spent two days in Singapore at his request, Lee wrote to the Chairman of the NU Council in March 1980, stating his own preference for the 'educationally ideal solution' of merging Singapore University (SU) with Nanyang, but outlining other alternatives. He set the terms of bargaining as follow: 'You have a responsibility to that generation of the Chinese Chamber of Commerce and Industry that raised public support and funds to found NU. I have a responsibility to ensure the best education of our students, without upsetting the sentiments of those older Chinese-educated generations who remember with pride their difficult struggle to set up Nantah [NU].'[25] Wee Cho Yaw, the banker Chairman of NU Council, duly replied with counter-proposals. Lee applied further heat in another letter that held out the establishment of a Technological University of Nanyang by 1992 as a sop to the merging of NU and SU. The letter resorted to sarcasm as it detailed the impasse NU had reached, partly by its own efforts: 'the Public Service Commission were left puzzled over the magic by which they [candidates] mesmerised their professors into awarding Firsts or Upper Seconds Honours.'[26] The NU Council held a day-long meeting and accepted the Prime Minister's proposals.

Lee was under no illusions that all his trials were over. He was faced with the need to treble teaching staff at the new National University of Singapore (NUS) by 1985 to meet rapidly expanding skilled manpower requirements. He told university staff on 20 May 1980, when introducing Tony Tan as NUS's first Vice-Chancellor: 'The public debate on merger, from a national viewpoint, totally missed the point.' Twenty thousand employment pass holders, Caucasian and Asian, had been propping Singapore up, 'If we remove them, the economy...will subside, like four punctured tyres.' The political issue had been resolved. The academic problems were a long way from solution.

Subduing a university was nothing new for the Prime Minister. He had never brooked nonsense from any Vice-Chancellor (except Toh Chin Chye), academic or student. His personal demeanour had often been astonishingly rude. During a forum once he became impatient with a lecturer's long-winded objection to the liberalising of abortion; he pushed the student chairman off the rostrum and took over the meeting. An undergraduate reporter noted that the 'supposedly intellectual crowd lapped up Mr Lee Kuan Yew's crude diatribes and jokes with glee.'[27] When for a short period leadership of the University of Singapore Students Union fell mainly into Singaporean Chinese-educated hands and the Union became vocal on social justice issues, its President, Tan Wah Piow, was gaoled on a civil disturbance charge* and his non-Singaporean colleagues were subjected to Special Branch harassment or expelled. Subsequently, student activities were reorganised to limit political discussion to the campus.

The picture in 1980 on the brink of the National University of Singapore's post-haste inauguration was not much different. In his address to staff quoted above, Lee expressed the suspicion that the average graduate stops reading after he has his degree, unlike the educated person who continues to probe and inquire into the causes and solutions of problems. He complained of inappropriate selection procedures in certain disciplines such as architecture and dentistry. He talked of his intervention to correct out-of-date

---

* The trial lasted 46 days, from mid-December 1974 to late February 1975. It took place before T.S. Sinnathuray of the District Court (now a High Court judge). The fact that Tan Wah Piow conducted his own defence was only one of many difficulties that beset the trial as a result of the Government's demands and the judge's rulings and interventions. The chief prosecution witness was none other than Phey Yew Kok, at the time General Secretary of the Pioneer Industries' Employees' Union (PIEU), outside whose headquarters Tan was alleged to have incited a riot. Phey and his offsiders added their note of intimidation to proceedings by stacking the court and its environs, thus complementing the Government's obvious desire to have Tan punished at all costs. The author interviewed several people connected with the NTUC and the PIEU; they all claimed it was common knowledge that the charges laid against Tan had been trumped up. Despite Phey's long and notorious record of 'fixing' opponents and despite his disappearance from Singapore five years later while awaiting his own criminal trial, Tan has had no chance to clear his name. Threatened with two and a half years' compulsory national service in the artillery regiment, Tan took advantage of the weekend respite he was grudgingly allowed after release from his eight-month gaol sentence and went into hiding. He made his way to London and was eventually granted permanent residence there.

teaching in public health. He lamented poor follow-up to examiners' reports. He made invidious comparisons between two groups present in his audience, the former Joint Campus staff from Bukit Timah and the first teaching staff to move to the new site at Kent Ridge. He attacked delusions of grandeur (about the university's national importance) on the part of the outgoing Vice-Chancellor and pretensions on the part of academics who wanted to unionise for the sake of better pay settlements. 'There is no place for petty xenophobics and little empire builders in Singapore. They cannot be allowed to stop us from building a good university quickly, with good teachers from overseas, Asians or Caucasians.'[28]

MORAL AND RELIGIOUS EDUCATION

Two realities that are barely compatible with one another haunt planning for the future. One is the dominance of English as the language of education. The other is expressed thus by Lee: 'It's not excellence that drove Singapore on. It is the cultural drive, something deep and fundamental.'[29]

There are those who fear that the fuel of Chinese culture, which has propelled the Singapore national rocket to this point of space and time, is nearly spent. The old Nanyang University, citadel of the Chinese-educated spirit, cultivated (in the words of a former Vice-Chancellor) 'a breed of highly motivated, socially conscious men and women, ready to work hard and take nothing for granted, a breed who, rather than look upon themselves as the elite in society, regard their being university graduates a privilege made possible by the generosity and social-mindedness of their fellow men'.[30]

Lee and his colleagues have tempered their earlier ridicule of Westernised Oriental Gentlemen (WOGs) in the fervent hope that the English-educated meritocracy can still combine national unity and cohesion with momentum towards higher living standards for the successful individual. 'Somehow,' Lee said in 1979, 'we must abstract and distil the essence of our Asian culture [N.B. not 'cultures'] and values so that English may be used for supplementary instruction in moral education.'[31]

Out of this seed (and following the Ong Teng Cheong Report) has grown Singapore's most curious and hybrid educational experiment. A set of syllabuses has been tested and is now being phased in to form a compulsory moral education programme from Primary 1 to Secondary 2. It supersedes the old civics courses. A local Roman Catholic priest has devised a major part of the syllabus, but has avoided grounding it explicitly in religion. For Secondary 3 and 4, however, a subject called Religious Knowledge is being implemented. Pupils will study the historical and philosophical aspects of the religion of their choice and the life and teachings of its founder, although proselytising and worship will be strictly barred from the classroom. The option of Confucian ethics is available for those preferring no religious affiliation (and in future there will be a subject called 'Study of World Religions').

Strong reaction to the Confucian ethics proposal has surfaced from those who suspect the PAP Government of wanting to rule in perpetuity with the mandate of heaven. Technically, as Goh Keng Swee has pointed out, that would be difficult without first disenfranchising everybody. Goh hopes Singapore can create her own version or school of Confucian thought adapted to modern circumstances and needs.[32]

The religious knowledge course has also been criticised for assuming that partition can be kept between faith and knowledge. Others have commented on the surprising choice of age in the target group—mid-adolescence—and wonder about pupils' receptivity.

There have been teething troubles in both moral and religious education programmes, namely the difficulty of producing interesting textbooks acceptable to different factions within each religion, the need to call on foreign help, confusion and disagreement among teachers and the problems of training them. Why has the Government persevered? Dr Goh has explained the leaders' thinking as follows: 'We see a society in Singapore where people with ability can get rich quickly. Having got the money, unless they have solid values based on what the great civilisations espoused, they could waste their money. Heaven knows what they will do. They will not bring up their children properly. Sooner or later society will degenerate.'[33] He also remarked that those with deep religious convictions or deep moral principles cope better with disappointment, family crises and work stress. Some are helped by a church support system. Others, agnostics, come to intense personal convictions without the benefit of religion. 'I know such people. Strong characters.'[34]

RELIGIOUS FAITH

Lee, Goh and Rajaratnam have their own very conscious but slightly different attitudes to religious faith. Lee has been one of Goh's agnostics since childhood, notwithstanding some Christian influence from family members. Goh has come to identify himself in broad terms with his Christian heritage. Rajaratnam believes religion is man-made. But all three accept that it is given to only a few to develop a moral code without dependence on a community of faith. What is essential for the sake of the economy, an ordered society and one's own self-esteem is the solid sense of what is right and what is wrong.

Singapore is in fact quite a religious society, with strong undercurrents also of superstition. Mediums and soothsayers are widely consulted. There are temples, mosques and churches all over the island, and many homes have their statues and shrines. On several occasions government-contracted bulldozers sent in to level sacred sites and buildings for urban development have been challenged by devotees.

Christianity and Islam have experienced more substantial renewal and revival over recent years than have Buddhism/Taoism and Hinduism, although the enthusiasm in certain Western quarters for Eastern religions has given Singapore's young Buddhists and Hindus some impetus to adopt a more actively proselytising style. A mysterious and fast-growing Chinese cult was banned in 1981. There is little evidence of progress being made by groups purporting to combine all religions; the spirit is more one of competition. Although Lee has decreed that Christians must leave Muslims out of their evangelistic sights, not all of the church groups are happy to observe the edict.

The growing edge of religion in Singapore lies with two Christian movements, one fundamentalist in its use of the scriptures, the other emphasising the empowering gifts of the Holy Spirit in believers—the charismatics. There have been moments of overlap and co-operation but, on the whole, little love is lost between the two. Roman Catholic numbers have continued to increase, less spectacularly. Many 'liberal' Protestant congregations and pastors have been affected by the charismatic movement, but the Methodist Church in particular has absorbed the new influence, without abandoning its traditional, broad-based English work. The churches whose ministry is based on a Chinese dialect are in decline. The 1980 census revealed that more than one-third of Singapore's tertiary-educated citizens are Christian. Undoubtedly the strong American missionary groups find reception easier where language and television culture have prepared the way. Singapore's expanding churches are exemplary in their zeal and opportunism; they are ready for whatever door opens—into the business world, the army, the civil service, the education system at every level, the health institutions and the prisons. Several of the new generation political leaders claim Christian allegiance. Some Singapore churches have reached the stage where they are sending out missionaries, not only within the region but to the ends of the earth.

Apart from supernatural explanations, it is evident that modernisation and the spread of English as first language have contributed to the helter-skelter cellular growth of Christianity. A host of desires may open people's hearts to the gospel message; the desire for a new context, for fellowship, for the assurance of sins forgiven, for the confidence that wealth is a sign of divine blessing. The abandonment of traditional Asian religions and the rifts this causes in extended family relations may need to be justified by appeal to drastic sanctions; idol-smashing and exorcism have been common in certain charismatic circles.

So far the churches and other religious groups have shown little inclination to be prophetic or critical towards the Government. One or two Christian MPs within the PAP, notably Professor Augustine Tan, have developed a somewhat quizzical stance. J.B. Jeyaretnam (Workers' Party MP) is a practising Anglican. The Roman Catholic hierarchy is quieter than it used to be, perhaps reduced to selective grumbling by the sheer range of fronts on which protest would be justifiable. There are, of course, Roman Catholic priests, religious and lay people with their finger on the pulse and they will act as seems best to them. Independent Christian groups still exist, despite the Government's heavy hand never being far away and despite charges of heresy from other Christians.

For the time being the nation's leaders can cast a watchful but approving eye over the religious scene. There are too few Muslims in any position to pose a threat to the Government's authority. Practice of Islam is unhindered but contained on an Indonesian rather than Malaysian type of basis. The churches for their part seem mostly to be producing good, honest citizens who have built into their faith a willingness to render all things lawful unto Caesar—by Caesar's definition of 'lawful'.

Goh Keng Swee gave a light-hearted speech a decade ago at a reunion dinner of fellow Anglo-Chinese School (ACS) old boys. He spoke of a Catholic function he had attended where, to his surprise, there were many battalion and brigade commanders present. He also discovered what a good grasp of political affairs the priests had who sat at table with him. 'By contrast, ACS annual dinners are distinguished by the large number of limousines that converge on the school each year causing an enormous traffic jam.'[35] From his point of view, it would be ideal if the Singapore citizen could translate both religious heritages—the Puritan ethic and the Roman Catholic instinct for stability and authority in a troubled world—into business capacity, political acumen and the readiness to defend the nation from malevolent neighbours.

Social engineering

Social engineering has been a process with varying degrees of deliberate planning about it. Lee prides himself on the helicopter view that he has of Singapore and on his ability, untypical of a politician, to evaluate opportunities without an eye to personal gain. As a result he can judge where society needs to go and how to conjure with the forces of potential support or opposition. Where the prospects of change are long-range, he can calculate a schedule, assemble statistical data and arrange for legislation, back-up and propaganda to assist the transition. The need to consult the people is reduced because he can see clearly what is in their best interests; all he may need is a little expert advice by way of confirmation.

The belief of Singapore's leaders that they do not have an ideology is an example of taking for granted the very air that they breathe. After all, their views constitute the interpretative framework for all legitimate intellectual inquiry and the measure for all planning. Lee and Goh in particular base the supremacy of the state upon the strength of the economy. That it is their version of the state is obscured by the technical nature of modern economic management giving the appearance of being mathematically foreordained, ascertained simply by applied intelligence. The place of culture and religion is to serve the state, to affirm and validate values the state is not yet strong enough to evoke in its own right. The role of those in command is to define and locate all the elements that make up the body corporate and its life, to specify their moral and utilitarian worth and to apportion reward or punishment.

The choice of pattern in policy planning and execution is governed by Lee's stern blend of principle and pragmatism. Where policy was inherited from the British or his local predecessors and no better alternative existed, the PAP took it over, perhaps refining or tinkering with it until such time as circumstances became more propitious for any out-and-out reform. Where the maintenance of colonial policy was desirable but politically difficult, some future goal or external justification could always be found. If all else failed, the catch-all, national security, was invoked.

Where Lee is convinced that a new direction must be taken, one or both of two methods are followed: soften the ground slowly, then act boldly; or put up an extravagant and unworkable proposition, then back down somewhat, having meanwhile secured better parameters for debate. The last few years have seen a variant on the second method; Lee has allowed others to propose or modify reforms, and if he does not like the resulting trend, he has stepped in to moderate or correct.

Many programmes have been executed despite opposition from professionals in the discipline concerned. Fortunately, the wonderful world of specialisation always produces some expert who will endorse the Government's position. Private disagreement is allowed if the person expressing it is in good standing with Lee or Goh. Any hint of technically based misgivings being made public is pounced on and the critic ridiculed or embargoed. The Government, however, has become adept at stopping just short of turning critics into martyrs.

Lee's own evaluation of Singapore's development veers between wonder and puzzlement, even dismay. He described the first decade of independence as 'the most spectacular in Singapore's history, the landscape transformed out of sight'.[36] Yet he is troubled by some of the conundrums of modernisation. What is he to make of the flaunting of wealth, the fecklessness of the elite, the lack of religious and racial tolerance despite higher education, the poor quality of teachers, the incidence of drugtaking, lawlessness and suicide in Singapore, even within the armed forces? He also ponders the fate of societies built on hard work that reach the point of technological sophistication where only a few need keep working. His way of handling the nub of these challenges is to look to the future for resolution, or to redouble efforts to inculcate remedial values, or to pass laws. His Singapore does not stand for irony.

Democracy has survived because the Government of Singapore has neither tried nor managed to classify and engineer its citizens totally. Some integral part of them has remained untouched, outside the process. Given the reliance of nations such as Singapore on global and local capitalism to generate a prosperous modern society, the survival of democracy may seem a miracle. Capitalism always takes a heavy toll of the people and the environment it requires for its expanding purposes. Yet it is undermined in the real world not only by its internal contradictions—the market forces on which it professes to thrive subvert or even destroy each other— but also by its practitioners' inconsistencies. There are money owners and speculators ('moneytheists' as Rajaratnam tags them) who occasionally lapse into human generosity and compassion. This is apart from the diversions and frailties to which any big spender is prey. If so, then even less may ordinary citizens be defined simply as capitalists or lackeys. The ebb and flow of social life are not determined only by national ideology or economic factors.

Nevertheless, a visitor or observer may wish to point out some worrying effects of Singapore's social engineering in case they pass unnoticed for too long.

One is the coarsening of a population subject to widespread militarisation. The prevalent models of masculinity and soldiering are not necessarily conducive to social harmony or sanity. Goh Keng Swee believes that the inflated ego which early studies indicated was a common feature of the demobbed national serviceman was preferable to a low self-esteem. But, as Major Leong Choon Cheong's book, *Youth in the Army* (produced in 1978 on Dr Goh's suggestion), has shown, attitudes to women and the society one is supposed to defend can turn grotesque in those whose only sense of worth and belonging derive from the camaraderie of the barracks.

Singapore women have attained a greater degree of choice about their role in life. Education, propaganda and family planning have played a part in bending their minds more towards a career or a job. But now the Prime Minister is asking them, especially the better educated, to invest more of themselves in having and rearing children. Whatever response there is to his request, the politicisation of women is not the only consequence the Government will have to worry about.

Singapore has gone even further than most developed countries in an astonishing and uncontrolled experiment. Radical changes have cut across all the Asian traditions of child rearing represented among the island's population. Bottle-feeding almost from day one is now normal, and deepseated family nurture patterns have largely been replaced by such arrangements as surrogate motherhood, weekend reunions with children, creches and foster care for years before forcible return to natural parents. The path to these changes was eased by the experience of networks of support for child rearing offered from within or beyond the extended family; but there is a world of difference between a centuries-old social art practised at village level and the dictates of modern urban commerce. No doubt efforts are being made to anticipate or palliate difficulties. Yet, to put it at its lowest, it is puzzling that a Prime Minister so concerned to improve productivity and intelligence to their utmost should have paid so little attention to those elements of nurture most likely to achieve his heart's desire.

Singapore's social engineering record shows not only the marks of its successes and failures but also the gaps of significant areas untouched. The nation's leaders have not set out to tamper with every existing custom. Yet it is also true that their vision has blind spots where principle flies in the face of popular tolerance, or where the machinery of pragmatism is preset to proceed on the basis of abstracted statistics, rather than of ongoing two-way contact with the people. The capacity of men and women to change and sacrifice their inheritance is finite, depending ultimately not on their experience of powerful leadership but on their inner consent to what they expect will benefit them or their children.

YUSOFF THE BOLD

It is time to pay tribute
To the ex-student Yusoff
For courage in the face of

The face of Mr Lee
Prime Minister and Stepfather of his people
Who visited the University
Stalking through its whitewashed cloisters
Like a dyspeptic tiger
In pursuit of Utility
And the filling of the national belly

What role will they play in the future?
Student after student
Answers wisely 'Teacher'
Until it comes to Yusoff
(The race is to the swifter race!)
Who croaks 'Er — me?'
Like a goat face to face with a tiger
'A poet'

An awful silence
Except for the palsied gasps of the retinue
It is seldom that Mr Lee Kuan Yew
Encounters such impertinence

And yet and yet
They who declared an intention to teach
Are now Administrative Officers
Administering whoever can be found to teach
While Yusoff
Still croaking like a tethered goat
Writes poetry.

D.J. ENRIGHT

11

Words and the Man

> A surgeon's primary instrument is his scalpel, a politician's is his word.
>
> LEE KUAN YEW,
> to the Royal Australian College of Surgeons, Singapore, 6 May 1973

> You know, Singapore is a volatile place: people speak up; they are anti-colonial; they are fervent; they are prepared to fight; they talk in a very robust and vigorous way. So the British thought in terms of a wider whole with people who are more accustomed to courtly gestures rather than with the open, rabble-rousing type of political society which we have in Singapore where everybody speaks his mind. In that way, they thought they were safer. But it was not to be.
>
> LEE KUAN YEW,
> address to workers at the British naval base, Singapore, 21 December 1965.

If 'morals are fists' (Jeremy Bentham) then words can be sharp instruments, at least when a master craftsman is at work. Every page of this book registers the extent to which Lee Kuan Yew relies upon words and has refined their use. They are not just instruments but his chief weapon, defensive and combative all at once. His life and experience, his intellectual pilgrimage, have marked him as a man apart, and he needs the means to protect his position, to secure co-operation and to vanquish foes. A.P. Rajah once complained in the Legislative Assembly that the Prime Minister was claiming to play all his cards openly: but he had put them face downwards. Lee retorted, 'Only fools place all their cards face upwards!'[1] Words are subtle enough, if chosen carefully, to reveal and conceal, tantalise and disarm. They create a bond where one may not naturally exist; at the same time they define the bond and give it a friendly or adversarial tone as required.

In the case of Lee, we are talking of prowess in the English language. He does not claim the same ease or compel the same attention with his Mandarin or Hokkien or Malay, even though he has laboured to acquire the proverbs, epigrams and polished turns of phrase that belong to these other tongues, relying on a teacher, a 'native' speaker or a tape recording. His early public forays into Mandarin must have been quite an ordeal for him. A journalist reported of a 1956 rally at Bukit Timah that Lee was brilliant in English, very effective in Malay, and so halting in Chinese that he had to interrupt himself constantly with the cry *'Merdeka!'* ('Independence!') to keep his audience's attention, let alone enthusiasm, for what he was saying. Yet all this costly effort has long since paid off and given him the bonus of an edge over his compatriots.

'When I started learning Mandarin, I made it a point of getting native speakers of Mandarin, people born and bred in Peking.* I do not speak Mandarin as fluently as the Singaporean Chinese-school graduate. But when abroad, in China, Taiwan, Hong Kong, or US, my Mandarin is better understood than Singaporean Mandarin; I had chosen native Mandarin speakers to be my teachers,' Lee has said.[2]

He is a speaker rather than a writer. His writings mostly read as if they are dictated onto a machine and then transposed and corrected into printed form. He gives lack of time as the explanation for not writing more, and says he is looking forward to redressing the balance when he retires. But it is also true that writing is far less direct in its impact. Besides, why not have the best of both worlds? Many of his speeches have been given wider circulation through the press, as propaganda booklets or in Alex Josey's volumes.

What of the quality of his English? Anyone familiar with his pronouncements over the years would give the same answer to that question: superior. Even when he gets excited and loses the careful accuracy that comes of thinking and preparing before delivery, the clear meaning of Lee Kuan Yew's message is rarely in doubt. He generally expresses his thoughts with economy, although obscure or technical words sometimes crop up and remind the audience of his learning.

When Lee speaks, the cut and thrust of his words have an unmistakable ring. Goh Keng Swee was proud that he and his colleagues prepared their own speeches, maybe 'the few remaining members of a vanishing breed of political leaders'[3]. The spoken

---

* One of them was Ching Ping, wife of the writer Dennis Bloodworth.

word is Lee's expression of piety, of 'loyalty to the sources of his being'. It connects him back to his childhood and education by doing now what it did then—creating his own world and purging it of undesirable elements. The resonances of Lee's speech are too rich to have been acquired by latter-day imitation. His extraordinary four-and-a-half-hour diatribe to the Parliament on 23 February 1977 played fast and loose with syntax and orderly presentation, but it was spellbinding and crystal clear as communication—the making and mocking of reputations, the weaving and debunking of history, the disclosing of Party secrets and memories—all with an ostentatious overlay of pithy Chinese sayings. It was tough, vulgar, didactic, irreverent, self-righteous by turn, a personal idiom well and long learned. Lee's loyalty is to himself and to his Singapore, and his speech marks out his distance from other group or private loyalties, often overriding them in the process.

The 'music' of Lee's way with words is bereft of literary allusion and psychological insight. It is designed to communicate its message as straightforwardly and efficiently as possible. It moves between two poles—from being rationalistic, information-laden, impersonal, to being dramatic in the fashion of street theatre, the courtroom or the cathedral pulpit. There are striking echoes of the Old Testament prophet or the Victorian preacher in Lee's blend of fire and homeliness when he prescribes the morality that Singaporeans should display at all levels of society; and in his persistence against the odds.

Long ago, Lee chose how he would learn to speak. At home English was a major language, interspersed with Malay and Cantonese. As a small boy, Harry refused to memorise Mandarin and, furthermore, decided he would adopt 'proper' English, not the patois of the Straits-born Chinese. 'I was taught English by Chinese, Indian, Malay, and Eurasian teachers ... from 1928 ... to 1937. For my last two years in Raffles Institution [RI], I had native English teachers to teach me English: an Englishman in Junior Cambridge [1938], two, an Australian and a Scotsman, in Senior Cambridge [1939]. For the four years I was in RI, the principal was a Scotsman. He addressed the school every Monday. I have little doubt that my spoken English improved immeasurably because of their attention and example, especially in accent, diction and rhythm.'[4]

His time in England (1946–50) and specifically at Cambridge gave him more models to imitate. 'I consider myself fortunate to have learned the classical version of the language to my continuing joy and advantage.'[5] It is interesting that his speech is not more completely Anglicised: together with accurate usage of standard English, some of his pronunciations have been fixed from over- or under-exposed snaps of the original. Now and then signs can be detected of his Singapore childhood environment; for example, the dropping-out of auxiliary verbs, the indiscriminate 'isn't it?', disagreement in number between noun and verb.

E.W. Barker, a Cabinet Minister, ascribed to Lee 'the gift of the gab'.[6] At school, at Raffles College and at Cambridge, people such as Barker observed the young man acquiring the skills of debate and of thinking on his feet. Like an oral poet, Lee has at any time a stock of phrases on particular themes that he can retrieve. He often practises and refines his current stock on visitors and colleagues for some time before and after the occasion for which they are primarily intended. Key words and phrases derive from his conversation or reading and in using them he makes them his own. For instance, he examined Gordon Means' doctoral thesis of 1964 on Malaysian politics, and circled the word 'ultra' referring to Malay extremists: it then became part of a catchcry he raised constantly until well past Separation.

His choice of expression is better informed now than in the early 1960s, when he would sometimes repeat phrases without recognising the freight of irony they carried. For a time he advocated the permissive society and a brave new world! Even in the corrected record a few slips of the tongue remain. A 'duplicity' of professors would result from dividing the University of Malaya in two. Apparently he said to the Advocates and Solicitors' Society in March 1967: 'No one doubts that anyone will be executed at the whim and fancy of somebody else'! To BBC television interviewer, Ludovic Kennedy, he made a startling confession on 5 March 1977: 'Never have the people of Singapore had a government which they can kick out of office freely, without hindrance, just by crossing them off the ballot. And never have they had a government which had to tend to their needs—every grumble, every bellyache, to make sure that the vote is on the side of the angels every five years.'

How does Lee replenish his store of ideas? By selecting subjects to pursue from the array of information and opinion presented to him. He makes a quick judgment about the value of a particular source. He is inclined to read and converse, either to indulge his mood and link it to a grander world of discourse or for utilitarian purposes with a bias towards quasi-technical material. He will quiz colleagues and local or visiting experts, sometimes to the extent of disregarding other table guests or people present.

Apart from tuning in habitually to the BBC's World Service news broadcasts, he reads newspapers in up to three languages each morning. He demands a précis or digest of the best available literature in whatever subject is concerning him at the time. Woe betide anyone who produces a shoddy or badly presented and argued Cabinet brief! He is fascinated by medical and health matters, by the hardware of defence and security, and by intelligence gathering. He enjoys works on statecraft, whether European or Asian, classical and modern, and likes to read history of the epic variety.

An Indonesian newsman asked him once at a press conference in Jakarta what kinds of books he read. The *Straits Times* of 10 September 1982 recorded Lee's answer:

>The Prime Minister hesitated for a moment, then said: 'That's a subject really for my psychoanalyst.' Another pause, and he launched into his longest reply of the session ... 'I will tell you the book I'm reading at the moment. It's called *From The Centre Of The Earth* by Bernard Bernstein. He gives the other side of the coin, the other side of the brochure of China today—you know, all the glossy pictures and all the strong, muscular men and vigorous women pointing to The East is Red and so on ...
>
>'I find it therapeutic because many of the questions I wanted to ask my hosts when I was there but for reasons of the niceties of protocol I never did.
>
>'It's an interesting book.
>
>'I'm also reading ... I decided to finish reading a book by Moritani called *Japan: The Most From The Least*. A very modest Japanese approach. But it was highly effective ... I'm afraid I don't read one book at a time. I find that becomes a kind of duty, an imposition to finish it from cover to cover.
>
>'So I pick up two or three books, and as the mood and fancy takes me, I pick up one or the other.
>
>'The third book I'm reading is *The Third World War*, revised edition. I read the previous one by Sir John Hackett.
>
>'It's a scenario of what happens when the major powers get into conflict and how the third world war takes place.
>
>'That's an apocalyptic picture of what could happen to the world ... Now we have so many weapons with radioactive capacity that even if we are not participants in a war, the radioactive fallout will finish us all off.
>
>'It is a sobering thought which gives us all an interest in preserving peace. Not to surrender to the enemy or to be intimidated or to be blackmailed. That's another series of books worth reading ...

'So [the books] range from the total apocalyptic annihilation of mankind to the hope of a better tomorrow from the miseries of life.'

Around the time that Singapore was cast out of Malaysia, Lee remembered: 'I had to read either Jane on fighting ships or Arnold Toynbee on challenge and response'. Toynbee's vision of civilisation transcending national boundaries and relying on a creative minority must have been a reinforcement to him, as well as the prediction of the Malay-Chinese flashpoint in Southeast Asia and the future of the Pacific basin. But, Lee added, he didn't want too much challenge: the thought of a civilisation uprooted, as on Easter Island, was a bit daunting!'

One of Lee's vital assets is his intellectual and legal training. He has the capacity to differentiate and analyse language. 'I am rather choosy about the form of words one puts ideas in and dresses one's ideas in.' It is 'part of my long education in the British tradition'. What is the meaning intended by the speaker who uses a certain term? What is the meaning interpreted by the listener? And what is the widely accepted 'majority' meaning? When Lee follows his own maxim, he gains insight into the relative positions he and his interlocutor occupy. Such a simple device can give considerable advantage: not just to score a debating point but to turn slogans to good account and trap one's enemy in contradiction. This is what happened in the controversy over merger with Malaya (1961–62). The *caveat* again is that Lee thinks instinctively in English, and has not always been good at gauging the nuances or mental drift of his colleagues or opponents whose mother tongue is different.

It is the ability to get purchase on basic political concepts as used in practice that has contributed to Lee's reputation as a Machiavellian. He quotes Humpty Dumpty: in Lewis Carroll's *Through the Looking Glass* 'a word means what I choose it to mean', and seems to cock a snook at those who are trapped in the web of unexamined or conventional wisdom. His advocate's mind probes the interests of his adversaries, and many find they have been outwitted. Ideologues who freeze insight into dogma lose Lee's freedom to pursue and maintain power by virtue of his constant analysis of what is happening.

Improvising and settling arguments definitively are skills Lee has always coveted. So is teaching, although his practice of it is informal and his aptitude unconsciously learned. John Strachey, a British Fabian, one of many such to visit Singapore over the years, cast his approving eye over Lee and described him as one of two tutor politicians in the world during the 1960s (Nehru being the other). Quoting Strachey, the late George Thomson, a civil servant turned teacher who knew the Singapore scene well, added that Lee had become more avuncular with the passage of time.[8]

The linkage of Lee the leader and Lee the instructor or tutor is quite basic. He is constantly trying to persuade people to his viewpoint as being the most accurate picture they could have of the real world, warts and all. Whatever else they do, they must take it into account. He makes available the fruits of his mental processes to whomever will receive them. Not everything is dispensed at once—only enough to assist the learning needed by that particular class at that stage. Harder or more esoteric material is reserved for brighter and worthier students. Statistics are used liberally to make his case watertight. Object lessons are given in the use of language. The tone is a mixture of sweet reasonableness, warning and urgency: the time of testing is ever near to hand; progress is not to be hindered by the slowness or misbehaviour of a few. But perhaps 'schoolmaster' is a more faithful metaphor: there is a commitment to pupil or student with both, but 'tutor' conveys the image of an older adult in the intimacy of his study listening first to a younger one before drawing him or her out, and the scale is too small to represent the Prime Minister's situation, except with his Cabinet juniors.

Another important characteristic of Lee's treatment of words is his retention of control over their consequences, as far as possible. Many of the most controversial interviews or speeches he has given are filed separately and do not appear in the public dossier. To pressmen he makes a clear distinction between attributable and non-attributable remarks and insists on all their recording devices being switched off for the latter. Some interviews are checked, and corrected if necessary, before release. With civil servants and underlings he eschews written instructions, particularly in sensitive or questionable matters. There must be no avoidable hostages to fortune—private and unrecorded words evaporate into thin air, and no amount of allegation that they were uttered, even by their original audience, can summon them back.

What are the settings in which Lee performs as a speaker? Parliament has given him scope to reveal most of the facets of his skill. The Legislative Assembly contests between him and David Marshall 1955–57 had no great impact on the masses because the only language allowed—and available to the two British-trained lawyers—was English, but they provided entertainment for the devoted gallery crowds and journalistic copy for the international community. Statements of lofty principle crossed the chamber to and fro, as did shafts barbed with insult, sometimes good-humoured, sometimes not; interjection and exposé tested the limits of the Speaker's leniency. With Marshall's resignation, Lee became undisputed master of the Singapore house and has remained so.*

During the Malaysia period, Lee's English and Malay speeches to the federal Dewan Ra'ayat or Rakyat (People's House) were characterised by a defensiveness hardly ever perceptible in Singapore. His eloquence in Kuala Lumpur was politically counter-productive.

Although Lee's parliamentary appearances and interventions have become even less frequent than the sittings themselves, they are memorable. His attacks upon J.B. Jeyaretnam, first Opposition Member since 1966, must have dispelled any illusion that he is mellowing. In one such he said '... make believe is, to a certain extent, necessary. We treat the Member for Anson with the necessary courtesy ... he has this irresistible urge to inflict damage upon himself ... He conducts himself with utter disregard for rules of decency ... He is a continuous purveyor of untruth ...'[9]. And, during another speech: 'Two allegations have been made of misconduct. I offer an open forum for all details. Instead, I have an unseemly, disgusting, wriggling retreat.'[10]

The former excerpted remarks were made on the same day as the Prime Minister 'with a heavy heart' paid a very personal tribute to Hon Sui Sen, the Finance Minister who had just died.

Having dominated the parliamentary arena, Lee can afford to disparage it a little. He once told MPs: 'Meanwhile, do not forget that the real action is in the constituency. My first lesson in politics was that the speeches made in Parliament did not count as much as the speeches I made *fang-wen*, on constituency tours. The speeches made in Parliament were of more interest to the press, the public gallery, and some of the intelligentsia. But when I went down and explained to people in the streets, in the *kampongs*, and when I solved their constituency problems: roads, drains, schools, community centres, veterinary stations, clinics, jobs and housing, that was what settled the issues and enabled us to win.'[11]

There is no doubt that the rallies, conducted at constituency level and given a larger audience through television, put Lee Kuan Yew

---

* Marshall returned in 1961 after the Anson by-election but was defeated at the September 1963 poll. The Singapore Legislative Assembly became the Parliament in December 1965 after the island achieved full independence.

for many years firmly in command of the popular political agenda.

Some of Lee's speeches to his Party have been released subsequently through its publication *Petir*. They show not only his supremacy as Secretary-General but a quite habitual and unselfconscious freedom about bestowing demands and favours on people. On 17 November 1981, following the loss of Anson constituency at a by-election poll, he said, 'Had we won in Anson, I would not have come to this gathering. Victory would have been sufficient reward. We shall fight again and I shall fight with you.' Three months earlier, at a farewell dinner, he summed up one of his earliest colleagues, Jek Yeun Thong: 'Amongst my documents I treasure one sheet of paper in simple Chinese, the first and simplest speech I have ever made in Mandarin for general elections in April 1955 at the Bandar Street square. It was before the biggest crowd Singapore had ever seen, around 60 000. With Jek's one sheet of paper, I tried to prove I was Chinese and Jek kept on writing speeches and pamphlets. Now, it does not matter much. Then, when I could not speak Chinese, he was crucial.'

Lee continues to accept speaking engagements associated with prestigious international bodies. In most of them he presents his political overview or wisdom on particular issues as an elitist who has long practised dealing with the grassroots. Some of the most personally involving of his speeches have been at medical congresses where he has waxed philosophical and displayed the fine detail of exceptional curiosity about a specialised area of research or knowledge.

His tough talking is reserved for occasions such as the Commonwealth Heads of Government meetings or Singapore National Day rallies, or wherever he decides to be elder statesman. He rebuked the CHOGM delegates in Kingston, Jamaica, for 'talking at each other, not to each other'. Heads of government vary in their response to his 'off-the-cuff' analyses of world affairs: Harold Wilson described them as enthralling; others have found them tiresome. At home, civil servants, university members, professional groups or trade unions expect to receive the Prime Minister's wisdom without gilt wrapping.

Press conferences and interviews have become a particular art form within Lee's repertoire. He often conducts them with the air of enduring a necessary evil and he does not hesitate to turn the tables on a questioner or to ridicule him. (At several such conferences he has ignored the women present.) The official transcript discreetly omits much of the repartee. Television interviews have been a fruitful source for this book, particularly those one-to-one sessions where skilful questions bring Lee to life. The interviews with Gerald Stone in July 1972 or with Ludovic Kennedy in March 1977 are two outstanding examples.

When Lee first saw himself on television, Josey tells us, he was momentarily shocked into silence. He was appalled at the fierce and unsmiling figure on the screen, clearly spoiling for a fight. 'This was not the figure the political Lee wanted to present to the electorate,' wrote Josey.[12]

He set out to soften the image. The result is not an unqualified success: when he is not tensed up to rebuke or attack, he tends to appear bored or chemically over-relaxed and his official smile is not unlike that of a crocodile tenderly anticipating its prey.

Lee the advocate was very successful. In latter years he claims to have been dismayed by some of his victories. He is conscious of the lawyer's tendency to play with words, and affects to be contemptuous of it. Nevertheless, the old habits of cross-examination die hard in him: Josey records two episodes in which Lee interrogated lawyers on behalf of the Government; Lee's hectoring showed little of the civility he demands of others.[13] On his overseas trips or with visiting or resident experts in Singapore, Lee pursues particular preoccupations of the moment by setting up a private session with an individual or panel. A Harvard academic who took part in a session on Japan was impressed both by Lee's extensive knowledge and by the stubbornness of his pessimism about Japanese military resurgence.

He has developed a unique line in praising and burying VIPs. His efforts to understand friends and acquaintances who have died are kindly but thin, to say the least, or even strange. He recalled Raffles College classmate Kwan Sai Kheong's 'high-pitched and chirpy voice'; he paid a parliamentary tribute to Benjamin Sheares that went into the President's last weeks on earth and medical self-diagnosis. Whether talking of the dead or the living, Lee apportions approval according to the measure of a person's usefulness or, as lesser alternative, goodwill to him. Of Pham Van Dong he said, 'I have learnt more about Vietnam and her distinguished Prime Minister from our two-hour meeting this afternoon than if I had read two books on the subject;'[14] Of Ratu Sir Kamisese Mara: 'I never dreamt that I would be visiting it [Fiji] ... as guest of my favourite Prime Minister in the Commonwealth.'[15] He specialises in the culturally backhanded compliment: for instance, to Japan's Nakasone: 'Most of your predecessors had made a virtue of soft and misty language making you appear so clear-cut by comparison';[16] of Fukuda (remembering the Japanese Code of

Honour—to die rather than be captured and vanquished): 'Our guest of honour tonight ... belongs to that generation ... of rare distinction. Their courage in the face of defeat and adversity ... brought about the miracle of Japan's rebirth ...'[17] (Let the reader who doubts that the Prime Minister's words are often loaded seek confirmation from any one of Singapore's coterie of Lee-watchers who examine what their Prime Minister has said or neglected to say and then read between the lines.)

What are the distinctive features of Lee's language and the inner workings it reveals?

There is a strong streak of sarcasm, ridicule, verbal sadism in many of Lee's speeches, and he appears indifferent whether the recipient of his contempt is present or not. At the opening of the Chung Cheng High School auditorium, Lee declared that the building was too grandiose.[18] In the 1950s and 1960s, his meetings with University members were often heated: on one occasion he called students 'goons' and said he was not interested in meeting them; he described a former Vice-Chancellor and PAP sympathiser as a 'good medicine man'.[19] At a joint press conference with President Marcos, Lee said he did not try cosmetic techniques to improve his image, knowing full well that Marcos dyed his hair.[20] He poked fun during the Jamaican CHOGM at those who 'bred like rabbits': sitting next to him was Khir Johari from Malaysia, with twenty-two children. He taunted the late Herman Kahn for his corpulence.[21] He advised Australian politicians to get over the temptation of the media.[22]

Lee's talk is dotted with scatological and phallic references: people squatting on others, looking at a man's pants when he is under fire; sucking the Singapore banana; thrusting, virile Singaporeans. He occasionally employs quasi-erotic imagery: 'Repression is ... like making love—it is always easier the second time'. 'When the elephants flirt the grass is trampled; when they make love, it is disastrous.' But he is not at ease with it, as was evident at a farewell dinner for Alex Josey in 1965: Lee launched out into a description of Josey's preference in women, their race, their lubricity, and so on; someone present recalled that 'none of us knew where to look'. Lee's customary swing between prurience and distaste showed up once when he told civil servants that, on a country trip with a hundred thousand other soft-living Italian families, he saw 'the young make love while the old drank mineral water in the sun'.[23]

Lee does not like to be pinned down by his words, and he can be very evasive in press conferences. He is proud of not contradicting his basic stand, yet he does so time after time. During a 1967 television conference he asserted, 'I am not saying intense people are better than unintense people' and immediately went on to say of the Thais, whom he classified as 'unintense', 'If you give them a sophisticated surface-to-air missile, you will have to have the instructor there till the end of time.'[24]

An interesting example of this refusal to be bound by the rules one sets for others is his solemn vow of Cabinet solidarity in one breath, whilst in the next he makes pointed reference to disagreements involving his colleagues or his correction of them. Special pleading is his stock-in-trade: he has exhorted citizens to filial piety, manual labour, males helping in the house and being willing to marry women educationally superior, *gotong royong*, [mutual co-operation], all without any sign of heeding his own advice.

Lee's vantage point is singular. He was not a 'hawk' or a 'dove' with regard to the Vietnam war, but an 'owl' glaring balefully at all sides.[25] Only rarely has he had the opportunity to experience ordinary Singaporeans' reaction to one another: 'I . . . have had to deal with telephone operators who did not know who I was and treated me just like a member of the public.'[26] He does talk of 'us' and 'them' when praising the intense or fearing the slothful. But if he is emphasising a misdemeanour by Singaporeans, he stands over again, saying, 'This will not do.'

Another more neutral device of Lee's is to describe Singapore in cybernetic terms—digits, ciphers—whilst still implying that he is outside it, the operator of the machine. His sense that things are not turning out the way they were meant to is harnessed to a renewed purposefulness, to make sure that they do.

With all this, there remains a flame of inspiration. Lee's vision is not one all would find captivating, but it can kindle his speech to touch the heights. His picture of Singapore in the year 2019 is euphoric: 'Singapore has been and will remain more than a place on the map . . ., this climb up the face of the cliff to a higher level of civilization . . . depends on man's restless, organized, and unending search for perfection.'[27] Or consider this passage, more practical in import, on the greening of Singapore, delivered at the opening of a horticulture and aquarium fish show on 17 September 1980.

> Can we not get tall equatorial forest trees, like the jelutong or teak, that grow to 30 or 40 metres to grow alongside the 30 or 50 storey buildings sprouting all over the city? They will keep their proportions against these high-rise. Such tall trees are slow-growing. All the same, experiments in America with tree

hormones have proved that tree growth can be speeded up. The challenge for Parks and Recreation is to give that touch of quality and originality in maintaining a balance of flora and fauna in our city, despite the bulldozer, despite the reinforced concrete structures and tarmac'd motorways. Both brain power and aesthetic sense, and more resources are the keys to success.

We have noted the Prime Minister's approach to the task of offering spoken or written condolence, welcome and official gestures to colleagues or foreign counterparts. We can also detect that once his own position is acknowledged, Lee willingly pays tribute to the team that has worked with him over the years. He is openly affectionate towards some, openly affirmative towards others. They and his immediate family constitute the privileged sphere within which Kuan Yew's language can slip into a human idiom. Sometimes when he is honoured at home and always when abroad, he responds graciously and with becoming modesty. At dinner parties, too, he can be a charming and hospitable conversationalist.

Anyone wanting to understand the use of rhetoric and the place of language in the twentieth-century political leader's armoury will be hard pressed to better the insights of American philosopher Kenneth Burke. His book *Permanence and Change*, first published in 1935, offers a telling account of the stresses under which inherited patterns of speech and communication labour when they are bedazzled and propelled into the unknown by the achievements of scientific reasoning and technology. Precisely because societies are in transition from the old to the new, it is not yet possible to assess the effects of classifying people by their economic status or organising them along the lines of a machine or computer. Those on the road are still likely to be conscious that race, religion or culture are their guiding lights, however flickering and feeble, rather than the dictates, for example, of modern consumerism or militarisation.

At such a stage of history there is an above average chance that non-traditional leaders will arise. Their private struggles, however personal and atypical—whether to establish an identity, vanquish enemies, realise grand dreams or attain some other all-absorbing goal—may match the prevailing public mood of the moment, the longing for direction and stability amidst bewildering change.

The full import of Burke's thesis goes far beyond our concerns here. One of his asides, however, may be a particularly pertinent (if unwitting) clue to Lee Kuan Yew's exceptional way with words; it can therefore serve as a fitting conclusion to this chapter. Burke believes that eloquence is given incentive by pain and is a strategy of appeal, of radical evangelism. The sufferer attempts to socialise his position by inducing others to repudiate the orientation painful to himself. This is difficult in a time of pronounced social conformity, but when normative influences are lacking and people's orientation weakened, his appeal may be more successful.[28]

LINES

let the gifted who discern
our pain and our belonging
say it for us:

words are only wind
children of the mind
give nothing if nothing
is accepted

LEE TZU PHENG

12

Lee the Man

> Well, I am very intrigued when people try and explain me away because I think it is an exercise in psychiatry.
>
> LEE KUAN YEW,
> press conference, Ottawa, 9 August 1973

Lee has always rejected attempts to classify him as one of a type or on a par with others. When Gough Whitlam lumped him and Edward Heath of Britain together as the two conservatives in the ranks at Ottawa's 1973 Commonwealth Heads of Government Meeting and made some critical remarks about Lee's island republic he earned the Singapore Prime Minister's undying dislike. Lee feels that no one is entitled to practise psychiatry on him, to shape him into some merely human mould where his behaviour conforms to norms set by outsiders, would-be authorities and self-appointed commentators. That would be to explain him away.

Our investigation so far has revealed a leader who has made an exceptional investment of himself in his political career. Lee Kuan Yew bestrides the modern history of Singapore, elevating it 'to a new path and new conclusion'[1]. No other leader stands out to anything like the same extent.

David Marshall, Singapore's first Chief Minister, devoted enormous energy to the tasks of his office. He resigned it, a little wistfully, and months later blundered right out of the Assembly. His political views undermined his already isolated position. He made several attempts to return to the public arena and succeeded only when useful to forces behind the scenes. No one who has met him could imagine Marshall emptying himself entirely into the planning, the machinations, the single-minded pursuit of leadership. He has been wealthy champion of the underdog, defence barrister with flamboyant forensic manner in crimes of passion and murder, ardent advocate of civil liberties. He is expansive and entertaining, a great raconteur, enjoying good food and company and the pleasures of life.

Marshall was succeeded by Lim Yew Hock, who died Haji Omar Lim in Jeddah on 30 November 1984. An English-educated clerk and founding member of Singapore's Labour Front and Trade Union Congress, Lim found himself in power 'by a fluke'[2] to use Lee Kuan Yew's words. 'He is quiet, small, unobtrusive, cracks jokes, plays practical jokes, puts balls into pockets and takes them out. But he is a very deep fellow and I knew that.' Lee summed him up: 'I thought that he was a very wily operator.'[3] Popular in some circles, Lim appeared to have limited political goals, often those defined, developed and turned into speeches for him by colonial officers. He allowed himself to be manipulated both by Lee and by those hostile to Lee such as Khaw Kai Boh (a police officer with Special Branch experience and later a Malaysian senator for the MCA). His backing increasingly came from right-wing circles at home or abroad. His enthusiasms for gambling and women distracted him and he was also compromsied by his connections with Chinese secret society and gangster elements. After leaving Singapore's Assembly in 1963, he was appointed Malaysian High Commissioner to Canberra, where he cut a curious figure. Eventually, stripped of the high honours he had received, and estranged from the Singapore scene, he became a Muslim and took up a position that the Malaysian leaders secured for him in the Middle East.

There were others who sought leadership or had it thrust on them. They, too, are men of another age. Lim Chin Siong achieved prominence in his early twenties: born in 1933, he was educated at Chinese High School where he came under Malayan Communist Party influence through Fang Chuang Pi (called *'the Plen'* [short for plenipotentiary] by Lee Kuan Yew when referring to Fang's alleged secret negotiations with him) and others. He was detained for his Anti-British League activities in 1950. Following his release, he and his lieutenant, Fong Swee Suan, began to organise Chinese school students and Chinese-speaking unionists. His strengths were his dedication to the struggle, his feel for organisational detail, his charismatic popularity and his public speaking skills in Hokkien and Mandarin. His weaknesses lay on the obverse side of his strengths: the difficulty he had in matching ideological purity with impure reality—the reality of domestic communal tensions and, later, the rift between Moscow and Beijing; his lack of fluency in English and above all, his dependence on others' counsel—whether via the MCP chain of command or from fellow-travellers such as Devan Nair whose vehemence often masked poor forward planning. Lim was not the sort of person who would instinctively go for the jugular, and to make matters worse he had too many well-equipped enemies to contend with at any given moment. Detained in October 1956, he emerged from prison only after the PAP had claimed electoral victory: Lee Kuan Yew had done everything he could to minimise Lim's potential to recapture the masses. Even so, he was the focus for an alternative government when the PAP split, and he became the Secretary-General of the new Barisan Sosialis. Had he remained in the arena, Singapore might have traversed a very different history. His detention for the third time in 1963 almost broke his spirit. He was isolated and deprived of his wife-to-be. He was confused by China's bitter animosity towards the USSR. He was frequently at odds with Lee Siew Choh and party leaders outside—sometimes being accused by them of betrayal. The Malaysian government extracted his promise to fight Lee Kuan Yew for control of Singapore if he were released by Kuala Lumpur.[4] Subject to drug treatment for hypertension, he plumbed the depths of depression and attempted suicide. By 1969 he was ready to admit defeat and, after proclaiming the folly of his stance, he was released, to the accompaniment of government publicity and Barisan condemnation. He went into voluntary study exile in the United Kingdom and by the time he returned to Singapore, the change in circumstances and his own disposition ruled out any further political ambitions. He now pursues a business career.

By contrast, Dr Lee Siew Choh, the Chairman of the Barisan Sosialis from its inception, could never be described as a likely contender for high office. He came to the PAP and the Assembly a cultivated man, bilingual, a doctor who patently cared about his patients' welfare. When Lee Kuan Yew's group precipitated the PAP split, the other defectors considered Lee Siew Choh the best of the parliamentarians available to lead them. His choice of a path through the minefields carefully laid by the PAP was nothing short of dismal, and he reacted wildly to each new challenge. He happened to be in Tokyo on 9 August 1965, and after sounding out communist opinion he condemned Singapore's independence as fraudulent. Having lost his 1963 electoral fight against Toh Chin Chye by 89 votes, his later determination that the Barisan boycott the legislature was readily attributed to mixed motives. Some even put forward a sinister explanation for his erratic behaviour—that he was a PAP 'plant' from the beginning. PAP plants there were, but Lee Siew Choh himself was the victim of a tantalising cat-and-mouse game the government found it easy to play once his more substantial colleagues were out of the way.

The only PAP person who came close to being Prime Minister was Ong Eng Guan. He was assisted by his high City Council profile and his popularity, much greater than Lee's inside and outside the Party. Ong's bid for power proved his undoing and revealed a singular lack of foresight—the British would never have entertained the prospect of him as premier.

At various stages Lee named Goh Keng Swee and Toh Chin Chye as deputies or alternatives to himself. Goh never seriously wanted or strove to be Prime Minister and occupied himself with the very substantial semi-public role he had. He did not envy Lee's constant exposure to the spotlight. Similarly Toh Chin Chye preferred not to be up front; his Party work and his academic research would have suffered. He did not have the drive or the presence to be at the helm of government.

None of the PAP's Indians could have been Prime Minister, unless Rajaratnam had been forced to head a government-in-exile from Phnom Penh, a plan that remained in the realms of fantasy. He and Devan Nair were always content to play second fiddle to Lee.

Of Malaysia's politicians, Tunku Abdul Rahman has been the only one with staying power comparable to Lee's. Born to a princely title in Kedah state, he ambled through his education in Malaya and Cambridge. After some political organising in Kedah during the Occupation, he rose to political prominence, succeeding Dato Onn to the presidency of UMNO in 1951. (Dato Onn was respected by many, including Lee, for his rebuke of Malay extremism however it manifested itself; at the same time, Lee recognised that Onn was marginal to Malay politics and that it was the Tunku with whom he would have to negotiate.) The Tunku became Chief Minister in 1955 and Prime Minister of independent Malaya in 1957, remaining so for almost all of the next thirteen years. His domain was extended by the formation of Malaysia in 1963. He became the father figure of local politics and alternated between 'divide and rule' and 'unite and rule' in a way that was only possible because of his personal network of friends and beneficiaries who commanded their respective communities. May 1969 sounded the death knell of his particular style. In retirement he has assumed the mantle of elder statesman and offered advice, whether it was sought or not; through his writing and contacts he has continued more or less publicly to exert influence. He had a brief spell as Secretary-General of the Islamic Conference. As was the case with Lim Yew Hock, his leadership did not require the sacrifice of many private pleasures.

Because of the size and multiracial composition of Malaysia—contrasted with Singapore's smallness and greater homogeneity—it would be foolish to expect any one man to dominate the scene there. Be that as it may, Lee remains unique in local history because he has spent himself fully in the business of being a politician and leader.

Nowhere is Lee's orientation more evident than in the crisis that came near to denying him, or actually did deny him, a role he had carved out. On 9 August 1965 and for months afterwards he was in a state of severe shock. Rational considerations might have consoled him that all was not lost, but it took a long time before the logic of the future could resume its sway over his heart.

There are abundant less dramatic instances. Lee might have felt helpless when confronted with the vitality of the Chinese-speaking 'ground' and the well-developed MCP taproot system going down into it, but he faced the challenge, gaining admiration as well as ridicule when he tried to master a language he had rejected imperiously in childhood. After creating the PAP, he soon came to accept the need for safeguards to keep control of it without letting it degenerate into a boneless wonder; yet when his control was eroded, his leadership and the Party's unity under fire, he never let go—except once, briefly, 'thereby saving' himself and his friends 'a great deal of trouble'. Even in the breathless days of 1961–63 after the split in the PAP, when planning for Malaysia could have collapsed, the PAP's position in the Assembly been destroyed by one more death or defection, or internal security become unmanageable without massive intervention, Lee quickly took heart from Toh Chin Chye and Rajaratnam; years later, he remembered how Rajaratnam in particular 'fought back ferociously, indefatigably, never losing much sleep on the consequences and penalties if we lost.'[5]

Notice also Lee's instinct for converting difficulties to good account. He had shown this skill during the Occupation by becoming first (to use David Marshall's droll description) a 'Nihongo [Japanese] functionary'; within a couple of years he was behaving as a 'Kuoyu [Chinese] patriot', the one who relayed to fellow Malayans news of crumbling Japanese fortunes and bathed in the reflected glory of RAF advances.[6] Later, when he reached England and found life in postwar London unbearable, he abandoned economics and somehow got into law at Cambridge, giving himself a more independent position from which to construct a political career. In the early 1950s, back home, his isolation and lack of a mass base, worrying to a man contemptuous of parties that sheltered under colonial wings, nevertheless provided a breathing space for him to calculate where to plunge in and on what terms. When he managed to gain *entrée* to Singapore's Chinese-educated, he knew he would not win their loyalty; so he kept the Party under tight control or, in government, entwined it with the administration.

The practice of statecraft demands that leaders find their own rhythm of work and rest. Dealing with the public from above needs to be offset by leisure and by strong, one-to-one personal relationships. In Lee's case, there are such relationships, but they have multiple purposes and are at a premium, as are all forms of relaxation and recreation. Everything is politically consequential. The two-month trip to Australia and New Zealand in 1965 was lamely declared to be for a 'personal'[7] holiday, not to 'perform'[8]: there followed an incredible itinerary of speeches and interviews, almost all directly about Malaysia and its troubles. Lee talked at length with the Australian Prime Minister, Robert Menzies, and followed up his visit with a seven-page handwritten letter of vivid analysis and forecast. The tenor of Malaysian politics was echoed on tour by the friction between Lee and High Commissioner Lim Yew Hock and both sides provided a running commentary. If Lee had thought to remove himself from the domestic scene to help quieten things down, he was being unusually obtuse.

When there is no inescapable demand or crisis on hand, daily routines allow for several hours of dawdling and incidental activities. Even these may have an ulterior purpose. Golf used to provide exercise and privacy; it also signalled to foreigners and locals alike Lee's prowess in an elite world that was not his by birth. A game such as poker, which he would have abandoned as frivolous, became useful in coaxing the Tunku towards merger. Chess sharpens the mind's skills of calculation and anticipation, and Lee has sometimes noted that his and Singapore's style of politics is of chess calibre rather than the draughts' level of opponents. Whatever other benefits physical fitness and health or dietary fads confer, at least they equip Lee for the rigours and potential threats of each day.

Two political friendships used to occupy large portions of his time and leisure: Devan Nair's and Alex Josey's. It is not possible, of course, to delve too far into the quality of the friendships, but a few passing remarks should be made about them.

Devan's longing for a venerable ideal of social commitment and his esteem of fluency found some sort of secular incarnation in Lee Kuan Yew. For many years he enjoyed regular and lengthy lunch meetings with the Prime Minister. We may guess that the topics of conversation ranged far and wide: the quality of a particular hawker's fried noodles, the personalities and events of politics and the higher reaches of literary analysis. Others came and went, but Devan was a constant companion until soon after his ill-fated Presidency began.

The link with Alex Josey is more puzzling. What kept the two men in virtually daily contact over so many years? Assembling the clues would suggest the following explanation: Josey had official duties as a press agent, he was a keen sportsman and an agreeable companion, on good terms with Rajaratnam and other PAP leaders. He made no demands on Lee, sought no favours, initiated no conversations and was reasonably tight-lipped. Lee could test out ideas on him as an expatriate who knew the local scene. The two played golf and enjoyed a casual drink. On occasions, they must also have discussed Josey's well-known amorous pursuits, given Lee's locker-room talk at the 1965 farewell dinner referred to in Chapter 11. To pursue such topics of conversation with peers or subordinates would have been beyond the pale for a man preserving his reputation and professional distance. Lee's desire for an outlet, however, could be satisfied if he kept the rule he set for others—that discretion prevail. With Josey, the foreign bachelor, the maverick intelligence operative, journalist and socialist, Lee could afford a little more latitude, a little more dropping of the guard. If this explanation is correct, some of those who knew of Josey's access to Lee must have resented it—not least the Prime Minister's wife and some of his close colleagues. For whatever reasons, and age would have played its part, the relationship had tapered off by the late 1970s.

It is when we come to Lee's personal life that we see his political dedication in sharp relief. His family constitutes a kind of social laboratory. He and his wife were outstanding students in their time, and it is clear that intellectual attainment was one of the principal factors bringing them together. Between them they have bred and reared three exceptionally accomplished offspring. The children were brought up and schooled with unswerving discipline to conform to the image of the new citizen. Each morning they would queue up for the bathroom with their books; schools, languages, musical instruments, sports and hobbies were chosen to push to the limit their talent and capacity. Hsien Loong helped his father by translating Jawi-script Malay during the darker days of Malaysia. The whole family went to Cambodia in 1967 and has visited certain other overseas countries to see and judge them at first hand; and in 1976 Lee took his daughter, Wei Ling, to Beijing for 'definite specific political reasons, one of them being to test how a Chinese-educated girl, but bilingual, would react to this situation'.[9] They have each functioned at some time or another as eyes and ears for their father, and he has used their reports as the basis for correcting defects in public institutions and policies.

Although Lee's wife, Kwa Geok Choo, has come to assume great significance behind the scenes in Singapore's political life, she has waged an energetic campaign to stay out of the limelight. Lee described his wife in 1978 as a 'frugal woman, a competent lawyer who has considerable wealth in her own right, made honestly'[10]. She rarely grants interviews to the media, and when she does, she does not discuss political questions. She declared in 1971 that she had never set foot in her husband's office. Only testimony from many quarters over recent years makes it impossible to characterise her simply as a brilliant and charming woman who accepts her subordinate wifely role.

Lee has been scrupulous about preserving his reputation for incorruptibility. He resigned as senior partner in his law firm, Lee and Lee, when he became Prime Minister in 1959. He has ordered no favours to be granted to members of Lee and Lee or associated family ventures. Despite these handicaps, his wife and his brother Dennis have built a flourishing practice, with conveyancing and consultancy its specialties.

Family members have likewise been served notice many times not to expect privileged treatment because of kinship with the Prime Minister. Moreover, they have been instructed not to talk out of turn. Lee Chin Koon, the Prime Minister's father, told a Filipino interviewer, 'A thousand pardons, but no, no, I am not free to say anything.'[11] But both parents were far too well known for harmless anecdotes about their son not to slip out. Lee Chin Koon still attends customers at a city jewellery store and sees friends through his swimming club or social contacts; Madam Chua Jim Neo, the Prime Minister's mother, was famous for her teaching of Nonya [Straits-born Chinese female] cuisine, her charitable work and her gregarious personality, and her death in 1980 deprived Singapore of a much-celebrated character.

'My public behaviour and my private behaviour cannot be compartmentalised. I am on parade all the time.' This was Lee's answer to the question, 'Would it be true that you are ... a kind of "enlightened dictator" behind the scenes?'[12] It is a source of amazement and annoyance to Lee that he is perceived to be a wilful authoritarian. We cannot know exactly what is going on in his mind, but the above answer points to his sense that each aspect of his life belongs to an indivisible whole. Rather than talking of his investment of himself in politics, it may be truer to say that his own identity is defined by exercising power over himself and others. His leadership derives not from choice but from a natural reflex, and who could fairly condemn a man for that?

This may help explain why Lee has not demanded personal loyalty from the PAP or sought to promote himself as a personality in Singapore. He is where he is because it is right that he should be there. All that has been required at each juncture is the recognition, by those that count, of the task that destiny has allotted to him.

Goals for a lifetime

Lee has never pretended to lack ambition. But he would deny, with justice, that his ambition is egotistical: he does not set out to gain his contemporaries' recognition, titles or eulogies; and he hates flattery. His New Year message of 1973 stated: 'The greatest satisfaction in life comes from achievement. To achieve is to be happy. Singaporeans must be imbued with this spirit. We must never get into the vicious cycle of expecting more and more for less and less. Sensual pleasure is ephemeral. Solid satisfaction comes out of achievement, the overcoming of obstacles which lie in the path of an individual or a nation seeking success. It generates inner or spiritual strength, a strength which grows out of an inner discipline.'

What are the goals that Lee Kuan Yew has striven to realise? We are no longer obliged to label them as exclusively political or personal, so we can look for continuity between his past—his youth and further back—and the period of his public career.

One recurrent objective has been the pursuit of autonomy and control. Their attainment is not necessarily at others' expense—Lee has always been willing to form a coalition with like-minded people beyond reasons of expedience, and he invests any long-standing coalition with an almost mystical value. However, if circumstances arise where others do not match the challenge, betraying or failing it, their liberty must be sacrificed a little to the masters of history. In earlier days Lee believed that coercion should be avoided except in emergency: show of force would normally be sufficient to deter the hostile. Latterly he has moved to a more 'realistic' position: the old line between defensive and offensive warfare has been obscured, and prudence may dictate a pre-emptive strike. This is true at individual and national levels.

Another goal is to prepare for the future or rather to embrace it; thereby one can modify it, make it more congenial and claim the favourable verdict of history for doing so. The past has been unsatisfactory and is in need of correction. Some have been misdirected, as was Lee himself, towards the dead end of being imitation English gentlemen, minions serving a foreign firm or colonial government. Others have been educated to look back, to be trapped in the web of language, religion, custom and race memory. For Lee, only those values must be instilled and practised that get as much purchase as possible on the forward momentum of technology and material progress.

The pushing back of frontiers, the discovery of new worlds to conquer—these are concerns visible in Lee's personal diplomacy, in Singapore Incorporated's international activity, in the grand designs for Singapore's people, economy and landscape and in the fluidity of legislative and constitutional norms. It is somehow a matter of seeking ever-larger contexts and an ever-new identity to fill them. Singapore is not just a 'transformed Chinaman' but an entity of the future. Several races and civilisations have made their contribution, in some cases desirable, in some not; but, according to Lee, 'No geographical or political boundary can contain the implications of what we set out to do when we succeed.'[13]

The final specific goal to be recognised in Lee's life is his struggle against the forces of entropy—chaos, slackness, irrationality and death. It has required from him and from the people of Singapore superhuman energy to counteract the heat of the Equator and the power of sloth, obscurantism and sensual degeneracy. Civilised living, an end in itself, is possible only where it is actively entrenched in the structures and behaviour patterns of a nation. The search for a successor generation is intended to deflect the impact of mortality—if Lee goes, at least his Singapore will live. His preoccupation with health and with the way in which his peers and colleagues die may seem morbid at times, but it has been the catalyst of renewed dedication to the daily round and the viability of good government.

In sum, the objective of Lee's life seems to be twofold: the creation of a polity that is properly ordered, yet open to renew itself and to blend into a larger territory wherever sought or accepted and the construction of his own place in history. But although the objective may appear twofold to the beholder's eye, it is for Lee, quite simply, one and undivided.

A style revisited

> ... Hakka Lee is an admixture of aggression and wary defences. In 1963, his public speeches, if not his television smiles, were punctuated with evidence of his true personality. 'I am prepared to meet you anywhere, any time', he said. 'I'll fix you', he threatened. To some, this fighting spirit, always apparent, was a symptom of latent inferiority, or basic insecurity ...
> Entering the 1970s, Lee Kuan Yew is more confident. The battles are over and won and the enemy routed, and he is less threatening, more philosophical, older and wiser. Lee's aggressive personality is noticeable and immediately felt ...
> Alex Josey, *Lee Kuan Yew: The Struggle for Singapore*, p. 35

Just as the reader prepares to contemplate a more relaxed Lee, Josey changes tack: the aggressive Lee returns to centre stage, quite unreformed after all. Over the last decade or so, efforts have been made to contend that he has mellowed. It is true that a certain weariness has marked some of his public appearances over the period, especially on solo television when there is no direct personal stimulus. But behind the scenes, and out in the open when a public enemy has had to be identified and fought, the old fires have flared up.

However much the experience of long-held power might be expected to change a man, the evidence so far admits of only one conclusion in the case of Lee Kuan Yew. Power has simply provided the resources to expand or consolidate the character and the style of the man along lines fixed well in the past.

From the time Lee was a schoolboy, his aggressiveness has been the subject of comment. A story in circulation during the 1960s came from a family source. The eleven-year-old Harry asked an uncle for one of his canaries. The uncle refused and thought no more of it until he discovered the bird dead: the boy had pulled all its feathers out. 'If he could not have it, no one else would.' 'Lee would hit anybody' was the testimony of another old family friend.

Since coming to office, Lee has tended to indulge his instinct to bully and demolish. The need to flee from untenable situations has been reduced and dignified by the mechanism of physical or mental withdrawal. Power mostly removes the humiliation of being bested.

Within this dominant characteristic of aggression we may trace elements of rage, fear and self-aggrandisement. They may be proportionate to what arouses them, or they may carry an extra force derived from a previous injury. They make a negotiated settlement so much harder.

Two quite separate sources related the following story: 'A former Singapore newspaper proprietor, now retired, was having an audience with Lee and apparently not toeing the line. Lee leaned over, grabbed him by the collar, and said "I'm a thug, you're a thug, and as one thug to another, you'll do what I say".'

Lee's close colleagues have responded in various ways to his aggressiveness. If they have agreed with its objective, they have gone along with it, perhaps seeking moderation or taking up some of its passion themselves. If they have believed it inconsistent with achieving its objective, they have kept quiet—maybe hoping that his fury would spend itself—or protested and argued. We can only guess at the outcome if and when there has been profound disagreement. Has there ever been a showdown? Has Lee always got his own way because he has the best cards as well as the hottest temper? Two Cabinet ministers indicated to the author that Lee was able to pull back before it was too late: but their tone suggested that capitulation was grudging, without further mention of the matter or apology for harsh words. Another close family business associate was quite blunt: the Lee he knew 'never recants'.

The miracle of Singapore's economic growth has been achieved both because of and despite Lee Kuan Yew. His interference in planning may highlight some basic problems otherwise neglected or underestimated. It also raises the temperature and reduces the efficiency of his staff, who are compelled to take all his commands with indiscriminate seriousness.

T.J.S. George cites a Filipino journalist, Juan Gatbonton, who wondered if 'the morbid suspiciousness, the bravado; the irascibility and the introverted intellectuality that make up the tightly wound personality of Lee Kuan Yew' might stem from the 'tragic realisation' that 'the ultimate fate of Singapore lies out of its hands'.[14] Lee's behaviour traits developed long before his political awareness; a constant feature of them has been the attempt to outwit or overturn 'tragic realisations'.

Inspection reveals a classic paranoia at work in Lee, and it finds powerful external focus in his demand that intense, calculating, tough little Singapore be on guard against the 'low-compression', spontaneous unthinking peoples who surround her. When the world is changing rapidly, when there is a situation of encirclement, the crisis mentality sets in and sets in deep: people's identities are under threat as traditions collapse and a strong, confident leader is needed to guide them forward. The threat is all the more plausible for being articulated by hint and allusion, rather than in loud rhetoric which might draw enemy fire. As Lee wrote for the PAP's 25th anniversary souvenir publication, 'I am inhibited by social conventions and political sensitivities from being specific.'[15]

It must be emphasised that to notice Lee's paranoia is not to explain him away. It is to name one of the forces at work deep inside him gearing him beforehand towards crisis, a force that, by its very nature, reaches out to fuse the fears of one man with the fears of a whole society; the latter may be a little weaker and less clear-cut than their leader's, but they still cry out for rescue. Perceptions riddled with fear are notoriously introverting and apt to lessen a person's or group's accuracy of reaction, but Lee manages to offset his paranoia with constant reality testing and so its regressiveness is held in check. Although he remains ever watchful, he can rise to a guarded optimism and even to momentary exultation when he and his Singapore appear to have triumphed over adversity.

Another distinctive feature of Lee's style is its innovativeness. Almost automatically he moves to seize the initiative, set terms, define reality, order life according to his vision and under his dominance. A particularly telling illustration of this was his first approach to the woman who became his wife, Kwa Geok Choo. Both of them had topped the Senior Cambridge results for all Malaya.* He let it be known quite loudly that she was the only woman intellectually worthy of him. Her reaction, sustained for some time, was one of distaste and when he persevered in bestowing his favours it was for battle that she first took him seriously. A throwaway remark, on the record and made in 1973, rounds the story off: Richard Nixon, at a White House dinner in honour of Lee, spoke to the toast and disclosed that over the meal he had been discussing husband's and wife's academic performance. 'I said, "Mrs Lee, tell me, is it true that you were number one in the class at Cambridge Law School and your husband was number two?", and she said, "Mr President, do you think he would have married me if that were the case?" '[16]

Lee has often talked of friends and his obligations to them. He gives the designation a special meaning, since he is the one that initiates a friendship and he is the one who breaks it off should the friend prove unworthy or not freely concur with his basic percep-

---

* Lee Kuan Yew in 1939, Kwa Geok Choo in 1938—she is three years older than he.

tions. It is as if he draws people and ideas into himself and then forgets that they come from outside until such time as something they say or do upsets him. Lim Kim San described the relationship between Lee and his colleagues as one of symbiosis between equals, possible because there was sufficient intellect and 'ballast' in each person for give and take to occur.[17] Lee's style and Lim's view of it are compatible, so long as it is remembered that Lee alone determines who will be admitted to his circle. His sense of inner resourcefulness makes him profoundly unwilling to be led by how others regard him or his views. It requires a mental adjustment for him to show an interest in most people's opinions: when he and David Marshall attended a student meeting at C. Northcote Parkinson's house in 1955, the historian and writer recalled that Lee showed none of Marshall's enthusiasm. 'He listened in grim silence, said nothing in compliment . . . When he eventually voiced an opinion it was more with the object of exposing folly than revealing wisdom.'[18]

Lee believes, according to Josey, that he could 'make a good film, write a good book, produce a good newspaper, build a good house or road, as well as or better than most'.[19] Life is too short for him to show his proficiency in such endeavours so he allocates them to other people, thus incorporating them into his plan. Those who lie outside the scope of his management are competitors and he is forever measuring himself against them. 'I speak to Harold Macmillan and Duncan Sandys as equals. At Cambridge I got two firsts and a star for distinction. Harold Macmillan did not.'[20]

It is the marked and repeated application of Lee's energy to all his objectives that demands notice—his obsessiveness. Fetishes about cleanliness and health, clothing and food, have been amply documented by Josey and others. They result in a long list of required living conditions. Some of them are explained in a decidedly strange way. 'I'm extremely sensitive to changes in temperature, humidity', Lee told interviewer Gerald Stone during a national Australian television programme, 'mainly because I think after four generations here I'm still not acclimatised.' 'You came from northern China?' asked Stone. 'Northern China,' replied Lee.[21] His Hakka ancestry is certainly persistent!

When the 'Use Your Hands' campaign was launched in 1976, Singapore's citizens beheld their Prime Minister manhandling a mop and bucket over the floor of a government school. Every year he has planted a couple of trees to give a lead in the greening of the Republic. But his shining footwear and nice clean clothes have taken the dirt out of these brief excursions into manual labour.

There has been little change in a man who long ago used up twelve people's share of water each day to keep himself thoroughly clean on his first voyage to England.

Finally, Lee is a man with an unusual sense of obligation. He is willing to observe the niceties of protocol and shake hands with dignitaries and commoners alike, a fixed and steely smile on his face. He maintains Cabinet solidarity. He keeps honour with ex-colleagues: 'With us, personal friendship and sentimental regard for old friends matter.'[22] All up to a point. The obligation Lee displays is to his own code, whose principles can be a little elusive to others. One of the main problems the Malaysian leaders experienced when dealing with Lee was his unpredictability.

Whether it is in Lee's personal dealings or in affairs of state, we see a man whose life force and style automatically demand the leader's role. Whether by instinct or calculation, he is always a step ahead, somehow not yet trapped by his enemies or by his own mistakes and 'trained incapacities'. No wonder he is doubly disturbed at the prospect some years hence of the adrenalin pumping more slowly should he and his ageing colleagues be aroused after two or three hours' sleep to deal with an emergency.

Whence such a man?

> Lee Kuan Yew, as a student, was disinterested [*sic*] in politics ... He accepted what he found: his family was fairly well-to-do, and he was respectful to his parents and concentrated on his studies. This world came tumbling around his ears when the Japanese troops marched in and began slapping faces and beheading criminals. Forced like everyone else to learn Japanese and to work to eat, young Lee found himself working as a translator in the office of a Japanese newsagency. He was there during most of the Japanese occupation, and daily he became more politically conscious and determined that one day Singapore would not be ruled by foreigners.
> Alex Josey, *Lee Kuan Yew: The Struggle for Singapore*, pages 142–43

We have a reasonably full set of pictures of Lee as he is now and as he has been on his journey from 1942 to the present. Yet, apart from bald assertions that he is displacing unresolved personal problems into public activity or the hunch that Lee is an exception or mutation, we have so far encountered only one major explanation of Lee's career. The above citation from Alex Josey sums it up: Lee's wartime experience. The contrast between Lee before and after the Occupation is deemed sufficiently dramatic to signify the emergence of a powerful political ambition from nowhere. Lee himself normally falls back to this line.

The trouble with the theory is that it has to fudge or disregard the evidence. Josey, for instance, perhaps in order to point up the contrast, says that 'Lee accepted what he found' in life up until 1942. As we shall see, the record shows no such acquiescence. Nor was he always 'respectful to his parents'.

We should not dispute that the Occupation had tremendous impact: it forced Lee to focus both on the scale of his ambitions and his want of preparation and training to fulfil them. But the seeds of his desire to be an agent of change had been sown long before. Lee acknowledged this in passing during a speech he made to the Assembly on 12 April 1956.

> May I put it, without apologies, in a very personal way. We all like to live our lives again through our children. We know that we should do what is best for them. But unconsciously we do for them what we wish our parents had done for us. When I was born the British Navy ruled the waves. My grandfather, who was a *chin-chen* [purser] on a steamship between Indonesia and Singapore, had the greatest respect for the British Navy. He made a great deal of money because, he said, there was no piracy in Malayan waters. He lived until he saw the *Prince of Wales* sunk by Japanese aeroplanes! He died shortly afterwards. I am sure that the sinking of the *Prince of Wales* had nothing to do with his death, but I think an age had passed with him. I was sent to an English school to equip me for an English university in order that I could then be an educated man—the equal of any Englishman—the model of perfection. I do not know how far they have succeeded in that. I grew up, and finally graduated. At the end of it I felt—*and it was long before I entered politics, in fact it is one of the reasons I am here*—that the whole set of values was wrong, fundamentally and radically wrong. [Italics added]

His speech went on to endorse 'less emotionally' Nehru's lament: 'I cry when I think that I cannot speak my own mother tongue as well as I can speak the English language'. Of his own son, Lee declared, 'He will not be a model Englishman ... whatever the difficulties in family relationships, he is going to be part of Asia, part of Malaya.' In Lee's own upbringing there was an element of incongruity, like the speck of grit that irritates the oyster into producing a pearl.

We need, then, to quarry down into Lee's earlier years if we would respect the depth and longevity of his orientation towards politics and towards improving his environment as best he could. We will try not to forget that the distinction between Lee the person and Lee the political practitioner is hard to sustain.

There is one further preliminary lead to explore. Josey and George both make much of Lee being a Hakka. The Hakkas, 'guest people', are a 'tribe' originally from northern China, many of whom settled in the southern provinces and then migrated overseas. Hakka males are supposed to be pugnacious, individualistic and courageous, their women vigorous and hardworking. Unfortunately, such typecasting is neither plausible nor useful. Lee is a Hakka only through the male line, his blood 'diluted' by other Chinese and even possibly Malay ancestry. Again, why is Lee's father—as with many other Hakkas—'quiet and self-effacing' (T.J.S. George)[22]? Lee detects his Hakka origins in his sensitivity to Singapore's climate, but he must be one of the few who has not adapted to the tropics.

The specific value of noting the Hakka strain is to emphasise the self-conscious clannishness it entails, particularly as one of Singapore's minority dialect groups. This might have imposed added strains on the marriage between Lee's father and mother. (Although there has been an above average number of 'Hakkas' in the Cabinet, the reasons for their inclusion owe little or nothing to their ethnic classification. Because of his commitment to impartiality, Lee himself has loudly disowned clan loyalties.

What is far more suggestive is Lee's birth and upbringing in circles predominantly but not entirely Straits-born Chinese. These circles have not been notable for conferring a secure or stable identity on any of their members who have moved outside them—in other words, almost all of the males. How difficult it must have been to hear Chinese language or observe Chinese custom and not grasp them, to be outwardly a son of the Middle Kingdom and yet inwardly an alien to one's race and a dependant of the white man.

The Occupation destroyed the credibility of hanging onto the coat tails of the British. A profound surge of pride in China was felt by those who, however far back their exile had occurred, were able to follow with keen interest the accomplishments and respective political movements of Sun Yat Sen, Chiang Kai Shek or, later, Mao Zedong. China's resistance to the Japanese, her revolution and her entry into the atomic age were celebrated or reviled, as the case might be, among Chinese still tied to the motherland by language and custom. But the Straits-born held to an outlook and a set of preoccupations that were attuned to survival and advancement in colonial Malayan society. Even where their sons were sent to China for a 'finishing' education, even though the wealthy among them practised an elaborate and refined etiquette of clearly Chinese origin, they were kept at arm's length by the more recent and less assimilated immigrants, who suspected them of extravagance and dubious morals and despised them for their distinctiveness.

Return to the fount

Harry Lee Kuan Yew* was born on Sunday 16 September 1923, the first child of Lee Chin Koon and Chua Jim Neo, who were aged twenty and sixteen respectively. Both his parents were Straits-born Chinese; their families had lived for a number of generations in and around the Straits Settlements of Malaya.

Lee Chin Koon's father, Hoon Leong, was born in 1873 and received what was unusual at the time—an English-medium education. It was to be a vital factor setting the pattern for his grandson's life. Lee Hoon Leong rose to be managing director of a shipping firm; he married into the Indonesian Chinese community. He died just before the Japanese captured Singapore.

Chin Koon showed little of his father's go-getting spirit. Educated in English, he completed his secondary schooling and, through family connections, became a clerk in a ship chandler's firm. He then broke with tradition and entered the Shell Company, where he remained for several decades in a clerical or managerial capacity. He thus acquired a steady income and a way of staying safely, if none too adventurously, under British protection.

The languages spoken in the Lee home were English and Malay,[24] as well as Cantonese dialect from the servant who had responsibility for the children. Harry's mother was a superb cook, and her food would have been the distinctive and spicy Nonya blend of Chinese and Malay styles, with a few concessions to British habits.

Lee himself has confirmed that parents and grandparents united in wishing for him an exemplary education to help him scale the heights accessible to a colonial subject of the British Empire. Early in the piece his mother took to putting aside whatever she could from cooking lessons, household money and other sources to give her children a nest egg so that they could further themselves. Lee's

---

* 'Kuan Yew' means 'shining far and wide'; it was the name of a celebrated Chinese general, just as 'Hsien Loong' was.

father expected that when the time came he would take an advance against his retirement benefits for the same purpose.

Harry received the best of special treatment accorded to the first-born and the eldest son: choice food portions and a place to study undisturbed, even when the family was living in a two-bedroom house. He could withdraw, and often did, from the noise and intercourse of his lively Straits-born family.

The marriage between Chin Koon and Jim Neo was never an easy one. Communication deteriorated between wife, husband and his parents. Jim Neo was one of twelve girls and, as she told a reporter, 'their father tried his best to make sure they did not marry into a traditional Chinese home'.[25] She was fifteen when the marriage was arranged, and she moved into her mother-in-law's house, as was the custom. But problems arose and before long alternative accommodation had to be found—one of her parents' properties in Kampong Java Road. With Chin Koon something of a dropout and Jim Neo a free spirit,* their lives began to centre more on her parents, an indulgent father and a mother who did not want her grandchildren to lose touch with their Chinese origins.

It was the old lady's initiative that caused Harry to be sent to a Chinese kindergarten, where he was photographed for posterity in mandarin jacket and cap. When he started out at Telok Kurau English School, she insisted that he continue to have Chinese tuition outside normal classes. He rebelled, refusing, as he often put it years later, to 'slot' a language that had to be learned 'parrot-fashion'. He was allowed to have his way, not for the first or last time.

By the mid- to late 1930s the Lee Chin Koon family was under strain. Their home was a bungalow on Norfolk Road owned by Shell, for whom Chin Koon had started work in 1929. He was often away for protracted periods attending the depots at Batu Pahat, Kuantan or elsewhere. The Depression had hit even Singapore's wealthier folk hard, and Jim Neo was obliged to make extra money however she could. Sometimes a Harbour Board contractor, Tan Chong Chew, stayed in the house. He was deaf and the domestic noise levels rose accordingly. Boarders were also accommodated to supplement income. When Chin Koon returned to his wife and family in Singapore, quarrels often broke out and accusations flew to and fro.

When the seven-year-old Harry began at Telok Kurau school, he

---

* Befriended by a foreign woman, Jim Neo had received from her a modicum of education, something normally denied to a Straits-born girl.

was seen as an intelligent but otherwise normal sort of boy, a good mixer, not too zealous about his studies. By the time he reached Raffles Institution in 1936, he was well on the way to being a driven and studious individual, often absenting himself from extracurricular activities and preferring either solitude or the company of those, mostly younger, that he could dominate.

'All of us, to a larger or lesser extent,' he told Old Rafflesians in 1960 'are affected by our experiences during our formative years and the most important of these are the years the teenager spends in a secondary school.'[26] Harry enjoyed the 'student meritocracy', the 'diverse backgrounds' of the pupils, the 'consistently high performance' of the school and its well-rounded programme.[27] (He even took up, albeit rather self-consciously, cricket and scouting.) It was a refuge from the emotional mess of home. Raffles Institution did not offer the religious values and tone of a mission school; but it had many dedicated teachers, men such as the principal, Mr Macleod, who 'really cared',[28] and Lim Tay Boh. To a degree they fitted the image that would find its highest expression in Lee's revered Cambridge tutor, W.S. Thatcher.

Devan Nair was one of many who described the relationship of Lee and his parents as 'not close' or 'conventional'. The record suggests that the description is euphemistic. In a Chinese community where filial piety is enjoined, latterly by the Government itself, Lee's attitude to his parents and elders has been the subject of many stories. Without exception, they tell of an old man whose pride in his son is not reciprocated with more than a bare acceptance of his presence in the family home; greater warmth was clearly evident in Harry's feelings for his mother, but she lived away from him, off Bukit Timah Road, and apparently they saw each other only occasionally.

Harry is reputed to have taken his role as eldest brother more seriously. Of the other members of the family, Dennis (Kim Yew) is senior partner in Lee and Lee and holds directorships in several major enterprises. He is divorced and remarried. Freddy (Thiam Yew) was a police officer, then managed the Prime Minister's golf club, and is now partner in a stockbroking firm. Monica, the only girl, married a wealthy financier and real estate dealer who is an amateur gardening expert. Suan Yew, a doctor, the youngest brother, was coached for schoolboy debates by Kuan Yew; he is married to the daughter of a Hawaiian Chinese millionaire. All the siblings have had some measure of support and friendship from Harry, and he takes an active interest in the ways that their children are brought up.

Lee perceived his grandfather to be a major influence on his childhood. Yet he came to reject the values advocated by Hoon Leong who had pinned his hopes on the bright little boy, almost as a substitute for his own son. His attachment to his mother was also ambiguous. The great analyst of childhood, Erik Erikson, believes that infancy is the life stage at which mistrust is overcome, or not. If this is so, then it is probable that Lee was not strongly mothered: he is a self-contained person who only needs one or two reliable and trustworthy adult companions at any given time, being otherwise detached and cautious by nature.

The pattern of life in the Lee household seems rarely to have been peaceful. It was riddled with conflict when husband and wife were together, and stridently matriarchal in Chin Koon's absence. There was no need for Harry as first-born son to vie for pride of place at home, and his paternal grandfather reinforced the sense that he was the important link in the family chain. Towards Harry, there was from quite early on a mixture of negligence, indulgence, favouritism, awe—and occasional punishment, the more distressing because of its infrequency. Somehow a special creation was occurring before the others' eyes, a 'little white boy' skilled in language, very clever and soon announcing some kind of messianic vocation to protect and save his homeland.

Whatever teasing went on, whatever hurts came—from perceived marital infidelity (which is surely not unconnected with Lee's tendency to be both prudish and prurient) or nagging, for example—Harry lashed out in retaliation, sought the upper ground or withdrew. He moved in and out of the family circle at will. He chose the terms of belonging, he set the standards by which his parents and grandparents were judged and rebuked. The spiritual resources for his nurture came more from teachers and books than from family, and were selected for the purpose by the youngster. It was as if he were surmounting the insurmountable fact of being born his parents' child, his father's son.

At school, friendship was important, provided his leadership was accepted, but came second to study, the testing of which provided an objective measure of the boy's merit. In cultivating skills with words he learned how to make reality bearable, even occasionally to change it. Whether there, particularly as a debater, or at home, he could begin to arrange the world outside him as he wanted it to be, pushing the frontiers back to accommodate his need for a personal growing space.

Although the picture we have before us is still sketchy, its outline is fairly clear. Here is a young man creating himself as much as any human being can, and looking to the future when greater competence will permit grander achievement. Lee was not crushed by the conflicts and tensions of his childhood. They were fuel for his inner fire, whose flame is by no means yet extinguished.

Through a glass darkly

The interpretation of Lee's formative years would have been a risky business without the solid perspective of his adult career. It remains to sharpen our characterisation of Lee more precisely. There are three methods of accounting for political leadership which will not be entirely appropriate or feasible.

The first is the predictive, task-examining approach of James David Barber.[29] He has devised a graph system to map out the performance of each US President or aspirant; he uses one axis for leadership style—active–passive—and the other to measure enjoyment—positive–negative. The results are intriguing. They provide a morally 'cool' test for voters to use in deciding their own preference. But by stressing 'adaptation' as a psychological litmus test, Barber is bound to underemphasise what is already in the candidate's self and what inner resources and commitments he has. In Lee's case, this would be negligent.

Another approach is the fascinating one represented by Erikson's studies of Luther and Gandhi.[30] Too much specialised psychoanalytic skill is required for this to be within our reach. There are also formidable difficulties about writing a detailed biography of a living political leader without full access to him, to his intimates and associates, and to classified documents and correspondence.

At the opposite extreme is the class dialectic of Marxist–Leninist analysis. Here the personality of a leader is far less important than the ideological status of his political economics and his capacity to blunt or intensify the revolutionary process. The true leader will form a cadre sworn to the party line, foment discontent and build solidarity among the exploited masses. He and his officials will consult international comrades and then decide on the desirability and timing of a united front, negotiation or armed struggle. He will buoy himself with the thought that socialism will come as surely as day follows night. The self-serving nationalist leader, on the other hand, will fall victim to corruption or lack of strategic vision. Lee's communist opponents learned to repent of these doctrinaire views at their leisure.

Lee is too resilient to be defined by his origins and too pervasive for his personality not to matter. The racial realities of his part of the world have inhibited the growth of a proletarian or revolutionary vanguard, and only if the island fell on really difficult times could any brand of communism gain a footing. Besides, political processes, especially in a small place like Singapore, are not mechanical forces that roll on regardless of the individuals involved with them.

We must therefore seek a framework of interpretation that takes into account Lee the person and the politician, his relations with others and his context. Because our study is constrained by being unofficial and by approaching its subject from outside, there is no question of claiming more than a tentative status for what follows.[31]

All social arrangements start, continue and end with the nature of the bond between 'self' and 'other'. Any examination of a political leader, even more than any examination of a human being as such, has to do with how the individual concerned relates to the world around him and how he is allowed to operate. Although military force and media manipulation can sustain a man's nominal authority beyond his natural capacity to command allegiance, Singaporeans would laugh out of court any suggestion that Lee Kuan Yew rose to power and has remained there simply by virtue of coercion or skilful public relations.

On the domestic scale of family or friendship it is possible, although it may be comparatively rare, for people to relate to one another in a mature and non-possessive manner that enhances both those inside the relationship and those immediately outside it. On the larger scale of a society or nation, maintaining balanced communication is a much more difficult enterprise. Norms of personal development, leadership and loyalty, group ethics and economic pressures are peculiar to the constituent 'tribes' and all have their impact. Disorder can occur, marring individuals who act or are acted upon in the public domain and damaging the political fabric.

There are two well-recognised social arrangements observable not only at an interpersonal level but on the wider canvas as well. In the first, the self tends to blend into the other; in the second, the self keeps a wary eye on others and feels obliged to compete with them.

It would be tempting to assume that the only other alternative—apart from the mature model that is difficult to achieve among a varied and populous society—is for the individual to drop out and become a cultural fringe-dweller. But there is another arrangement whereby the unusual self establishes rapport with others electively and only as long as its individuality is not diminished. This mode is in fact the one most apt to evoke alternative and change-bearing forms of social activity.

The above ways of resolving the self–other dilemma originate in a child's relations to his mother and unfold through childhood and adolescence. They are projects whose nature and application may be investigated among leaders or, for that matter, followers within a society or community. A shorthand label would be helpful for each of those three projects that are most concerned with social engagement rather than social withdrawal: *'dependent'*, *'competitive'* and *'masterful'* are roughly appropriate. The point of departure for each is the discovery that the self is separate from (m)other. The projects are distinguishable to the extent that one of the three resolutions of self–other is accentuated.

The *prima facie* value of this approach is that it employs terms suited to the sort of information available to the concerned citizen. As with all social projects, there is a psychological world behind them, a hinterland to be explored, but by using language that attempts to be fair and unbiased the precise nature of the project and of its individual practitioner can be faced without presuming any significant underlying pathology or without having to avoid it.

To develop our analysis a little further: the *dependent* project is an habitual attempt to repair the breach between self and other, surrendering independence if necessary so that love can flow. The *competitive* project makes a virtue out of the breach between self and other, and musters strength to attain and defend self-sufficiency. Esteem is measured according to achievement. The *masterful* project, however, denies and transcends the self–other differentiation. It is paradoxical, for it makes the singularity of the self the condition of engaging with others: the self–other dilemma is resolved by synthesising a larger and grander future where the self incorporates others. Since our focus of attention is on leaders, we might expect that each of these projects is given rein by the appurtenances of power. But it is obvious enough that the *masterful* person is the one most likely to aspire and plan towards eminence.

A preliminary assessment of Lee Kuan Yew would describe him as clearly a *masterful* person, although with something of the *competitive* strain in his makeup. That is to say, Lee prefers to draw others into his vision of the future without personalising the bonds, except occasionally and on the basis of subordination. His is a project of great virtuosity, always claiming the higher ground in relationships through its vigorous and adventurous intellectualising. It also draws strength from charting the social changes necessary to realise its hopes. The changes, however rationally plausible and coherent they are, may be drastic and are likely to leave lesser mortals dazed, limping along behind. Where people resist even a minor part of Lee's vision and can no longer be brought into his sphere of control, they become a threat, and he deals with them as competitors who must be vanquished.

The mainspring of Lee's project is his exceptional capacity for self-starting. If we attempt to investigate his particular *masterful* project, we will be led, sooner or later, to theories of personal identity and the grand self, and to the clinical evidence on which the theories are based, in other words to the psychological literature on narcissism. Noting the social philosopher Kenneth Burke's wry observation that we accept psychoanalytic tracing of motives in cases where we are not involved,[32] let us see if the cap of narcissism fits Lee.

Remembering that Narcissus was, according to Greek mythology, a handsome youth whose energy of love was aroused when he became captivated by his own reflection in a pool of water, we may guess that it will not be too difficult to match the imagery and language of narcissism to a man whose character and personality were richly formed by his own initiatives.

Lee has an intense inner life possessed of its 'cerebral and visceral compulsions'. Those to whom he has been close—his Cabinet colleagues, Alex Josey, Devan Nair, his mother and siblings, and, above all, his wife and children—are like planets reflecting his concerns or suns radiating similar concerns of their own. At best they are freely in orbit or constellation around him. Those beyond the first circle whom he would define as loyal Singaporeans, from top civil servants to the man or woman in the street, are illuminated and contained. Their existence has meaning by extending and substantiating the Prime Minister's vision.

Relying on a 1972 article that summarises Heinz Kohut's thorough and archetypal study of narcissism, far from negative in its assumptions or conclusions, we can shed our earlier suggestion that Lee has secondary *competitive* accents to him.[33] Although no one person conforms strictly to a psychological type, the consistency of what we have observed of Lee's behaviour throughout his life from childhood onwards would square with Kohut's tracing of narcissism's roots back to the conflicts of infancy. Moreover, the *competitive* type seems to be shaped at a later stage when the young male child tries unconsciously to outbid his father for the favour of his mother: in Lee's case, that particular conflict was never real or necessary.

Kohut brings to light and affirms the 'ambitions', the 'wish to dominate' and 'to shine', the 'yearning to merge into omnipotent figures' of a narcissistic personality [page 365]. He also depicts the rage that erupts when injury is done or anticipated to the self and the world of the self's making. He envisages the capacity of an active participant in human affairs to achieve some conscious control over the narcissistic forces within himself. Under this regimen, rage can subside, a tantrum be averted, self-respect and even joy found in patiently naming and transforming one's tendencies to fragment or distort self and harm others [pages 387–8].

Kohut does not flinch from the dark side of narcissism, whether on the part of masterful leaders or their followers and the executors of their designs: 'The most gruesome human destructiveness is encountered not in the form of wild, regressive and primitive behaviour, but in the form of orderly and organised activities in which the perpetrators' destructiveness is alloyed with absolutarian convictions about their greatness and with their devotion to archaic omnipotent figures' [page 378].

It requires no mental gymnastics to locate Lee's destructive elements within the narcissistic band of the human spectrum. Consider, for example, his aggressiveness, his public and total humiliation of opponents and recalcitrants, showing them no empathy but only the ridicule and contempt that he perhaps feared from them. Consider his compulsive need to avenge a hurt, as Kohut says, 'by whatever means' [page 380]. We may also recall his hypochondria [page 390] or his unintentionally patronising judgments of giants such as Charles de Gaulle, Nehru and Mao.

If we were being pessimistic about Lee, we might agree with the more general observation of political leaders made by A.F. Davies quoting Harold Lasswell, that 'familial grudges are made over into public causes, and, in notable actors, a whole life is 'moulded in such a way as to give opportunity for the expression of these affects'.[34] That would be to concede that Lee's politics are basically vengeful, with hate their leading emotion. But the reality is far more positive and forward-looking. Nor may we overlook the checks and balances that have always given Lee Kuan Yew pause at the brink of disintegration—even in August 1965. They are checks and balances arising from his own resourcefulness, his familiarity with coping alone. And they are checks and balances brought to bear by those closest to him and by the people of Singapore.

Should the characterisation of Lee's project as *masterful* be correct, it helps us recognise the magnitude of his accomplishment. He has converted the permissive neglect, the kindly misunderstanding and the high hopes heaped on him by parents and grandparents into an all-consuming project of social reconstruction and punishment. Most of us would never once throughout our waking lives consider that such a project could exist or be feasible, therefore it remains veiled from our full view. Only when all the scattered bits and pieces of self-revelation and information are put together does the puzzle resolve into a startling picture. Here is a man willing to bring a whole nation under his protection and command. From his perspective, Lee Kuan Yew offers grandeur and glory to all those united with him as they seek virtue together from the rising sun of a better future.

ULYSSES BY THE MERLION
(for Maurice Baker)

I have sailed many waters,
Skirted islands of fire,
Contended with Circe
Who loved the squeal of pigs;
Passed Scylla and Charybdis
To seven years with Calypso,
Heaved in battle against the gods.
Beneath it all
I kept faith with Ithaca, travelled,
Travelled and travelled,
Suffering much, enjoying a little;
Met strange people singing
New myths; made myths myself.

But this lion of the sea
Salt-maned, scaly, wondrous of tail,
Touched with power, insistent
On this brief promontory . . .
      Puzzles.

Nothing, nothing in my days
Foreshadowed this
Half-beast, half-fish,
This powerful creature of land and sea.

Peoples settled here,
Brought to this island
The bounty of these seas,
Built towers topless as Ilium's.
      They make, they serve,
      They buy, they sell.

Despite unequal ways,
Together they mutate,
Explore the edges of harmony,
Search for a centre;
Have changed their gods,
Kept some memory of their race
In prayer, laughter, the way
Their women dress and greet.
They hold the bright, the beautiful,
Good ancestral dreams
Within new visions,
So shining, urgent,
Full of what is now.

Perhaps having dealt in things,
Surfeited on them,
Their spirits yearn again for images,
Adding to the dragon, phoenix,
Garuda, naga, those horses of the sun,
This lion of the sea.
This image of themselves.

EDWIN THUMBOO

13
No Man is an Island

> ... [A]s a leader of a newly independent nation, and the man most identified with it, I start out with a tremendous advantage over anyone else in Singapore. I would have to be pretty inept to dissipate this lead over other native politicians.
>
> LEE KUAN YEW,
> interview with Crocker Snow Jr, quoted in
> Alex Josey, *Lee Kuan Yew: the Struggle for Singapore*, 1974, p. 48

We have endeavoured to chart the course adopted by Lee Kuan Yew soon after new colonial masters, the Japanese, had swept down through Malaya, captured a complacent Singapore and begun brutal subjugation of her bewildered population. At that moment, Lee decided 'never again'.

We have observed the preparations that he made for each stage of his rescue operation, even though he could not always be sure that the preparations would produce the desired result or secure access to the levers of power. It was not at all a foregone conclusion that a man of Lee's background should rise to be a successful political organiser, front man and finally Singapore's Prime Minister. What drove him on was ambition. 1965's truncation of opportunity for him to go further and shape Malaysia's destiny left him the more limited but concentrated task of making Singapore over. On the world stage, he has performed a role far beyond what might have been anticipated from the leader of a small island of two and a half million people. He and his nation have striven to outshine their Malaysian and regional counterparts. Amidst troubled and uncertain times Singapore has been not only a latter-day Venice but a symbol of excellence in her own right.

The breadth and intensity of Lee's motivation are suggested by his career and revealed by his eloquence. They were not created by the Occupation, however much their political expression was a conscious choice triggered by his experience of those years. We have sketched enough of his younger days to intimate the development of an exceptional degree of self-determination well before the crucible of war could pour iron into his soul.

Two final tasks remain to complete our study—namely, to analyse Lee's relationship with the people of Singapore and to look to the future with or without him at the helm. Before embarking on them, it will be helpful to add some relevant detail to the contemporary picture of the Prime Minister pieced together in the first chapter. The last few years have wrought significant but not necessarily obvious changes to Lee's personal position.

His mother's death marked a break with his parents' generation that his father's continuing residence with him at 38 Oxley Road does not seem to repair. Lee might have been talking of his own situation when he said, 'I know that not all parents are easy to live with.'[1] The departure of close friends and colleagues from Singapore's 'court', whatever the individual causes, has thrown Lee even more than before upon the resources and security of his immediate family. His wife has become his principal anchor and lifeline, a situation that one imagines must be satisfying yet frustrating to both of them: Lee has said half-humorously that he is a 'kept man'.

Madam Kwa Geok Choo is remembered by her fellow Raffles College students as a clever, studious, calm and good-hearted person, simple in her habits despite the great wealth of her kinsfolk. While she was not considered the beauty of her year, she was well liked by contemporaries. She and her family won respect for their demeanour and resilience during the Occupation. Her competitive relationship with Harry Lee, her firm resolve, her academic and public speaking prowess and her sisterly encouragement and advice to others somehow inclined them to consider her just as suited in her own way as Harry to a political career. Her protestations to the contrary have been overtaken not by secret ambition or choice: rather, it has been the outworking of her marriage that has eventually made her so important a figure behind the scenes.

Lee's bond with his children has been close. Within the limits of time and energy available he has tried to be a good father to them. He has interacted with them as a doting instructor who expected to be instructed by them in turn. They have rewarded him by living out and embodying many of the virtues and hopes he has wanted for Singaporeans at large.

Hsien Loong (born 1952) is a lanky, patrician figure, now very much at the centre of attention. When he speaks, his mouth movements are reminiscent of his father's, but his delivery is more rapid and less aggressive, his style is not nearly so much the advocate's and his humour is gentler and more earnest. His glasses slip down his nose and give him a bookish appearance. He has already undergone several ordinary lifetimes' worth of experience. He coped with ten or eleven years of the school and home language environments being quite different from one another. He has acquired a wide range of academic and artistic skills, and has had the best tuition available to help him do so. He is physically disciplined but not enthusiastic about team sports. His thirteen years of regular army life dovetailed with tertiary studies in mathematics, computer systems, nuclear physics and business administration. Meanwhile, he gained political exposure by providing briefings and counsel to the Government and sitting in on Cabinet discussions of domestic, regional or global strategy. His marriage to Dr Wong Ming Yang of Kuala Lumpur was tragically shortlived—only four and a half years; she died of a massive heart attack a month or so after giving birth to a son (there is an older surviving child, a daughter). Hsien Loong has a depth about him that suggests a 'coming to terms with his own soul' (to paraphrase his words about the modern Singaporean's responsibility). He bases his offer of leadership on the conscious attempt to see his father's vision through to a new stage, where the well-educated and affluent of the younger generation will put meaning into their lives by striving for excellence and by contributing to the welfare of the nation's less accomplished citizens.

Wei Ling (born 1955) is a paediatrician trained in Singapore and overseas. She is described by many acquaintances as 'hard-working' and 'reserved'; she is apparently very fond of animals. Proficient linguistically, she is also versed in the martial arts and self-defence. Her time as a medical student aroused not only respect but a certain nervousness toward her among teaching staff. Having her father's ear, she could and did voice complaints about particular courses, which led to remedial action by the Prime Minister. From a parent's perspective, there are real problems for a highly trained woman such as Wei Ling. Will there be a Chinese Singaporean male worthy of her, and, if not, will she find a suitable foreign partner to ensure the transmission of her unique genetic endowment and nurturing capacities?

Hsien Yang (born 1957) is tall for a Singaporean, robust of physique yet with a slight stoop. He is a major in the Singapore Armed Forces and commands an artillery battalion. A fairly full word portrait of him as he was some eight or nine years ago appears as a chapter of the book *Youth in the Army* (which surveys the psychological impact of national service on officers and other ranks).[2] He read engineering at Cambridge, taking out first class honours. According to the portrait, he considers himself 'more at home with numbers than with words' [page 188]; he has been keener than his brother or sister about sports, especially swimming. His mother thought that his involvement with extra-curricular activities at National Junior College, where he spent two years on pre-university studies (as his brother had done), was 'a bit excessive' [page 188]. His school friends were all similar to him in temperament—equable and moderately outgoing—and similarly inclined to the hard, precise sciences. Hsien Yang said, 'I can't tolerate a poet friend' [page 189]. From having expressed little interest in girls before he went to Cambridge, Hsien Yang soon found a partner there, a Singaporean whom he had known casually from pre-university college days, Lim Suet Fern; they were married in a Christian ceremony in mid-July 1981. She is a talented lawyer* who epitomises the new breed of young Singaporean women willing to argue things out with men, including their elders, on an equal footing.

The children breathed a quite exceptional domestic atmosphere of political awareness and discussion. Security guards constantly watched over them and their parents. Being subject to rigorous disciplinary demands they had little experience of the idle games, the chatter and the carefree mixing that other youngsters would have taken for granted. Although sheltered from commercial media and consumer blandishments, they were trained to the highest pitch that current methods, aided (not uncritically) by parental pressures, could muster. Not for them the education of an ordinary Singaporean. Even less did they learn how to grow food, tend machines or beasts of burden and farm earth and sea. Not for them the responsibility of providing for one another and helping produce the family's basic necessities; not for them membership of a community enacting and celebrating its seasonal and ritual rhythms. Parents, teachers and special tutors taught them more sophisticated lessons: how to speak and use several languages properly; how to maximise their individual potential; how to convert mental agility to competitive advantage; and how to moderate the effects of wealth and eminence by personal decency. It is a tribute to the strength of their home life and their own characters that the three young Lees, Hsien Loong, Wei Ling and Hsien Yang, have successfully weathered the effects of modern urban education, so

---

* Her father, Lim Chong Yah, is a professor of economics and Chairman of the National Wages Council.

often conducive to privatism, prolonged immaturity and self-indulgence. There is no doubt that they are willing to put back into society some of what they have received.

The extent to which they still contribute to their father's thinking or reinforce his sense of well-being is not for us to know. On many occasions in the past he has gladly acknowledged their contributions. He has described them as his 'hostages to fortune', the only kind whose existence he is proud to admit (along with his grandchildren, whom he has confessed a certain awkwardness about handling). Probably, having left home for study overseas or marriage, the three have developed their own distinctive outlook and preoccupations. It must always be a stark moment of truth when busy, accomplished and dogmatic parents face the fact that their children have ceased to be an extension or reincarnation of themselves and their ideals.

Lee's values and beliefs do not derive from a traditional religious faith. Until he reached Cambridge his upbringing was almost devoid of any religious input directed specifically to him. He was exposed to the nominal Buddhism of his family and to the openly secular emphasis of the government institutions of learning that he attended. What he experienced in England was not likely to have been more than the genteel hallowing of national history and ideals represented by Church of England college chapels and chaplains. But he has observed the inner strength of his more religious friends and the dedication of many of the teachers and principals associated with Singapore's mission schools. A few allusions indicate that he has begun to toy with the hypothesis that there is some kind of supreme Being. It was said that his mother became a Christian before she died and asked him to promise that he would do likewise. Whatever his attitude to the God disclosed by Jesus of Nazareth or to any other expression of deity, he could not be content with a religion that constrained him within narrow and petty limits for the sake of some drug-like consolation. He has been fascinated by the big questions of authority, of death, of the human body and its workings, of the ingenuity yet frailty of technological progress, of civilisation and language; he would not lightly abandon the insights that he has won as a result. Nor would he be likely to purchase respectability and orthodoxy at the price of pretending that his negative judgments and hostility towards certain people are not important to his identity and the survival of the nation.

There is a sober and soul-searching side to Lee that has come to the fore through political and personal vicissitudes of recent years. Nevertheless, anyone who examines the man's leadership will discover that one rock-solid feature of the psychological landscape is always in evidence. It is that Lee does not, perhaps cannot, criticise or doubt himself. When he was asked by *Leaders*, an American quarterly magazine, 'What are your biggest faults?', he replied, 'I do not know or I would have tried to minimise flaws which could be fatal. My friends are too kind or too polite to tell me; my enemies mislead me by naming fictitious ones.'[3]

Whatever Lee finds looking back at him from the mirror is sufficiently wholesome that his conscience is untroubled; at least his reflection is bright by comparison with other leaders' and is not disfigured by the scars of corruption or sycophancy. One of the reasons why he resents attempts to probe his character is that he sees his motives as quite straightforward, his ambition as directed not to his own but to his nation's advancement. All along, he has been doing his duty, ensuring that the Singapore experiment works, whatever historical accidents have affected its progress for good or ill.

The man and the people

> There is no cringe in Singapore ... I wave at them, they wave back at me. We are equal. They are prepared to stand on their two hind legs and bark back at you.
> Lee Kuan Yew, BBC interview, quoted in Alex Josey, *Lee Kuan Yew: the Struggle for Singapore*, p. 205

When Harry Lee was a child, he would often be missing from the meal table. A paradoxical sign of family membership was his freedom to go off, withdraw to his room—to read or dream, or just to escape what was unsatisfactory and upsetting.

Prime Minister Lee Kuan Yew still claims that right. Sometimes he finds Singapore 'intellectually debilitating, introverted, because of the lack of a world picture.'[4] He seeks stimulus and grandeur elsewhere.

The home life of childhood days and the island of Singapore share the charm and the staleness of familiarity. They have been skins that Lee has shed at crucial moments, stepping out of them more splendid and more powerful each time.

Meanwhile the people of Singapore make their lives and work out their own personal and group projects. Between them and their Prime Minister is something of the same ethos of commitment yet distance that characterised the boy's household. Few would doubt that Lee wants the best for Singapore: an honourable name, a persuasive voice, room to grow and to offer an exemplary contribution to civilised and rational living. However, his reaction to the history that he has shaped and shared with his people has often been quite different from theirs.

His rage at stupidity within the gates and malevolence outside has exploded time and again and made it hard to live with him. At the most visibly traumatic point in his life, when everything he had worked for seemed to be cut short, there were crackers of glee in Chinatown and the stock market boomed; Singaporeans were bemused by their leader dramatically unable to control his emotions and be his usual calculating self.

Equally, some of Lee's triumphs have put him out of kilter with all but his most ardent followers or close-bound colleagues. Among the Chinese, the Referendum of 1962 or, among the Malays, the election of 1963 showed Lee what could be done 'to lead people against their own racial, language and religious prejudices towards a more tolerant, rational and cohesive society'.[5] Yet we may wonder if voters surveying the results learned the same lessons as their Prime Minister.

Who could deny that there have been many moments of rapport between Lee and the crowds who have joined him for various national celebrations? Surely there must be joint pride in having turned sparsely inhabited swampland into a populous, modern habitat 'without killing Red Indians or Aborigines', in having created a city whose public areas are both gracious and full of vitality, in beating down the climate so energetically. There are many reasons for collective self-congratulation: the new sophistication of port and airport; the recomposed landscape; the cosmopolitan coexistence of race and race, foreigner and local-born, private purpose and public good. Here is a *yin–yang* harmony of opposites interacting without assimilation.

Moreover, the elite mentality that has enabled Lee and Goh Keng Swee to mobilise close associates and subordinates has seeped down through the upper levels of Singapore's education system and social structure. The numbers of followers who have responded to the rhetoric of Lee's patriotism and the call of the PAP are much higher than the Prime Minister decreed to be the essential minimum; not all are scoundrels seeking a last refuge or that special breed of clones whose voice and signature resemble those of their leader.

Might not the basic mode of relationship between Lee and the people of Singapore, at its best, be likened to that of a star actor–writer–director and a supporting cast on stage together each night for the performance of a series of plays, then going home to their very different private worlds? The scripts have been sufficiently to the cast's liking, and the theatre management and production staff have been so competent that the plays have continued to attract audiences. The versatility of the whole cast has won acclaim; they have worked well with their star, whose talent is matched only by the volatility of his temperament.

The simile is too unambiguously favourable to merit further exploration. After all, Lee has not relied solely on the persuasive power of his vision and his verbal skills to gather support. He has brought into play the sanctions of law and the forces of order. He has resorted to bullying, petulance and vindictiveness. He has affronted, both deliberately and involuntarily, almost all the spiritual orientations and pieties of all his people at one time or another. He has nonetheless succeeded because in the nature of Singapore, especially a modernising Singapore, the normative influences of one traditional group are abhorrent or irrelevant to another. The cost has been high: a damaging of the social habits that render civilised co-operation a reflex and not an endless and gruelling effort.

Paradoxically, it is Lee Kuan Yew's inability to work with most people in an equal and mutually encouraging way that has lent him great political strength. He has not been beholden to personal loyalties or vested interests and people have long since ceased to expect that he will pay much attention to their feelings. So he can apply his energy to exploit his citizens' need for structure within which the risks of their private ventures can become bearable. Almost palpably he is outside their lives, overarching them in expression of his own need to control and dominate and yet thereby providing protection for them to forget him 'up there' and get on with their own concerns.

A masterful project such as Lee Kuan Yew's is at constant risk of destroying itself. It feeds on the awareness of its subject's own singularity and the hope that the future inspires. When communication with others is fitful, the delicate art of communication has been weakened or forgotten and singularity can become a form of talking to oneself. The masterful person's hope can become faint when sickness and setback strike, or sterile because it looks to create a haven far above the earthy mess of humankind, the acceptance of being a man or a woman and therefore incomplete. The greater indulgence of power open to Lee since 1965 has accentuated the compulsiveness of his personality; at the same time, the greater urgency and unity demanded of him and his team in order to cope with rapid change have had a restraining effect.

There are signs that the people are tiring of the paternal treatment that has been meted out to them. Some are upset over the Government's attitude to such issues as citizens' capacity to manage their own savings. Others are weary of hectoring lessons in history and sermons on social and industrial behaviour. Others are shocked by evidence of Government vengefulness towards an ungrateful electorate. Some are even willing to believe that Lee's Machiavellian hand was behind the economic downturn of 1985, seeking to manipulate Singaporeans and bring them to their senses.

Politics has always implied a struggle between the interpersonal forces of cohesion, competition and eagerness to change. Of its nature, it is a function of people acting outside their immediate circle on the scale of tribe, city, nation or region. Although affected by the ebb and flow of history and obliged to contend with war and revolution, politics could, before the shocks of the industrial and communication revolutions, expect periods of relative stability and isolation from wider conflict. Only from time to time did a surge of new ideas and techniques cause a major, even fundamental shift in social structure. Today, change is an almost ceaseless pressure, indifferently and whimsically uprooting community and flattening or elevating those who bid for power and wealth.

Our study has shown that Lee has been unusually well served by his training and inclination to move with the thrust of change towards the future. He is the enemy of parochial community—its peace about living in the present and accepting things the way they are, the languor of folk dance and celebration, the oneness with land and with ancestors, and the willingness to work only long enough to secure basic necessities or to help a neighbour. He has sought to overcome what he chooses to call the backwardness of the Malays, the clannishness of the Chinese-educated and the Indians, and the grubbiness of rural villages or city slums. He is more attuned to the incentive mentality and to the acquisition of wealth or technique without counting the personal and social costs involved. His didactic methods elicit from those responsive to them an identity based on achievement and competition. Duty is a convenient catchcry by which people are marshalled within his organising sweep. Needless to say, he despises almost equally those who, on command, surrender their selfhood to become efficient robots of administration and those who, despite his warning, turn in on themselves and become devotees of conspicuous consumption.

Lee has never had a faction of his own followers to preserve him in government. Quite apart from rarely needing that kind of support, he is too harsh a judge of adulation and too demanding a taskmaster. As far as he is concerned, the PAP vision (increasingly his vision) of Singapore is to be implemented for the highest of motives. That is why the island and compatible foreign societies are being scoured to find people with the right combination of talent, skill and character. Yet, on the whole, those who are spontaneous admirers of Lee Kuan Yew can remain so only if they have at most fleeting personal contact with him and only if they are deaf to whatever parts of his wide-ranging attacks upon defaulters apply to them.

He is a 'messianic' rather than a 'charismatic' figure, to use the distinction suggested by the psychoanalyst Ernest Wolf.[6] Lee's call is for citizens to obey his vision, not to make him the centre of their lives. Much of what he offers is of limited appeal: the repeated emphasis on discipline and grit, or the challenge to be a 'stayer' rather than a 'quitter'. But at times of crisis, when the old order was seen to be collapsing, Singaporeans have been willing to sink their differences and trade their own dreams for those of their Prime Minister. Of itself, however, the sway of a messianic leader is hard to sustain, let alone recapture. When a crisis is over, people may revert to type. When a new crisis is alleged to be imminent and new obedience is demanded, it is touch and go whether they will again respond as required.

President Yusof Ishak, delivering a speech prepared for him by Lee Kuan Yew, once said that two million people in the modern age could achieve as much as twenty million through rational organisation and determined and disciplined effort.[7] Singapore has been a powerful vindication of such a possibility. What is not yet clear is how long the majority of Singaporeans will be willing to subscribe to the kind of rationality and effort proposed by their government.

Attempts to wean Singapore's political culture from its indigenously evolved base of democratic participation and persuasion onto supposedly more effective and productive forms of governance must surely fail. It would be equally forlorn to claim that Singapore is a Confucian state or that a particular ruler has the mandate of heaven. A multiracial and multicredal set of people can find common cause only if constituent groups, especially minorities, have guaranteed rights, fairly distributed responsibilities and the protection of universally applicable checks and balances. For a predominantly immigrant and composite society, stability and democracy, once linked, go together with a logic of special intensity. The experience both of British and Japanese overlordship and of the daily conflict between Malaysia's and Singapore's governments from 1963 to 1965 has rendered allegiance to any leadership, even Lee's critical and provisional. 'Pragmatism must be kept within limits' is a truth brought home to Singapore's governed no less personally than to their Prime Minister.

Planning for an uncertain future

> The 'old guard' will progressively—I choose the word 'progressively' with a sardonic sense of the inevitable—step aside as the young take charge. Several of my senior colleagues have urged me to replace them. They have done this too vehemently for me to treat these urgings as just a natural desire to be reassured of their indispensability. I have refused to let them go, at least not until I have new ministers of comparable capacity, with some on-the-job experience.
> Lee Kuan Yew, PAP 25th Anniversary rally, Singapore, 20 January 1980

Few governments have bent their energies towards providing a succession quite so assiduously as Singapore's. Thinking carefully about the dynamics of political control and studying the post-war experiments at independence. Lee recognised before he came to office that the democratic process did not necessarily produce the stable, long-term administration that a developing economy needed. Even more clearly was it borne in on him by his first six years at the helm of the PAP Government (1959–65) that shoals and rocks were never far away from the barque of state.

During a long interview he gave to three foreign correspondents in 1966, Lee said, 'The real problem now in Singapore politically ... is, how do we, over the next ten years, allow a new generation to emerge to take over from us? ... in about ten years, we will no longer have that rapport with the younger mass base.'[8] Rajaratnam expressed the leadership's problem as a dilemma: whether to pull out and run the risk of lightweights taking over, or to stay and overshadow.[9]

It emerged in Chapter 9 that the timetable for grooming a succession has been revised and extended several times. Despite declarations of confidence that the problem was close to solution, there has been a dearth of talent arising naturally from the ground or willing to be selected and taught by Lee and tested in the arena under his beady eye.

Lee and his senior colleagues used to acknowledge freely that they could not designate their successors: 'Even kings cannot,' he admitted to the 1971 National Day rally.[10] A few months later he told the Polytechnic students, 'You know, I am not here because my father was a prime minister. And my son has no hope of inheriting my position. He knows it and you know it.'[11] Nowadays that rueful incantation has been replaced by a concerted effort to prove it wrong.

According to his son, Hsien Loong, two other problems occupy the attention of the team that Lee has assembled to carry on his work. The first of them is 'to continue generating imaginative and sensible policies'. The more difficult problem is 'how to renew the faith' and build confidence in the new team. The 1984 elections demonstrated to Hsien Loong that 'many voters, particularly the younger ones, are beginning to have less than absolute faith in the Government'.[12]

He added, 'There is nothing uniquely Singaporean about this loss of faith, this restlessness with the *status quo*, and particularly with the powers that be. It happens to every generation, in every age, in every country. What makes it a serious problem for us is that its consequences are uniquely disastrous. In Singapore, as a result of the close rapport between rulers and ruled, we have for almost a generation done better than this. We have performed close to our full potential—perhaps 95 per cent. But if Singaporeans lose faith, we will not simply drop to 70 per cent performance, like the US or the Soviet Union. We have not the ballast of geographic size or the wherewithal to muddle through, enduring stoically as a natural disaster what is in fact a humanly inflicted disaster. Our performance would drop precipitously, to 10 per cent or 20 per cent. Far from cheerfully muddling through, we would vanish without trace, submerged into the mud of history.'[13]

Some years ago Lee Kuan Yew described ASEAN, and therefore Singapore, as an 'exception' in the Third World. Instead of having to lament resources wasted on war, rivalry and hatred, he was able to rejoice that ASEAN members had contrived, as much by 'divine providence as diplomatic foresight', to build a framework for consultation and co-operation. Economic development was to be their focus of attention. 'We give our peoples fuller lives, and thus ensure political continuity and stability.'[14] This statement may be an unwitting clue to why Lee's perceptions and expectations differ so much from those of his people and make it so difficult for him to stage-manage a succession. Lee views the nation as an organism whose very health—'continuity and stability'—depends on the nourishment of its members. To be sure, the people have reached the point where the attainment of what Lee means by 'fuller lives' has replaced the more tribal and more modest ambitions of their ancestors. But ensuring the nation's survival and stability is not their chief preoccupation. 'Immigrants or their children are keener or emotionally more ready to try out new ideas for better results. This is the main reason for the progress we have made.'[15] By trading on the immigrant mentality in order to supersede it, just as he has done with Chinese education, Lee has bought his nation—at a price. His claim to know what the older generation wants may be little more than self-praise for having divided and ruled. Now the ploy is breaking down and the younger generation shows signs of forgetting or forsaking its redeemer.

What none of the second-echelon leaders has openly said, although some of them have almost certainly thought, is that the Prime Minister has contributed substantially to the problem. He has fixed the framework of political activity so firmly that policy debates have generally turned into attacks by the Government on the integrity, intelligence and independence of its critics, even those occasional muted voices of dissent within the PAP. 'There is no leeway but Lee's way' is a popular slogan that summarises what has happened. When he was alleging trespass of Singapore's sovereignty through manipulation of the press, specifically the *Singapore Herald*, Lee warned the Washington CIA bureau chief for Southeast Asia, 'Mr Nelson, the last thing you want to do is to undermine me because then you will be in deep trouble. You either have the communists or you have a lot of incompetent people who will bring about chaos and communism.'[16] The public might have permitted him to categorise the situation in such a fashion because they consider that he has worked hard to earn the right. But if he has got away with interpreting their silence as consent, he is the exception that proves the rule. No one else will do so.

Despite fears or predictions to the contrary, Singapore's one-man one-vote system, which brought the PAP to power, is still intact. This puts Lee and the younger team in an exquisite bind. On the one hand they are sure that what has generated Singapore's wealth is not the universal adult suffrage but the careful husbanding of the economy and the keeping of consumption below income. Did not Britain and other advanced industrial countries first modernise by exploiting their labour force and their colonies and only then introduce democracy? On the other hand, short of constitutional upheaval, the citizens cannot be prevented from playing what the PAP regards as an insincere and risky game:

voting individually for an opposition candidate in protest at particular government policies while wanting the PAP to retain office overall.

Lee Hsien Loong drew attention to this danger when he told the story of ten men invited to bring wine for a festivity; each one decided that he could get away with bringing water instead. 'Singaporeans would be ... rueful if they woke up one morning to find that they too had accidentally turned their wine to water. The danger is a real one. The question is what to do about it. The problem is that the link between one vote and the outcome, determined by more than one million votes, is too tenuous to provide a strong incentive to vote sincerely.'[17]

With or without Lee

> There are no such things in real life as what Herman Kahn calls 'surprise-free, multifold projections' ... The Republic of Singapore is a surprise ... There is a danger here, you know, of people like me not minding their Ps and Qs and being accused of uttering self-fulfilling prophecies.
> Lee Kuan Yew, question-and-answer session at the Hong Kong Foreign Press Club, 19 February 1970.

Sometimes over the years the Singapore stock market has fluctuated according to rumours about Lee's sickness or even death. Those Singaporeans and foreign admirers who dread Lee's departure take comfort in the rising statistical average life expectancy of a healthy male. Many others are puzzled by the sense of urgency and anxiety that the government feels about the future leadership, its pattern and personnel. Regarding the talk of constitutional amendments to allow for an executive President, David Marshall, the former Chief Minister, remarked in a 1984 interview: 'What fascinates me is what seems to me to be a premature debate ... I have not the slightest doubt that he [Lee] is equal to the battle, in the heat and dust of the valley, for at least another ten years.'[18]

Despite the delicate nature of the subject, Goh Chok Tong and certain others have advertised both their readiness to meet the current challenges and, if anything, their superior ability to handle the younger voters. They refuse to be portrayed any longer as pupils taking every cue from instructors. The old guard, however, Lee and Rajaratnam in particular, have signalled a contrary view of the situation. Lee is not going to be ousted by the younger team; if he goes anywhere, it will be to the box seat of an upgraded

Presidency from which he can supervise the scene. Late in July 1985 Rajaratnam chose to break seven months of 'exasperated and restless silence' (why was he unable to speak frankly in private?) and instruct the younger ministers to put on knuckle dusters, rubber ones 'if they are finicky', before the Opposition grew reckless, played the politics of envy and spread gloom, doom and confusion. He did concede that the 'street-fighting' methods of the old guard might not be appropriate as they had been during the days of 'Queensberry rules, revised and edited, to cope with communists, communalists, racialists and gangster-backed politicians'.[19]

These flashes of irritation may indicate a less stable future than many Singapore commentators seem willing to contemplate. If our assessment of Lee is accurate, his investment of himself in the project of leading Singapore has taken him past the point where he could relinquish power, as he used to talk—speculatively and at a distance—about doing. Josey's 1974 book, *Lee Kuan Yew: the Struggle for Singapore,* twice refers to the possibility of Lee retiring while still in his fifties. '... he is determined to lay down his burden in ample time to prevent himself from becoming old and crusty with power, and to enjoy another more leisurely sort of life. He would like to write books, about Southeast Asia and about politics. It is unlikely that he will ever return to the law' [page 11], '... content that he has done his best and that the Republic he conceived is going to prosper ... he might want to join the Establishment he is trying now so hard to create (become a don, or the chairman of a statutory board) to help provide the continuity which Lee believes Europe has shown to be essential if a nation, no matter how tiny, is to have some sort of heritage, tradition, background, if the nation is to be bigger and more lasting than current personalities' [page 40]. This sort of talk has not been heard for years.

What kind of successor would Lee tolerate if he became President or was still calling the shots? Not a person whose style and project were predominantly dependent (to use our categories from Chapter 12). The times demand someone strong and tough. Yet too much toughness, too great a tendency to threaten would also be unacceptable—it would not carry the people and it would pretend to a base of more independent power than would really be the case, even if the outgoing Prime Minister were willing to hand it over. What of Lee's own masterful project? Could another leader more charismatic than Lee or similarly messianic come to the fore? Speaking generally, the answer must be no. He is too brittle to bear the friction of another visionary or an alternative vision nearby. His fierce vigilance and the presumption that he monopolises rationality and dedication are factors that must nip someone else's creative leadership in the bud.

The most likely turn of events by the end of the decade is for Lee's own son, Hsien Loong, to follow his father as Prime Minister. He has the correct vision, the stamina and the charisma needed. The present First Deputy Prime Minister Goh Chok Tong's efforts to be strong and flexible all at once do not seem to have compelled citizens' respect. We might guess that Goh's usefulness to Lee Kuan Yew is impartial: whether he succeeds or fails—although neither should occur on a spectacular scale—he is a forerunner and a convenient scapegoat.

Lee Hsien Loong represents a particular question mark over any generalised analysis. The Prime Minister reacts vigorously to the suggestion that he is establishing a Lee dynasty. Appearing before the National Press Club in October 1985 while visiting Washington to address Congress and consult with President Reagan, he said that the suggestion 'is a subject of considerable amusement in the Lee family because my son feels he is a person unto himself and not an object to be manipulated by his father. I have no desire to fulfil myself vicariously'.[20] Even if these words show that Lee Kuan Yew is once again failing to be aware of himself and those nearest to him, even if it was his colleagues rather than he himself who recommended that his son not delay any longer coming into public politics, no one would want to deny Lee the thrill of watching his own flesh and blood sail through the early lessons and grades of national leadership. It is intriguing to ponder, and impossible as yet to decide, which of the three projects we have described may be personified by Lee's son once he is free to act in his own right.

Meanwhile, it should not be assumed that Hsien Loong will automatically have an easy time of it. He has been served notice by Goh Chok Tong and others that he will have to convince them that he has earned his spurs. Even more important would be the first challenge he offered to Lee Kuan Yew's taking him for granted. Whatever admiration Hsien Loong has for his father, and it comes across as warm and genuine, he has been through too much not to be his own man; besides, he is his mother's son as well.

There are others, of whom Dr Tony Tan is the most outstanding, likely to figure prominently in any rearrangement of top posts undertaken by Lee Kuan Yew. Tony Tan's strengths, as earlier chapters of our study have enumerated them, are his intellect, his background and his rapid but thorough formation in key areas of political management. Whether he would continue to appeal to the public if Lee Kuan Yew were his only foil is a question not yet able to be answered.

What could happen to the PAP while the leadership succession is being sorted out? The political scientist Chan Heng Chee foreshadowed four possibilities in her *Straits Times* article 'The PAP in the 1990s—the Politics of Anticipation (27 April 1985). They are:

1. The PAP to recapture lost ground. As Professor Chan says, this will be very difficult because of the growing belief that parliamentary democracy is incomplete without an Opposition.
2. The PAP to dominate Parliament with an institutionalised presence of one to twelve Opposition MPs. She believes that this is the most likely middle- or even long-term development.
3. The emergence of a serious alternative to the PAP. According to Professor Chan, this would be contingent on the ruling party's tolerance. If so, and given the recent behaviour of the PAP towards the two Opposition members, the possibility is not really worth considering.
4. More support for a fragmented Opposition, seats becoming marginal and the PAP faced with the prospect of forming a coalition government.

At least two further possibilities arise logically from the way Lee Kuan Yew operates and should be added to Chan Heng Chee's list.

5. The Prime Minister to purge the PAP of some of its present leaders, who would then form an Opposition party. They would probably attract support from those on the sidelines not willing to join an existing Opposition party or to express their ambitions while Lee controls the PAP.
6. The Prime Minister to lose control of the PAP and set up another party—or even system of government—to hold power. If allowed to exist, the non-Lee remnant, in this case the PAP, would attract support as specified in (5) above. This is less plausible than the scenario of (5).

One lesson that Goh Chok Tong and his colleagues have taken to heart from the old guard is the perfectly reasonable one that political stability is essential to economic success. They also seem to accept Lee Kuan Yew's more contentious corollary that the people of Singapore are now playing fast and loose with stability and must be called to account. Goh translated it into rhetorical questions that he put to National University of Singapore students: 'Does prolonged peace and prosperity contain the seed of its own destruction? Have we so quickly forgotten our painful birth and poverty years? Have we reached the peak of our political stability? Are we suffering a rich man's disease? If every General Election from now on is like flipping a coin, then we have reached the upper limit of our prosperity.'[21]

This overcharged crisis atmosphere will furnish ample justification for the old man—and for some of the younger team—to bring matters to a head. Even a showdown is not out of the question. Only if the economy shapes up and improves will the moment of reckoning be delayed, but Lee's remaining means that it will inevitably come.

Should death or terrible illness befall the Prime Minister, or should he somehow depart from office, developments would be even less predictable. One of the three current favourites—Goh Chok Tong, Tony Tan, Lee Hsien Loong—would be odds-on to take his place; Goh Chok Tong's chances of doing so would improve. Chan Heng Chee's (2), (3) or (4) would be real possibilities. But the PAP's internal cohesion could be under such strain that (5) or (6) might occur under the aegis of the new Prime Minister.

In the absence of Lee, it is not inconceivable that another masterful leader may arrive on stage. Somewhere there may be another Singaporean who has been provoked by the fitful cherishing of creche and foster care and mother, of exhausted parents and inattentive but indulgent surroundings, to dream and intellectualise and expand mental horizons, as Lee did. This leader-in-the-making might also have sought out teachers and mentors, poring over books (and computers) and drafting friends and associates into his—or her—vision. What an ironic twist it would be to Singapore's social engineering and slogan of equal opportunity!

Lee's departure will open the way for traditional groups to raise their voices more loudly. There are clusters of people in Singapore who are willingly dependent on religious or cultural bonds to sustain them, and they can expect to flourish once their predator has gone. Some of the dropouts who have failed the present norms and tests of social worth may regain a sense of dignity. There will be new leaders who spontaneously resonate with the traditional groups; there will be ambitious men whose appetite for power has been whetted and they will try to contrive their way to popularity. In either case, the Sino–Malay tensions would be likely to increase and be more susceptible to regional exploitation.

Figureheads for another generation

To conclude our study, let us gaze a little further ahead. With each addition of young voters to the electoral rolls, maintenance of the current vision and values will become harder. As the Prime Minister stated in his 1982 Eve-of-National-Day address: 'My deepest concern is how to make the young more conscious of security. By security I mean defence against threats to our survival, whether the threats are external or internal ... Civilisation is fragile. It is especially so for an island city state.'

The statistics of Singapore—second busiest port, third biggest refining centre in the world, etc., etc.—and the timeliness and success of her adaptation to external events cannot conceal the limitations under which she labours: of space, of dependence on foreign countries for food, water and other material resources. Singapore has to stay valuable to the world for her sovereign future to be guaranteed and renewed. She must expend constant effort and ingenuity.

It is not difficult to catalogue some of the global roles Singapore can fill in the immediate future. A diplomatic stalking horse for ASEAN and a refuge for failed coup-makers. An offshore trade zone and money haven. An independent 'think tank' facility and convention centre. A consultant and exemplar for many urbanising nations. An operations or service headquarters for transnational corporations. A go-between for China and Taiwan. A lighthouse for the Straits of Malacca. A breathing-space for tourists and expatriates. A profitable and discreet base for armaments to be manufactured or sold by import–export procedures to a comprehensive range of combatants. A clever producer of commodities, most of which are above board but some of which may depend on contravention and circumvention of other countries' laws and bans. A 'pirate' city where copyrights and patents may be in suspension.

Where an ethic of self-interest prevails among foreign dealers, the risk is that Singapore may be bypassed as easily as she is used. Where a more international morality comes into force, however selectively, she may be punished for other people's sins, as well as her own.

Are Singapore's days as a separate nation numbered? Will her fate be like that of Hong Kong? Will the time come for Singapore to rejoin Malaysia? Asked the last question at a Harvard Club dinner in Kuala Lumpur, Goh Chok Tong paused for a few seconds and replied, 'Nothing is impossible in politics.'[22] All other options—such as enhanced links with Brunei or East Asian countries or Australia, New Zealand and the Pacific—are too awkward to be feasible for Singapore unless she acts with the full consent of other ASEAN members. The only thing that can be said with some certainty is that while the present leadership of Singapore continues to imprint itself so vividly and totally upon the affairs of the island, there will be no yielding of autonomy or control without an almighty battle.

What elements should be borne in mind when guessing domestic political developments? Apart from the suggestions already made, there are two or three indicative signs to look for. One is ferment within the PAP and, to a lesser extent, within the trade unions (and the wider workforce) and the grassroots organisations. Will some new movement bubble up from the discontent of former leaders such as Toh Chin Chye, Jek Yeun Thong and Ong Pang Boon; from a backlash to the farcical treatment of Devan Nair following his resignation (the unacceptable conditions laid upon his eligibility for a government pension, and so on); from the clash of ambitions among current or recent leaders and cadres? Another facet of Singapore politics—an unintended consequence of racial integration—may be a heating up of class antagonisms: a bourgeoisie with expectations that can no longer be met and a proletariat defined to the point of consciousness (and envy) by long years of educational and military training for a subordinate place in society. Lastly, a futurologist would have to assess the probable significance of military and paramilitary forces for the various scenarios that can be constructed.

Rajaratnam has his own version of Singapore's future. At the opening of the Fidic annual conference at the Shangri-La Hotel on 14 June 1982 he said, 'The only certainty I am prepared to vouch for in this so-called Age of Uncertainty is that the future belongs only to those nations which are prepared to serve as partisans of the new Technological Society emerging out of the crumbling structure of the First Industrial Revolution ... I have ... stressed that the Europeans succeeded because they had no great but irrelevant past to uphold and preserve. But today the Western Europeans, too, have outmoded ... traditions ... the social, political, economic and ethical beliefs which though they harmonised with the needs of the First Industrial Revolution are today increasingly in conflict with the requirements of the Third Wave* technology. So as of now I do not know who is going to inherit the Third Wave Revolution, but as far as Singapore is concerned its ambitions are

---

* The 'Third Wave' is a phrase devised by Alvin Toffler, author of *Future Shock*, to serve as the title of a subsequent book of his. (London: Collins, 1980) The first wave—a mighty force on a collision course with history—was the agricultural revolution; the second wave the industrial revolution. The third wave promises to overtake the present relatively clumsy and mechanical structures of state and corporation and recover more personal dimensions for human society.

modest. It is to be in the race and to be somewhere in the middle of the line of runners.'

Rajaratnam's words draw together many of the themes that we have canvassed in this book. We do not have to be committed to his view of 'the static and cyclical world of Asia' or to his historical analysis where it is questionable: 'For Western man the Golden Age lay in the future simply because his past until then was lowly as it was inglorious. The European was the first to conceive of the idea of human progress and of the possibility of the improvement of the lot of man in this world and not in the hereafter.' [!]

But his attempts to characterise the Renaissance and the Enlightenment make it easier to understand Lee's philosophy and Rajaratnam's support of it. 'The hallmark of this new type of man was insatiable curiosity about himself and about other people. From the Age of European Enlightenment he absorbed a cluster of new ideas—the rights of man, government based on the consent of the governed and the right to free rational enquiry. From the Reformation he imbibed another novel idea, termed the Protestant Ethic. Its essence was that work was a holy thing and no man should be denied the right to work and enjoy the fruit of his labour. And most important of all European man was moved by what one writer has called the "Faustian spirit", that life is a matter of will, discipline and dedication and a sense of personal responsibility to transform the world according to Man's wishes.'

We have already encountered the language of myth in linking Lee Kuan Yew's masterful project to the figure of Narcissus. There is an ambivalence about those who live with exaggerated images of what they and their world might be. They are impelled by hope, yet each gesture of reaching out to embrace the hope may be defied and confounded by the pool's reflection. The seer Tiresias prophesied: 'Narcissus will live to a ripe old age, provided that he never knows himself.'

And now Rajaratnam summons up for us another character more recently lodged in the pantheon of mythology: Faust. Legend portrays this doctor of magic in two ways: a man possessed by an insatiable thirst for scientific knowledge; and a man who bargains with the Devil. Artists have not yet devised a convincing final resolution of these divergent elements. Is Faust a hero who atones for the sins of a lifetime by his active pursuit of truth, or is he to be consigned to annihilation because of his *hubris*, his pride?

Out of the vast array of human behaviour, Narcissus and Faust symbolise what is excellent and fascinating, and what is perilous and destructive, about the spirit of Lee Kuan Yew's Singapore.

There is no reason to doubt that the people of the island republic will choose or be offered other figureheads for their journey into the future.

> Singapore has no history to speak of. We can show the Raffles statue. I can tell the people what we have achieved. Tomorrow? The MRT. Yesterday? Maybe Lee Kuan Yew, that's all.
> S. Rajaratnam, 1984 speech to university students, in *Far Eastern Economic Review Asia 1985 Yearbook* p. 232.

Postscript

> We argued and thrashed out our differences in private. In public we never contradicted each other.
>
> LEE KUAN YEW,
> *Petir*, 1979, page 38

Events since late 1985, when *No Man is an Island* was finished, have given some of the more apocalyptic predictions in chapters 9 and 13 greater plausibility. The economic downturn, while immediately devastating to those thrown out of work or business (Singaporeans' very *raisons d'etre*), has also impinged on the leadership situation. Lee Kuan Yew's recent hint that he may stay on longer as Prime Minister is but one of many signs that the succession is not progressing satisfactorily. There are others. Lee's personal performance has been less than commanding. His 1986 international commentaries and overseas trips have continued to make idiosyncratic ripples or waves. Domestically he has tended to provoke rather than damp down popular opposition: early in June, for example, he told a Tanjong Pagar gathering that wage earners must be the last to benefit from any economic recovery. In March he failed to win a marathon impromptu joust with J.B. Jeyaretnam (televised from Parliament) over judicial independence.

Moreover, several of Lee's political progeny are ringing in the changes of a different generation. At the lowest level is the imitation of the master practised by various PAP functionaries criticising foreign academics or threatening action against foreign media for alleged bias. This self-serving appeal to xenophobia is under fire from citizens previously silenced.

Chairman Ong Teng Cheong has pledged the PAP to recruit members, improve the Party's image and finances, and 'sell' its policies. He is defying the trend towards improved political representation, seen in the new opposition party being started by a former PAP MP. The punchline of a current joke has it that in the 1990s 'PAP' will stand for 'passed away peacefully'! At the time of writing Ong also remains at the NTUC as Secretary-General. There is no one well-based in both Party and labour movement to take his place.

Dr Richard Hu is the Minister for Finance. Invited by Lee himself to join the Executive on the strength of his 'pukka' accent and his career as an academic and head of Shell (Singapore), Hu polled the highest vote in December 1984 to win Goh Keng Swee's old seat of Kreta Ayer. His easy entry to office soon gave way to conflict with Goh. The 1986 Budget and other measures show that Hu has challenged or dislodged some of the old guard's sacred cows, reducing regulation of the economy and financial system. There is also more vigorous and far-reaching dialogue about policy within government circles.

In August 1985 Lee painted a grim picture of national housekeeping problems while describing the CPF as 'the nest egg of last resort.' Yet before year's end Dr Tony Tan exhorted civil servants to 'bring unpleasant facts to the attention' of their political masters rather than allow the folly of persistence with erroneous policies. His illustration was precisely that of keeping CPF levels high when the economy turned sluggish. Within three months the Government had implemented a 'temporary' reduction, if only of employers' contributions.

Lee Hsien Loong, now remarried (to Ho Ching, an official of the Defence Ministry) and appointed Acting Minister for Trade and Industry (with Tony Tan falling back to Education), appears to be going from strength to strength. The very formation of the economic committee he chaired was remarkable enough, let alone its broad consultative scope. More was to come. Despite fears by some participants that Hsien Loong was at times out of his depth or rattled by media pressure, his Committee's findings, which were tabled in February 1986 and largely accepted, admitted no self-doubt: 'Whether the Report is successful in bringing about the desired objective must ultimately depend on how effectively its recommendations are implemented.' It commits Singapore's planners to forswear the 'rigidity' of an insulated political leadership manipulating a mixed economy through a dirigiste bureaucracy, and opt instead for greater openness to market forces.

Relations with Malaysia have deteriorated. There was a fracas late in January after the huge Pan-Electric Industries conglomerate collapsed and its boss, Tan Koon Swan, also President of the MCA, was charged with serious malpractice. When the Johor MCA threatened to retaliate and hinder renewal of a water supply contract between the two countries, Goh Chok Tong averred that

Postscript

the MCA was not in charge of Malaysia. His statement was called 'irresponsible' by the Malaysian Cabinet and drew a formal protest note.

Over and above this irritant, Malaysia's burgeoning internal problems are bound to affect Singapore. Musa Hitam has resigned from the Deputy Prime Ministership, and has been replaced by Ghafar Baba. As chapter 8 partly adumbrated, there are other indications that trouble lies in store for Dr Mahathir and his nation.

Besides a renewed bout of instability in Thailand, major regional concern has centred on the Philippines. Lee signalled his view of the drama there with an extraordinary letter to the chameleon Defence Secretary, Juan Ponce Enrile: casting him and General Ramos, not the people or even the Church, as the heroes, the letter implied relief that Marcos was gone and conviction that a woman President needed strong men with military resources if she were to 'put things right'.

The wisdom of cultivating Brunei is becoming more obvious by the month. Excess liquidity can be soaked up in Singapore investment and market rescues, and whatever the world price fluctuations Brunei's oil reserves provide feedstock for Singapore's manufacturing, refining and petrochemical industries.

For thirty years, more or less, PAP leaders stayed behind closed doors when they argued. Lately the process of power transfer and the stress of perceived circumstance have undermined this discipline. The fact that the crossfire of disagreement remains sporadic, muffled or punctuated by lulls seems to mean neither that the Prime Minister is straining to preserve solidarity nor that his junior colleagues are cowed into submission. More likely there is a moderating influence still at work, encouraging travel and other safety valves, urging each side to contain conflicts and delay head counts. All that can be said with certainty is that the old order has now gone beyond recall.

Abbreviations

ABL Anti-British League
ACS Anglo-Chinese School
ANZUK Australia, New Zealand and the United Kingdom (defence force)
ASEAN Association of Southeast Asian Nations
Barisan Barisan Sosialis (or Barisan Socialis in original spelling) = Socialist Front
B-G Brigadier-General
BMA British Military Administration
CCP Chinese Communist Party
CEC Central Executive Committee
CHOGM Commonwealth Heads of Government Meeting
CHOGRM Commonwealth Heads of Government Regional Meeting
CJA Council of Joint Action
CPF Central Provident Fund
CPM Communist Party of Malaya (also MCP)
DAP Democratic Action Party
DP Democratic Party
EDB Economic Development Board
HDB Housing and Development Board
HUDC Housing and Urban Development Corporation
IMP Independence of Malaya Party
INTRACO International Trading Company
ISC Internal Security Council
ISD Internal Security Department
LF Labour Front
LKY Lee Kuan Yew
Maphilindo a proposed grouping of the so-called Malay nations: Malaya, the Philippines and Indonesia
MCA Malayan/Malaysian Chinese Association
MCP Malayan Communist Party (also CPM)

MDU Malayan Democratic Union
MIC Malayan/Malaysian Indian Congress
MLA Member of the Legislative Assembly
MNP Malay Nationalist Party
MRT Mass Rapid Transit (transport system) planned for Singapore
MSC Malaysian Solidarity Convention
NAM Non-aligned movement
NBLU Naval Base Labour Union
NTUC National Trade Unions Congress
NU Nanyang University (also Nantah)
NUS National University of Singapore
NWC National Wages Council
PAP People's Action Party
PIEU Pioneer Industries' Employees' Union
PKI Communist Party of Indonesia
Plen (the) Plenipotentiary, LKY's cover name for Fang Chuang Pi, the high-ranking MCP cadre who negotiated through him with the PAP from 1958 to 1961
PP Progressive Party
PPP People's Progressive Party
PPSO Preservation of Public Security Ordinance
PSC Public Service Commission
RI Raffles Institution
RTS Radio and Television Singapore
SATU Singapore Association of Trade Unions
SBC Singapore Broadcasting Corporation
SCBA Straits Chinese British Association
SEATO Southeast Asian Treaty Organisation
SLP Singapore Labour Party
SPA Singapore People's Alliance
SU Singapore University
UDP United Democratic Party
UMNO United Malays' National Organisation
UPP United People's Party
ZOPFAN Zone of Peace, Friendship and Neutrality

Endnotes

Introduction
1 Singapore *Sunday Times*, 11 June 1984
2 R.M. Nixon *Leaders*, New York: Warner, 1982, p. 336
3 Kamarkar, MP, New Delhi, 3 September 1966

Chapter 1
1 LKY, broadcast, Singapore, 5 June 1959
2 LKY, off-the-cuff speech to the Royal Society of International Affairs, London, May 1962
3 LKY to People's Association, 21 July 1968
4 S. Rajaratnam, author's interview, 23 March 1976
5 LKY, closing speech to the Commonwealth Heads of Government Meeting (CHOGM), Singapore, 22 January 1971
6 LKY, interview with Gerald Stone, ABC-TV (Australia), July 1972
7 *Straits Times*, 29 March 1985
8 *Straits Times*, 24 December 1984
9 *Straits Times*, 20 December 1984
10 LKY, National Day rally, 14 August 1983
11 *Straits Times*, 11 August 1980
12 T.J.S. George, *Lee Kuan Yew's Singapore*, London: Andre Deutsch, 1973, p. 30
13 LKY, speech at Everton Park, Singapore, 8 November 1965
14 LKY, question and answer session with the press, Helsinki, 9 June 1971
15 Quoted in A. Josey, *Singapore: Its Past, Present and Future* Singapore: Andre Deutsch, 1979, p. 88
16 LKY, press conference, Indonesia, quoted in *Asiaweek*, 19 April 1985
17 Goh Keng Swee, author's interview, 3 October 1985
18 LKY, letter to Goh Keng Swee printed in *Straits Times*, 29 December 1984

19 Lim Kim San, author's interview, 1 April 1976
20 C.V. Devan Nair, 16 September 1973
21 Iain Buchanan, *Singapore in Southeast Asia* London: Bell, 1972, pp. 310–11

Chapter 2
1 LKY, *The Battle for Merger*, pp. 10–11
2 LKY, mass rally over Japanese blood debt, 25 August 1963
3 George, *op. cit.*, p. 23
4 *Ibid.*
5 LKY, mass rally, Singapore, 25 August 1963
6 T.H. Silcock, author's interview, 14 October 1982
7 LKY, *Petir*, Singapore: PAP, 1979, p. 31
8 George, *op. cit.*, p. 21
9 John Drysdale, *Singapore: Struggle for Success* Singapore: times, 1984 p. 20
10 George, *op. cit.*, pp. 23–4
11 LKY, Freedom of the City acceptance speech, London, 15 July 1982
12 Cited in A. Josey, *Lee Kuan Yew: The Struggle for Singapore* Sydney: Angus and Robertson, 1974 and 1976, p. 31
13 *Ibid.*, p. 32
14 *Ibid.*
15 A. Josey, *Reynolds News*, 1956 (no specific date visible on photocopy in files)
16 LKY, interview with Ludovic Kennedy, BBC-TV, 5 March 1977
17 LKY, *The Battle for Merger*, pp. 11–12
18 Cited in A. Josey, *Lee Kuan Yew: The Struggle for Singapore* Sydney: Angus and Robertson 1974 and 1976, pp. 32–3
19 Speech extensively excerpted in A. Josey *Lee Kuan Yew* Singapore: Donald Moore Press, 1968, pp. 30–36

Chapter 3
1 LKY, *The Battle for Merger*, p. 15
2 A. Josey, *Lee Kuan Yew* Singapore: Donald Moore Press, 1968, p. 47
3 Cited in Drysdale, *op. cit.*, p. 84
4 *Ibid.*, p. 36
5 LKY, *Petir*, Singapore: PAP, 1979, P. 33
6 *Ibid.*, p. 34
7 *Ibid.*, p. 34
8 *Ibid.*, p. 33
9 Yeo Kim Wah, *Political Development in Singapore 1945–55* Singapore: Singapore University Press, 1973, p. 119
10 LKY, *Petir*, Singapore: PAP, 1979, p. 31
11 Author's interview
12 LKY, *The Battle for Merger*, p. 18
13 Note the discussion of this matter in Richard Clutterbuck, *Riot and*

Revolution in Singapore and Malaya 1945-1963 London: Faber, 1973, p. 99
14 LKY, *Petir*, Singapore: PAP, 1979, pp. 31-2
15 *Straits Times*, 18 May 1954
16 Richard Harris, 'Portraits of our Time', BBC radio 17 May 1971
17 LKY, *Petir*, Singapore: PAP, 1979, p. 32
18 Report of Rendel Commission, February 1954, p. 35
19 LKY, *Petir*, Singapore: PAP, 1979, p. 32
20 *Ibid.*
21 Toh Chin Chye, *Petir*, Singapore: May 1960
22 Tunku Abdul Rahman, author's interview, 19 September 1975
23 LKY, *Petir*, Singapore: PAP, 1979, p. 31
24 The Manifesto is reproduced in Fong Sip Chee, *The PAP Story*, Singapore: Times Periodicals, 1979, pp. 15 ff
25 Rajaratnam, cited in Fong, *op.cit.*, p. 14
26 LKY, election rally, 20 December 1976
27 PAP 6th anniversary souvenir, 1960
28 LKY, *Straits Times*, 5 May 1955
29 Singapore Legislative Assembly Debates, 16 May 1955
30 *Ibid.*, 26 April 1955
31 *Ibid.*, 21 September 1955
32 *Ibid.*, 26 April 1955
33 *Ibid.*, 22 July 1955
34 James Puthucheary, author's interview, 5 November 1975
35 Singapore Legislative Assembly Debates, 4 October 1956
36 Toh Chin Chye, *Straits Times*, 29 November 1955
37 David Marshall, *ibid.*

Chapter 4
1 LKY, interview on BBC-TV, 5 March 1977; and many other times
2 LKY, *ibid.*, also Helsinki, 9 June 1971; and often
3 LKY, Canberra, 21 October 1976
4 LKY, Parliament, 23 Febuary 1977
5 *Ibid.*
6 The Speaker, George Oehlers, stopped the Chief Minister, Lim Yew Hock, as he was divulging these machinations (Singapore Legislative Assembly Debates, 4 March 1959). Lee's counter, 'a downright lie' (*ibid.*), need only be taken to mean that he and Lim did not see the Colonial Secretary, Alan Lennox-Boyd, *together*. See also LKY, Legislative Assembly Debates, 14 and 19 March 1959.
7 The words of a senior Singapore official, author's interview
8 Lim Yew Hock, Singapore Legislative Assembly Debates, 4 March 1959
9 A. Josey, *Singapore: Its Past, Present and Future* Singapore: Andre Deutsch, p. 24
10 LKY, Singapore Legislative Assembly Debates, 12 September 1957

11 LKY, *The Battle for Merger*, p. 17
12 *Ibid.*, p. 22
13 *Ibid.*, p. 17
14 Thomas Bellows, *The People's Action Party of Singapore*, Yale University: Southeast Asian Studies No. 14, pp. 24-8
15 *Ibid.*
16 *Ibid.*, p. 26
17 Cited by H.E. Wilson, *Social Engineering in Singapore*, Singapore University Press, 1978, p. 216
18 Stated in Clutterbuck, *op. cit.*, p. 137
19 *Ibid.*, p. 141
20 LKY, *Straits Times*, 7 June 1957
21 *Ibid.*, 22 August 1957
22 *Straits Times*, 21 December 1957
23 W.A. Hanna, *Sequel to Colonialism* New York: American Universities Field Staff, 1965, pp. 71, 74
24 LKY, *The Battle for Merger*, p. 26
25 *Ibid.*
26 A.C. Brackman, *Southeast Asia's Second Front* New York: Praeger, 1966, p. 26
27 LKY, *The Battle for Merger*, p. 22
28 *Ibid.*, p. 23
29 *Ibid.*
30 *Ibid.*, p. 30
31 LKY, *Straits Times*, 19 May 1959
32 *Ibid.*
33 LKY made this point in a speech to foreign correspondents, Singapore, 16 September 1959
34 LKY, *Straits Times*, 12 May 1959

Chapter 5
1 Fong, *op. cit.*, p. 77
2 LKY, quoted by Alan Blades and cited by Clutterbuck, *op. cit.*, p. 293
3 LKY, *The Battle for Merger*, p. 24
4 LKY, press interview, 30 August 1965
5 Cited in Hanna, *op. cit.*, p.177
6 Bellows, *op. cit.*, p. 37
7 LKY, Singapore Legislative Assembly Debates, 3 August 1960
8 LKY, *The Battle for Merger*, p. 41
9 *Ibid.*
10 Tunku Abdul Rahman, *Straits Times*, 1 February 1961
11 LKY, *Straits Times*, 31 March 1961
12 M.N. Sopiee, *From Malayan Union to Singapore Separation*, Kuala Lumpur: Penerbit Universiti Malaya, 1974, p. 140
13 *Ibid.*, p. 141
14 LKY, *The Battle for Merger*, pp. 35-6
15 *Ibid.*, p. 37

16 *Ibid.*, p. 43
17 *Ibid.*, p. 35
18 LKY, *Straits Times*, 22 July 1961
19 James Puthucheary's mocking description in a letter to the editor of the *Straits Times*, 21 August 1961
20 C.M. Turnbull, *A History of Singapore 1819–1975*, Kuala Lumpur: Oxford University Press, 1977, p. 294, note 30
21 Goh Keng Swee, author's interview, 31 October 1975
22 Pang Cheng Lian *Singapore's People's Action Party*, Singapore: Oxford University Press, 1971, pp. 14–15
23 Goh Keng Swee, cited by LKY at valedictory dinner August 1981 and reported in *Straits Times* 15 March 1982
24 LKY, radio broadcast, 26 July 1961
25 LKY, speech to parliamentarians, 21 July 1961
26 LKY, *The Battle for Merger*, p. 67
27 S.V. Lingam, who had defected to Ong Eng Guan in 1960, left Ong's United People's Party and returned to the PAP 'not of his own volition nor of his own free will' (Fong, *op. cit.*, p. 119)
28 LKY, Legislative Assembly, quoted by Hanna, *The Formation of Malaysia* New York: American Universities Field Staff, 1964, p. 117

Chapter 6
1 LKY, press conference, 9 August 1962
2 LKY to civil servants, 14 June 1962
3 LKY, press conference, 9 August 1962
4 LKY, 28 September 1962
5 LKY, interview with Hylda Bamber, 13 March 1965
6 LKY, *Straits Budget* (newspaper), 3 July 1963
7 Goh Keng Swee, author's interview, 31 October 1975
8 LKY, *Straits Times*, 4 February 1963
9 Elwyn Jones QC, *Straits Times*, 30 August 1963
10 LKY, *Straits Times*, 10 August 1963
11 LKY, 3 September 1963
12 LKY, *Petir*, Singapore: PAP, 1979, p. 35
13 LKY quoted by F.L. Starner in K.J. Ratnam and R.S. Milne, *The Malayan Parliamentary Election of 1964*, Singapore: University of Malaya Press, 1964, p. 331
14 See the *Straits Times* election issues of September 1963
15 LKY, eve-of-poll broadcast, 20 September 1963
16 PAP election manifesto, cited by F.L. Starner in Ratnam and Milne, *op. cit.*, p. 346
17 LKY, eve of poll broadcast, 20 September 1963
18 LKY, Singapore Legislative Assembly Debates, 1 August 1963
19 LKY: September in Ratnam and Milne *op. cit.* pp. 23–4; December in A. Josey, *Lee Kuan Yew* (revised edition) Singapore: Donald Moore Press 1971, pp. 198–9
20 Fong, *op. cit.*, p. 123

21 LKY, *Straits Times*, 19 September 1963
22 LKY, *Dewan Ra'ayat* (Malaysian lower House of Parliament), 21 December 1963
23 LKY, 17 October 1965 and August 1981 (reported in *Straits Times*, 15 March 1982). See also Chan Heng Chee, *Singapore: the Politics of Survival*, Singapore, Oxford University Press, 1971, p. 10
24 S. Rajaratnam, *Straits Times*, 18 January 1964. LKY left Singapore on 20 January 1964
25 Tunku Abdul Rahman, author's interview, 19 September 1975
26 LKY to university members, 20 May 1964
27 LKY, *Straits Times*, 27 April 1964
28 LKY to Cantonese and other civic organisations, 14 March 1964
29 LKY, rally at Jinjang, West Malaysia, 5 April 1964
30 LKY, *Sin Chew Jit Poh* (newspaper), 6 April 1964; cited in Ratnam and Milne, *op. cit.*, p. 150
31 Socialist Front regarding LKY, *Malay Mail* (newspaper), 28 March 1964. The comparison of Rajaratnam to Goebbels is in *Sin Chew Jit Poh*, 28 March 1964
32 Tan Siew Sin, *Sunday Mail* (newspaper), 29 March 1964
33 Quoted in Ratnam and Milne, *op. cit.*, p. 143
34 *Ibid.*, p. 151 note and p. 147
35 Tunku Abdul Rahman, *Sunday Times*, 15 March 1964
36 LKY, *Straits Times*, 25 April 1964
37 M.N. Sopiee, *From Malayan Union to Singapore Separation*, p. 193
38 Khir Johari, quoted *ibid.*, p. 225 footnote 202
39 Tunku Abdul Rahman, *Sunday Times*, 18 April 1965

Chapter 7
1 Tunku Abdul Rahman, *Straits Times*, 7 September 1964
2 Sopiee, *op. cit.*, p. 195
3 *Ibid.*, p. 197
4 Toh Chin Chye, *Straits Times*, 2 November 1964
5 Tunku Abdul Rahman, cited in Sopiee, *op. cit.*, p. 199
6 LKY, quoted by A. Josey *Lee Kuan Yew* (revised edition), Singapore: Donald Moore Press, 1971, pp. 235–6
7 Tunku Abdul Rahman, *Straits Times*, 8 March 1965
8 Tunku Abdul Rahman, *Straits Times*, 3 March 1965
9 Tunku Abdul Rahman, *Straits Times*, 12 June 1965
10 LKY, 13 September 1965, cited in A. Josey *Lee Kuan Yew* (revised edition), Singapore: Donald Moore Press, 1971, p. 271
11 Tunku Abdul Rahman, *The Star* (newspaper), 9 April 1975
12 S. Rajaratnam, quoted in A. Josey, *Lee Kuan Yew*, Singapore: Donald Moore Press, 1968, p. 405
13 *Ibid.* p. 415
14 LKY, press conference, 9 August 1965
15 LKY, quoted in A. Josey, *Lee Kuan Yew*, Singapore, Donald Moore Press, 1968, p. 421

16 e.g. Bellows, *op. cit.*, especially pp. 52-66; Noel Barber. *The Singapore Story*, London: Fontana, pp. 183-7.
17 Dennis Bloodworth, *The Chinese Looking Glass*, London: Secker & Warburg, 1967, pp. 256-7
18 A. Josey, *Lee Kuan Yew* (revised edition), Singapore: Donald Moore Press, 1971, p. 608
19 LKY, press conference, 9 August 1965
20 *Ibid.*
21 LKY, 12 August 1965
22 LKY, 14 August 1965
23 LKY, 1 September 1965
24 LKY, 26 August 1965
25 LKY, 11 August 1965
26 LKY, 30 August 1965
27 LKY to Malaysian and Singaporean students, London, 22 April 1966, quoted in A. Josey, *Lee Kuan Yew*, Singapore: Donald Moore Press 1968 p. 465
28 LKY, 14 August 1965
29 Alan Blades, quoted in Richard Clutterbuck *Riot and Revolution*, p. 162
30 LKY, 11 December 1965
31 LKY, 8 November 1965
32 LKY, 13 September 1965
33 LKY, 30 August 1965
34 LKY, 5 November 1967
35 Lim Kim San, author's interview, 1 April 1976
36 LKY, Raffles Institution, 6 June 1969
37 LKY, August 1981 valedictory dinner speech in *Straits Times*, 15 March 1982
38 *Ibid.*
39 Toh Chin Chye, *Petir*, Singapore: 1979, p. 29
40 LKY, rally, 8 August 1966

Chapter 8
1 See Creighton Burns (formerly Southeast Asian correspondent of the Melbourne *Age*) cited in R. Tiffen *The News from Southeast Asia* Singapore: ISEAS 1978 pp. 140-1
2 LKY, university seminar, 9 October 1966
3 LKY, interview in *Asian Wall Street Journal*, 9 February 1979
4 LKY, 22 October 1965
5 LKY, quoted in *Far Eastern Economic Review*, 16 October, 1981
6 LKY to American Association, Singapore, 10 November 1967
7 See Lee Khoon Choy *An Ambassador's Journey* Singapore: Times Publications, 1983, pp. 213-20
8 A point made by Harold Crouch in his ASEAN political study *Domestic Political Structures and Regional Economic Co-operation*, Singapore: ISEAS, 1984, pp. 95-6

9 S. Rajaratnam, *Straits Times*, 16 December 1970
10 LKY, speech 'We want to be ourselves', Singapore: Ministry of Culture, 1966, p. 9
11 LKY, Commonwealth Heads of Government Meeting (CHOGM), Lusaka, Zambia, 1 August 1979
12 LKY, A. Josey *Lee Kuan Yew*, Singapore: Donald Moore Press 1968, p. 428
13 LKY, 21 October 1965
14 Toh Chin Chye, interview in *Asiaweek*, 7 September 1984
15 LKY, 7 June 1966, quoted by G.P. Means, *Malaysian Politics* London: London University Press 1971, p. 365
16 For a report on the Prime Ministers' Conference, see *Sunday Times* (London), 13 September 1966
17 LKY, CHOGM, Lusaka, 1 August 1979
18 LKY, TV interview with four foreign correspondents, Singapore, 5 November 1967
19 LKY, 16 September 1973
20 LKY, 12 May 1975
21 LKY, ASEAN Summit, Bali, 23 February 1976
22 LKY to acting Prime Minister of Malaysia, 14 January 1976
23 LKY, A. Josey *Lee Kuan Yew* vol. 2 Singapore; Times Books International, 1980, pp. 298–302. See also C.V. Devan Nair (ed.) *Socialism that Works* Singapore: Federal Publications, 1976
24 LKY, TV interview taped 25 September 1967
25 e.g. *Time* magazine, 25 January 1982, p. 11
26 LKY, CHOGM Melbourne, 2 October 1981
27 LKY, press conference, London, 21 June 1979
28 S. Dhanabalan, *Straits Times*, 8 November 1983
29 S. Rajaratnam in a pamphlet, cited in *Asiaweek*, 25 March 1983
30 LKY, CHOGM Melbourne, 1 October 1981
31 LKY, interview with Padraic Fallon of *Euromoney* magazine, 2 May 1978

Chapter 9

1 LKY to PAP MPs, 17 November 1981
2 Goh Chok Tong, interview quoted in feature by Michael Richardson, Melbourne *Age*, 18 July 1985
3 Goh Chok Tong, *Straits Times*, 4 November 1984
4 LKY to PAP Conference, 7 December 1980, reported in *Straits Times*, 25 March 1981
5 LKY to PAP Conference, 15 November 1982, reported in *Straits Times*, 27 December 1982
6 *Ibid.*
7 *Ibid.*
8 LKY, 7 December 1980, in *Straits Times*, 25 March 1981
9 LKY, 15 November 1982, in *Straits Times*, 27 December 1982
10 LKY, 7 December 1980, in *Straits Times*, 25 March 1981

11 For his MA thesis on Lee Kuan Yew, the author ran a check to ascertain the most probable voting behaviour of each member of the 1959 CEC (listed by Fong, *op. cit.* It emerged that Madam Chan almost certainly voted for Ong Eng Guan)
12 Reproduced in the *Asia Research Bulletin*, Singapore, 31 December 1982, p. 997
13 LKY, Parliament, 25 July 1984
14 *Ibid.*
15 Goh Chok Tong, *Straits Times*, 29 September 1984
16 LKY, Parliament, 25 July 1984
17 LKY, quoted in the *Bulletin* magazine (Sydney), 16 September 1972
18 Teh Cheang Wan quoted in the *Far Eastern Economic Review*, 11 April 1985
19 Poh Soo Kai, interview with Bill Gray, Melbourne *Herald*, 11 September 1982
20 Said Zahari quoted in the *Far Eastern Economic Review*, 14 September 1979
21 R.E. Gamer *The Politics of Urban Development in Singapore*, Ithaca: Cornell, 1974, p. 82
22 LKY, Canberra, 21 October 1976
23 LKY, 26 April 1967
24 Raj K. Vasil, *Governing Singapore* Singapore: Eastern Universities Press, 1984, p. 137
25 LKY, 15 July 1972
26 Report in the Melbourne *Age*, 20 April 1982
27 LKY, 1982 Courtesy Campaign, 29 June 1982
28 LKY quoted in feature by Michael Richardson, Melbourne *Age*, 28 May 1982
29 Lee Hsien Loong, speech excerpted in *Australian Financial Review*, 12 August 1985
30 LKY, interview with *Asahi Shimbun* correspondent, 5 January 1981
31 LKY, National Day rally, 15 August 1967
32 LKY, National Day rally, 17 August 1980

Chapter 10
1 Lee Soo Ann 'The economic system' in Riaz Hassan (ed.) *Singapore: Society in Transition* Kuala Lumpur: Oxford University Press, 1976, p. 3
2 LKY, interview with Takuhiko Tsuruta of *Nihon Keizai Shimbun*, 25 November 1981
3 Augustine Tan, MP, quoted in *Far Eastern Economic Review*, 25 April 1985
4 Dennis Bloodworth *An Eye for the Dragon* Harmondsworth: Penguin, 1975, p. 324
5 Goh Keng Swee, Parliament, quoted in *Far Eastern Economic Review*, 9 February 1984
6 Cited by Saw Swee Hock in Chapter 5 of You Poh Seng and Lim

Chong Yah (eds) *Singapore: 25 Years of Development*, Singapore: Nan Yang Xing Zhou Lianhe Zaobao, 1984, p. 146
7 LKY, National Day rally, 19 August 1984
8 LKY, 10 December 1962
9 Quek Shi Lei, quoted in A. Josey *Singapore: Its Past, Present and Future*, Singapore: Andre Deutsch, 1979, pp. 62–3
10 LKY, 31 January 1971
11 A. Josey *Lee Kuan Yew: The Struggle for Singapore* Sydney: Angus and Robertson 1974 and 1976, p. 115
12 D.J. Enright, *Memoirs of a Mendicant Professor* London: Chatto and Windus, 1969, p. 127
13 LKY to university staff, 20 May 1980
14 LKY, Parliament, 23 February 1977
15 Goh Keng Swee to Singapore Teachers' Union, 26 July 1975
16 '*Report on the Ministry of Education 1978*' Singapore, 1979, p. 51
17 *Ibid.*, p. iii
18 LKY, seminar with principals on education, 24 January 1979
19 '*Report on the Ministry of Education 1978*', Singapore, 1979, p. vi.
20 '*Report on Moral Education*' Singapore, 1979, p. iii
21 LKY, opening of new Polytechnic, 7 July 1979
22 LKY, National Day rally, 19 August 1979
23 LKY, *Straits Times*, 24 November 1979
24 LKY to university staff, 20 May 1980
25 LKY, *Straits Times*, 11 March 1980
26 LKY, *Straits Times*, 2 April 1980
27 Mahbubani Kishore, *Singapore Undergrad*, 10 June 1969
28 LKY, 20 May 1980
29 LKY, 24 January 1979
30 Rayson Huang, cited in article by NU graduate journalist, *Straits Times*, 14 March 1980
31 LKY, 5 January 1979
32 Goh Keng Swee, *Straits Times*, 27 December 1982
33 *Ibid.*
34 Goh Keng Swee, *Straits Times*, 29 December 1982
35 Goh Keng Swee, 1 March 1976
36 LKY, National Day rally, 17 August 1975

Chapter 11
1 A.P. Rajah and LKY, Singapore Legislative Assembly Debates, 11 December 1959
2 LKY, 26 March 1980
3 Goh Keng Swee *The Economics of Modernization*, Singapore: Asia Pacific Press, 1972, p. vii
4 LKY, 26 March 1980
5 LKY, 30 September 1974
6 E.W. Barker quoted in *Straits Times*, 23 April 1983
7 LKY, state dinner, Tanzania, 5 September 1970

8 George Thomson, author's interview, 16 October 1975
9 LKY, Parliament, 20 December 1983
10 LKY, Parliament, 22 December 1983
11 LKY, Parliament, 23 February 1977
12 A. Josey, *Lee Kuan Yew: The Struggle for Singapore*, Sydney: Angus and Robertson 1974 and 1976, p. 34
13 *Ibid.*, i.e., David Marshall, pp. 132 ff; Thio Su Mien, pp. 237 ff
14 LKY, state dinner, Singapore, 16 October 1978
15 LKY, CHOGRM, Fiji, 14 October 1982
16 LKY, state dinner, 4 May 1983
17 LKY, state dinner, 14 August 1977
18 LKY, 21 July 1968
19 LKY, 24 November 1966
20 LKY, 19 January 1977
21 LKY to Institute of Directors, London, 2 November 1971
22 LKY to Parliamentarians, Canberra, 21 October 1976
23 LKY, 14 June 1962
24 LKY, 8 November 1967
25 LKY to British Labour Party, Scarborough, 10 October 1967
26 LKY, Parliament, 16 March 1976
27 LKY, quoted in A. Josey, *Lee Kuan Yew* (revised edn) Singapore: Donald Moore Press, 1971, p. 497
28 Kenneth Burke, *Permanence and Change*, New Jersey: Prentice-Hall, 1977, p. 115 footnote

Chapter 12

1 LKY, interview with Crocker Snow Jr, Boston *Globe Sunday Magazine*, 1968, quoted in A. Josey, *Lee Kuan Yew: The Struggle for Singapore* Sydney: Angus and Robertson, 1974 and 1976, p. 50
2 LKY, Singapore Legislative Assembly Debates, 4 October 1956
3 LKY, *ibid.*, 19 March 1959
4 The Malaysians acted through Senator Khaw Kai Boh, formerly of Singapore's Special Branch. See Bloodworth, *op. cit.*, p. 348
5 LKY, *Petir*, Singapore 1979, p. 35
6 D. Marshall, Singapore Legislative Assembly Debates, 10 January 1957
7 LKY, TV press conference, Singapore, 5 March 1965
8 LKY to Malaysian students, Sydney, 20 March 1965
9 LKY, Parliament, 23 February 1977
10 LKY, trial of J.B. Jeyaretnam, December 1978
11 Lee Chin Koon, interview printed in *Straits Times*, 9 January 1971
12 LKY, interview with Ludovic Kennedy, BBC-TV, 5 March 1977
13 LKY, National Day rally, 8 August 1966
14 Juan Gatbonton, cited in George, *op. cit.*, p. 157
15 LKY, *Petir*, Singapore PAP. 1979, p. 40
16 Richard Nixon, White House dinner, Washington, 10 April 1973
17 Lim Kim San, author's interview, 1 April 1976
18 C. Northcote Parkinson, *A Law Unto Themselves*, London: John

Murray, 1966 p. 141
19 A. Josey *Lee Kuan Yew* (revised edition) Singapore: Donald Moore Press, 1971 p. 25
20 A. Josey *Lee Kuan Yew: The Struggle for Singapore*, Sydney: Angus and Robertson 1974 and 1976, p. 36
21 LKY, interview with Gerald Stone, ABC-TV (Australia), July 1972
22 LKY, *The Battle for Merger*, p. 12
23 George, *op. cit.*, p. 17
24 Mrs Lee Chin Koon (Chua Jim Neo) told a reporter: 'My mother tongue is Malay' (Melbourne *Herald*, 14 September 1976)
25 Mrs Lee Chin Koon, *ibid.*
26 LKY to Old Rafflesians, 29 June 1960
27 LKY, 28 July 1973
28 LKY, 29 August 1966
29 See J.D. Barber *The Presidential Character*, New Jersey: Prentice Hall, 1977
30 See E.H. Erikson *Young Man Luther* London: Faber, 1959, and *Gandhi's Truth* London: Faber, 1970
31 See the writings of Graham Little, particularly 'Leaders, followers and the self', an unpublished paper for the Conference on the Psychohistorical Meaning of Leadership, Chicago, 1980
32 Burke, *op. cit.*, p. 20
33 Heinz Kohut, 'Thoughts on narcissism and narcissistic rage', reprinted from *The Psychoanalytic Study of the Child*, vol. 27, New York Times Book Company, 1972
34 A.F. Davies, *Political Passions*, Melbourne Political Monograph No. 3, no date, p. 23

Chapter 13
1 LKY, Chinese New Year reception, 23 January 1982
2 Lee Hsien Yang is interviewed by the book's compiler, Major Leong Choon Cheong, and the resultant portrait appears on pp. 185–92
3 Quoted in A. Josey, *Lee Kuan Yew* vol. 2, Singapore; Times Books International, 1980, p. 532
4 LKY, 21 December 1972
5 LKY, *Petir* (1979), pp. 37–8
6 Ernest S. Wolf, 'Recent advances in the psychology of the self', reprinted from *Comprehensive Psychiatry*, Chicago: Grune & Stratton, vol. 17, No. 1 (Jan/Feb), 1976
7 Yusof Ishak, quoted in the *Mirror*, Singapore Ministry of Culture, 10 January 1966
8 LKY with Creighton Burns (Melbourne *Age*), Nihal Singh (New Delhi *Statesman*) and Dennis Bloodworth (London *Observer*), TV Singapura, 28 July 1966
9 S. Rajaratnam, author's interview, 31 March 1976
10 LKY, National Day rally, 15 August 1971
11 LKY, 5 June 1972

12 Lee Hsien Loong, April 1985 lecture, quoted in the *Australian Financial Review*, 12 August 1985
13 Lee Hsien Loong, *ibid*.
14 LKY, ASEAN Foreign Ministers' meeting, Singapore, 14 June 1982
15 LKY, inauguration of 1982 Courtesy Campaign, 29 June 1982
16 LKY, Helsinki, 10 June 1971
17 Lee Hsien Loong, *Australian Financial Review*, 12 August 1985
18 D. Marshall, *Straits Times*, 9 September 1984
19 S. Rajaratnam, quoted in *Asiaweek*, 30 August 1985
20 LKY, National Press Club, Washington, quoted by Nayan Chanda in *Far Eastern Economic Review*, 24 October 1985
21 Goh Chok Tong, *Bulletin*, Singapore Ministry of Culture, August 1985
22 Goh Chok Tong, quoted in *Asiaweek*, 6 September 1985

Bibliography

Apart from seventy or so interviews the author conducted between 1975 and 1985 (including the brief session with Lee Kuan Yew recorded in Chapter 1), this book is primarily based on the Singapore Prime Minister's own words. The public dossier of his speeches, press conferences, interviews, briefings, statements, press releases and dialogues is now on view at those of Singapore's major libraries with archival facilities. The author has also made use of video and sound tapes, transcripts of parliamentary proceedings, newspapers, magazines and occasional publications.
Listed below are the documents that have been of special importance as sources or references.

BOOKS AND BOOKLETS

Amin, M. and Caldwell, M. (1977) *Malaya: The Making of a Neo-Colony* London: Spokesman
Amnesty International (1980) *Report of Mission to Singapore 1978* London: Amnesty
Barber, J.D. (1977) *The Presidential Character* New Jersey: Prentice Hall
Barber, N. (1978) *The Singapore Story* Glasgow: Fontana/Collins
Bellows, T.J. (1970) *The People's Action Party of Singapore* Yale University, Southeast Asian Studies No. 14
Bloodworth, D. (1967) *Chinese Looking Glass* London: Secker and Warburg
—— (1975) *An Eye for the Dragon* Harmondsworth: Penguin
Brackman, A.C. (1966) *Southeast Asia's Second Front* New York: Praeger
Buchanan, I. (1972) *Singapore in Southeast Asia* London: Bell
Burke, K. (1935) *Permanence and Change* New Jersey: Prentice Hall
Chan Heng Chee (1971) *Singapore: The Politics of Survival* Singapore: Oxford University Press
—— (1976) *The Dynamics of One-Party Dominance* Singapore University Press

—— (1984) *A Sensation of Independence* Kuala Lumpur: Oxford University Press
Cheah Boon Kheng (1979) *The Masked Comrades* Singapore: Times Books International
Chen, P.S.J. ed. (1983) *Singapore: Development Policies and Trends* Kuala Lumpur: Oxford University Press
Clammer, J. (1985) *Singapore: Ideology Society Culture* Singapore: Chopmen
Clutterbuck, R. (1973) *Riot and Revolution in Singapore and Malaya 1945–1963* London: Faber, substantially revised as (1985) *Conflict and Violence in Singapore and Malaysia 1945–1983* Singapore: Graham Brash
Crouch, H., Lee Kam Hing and Ong, M. eds (1980) *Malaysian Politics and the 1978 Elections* Kuala Lumpur: Oxford University Press
Crouch, H. (1980) *Domestic Political Structures and Regional Economic Co-operation* Singapore: Institute of Southeast Asian Studies (ISEAS) Economic Research Unit, ASEAN Political Studies
Davies, A.F. (1973) *Politics as Work* Melbourne [University] Political Monograph No. 1
—— (no date) *Political Passions* Melbourne [University] Political Monograph No. 3
Devan Nair, C.V. ed. *Socialism that Works* Singapore: Federal Publications
—— (1982) *Not by Wages Alone* Singapore National Trades Union Congress
Drysdale, J. (1984) *Singapore: Struggle for Success* Singapore: Times Books International
Enright, D.J. (1969) *Memoirs of a Mendicant Professor* London: Chatto and Windus
Erikson, E.H. (1959) *Young Man Luther* London: Faber
—— (1970) *Gandhi's Truth* London: Faber
Fletcher, N.McH. (1969) *The Separation of Singapore from Malaysia* Ithaca: Cornell, Data Paper No. 73
Fong Sip Chee (1979) *The PAP Story; The Pioneering Years* Singapore: Times Periodicals
Gamer, R.E. (1974) *The Politics of Urban Development in Singapore* Ithaca: Cornell
George, T.J.S. (1973) *Lee Kuan Yew's Singapore* London: Andre Deutsch
Goh Keng Swee (1972) *The Economics of Modernization* Singapore: Asia Pacific Press
—— (1977) *The Practice of Economic Growth* Singapore: Federal Publications
—— and team (1979) *Report on the Ministry of Education 1978* Singapore Government
Hanna, W.A. (1964) *The Formation of Malaysia* New York: American Universities Field Staff
—— (1965) *Sequel to Colonialism* New York: American Universities Field Staff

Bibliography

—— (1968) *Success and Sobriety* New York: American Universities Field Staff Reports (Southeast Asia Series) vol. XVI No. 3 'Personalities without a Cult' and No. 4 'The Privacy of the Prime Minister'
Hussan, R. ed. (1976) *Singapore: A Society in Transition* Kuala Lumpur: Oxford University Press
Hon, J. (1985) *Relatively Speaking* Singapore: Times Books International
Indorf, H.H. (1984) *Impediments to Regionalism in Southeast Asia* Singapore: ISEAS Economic Research Unit, ASEAN Political Studies
Josey, A. (1968) *Lee Kuan Yew* Singapore: Donald Moore Press
—— (1971) *Lee Kuan Yew* (revised edition) Singapore: Donald Moore Press
—— (1974) *Lee Kuan Yew: The Struggle for Singapore* Sydney: Angus and Robertson [revised edition (1976) adding material on Lee Kuan Yew's views of the success of communist takeovers in Indo-China]
—— (1979) *Singapore: Its Past, Present and Future* Singapore: Andre Deutsch
—— (1980) *Lee Kuan Yew* (vol. 2) Singapore: Times Books International
van der Kroef, J. (1970) *Communism in Malaysia and Singapore* The Hague: Martinus Nijhoff
—— (1981) *Communism in South-East Asia* London: Macmillan
Lee Khoon Choy (1983) *An Ambassador's Journey* Singapore: Times Books International
Lee Kuan Yew (no date) *The Battle for Merger* Singapore: Ministry of Culture
—— (1965) *The Battle for a Malaysian Malaysia* Singapore: Ministry of Culture, Parts 1 and 2
—— (1965) *Malaysia—Age of Revolution* Singapore: Ministry of Culture
—— (1965) *Towards a Malaysian Malaysia* Singapore: Ministry of Culture
—— (1965) *Malaysia Comes of Age* Singapore: Ministry of Culture
Lee Ting Hui (1976) *The Communist Organization in Singapore* Singapore: ISEAS Field Report No. 2
Leong Choon Cheong (1978) *Youth in the Army* Singapore: Federal Publications
McKie, R. (1963) *Malaysia in Focus* Sydney: Angus and Robertson
Mahathir bin Mohamad (1970) *The Malay Dilemma* Singapore: Donald Moore Press
Marshall, D.S. (1971) *Singapore's Struggle for Nationhood 1945–1959* Singapore: Universities Education Press
Means, G.P. (1970) *Malaysian Politics* London: University of London Press
Milne, R.S. and Mauzy, D.K. (1978) *Politics and Government in Malaysia* Singapore: Federal Publications/ISEAS
Ministry of Culture ed. (1965) *Separation* Singapore: Ministry of Culture
Nixon, R.M. (1982) *Leaders* New York: Warner Books
Osborne, M. (1964) *Singapore and Malaysia* Ithaca: Cornell, Data Paper No. 53 (Southeast Asia Program)
Ong Teng Cheong and committee (1979) *Report on Moral Education*

Singapore Government
Pang Cheng Lian (1971) *Singapore's People's Action Party* Singapore: Oxford University Press
PAP CEC or Central Editorial Board (1959) *The Tasks Ahead* Parts I and II Singapore
—— (1960) *Sixth Anniversary Souvenir*
—— (1964) *Tenth Anniversary Souvenir*
—— (1979) *Petir—Twenty-fifth Anniversary Souvenir*
Parkinson, C.N. (1966) *A Law Unto Themselves* London: John Murray
Pritt, D.N. (1966) *Autobiography (vol. III) The Defence Accuses* London: Lawrence and Wishart
Ratnam, K.J. and Milne, R.S. (1967) *The Malayan Parliamentary Election of 1964* Singapore: University of Malaya Press
Rendel, G. (Chairman) (1954) *Report of Constitutional Commission* Singapore
Smith, J.B. (1976) *Portrait of a Cold Warrior* New York: Putnam
Sopiee, M.N. (1974) *From Malayan Union to Singapore Separation* Kuala Lumpur: Penerbit Universiti Malaya
Stenson, M.R. (1970) *Industrial Conflict in Malaya* London: Oxford University Press
—— (1980) *Class, Race and Colonialism in West Malaysia* Brisbane: University of Queensland Press
Thio Chan Bee (1977) *Extraordinary Adventures of an Ordinary Man* London: Grosvenor
Thomas, F. (1972) *Memoirs of a Migrant* Singapore: Universities Education Press
Tiffen, R. (1978) *The News from Southeast Asia: The Sociology of Newsmaking* Singapore: ISEAS
Toffler, A. (1980) *The Third Wave* London: Collins
Tunku Abdul Rahman (1969) *May 13th Before and After* Kuala Lumpur
—— (1978) *Viewpoints* Kuala Lumpur: Heinemann
Turnbull, C.M. (1977) *A History of Singapore 1819–1975* Kuala Lumpur: Oxford University Press
Vasil, R.K. (1979) *Public Service Unionism* Singapore: Times Books International
—— (1984) *Governing Singapore* Singapore: Eastern Universities Press
Wilson, H.E. (1978) *Social Engineering in Singapore* Singapore University Press
Yeo Kim Wah (1973) *Political Development in Singapore 1945–1955* Singapore University Press
You Poh Seng and Lim Chong Yah, eds (1984) *Singapore: Twenty-Five Years of Development* Singapore: Nan Yang Xing Zhou Lianhe Zaobao

ARTICLES, DISSERTATIONS AND ACADEMIC EXERCISES

Koh Tat Boon (1973), The University of Singapore Socialist Club, academic exercise, Department of History, University of Singapore

Kohut, H. (1972) 'Thoughts on narcissism and narcissistic rage', reprinted from *The Psychoanalytic Study of the Child*, vol. 27, New York Times Book Company

Little, G. (1980) 'Leaders, followers and the self', paper for conference on 'The Psychohistorical Meaning of Leadership', Chicago

Minchin, J.B. (1980) 'Patriot of the will: Lee Kuan Yew,' MA thesis, University of Melbourne

Peritz, R. (1964) 'The evolving politics of Singapore: A study of trends and Issues', PhD dissertation, University of Pennsylvania

Sweeney, G. (1973) 'Political parties in Singapore 1945–1955,' MA thesis, University of Hull

Wilairat, K. (1975) 'Singapore's foreign policy: A study of the foreign policy system of a city-state', PhD dissertation, Georgetown University, Washington, DC

Wolf, E.S. (1976) 'Recent advances in the psychology of the self', reprinted from *Comprehensive Psychology*, Chicago: Grune and Stratton, vol. 17, No. 1 (Jan/Feb)

NEWSPAPERS AND PERIODICALS

Singapore (from 1945–85)
Straits Times, Sunday Times, Singapore Free Press, Singapore Standard, Straits Budget, New Nation, Monitor, Petir (PAP), *Plebeian/Plebeian Express* (Barisan Sosialis), *Mirror* (originally *Malaysian Mirror*), *Bulletin, Singapore Undergrad, Asia Research Bulletin, Perjuangan* (NTUC), *Bakti* (civil service)

Malaysia
Straits Times and *New Straits Times, Straits Echo. The Star*

Foreign
The Times (London), *Sunday Times* (London), *Financial Times* (London), *Guardian* (Manchester)
Far Eastern Economic Review (Hong Kong) [including the late Richard Hughes' featured column], *Asiaweek* (Hong Kong)
Age (Melbourne) *Herald* (Melbourne) [including Denis Warner's syndicated column], *Australian Financial Review* (Sydney), *Bulletin* (Sydney)

Extensive use was made of the Singapore Legislative Assembly Debates (1955–65), the proceedings of the Singapore Parliament (1965–85) and the proceedings of the Malaysian lower house, the *Dewan Ra'ayat* or *Dewan Rakyat* [People's House] (1963–65).

Index

References to chapters rather than page numbers indicate frequent occurrence of the index item specified

Africa (including southern Africa) 130, 164, 195
Afro–Asia 180
Ahmad Ibrahim 75f, 19ff
Ahmad Mattar 214
Alliance (Malaysia) [made up of UMNO, MCA and Malayan/Malaysian Indian Congress] Chs. 6–7
Alliance (Singapore) 76, 133
Anson (parliamentary constituency) 110ff, 199, 205
Anti-British League (ABL) 54, 62ff, 69
ANZUK (Australia, New Zealand and United Kingdom defence force) 182
ANZUS (Australia, New Zealand and United States alliance) 193
ASEAN (Association of Southeast Asian Nations) xvii, 14, Ch. 8, 227, 243, 332, 339
Australia and Australians 145, 159f, 165f, 181f, 189f, 193, 212, 228, 245, 339
Azahari, (Sheikh) A.M. 57, 127

Baker, Maurice 173
Babas *see* Chinese Straits-born (Babas)
Bandung Conference 180
Bangladesh 15, 193, 244
Bani, S.T. 132
Bank Bumiputra 173
Barber, Noel xii
Barisan Sosialis = Barisan Socialis

[Socialist Front] 118ff, 125ff, 200, 215f, 241, 293
Barker, E.W. (Eddie) 13, 173, 202, 278
Bellows, Thomas xii, 88
Berita Harian 56, 232
Blades, Alan 63, 109
Bloodworth, Dennis xii, 155, 244, 276
Bose, Subhas Chandra ('Netaji') 32
Boyd, (Viscount) Alan Lennox 79, 82ff, 347 endnote 6
Briggs, Sir Harold 53
Britain and the British (including references to London, Westminister and Whitehall) 45ff, 159ff, Chs. 3–7, 166, 181f, 192, 245, 255, 330
British Military Administration (BMA) 38
Brunei 15, 110, 127, 167, 183f, 339, 343 *see also* ASEAN after 1984
Buchanan, Iain xii
Buddhism and Buddhists xviii, 267, 325
Bukit Ho Swee 249
Burma 193
Burke, Kenneth 287f, 315
Byrne, K.M. (Kenny) 53, 59, 61ff, 73, 87, 93, 102, 106, 109, 132, 203

Cambodia = Kampuchea 147, 180, 189f *see also* Indo-China
Cambridge University 41–4
Canada 212
Carter, Jimmy 15, 183, 185

369

Central Provident Fund (CPF) xviii, 245, 248, 250
Chan Choy Siong 203, 209, 253 endnote 11
Chan Heng Chee xiii, 4, 13, 337f
Chan Kai Yau 190
Changi airport 251
Chen, Bernard 206
Chew Swee Kee 93ff
Chia Thye Poh 216
Chiam See Tong 7, 209, 219
Chiang Kai Shek 38, 307
Chin Peng (Ong Boon Hua) 39, 79
China and Chinese 14, 15, 28, 105, 183, 186ff, 189f, 193, 243f, 252, 261, 339
Chinatown 252
Chinese overseas (Third China) 164, 166
Chinese (Singapore/Malaya): xvii, 27ff, 327; King's Chinese 27; Straits-born including Babas 27, 32, 38, 254, 277; towkays 27
Chinese (Singapore): Confucianism xviii, 266; Confucius 180; dialects & Mandarin language xviii, 8, 262ff, 283, 333
Ching Ping 276
Christianity and Christians (inc. Roman Catholics) xviii, 24, 102, 197f, 247, 255, 267f, 325
Chua Jim Neo = Mrs Lee Chin Koon 9, 298, 308ff
Chua Sian Chin 21, 259
CIA (Central Intelligence Agency) 53, 107, 158, 333
Citizen's Consultative Committees (CCCs) 13, 229
City Council 91ff
Clutterbuck, Richard 90, 346 endnote 13
Commonwealth (including Prime Ministers' Conferences, CHOGM [Commonwealth Heads of Government Meeting] and CHOGRM [Commonwealth Head of Government Regional Meeting]) 129, 150, 171, 181, 189, 191, 283
Communism, communists and Communist United Front 42f, 69, 78, 86, 115ff, 192f
Communist Party of Indonesia see PKI
Confrontation (Konfrontasi) [between Indonesia and Malaysia] Chs. 6–7, 163
Corridon, Richard 63, 85f
Council of Joint Action (previously Council of Action) (CJA) 65, 71

CPF 344
CPM (Communist Party of Malaya) see MCP
Critchley, Tom 154
Cuba 190f

Daim Zainuddin 173
Dalley, F.W. 85
DAP (Democratic Action Party) 55, 168
Davies, Derek 171
de Gaulle, Charles 316
Democratic Party (DP) 75
Deng Xiaoping 208
Devan Nair, C.V. (President) 6, 11, 23ff, 38, 43, 54ff, 66, 75, 77, 85f, 103, 114, 134, 137, 154, 155ff, 200ff, 213, 217, 223ff, 294, 296f, 310, 315, 340
Dhanabalan, Suppiah 7, 19, 175, 189f, 198, 210, 245
Domei 35, 232
Douglas-Home, (Sir) Alec 142
Drysdale, John 40
Dutch New Guinea 107
Dutch Labour Party 185, 187

Eastern Sun 232
Eber, John 38, 42, 44, 60ff, 68, 83
EDB (Economic Development Board) 176
EEC (European Economic Community) 189
Egypt 180
Elliott, Tom 65
Emergency Regulations 73, 78
English language xviii, 8, 194, 256, 262, 277
Enright, D.J. xii, 257
Enrile, Juan Ponce 345
Erikson, Erik H. 312
Eurasians 32, 255
Europe (including European Economic Community [EEC], Western and Eastern Europe and individual countries) 111, 180, 182, 189, 213

Fajar see Socialist Club
Family Planning and Population Board 247
Far Eastern Economic Review 171
Federation of Pan–Malayan Students 67
Fiji 284
Fitzwilliam Hall (later College), Cambridge 41
Five-power defence arrangements 180f
Fletcher, Nancy xii

Index

Fong Sip Chee 103
Fong Swee Suan 11, 70, 77, 103, 115, 127, 292
Fraser, Malcolm 8
Fu, James 9ff
Fukuda, Takeo 284

Gamba, Charles 65
Gamer, Robert xii, 219
Gandhi, Indira 195, 208
Gandhi, Mohandas (Mahatma) 23
Gatbonton, Juan 302
George, T.J.S. xii, 12, 35, 39, 40, 302, 307
Ghafar Baba 344
Ghazali Shafie, (Tan Sri) Muhammad 170f
Goh Chew Chua 75
Goh Chok Tong 7, 18, 19, 197, 204ff, 214, 245, 334, 336ff, 344
Goh Keng Swee (Dr) x, xi, 5, 21, 22f, 24, 34, 44, 51, 59, 61ff, 73, 81, 83, 87, 90, 93, 116f, 120, Chs. 6–10, 276, 294, 327, 343
Goode, (Sir) William 85, 94, 103f, 112, 115
Government (of Singapore) Investment Corporation 247
Govindaswamy, P. 24
Gurkhas 10, 228
Gurney, (Sir) Henry 53

Hakka (Chinese dialect group) 301, 304, 307
Hanna, Willard xii
Hartnett, (Sir) Laurence 245
Hatta, (Dr) Muhammad 36
Hawke, Robert 8
HDB (Housing and Development Board) xviii, 229, 246, 249f
Head, (Lord) 147, 153f
Heath, Edward 291
Hertogh, Maria [riots] 60, 62, 82, 97
Hinduism and Hindus xviii, 267
Ho Ching 343
Ho Kwon Ping 206
Hoalim, Philip, Senior 40
Hock Lee bus strike/riots 77, 97
Hon Sui Sen xiii, 11, 19, 21, 35, 221, 240, 282
Hon, Joan xiii
Hong Kong 188, 233, 243, 339
Hong Lim (parliamentary constituency) 109ff, 151ff
Howe Yoon Chong 17
Hu, Richard (Dr) 343
HUDC (Housing and Urban Development Corporation) 249

Hughes, Richard xii
Hussein Onn (Tun) 170f
Hyde, Douglas 89

Independence of Malaya Party (IMP) 60, 72
India and Indians 180, 193, 244
Indians (Singapore) xvii, 32, 164, 215;
    Tamil language xviii, 8
Indo-China *see also* Cambodia, Laos, Vietnam 164, 182, 243, 286
Indonesia (including Jakarta) 107, 110, Chs. 6–7, 163ff, 174ff, 195, 243f *see also* ASEAN after 1967
Internal Security Council (ISC) 83f, 113, 127f
Internal Security Department *see* Special Branch
INTRACO (International Trading Company) 176
Iran (including the Shah) 185
Islam and Muslims xviii, 32, 97, 105, 151, 159, 164, 255, 267f
Ismail bin Harun (Tun Dr) 147, 149, 154, 169
Israel and Israelis 159, 174, 180, 195, 239

Ja'afar Albar, Syed 141, 147f, 154
Jamit Singh 65, 81
Japan and Japanese 28, Ch. 2, 129, 167, 182, 188f, 193, 261f, 284f, 321, 330
Jardine Fleming 245
Jek Yeun Thong 21, 75, 81, 109, 168, 203, 283, 339f
Jeyaretnam, J.B. 74, 209, 215f, 219f, 268, 282, 343
Josey, Alex xi, 37, 53f, 64, 85, 113, 153, 155, 231, 256, 276, 284f, 296f, 301, 305f, 315, 326, 335

Kahn, Herman 285, 334
Keppel Shipyard 246
Khaw Kai Boh 84f, 292
Khir Johari, Mohamed 137, 285
Khmer Rouge 189
Kishore Mahbubani 177
KMT (Kuomintang) 232
Kohut, Heinz 315ff
Korea (including North and South) 28, 188
Kwa Geok Choo 18f, 43f, 59f, 213, 225, 297f, 302, 322
Kwan Sai Kheong 284

Labour Front (LF) 75, 88ff, 107, 131
Labour Party (Britain) 14, 42
Lai Teck 36
Lange, David 191
Laos 147 *see also* Indo-China
Latin America (including Central America) 15, 195
Leaders 326
Lee Chiaw Meng (Dr) 21, 207, 229, 259
Lee Chin Koon 9, 33, 298, 308
Lee Chin Koon, Mrs *see* Chua Jim Neo
Lee Hoon Leong 306, 308f, 311ff
Lee Hsien Loong (Brigadier-General [Reservists]) 7, 19ff, 146, 159, 204ff, 235f, 245, 297f, 308, 322f, 332ff, 336ff, 343f
Lee Hsien Loong, the late Mrs *see* (Dr) Wong Ming Yang
Lee Hsien Loong, the new Mrs 344 *see* Hong Ching
Lee Hsien Yang 323f
Lee Khoon Choy 21, 175, 231
Lee Kim Mon, Monica 310
Lee Kim Yew, Dennis 59, 82, 310
Lee Kuan Yew, childhood and adolescence 308–12; children *see* Lee Hsien Loong, Lee Wei Ling, Lee Hsien Yang; education 33, 40ff, 309–11; grandfather *see* Lee Hoon Leong; Hakka ancestry 301, 304, 307; law firm (Lee and Lee) 21, 82; learning of languages 8, 277; parents *see* Lee Chin Koon, Chua Jim Neo; Mrs *see* Kwa Geok Choo; siblings *see* Lee Kim Yew, Dennis, Lee Thiam Yew, Freddy, Lee Suan Yew, Lee Kim Mon, Monica
Lee Siew Choh (Dr) 118, 121, 128, 200, 293
Lee Suan Yew 310
Lee Thiam Yew, Freddy 310
Lee Wei Ling 298, 323
Leong Choon Cheong 271, 323
Liberal Socialists 83, 91, 93
Little, Graham (Dr) vii
Lim Chee Onn 11, 21, 55, 61, 205f, 225
Lim Chin Joo 109
Lim Chin Siong 69ff, 73, 75ff, 82ff, 89, 91, 103, 108, 114ff, 118, 127, 292f
Lim Hong Bee 44, 83
Lim Kean Chye 38, 42, 64, 127
Lim Kim San 5, 21, 152, 159, 201, 242, 304
Lim Tay Boh 39, 310
Lim Yew Hock (Tun) = Haji Omar Lim 83ff, 88ff, 92ff, 121, 128, 131, 146, 230, 292, 294, 296

London School of Economics 40f

Machiavelli 179
Mahathir bin Mohamad (Dr) 57, 148f, 171ff, 195, 344
Malay Nationalist Party (MNP) 56
Malaya (including Kuala Lumpur as seat of federal government) 36f, 45f, Chs. 3–5
Malayan Democratic Union (MDU) 40, 43
Malayan Forum 44f, 83, 97
Malayan National Liberation League 200
Malays (Singapore) xvii, 31f, 97, 141, 151, 199, 214f, 250, 327; Malay language xviii, 8
Malaysia Chs. 5–7, 163ff, 167ff, 183ff, 339 *see also* ASEAN after 1967
Malaysian Solidarity Convention (MSC) 147f, 159
Mao Zedong = Mao Tse Tung 38, 180, 186, 193, 199, 307, 316
Maphilindo 129
Mara, (Ratu Sir) Kamisese 284
Marcos, (President) Ferdinand 184, 195, 285, 343
Marshall, (Chief Minister) David xiii, 67, 76ff, 82ff, 95, 107, 111, 114, 120f, 211, 281f, 291f, 295, 304, 334
Marxism and Marxists (including Marxism–Leninism) 38, 42, 66, 86, 104, 117, 156, 192
Mass Rapid Transport (MRT) 247, 252, 342
May 13th riots (1969) 159, 168f
MCA (Malayan/Malaysian Chinese Association) 72, 75, Chs. 6–7, 164, 167ff, 233, 292
McKie, Ronald xii
MCP (Malayan Communist Party) = CPM 36f, 43, 46ff, 69, 86f, 89ff, 95, 115, 292
Menzies, (Sir) Robert 181, 234, 296
Middle East 189
MI5 116, 157
MI6 53
Monetary Authority of Singapore 246
Musa Hitam (Datuk) 57, 172f, 344

Nakasone, Yasuhiro 284
Nanyang Siang Pau 232
Nanyang University (Nantah) (NU) 88f, 96, 105, 131, 221, 263ff
Nasser, (President) Gamal Abd el 180
National Junior College 258

Index

National Stadium 252
National Union of General Workers 90
National University of Singapore (NUS) 263ff
National Wages Council (NWC) 244, 324ff
NATO (North Atlantic Treaty Organisation) 188
Naval Base Labour Union (NBLU) 65
Nehru, (Pandit) Jawarhalal 281, 306, 316
New Zealand 145, 165, 181, 191, 193, 212, 339
Ng Pock Too 20, 209
Nicoll, (Sir) John 66
Nixon, Richard x
Non-aligned movement (NAM) 190f
Noordin Sopiee, Mohamed 142
North Borneo *see* Sabah
NTUC (National Trades Union Congress) xix, 55, 120, 158, 197, 206, 223ff, 246

Occupation by Japanese (1942–45) 29, Ch. 2
Ong Cheng Sam 11, 151
Ong Eng Guan 78, 91ff, 102ff, 108ff, 118, 151, 209, 294, 353 endnote 11
Ong Pang Boon 81, 116, 119, 203, 207, 209ff, 259, 340
Ong Teng Cheong 7, 19, 197, 202, 225, 260f, 265, 343
Onn bin Jaafar 60, 72, 294
Operation Cold Store 127f, 217
Othman Wok 21, 64, 231

Pakistan 193
Palestine 47, 53
Pang Cheng Lian 116
PAP (People's Action Party) (including Central Executive Committee [CEC]) x, xvii, 1, 2, 7, 18, 21, 72ff, 78, 84ff, 88, 95, 101ff, 108, 114, 202ff, 236, 337f
Parkinson, C. Northcote xii, 25, 304
Peacock, Andrew 11
People's Association 13, 116, 229
Peritz, Rene xii
Pham Van Dong 284
Phey Yew Kok 20, 55, 206, 224, 264
Philippines, Republic of the 183ff, 193, 344 *see also* ASEAN after 1967
Pillay, J.M. 240
PKI (Communist Party of Indonesia) 111, 120, 200
Plato 179
Plen (Plenipotentiary) = Fang Chuang Pi 92, 113
Poh Soo Kai (Dr) 218
Preservation of Public Security Ordinance (PPSO) 77
Presidential Council (for Minority Rights) 218
Pritt, D.N., QC 68, 82
Progressive Party (PP) 5, 38, 59ff, 66, 73
Public Service Commission (PSC) 84, 241
Puthucheary, Dominic 11, 127
Puthucheary, James 65, 78, 84, 115, 127, 241

Queenstown 249

Raffles College 33f, 39, 40, 43, 278
Raffles Institution (RI) 197, 277f, 310
Raffles, (Sir) Thomas Stamford 106
Rahim Ishak 21, 62
Rahman, (Tunku) Abdul 62, 72ff, 83, 90f, 97, Chs. 5–7, 163ff, 167ff, 212, 294, 296
Rahmat Kenap 142
Rajah, A.P. 64, 275
Rajaratnam, Sinnathamby 5, 24, 43, 51, 63ff, 87, 103, 107, Chs. 6–8, 223, 266, 270, 294, 334ff
Ramos, General Fidel 345
Razak, (Tun) Abdul 33, 44, Chs. 6–7, 167ff, 185f
Reagan, Ronald 16
Referendum on merger 119–22, 125, 327
refugees 164
Rendel Constitutional commission and Consitution 67, 71, 81
Residents' Committees (RCs) 13, 229, 251
RTS (Radio Television Singapura/Singapore) [later reconsituted as SBC (Singapore Broadcasting Corporation)] 130, 232, 256

Sabah = North Borneo 110ff, Chs. 6–7, 163f, 173, 344
Said Zahari 218
Samad Ismail, Abdul 38, 56f, 62ff, 73, 86, 170f
Sandys, Duncan 129f
Sarawak 110ff, Chs. 6–7, 163f
SBC *see* RTS
SEATO (Southeast Asia Treaty Organisation) 68, 112, 193
Selkirk, (Lord) 112, 115ff
Sembawang (parliamentary constituency) 122
Separation 153ff
Sharma, P.V. 38, 54f, 60, 66

Sheares, (President) Benjamin 11, 213, 284
Sheng Nam Chin 118
Sihanouk, (Prince) Norodom 147, 189
Silcock, T.H. 38
Sin Chew Jit Poh 232
Singapore Association of Trade Unions (SATU) 120, 127f, 130
Singapore Bus Workers' Union 77
Singapore Chinese Chamber of Commerce 59, 104
Singapore Chinese Middle School Students' Union 89
Singapore Factory and Shop Workers' Union 61, 77
Singapore Herald 232, 333
Singapore International Chamber of Commerce 54
Singapore Labour Party (SLP) 61, 73
Singapore Monitor 232
Singapore People's Alliance Party 92
Singapore Traction Company Employees' Union 106
Singapore University (SU) 263f
Smith, J.B. 53
Social Democratic Party (SDP) 209
Socialist Club (University of Malaya) 65, 67, 119, 121
Socialist Front (Malaya/Malaysia) 136
Socialist International 185, 187
Soekarno = Sukarno, (President) 36, 174
Special Branch = Internal Security Department 13, 62ff, 71, 73, 84, 89, 113, 157f, 217f, 227, 292
Sri Lanka 15, 193, 244
Strachey, John 280f
Straits Chinese British Association (SCBA) 59f
Straits of Malacca xvii, 339
Straits Times 2, 52, 56, 213, 232f
Suharto, (President) 174f, 195, 243
Sun Yat Sen 307
Sunday Times (Singapore) ix
Switzerland 47, 158, 239, 243

Taiwan 105, 167, 188–233, 330f
Tamil *see* Indians
Tan, Augustine H.H. (Dr) 244, 268
Tan Chee Khoon (Dr) 148
Tan Cheng Lock 51, 72f
Tan Chong Chew 35, 309
Tan Eng Liang 21
Tan, Joseph 38
Tan Koon Swan 344
Tan Lark Sye 131, 173

Tan Siew Sin 51, Chs. 6–7, 164
Tan, Tony 344f
Tan Wah Piow 264
Tang, I.F. 240
Tanjong Pagar (LKY's parliamentary constituency) 1, 75, 121
Teh Cheang Wan 216
Thailand 167, 183ff, 244, 286 *see also* ASEAN after 1967
Thatcher, Margaret 16
Thatcher, William S. 41f, 310
Thio Su Mien (Dr) 12f
Thomas, Francis 86, 93
Thomson, George G. 109, 281
Toa Payoh 249
Toffler, Alvin 340
Toh Chin Chye (Dr) 5, 18, 21, 52, 62, 78ff, 81, 88, 90, 93, 103, 108, 114, 116f, Chs. 6–9, 259, 264, 294, 340
Toynbee, Arnold 280
Trade Union Congress 90, 114
Tregonning, K.G. 158
Turnbull, C. Mary 115
Turner (Fitzwilliam Hall, Cambridge) 41

UMNO (United Malays' National Organisation) (Malaya/Malaysia) 37, 62, 72, 75, 91, 94, 112, 120, Chs. 6–7, 167ff
UMNO (United Malays' National Organisation) (Singapore) 37, 91, 142, 200
UN (United Nations) 15, 26, 120, 125, 180, 190, 252
Uniformed Postal Staff Workers' Union 63
United People's Party (UPP) 108, 120
United States of America (US or USA) 150, 158f, 166, 182f, 189, 228
USSR (Union of Soviet Socialist Republics) = Soviet Union 180, 188, 332
Utusan Melayu 56, 60, 62, 73, Chs. 6–7

Vasil, Raj xiii
Vietnam 182, 189f, 195, 286 *see also* Indo-China

Wee Toon Boon 11, 24
Whitlam, E. Gough 291
Wilson, Harold 147
Winsemius, Albert (Dr) 201, 240, 244
Wolf, Ernest 330
Wong Lin Ken (Dr) 21, 203

Index

Wong Ming Yang (Dr) 323
Woodhull, Sandralsegaram] (Sidney) 65, 81, 115
Workers' Party 74, 209

Xun Zi 180

Yeo Kim Wah 66

Yeo Ning Hong (Dr) ix, 20
Yong Nyuk Lin 21, 203, 259
Yusof Ishak (President) 62, 106, 213, 330

Zhao Ziyang 187
Zhou Enlai = Chou E Lai ix, 185f

Background Notes:

SINGAPORE

> We the citizens of Singapore
> pledge ourselves as one united people,
> regardless of race, language or religion,
> to build a democratic society
> based on justice and equality
> so as to achieve happiness, prosperity and progress
> for our nation.
>
> CITIZENS' PLEDGE

Historically the port of Temasek or Singapura (Lion City) goes back to the thirteenth century. In 1819 the British adventurer Stamford Raffles established a trading base on the island, thereby inaugurating modern Singapore.

Today the island republic has a population of more than 2.5 million. It occupies a total area, including islets and reclaimed land, of 620 square kilometres (295 square kilometres built up). Being just north of the Equator, its climate is hot and humid, with abundant rainfall. Singapore is strategically located on the Straits of Malacca between the Indian and Pacific Oceans. The main island is linked to the southern tip of peninsular Malaysia by a kilometre-long causeway carrying a road, railway and water pipeline. Indonesian islands form an arc to the south a short distance across the Straits of Singapore.

A democracy with compulsory universal suffrage for all citizens over twenty-one years of age, Singapore has a unicameral Parliament comprising 79 members elected by the people in single-member constituencies. Twenty political parties are currently registered. The island has been governed by the People's Action Party (PAP) since 1959, was within Malaysia from 1963 to 1965 and became a sovereign state in 1965 and a founding member of the Association of Southeast Asian Nations (ASEAN) in 1967.

The executive of Singapore comprises the President as head of state, the Prime Minister as head of government, and the Cabinet. The President is chosen by Parliament for a four-year term; he is responsible for appointing as Prime Minister the member of Parliament who commands the confidence of the majority of MPs; and he acts on the Prime Minister's advice in appointing Cabinet members from the Parliament. The judiciary is independent of the executive in its administration of the law, and its power is vested in the Supreme Court (High Court and Courts of Appeal) and the Subordinate Courts. The British Privy Council remains Singapore's final appellate court.

The population can be classified into racial grouping as follows: Chinese 76.5 per cent; Malays 14.8 per cent; Indians (mostly of southern Indian origin) 6.4 per cent; other ethnic groups 2.3 per cent. Overall there are 1039 males per 1000 females.

English, Mandarin, Malay and Tamil are the four official languages in descending order of usage. Hokkien, Teochew and Cantonese are the principal dialects among the Chinese, still widely used, though Mandarin is becoming quite common among the young.

Islam (nominated by all Malays and some Indians, making up 16 per cent of the population aged ten years and over), Buddhism (56 per cent, nominated by more than two-thirds of Singapore's Chinese), Christianity (10–11 per cent drawn from all races except the Malays) and Hinduism (4 per cent, overwhelmingly Indian) are the main religious affiliations of Singapore's people. Most of the rest are 'free thinkers' not professing any faith. Singapore's Buddhism is predominantly of the Mahayana stream, and its beliefs and practices are mixed with those of Taoism and Confucianism. The state is secular but guarantees freedom of religious expression.

The average life expectancy is 71 years. Infant mortality at last reckoning was 9 per thousand live births. The birthrate has declined from 42.7 per thousand in 1957 to 16.2 per thousand in 1984. Health services are subsidised by the government, but there is a flourishing private sector that offers traditional Asian forms of treatment and medicine as well as Western health care.

The divorce rate has increased from 1 for every 48 marriages taking place in 1973 to 1 for every 11 in 1984.

Singapore is a sophisticated and well-equipped city state but is not self-sufficient in water, food, oil and most other resources needed to sustain a modern way of living or national economy. Primary production continues to decline and the economy depends mainly on trade, tourism, manufacturing, construction and service sectors (with a growing emphasis on 'brain' services and high-technology industries). Singapore is also a regional centre for communications, finance and banking, and entrepreneurial ventures. The port and airport are of the highest standard and are served by many international shipping and air lines, including Singapore's own flag carriers.

The indigenous gross national product per capita in 1984 was somewhat over S$12 300; it is not possible to give a realistic average figure for household income because of substantial inequalities among the population. Inflation for 1984 was 2.6 per cent. The economy's growth slowed down markedly in 1985; preliminary projections indicate a shrinkage of about 2 per cent. More than 81 per cent of the population now resides in Housing and Development Board flats, the great majority of which are being purchased rather than rented. The workforce's compulsory private savings are maintained at a high level, and can be drawn on before retirement only for housing, hospital or medical expenses and certain share purchases. Official calculations put foreign reserves at S$22.7 billion by the end of 1984.

In 1984, 66.8 per cent of the 1.8 million people aged between fifteen and sixty-four years participated in the workforce. Unemployment was running at 2.7 per cent. 1985's downturn would undoubtedly have had an adverse impact on these figures. About 16 per cent of the workforce was unionised as at the end of 1984, and 97 per cent of union members were affiliated to the government-backed National Trade Unions Congress. Government-provided financial assistance and welfare are more limited than in most Western countries.

The government promotes defence of Singapore as the responsibility of every citizen and every organ of society. Over 21 per cent of expenditure for 1984–85 has been allocated to the Ministry of Defence. National service has been made the basis of military defence, and is compulsory for all males aged eighteen and over.

Singapore has always coped with enormous pressures, a fact of life that her brilliant survival so far has perhaps tended to obscure. Some of the pressures are largely inescapable: climate, size, diverse population, nearness to neighbours and fluctuating levels of conflict in the region. Others are the consequence of choices made by government or people over the years, such as the determination to maintain sovereignty or to develop particular patterns of economic organisation and dependence. The present difficulties, symbolised by the collapse of major companies and the worsening glut of hotel rooms, may turn critical or may be overcome with Singaporeans' customary ingenuity. Much depends on what happens in the wider world. But while there is a perception that any pressures are deliberately chosen or accepted, the relationship between citizens and government may unfold as part of the problem and not just of the solution.